Anglos and Mexicans in the Making of Texas, 1836–1986

D1013864

Anglos and Mexicans in the Making of Texas, 1836–1986

by David Montejano

 UNIVERSITY OF TEXAS PRESS, AUSTIN

Sixth paperback printing, 1997

Requests for permission to reproduce material from this work
should be sent to Permissions, University of Texas Press, Box 7819,
Austin, Texas 78713-7819.

Library of Congress Cataloging-in-Publication Data

Montejano, David, 1948–
    Anglos and Mexicans in the making of Texas,
1836–1986.

    Bibliography: p.
    Includes index.
    1. Texas—History—Republic, 1836–1846. 2. Texas—
History—1846–1950. 3. Texas—Race relations.
4. Mexican Americans—Texas—History—19th century.
I. Title.
F390.M78 1987   976.4   86-27249
ISBN 0-292-77596-2 (pbk.)

The publication of this book was assisted by a grant from the
Andrew W. Mellon Foundation.

Pa' mis padres

por sus labores

por sus anhelos

Contents

Illustrations

Maps

Tables

Acknowledgments

THE FOLLOWING history represents a personal as well as an intellectual journey. It proposes answers to questions that "grew up" with me, questions about the Texas world I came to know as a fourth-generation native. The most prominent feature of this world was the sharp division between Anglo and Mexican in schools, neighborhoods, and social life generally. What were the origins of such segregation? And why, during the past twenty years, was this segregated order apparently breaking down? No explanations were immediately forthcoming. These were the seeds of curiosity that led me, gradually and perhaps inevitably, to write an interpretive history of Mexicans and Anglos in Texas. Although this particular interpretation is focused on Texas, the history reconstructed here does not describe an isolated or unique experience. In an immediate sense, this work suggests the outlines of a regional history that speaks of Mexicans and Anglos and the "making" of the American Southwest. In a more general sense, the history points to the experience of ethnic conflict and accommodation throughout the world, and to the manner in which economic development has shaped ethnic relations.

My acknowledgments reflect, besides debts of various sorts, an actual geographic odyssey. The friends and colleagues who have encouraged this work are scattered among the places where I have studied and taught, on both East and West coasts as well as in the Southwest. When a segment of this book was a doctoral dissertation, Kai Erikson, Stanley Greenberg, Wendell Bell, and the late Paul S. Taylor helped to shape the initial direction of the project. The support of Professor Taylor was especially important, for his collection of interviews with Anglo Texans during the 1920s and 1930s launched the entire project. The sharpening of my general argument was due in large measure to the many conversations with Andres Jimenez, Ron Balderrama, Felipe Gonzales, and Margarita Decierdo, who read several drafts but never lost their enthusiasm for the project. The comments of associates who read various chapter drafts—Martin Jankowski, Jorge Chapa, Emilio Zamora, Lew Friedland, Ricardo Romo, Tomas Almaguer, Patricia Zavella, Rodolfo Rosales, Antonio Gonzalez, and Regino Chavez—contained important suggestions.

Victor Zazueta and Steven Nechero were helpful assistants in preparing the bibliography and the maps, and Jacqueline Rodgers typed a good portion of the manuscript. Finally, several members of my extended family served, through their impatience, as a constant spur to finish the book. A todos estos amigos, colegas, y familiares, les doy un abrazo de gracias.

The project would have taken more years to complete had it not been for the institutional support I received. A grant from the Ford Foundation allowed me the time to start the project and, ten years later, a grant from the Rockefeller Foundation allowed me to bring it to a close. A modest faculty grant from the University of New Mexico provided for the collection of photographs and the reconstruction of maps. Librarians were, of course, indispensable, and I would like to thank the staffs of the following institutions: the Bancroft Library and the Chicano Studies Library of the University of California, Berkeley; the Chicano Studies Library of the University of California, Los Angeles; the Benson Latin American Collection and the E. C. Barker Library of the University of Texas at Austin; the Lorenzo de Zavala State Archives in Austin; the Daughters of the Republic of Texas Library and the University of Texas Institute of Texan Cultures Library in San Antonio; and the Texas Agricultural and Industrial University Library in Kingsville. From the above institutions, I must single out librarians Francisco García, Richard Chabrán, Bernice Strong, and Tom Shelton for their assistance. Timely logistical support was provided by Carlos Arce and his staff of the National Chicano Network, then at the University of Michigan, and by William Velasquez and his staff of the Southwest Voter Registration Education Project in San Antonio. The generous assistance of these individuals and institutions made the writing a pleasant experience. Needless to say, none of the above individuals or institutions is responsible for the interpretation contained in this history.

An early version of Chapter 9, "The Web of Labor Controls," appeared in *The World-System of Capitalism: Past and Present*, ed. Walter Goldfrank (Beverly Hills: Sage Publications, 1978), and portions of Chapter 11, "The Geography of Race and Class," appeared in the winter 1981 number of *Review* (Beverly Hills: Sage Publications).

Anglos and Mexicans in
the Making of Texas, 1836–1986

incorporation (1) Sp-Mex hacienda society, undermined by Mex War

reconstruction (2) Anglo-Mex ranch society, undermined by agric revolution at turn of century

segregation (3) segregated farm society, undermined by WWII & urban-industrialization

integration (4) pluralistic urban-industrial society

1. Introduction

TWO MAJOR concerns guided this work. One was to reconstruct a history of Mexican-Anglo relations in Texas "since the Alamo." In geographic terms, the focus was primarily directed to a 200-mile-wide strip paralleling the Mexican border from Brownsville to El Paso.[1] I considered this history important because of the fragile historical sense most people have of the American Southwest. The vestiges of a Mexican past are still evident. In the old cities of the region, the missions and governors' palaces, the "old Mexicos," the annual fiestas, and the like remind one that there is a history here, but it seems remote and irrelevant. There is no memory, for example, of annexation as a major historical event. What happened to the annexed Mexicans? The question points to a larger lapse in memory—what does the nineteenth-century frontier period have to do with the present?

There is, of course, a popular and romanticized awareness of southwestern history—Indians and Mexicans were subdued, ranches fenced, railroads built, and so on until the West was completely won. A "triumphalist literature" has enshrined the experience of the "Old West" in tales of victory and progress.[2] Drama, the easiest virtue to fashion for southwestern history, has long taken the place of explanation and interpretation. Because this history has seldom been thought of in economic and sociological terms, much of the road connecting the past with the present remains obscured. When the legendary aspects are stripped away from the frontier experience, for instance, cowboys surface as wage workers on the new American ranches and as indebted servants on the old *haciendas*; the barbed-wire fence movement of the 1880s becomes not just a sign of progress but an enclosure movement that displaced landless cattlemen and maverick cowboys; and the famed cattle trails commemorated in western folklore become an instrument by which the region was firmly tied into national and international markets. The failure of memory, then, is as much sociological as it is historical.

The absence of a sociological memory is nowhere more evident than in the study of race and ethnic relations in the Southwest.

The greater border region ▢

South Texas.

Compared with the significant literature on race relations in the American South, similar work in western Americana appears tentative and uncertain. An extensive literature has addressed the major events—the origins of the Mexican War, the founding of the cattle trails, and so on—but only rarely has the discussion focused on the consequences of these events for the various peoples living in the region. In recent years, a few notable works have begun to investigate this area, but this territory remains largely uncharted.[3] It was imperative, in this context, to present a different kind of history, an interpretive history that would outline the connections between the past and the present while maintaining a focus on Mexican-Anglo relations.

My second major concern, then, was to ask this history some sociological questions about ethnicity, social change, and society itself. In one sense, this book can be described as a southwestern history about nation building, economic development, and ethnic relations. In a more comparative manner, the history points to the familiar experience of conflict and accommodation between distinct societies and peoples throughout the world. In describing the situation of Texas Mexicans in the early twentieth century, for example, historian T. R. Fehrenbach has drawn parallels to Israel's West Bank, French Algeria, and South Africa.[4] In contrast to these parallels, the Texas history of Mexicans and Anglos points to a relationship that, although frequently violent and tense, has led to a situation that today may be characterized as a form of integration.

An interpretation that attempts to serve both sociology and history must invariably make some difficult decisions about the organization of the presentation. For the sake of the reader whose interest is primarily historical, I have placed the customary introductory discussion of sociological concepts and methods in an appendix. Those interested in theory and methods should refer to this appendix. Some brief comments about "race" and "development," nonetheless, are in order here.

A Sociological Overview

A critical limitation in the sociological literature consists of its inability to deal with the race question. Whether the process of social change has been called modernization or capitalist development, the subject of race has been considered a temporary aberration, an irrelevancy in the developmental experience. Industrialization and urbanization were expected to weaken race and ethnic divisions because such distinctions were considered inefficient and counterproductive. As social life underwent a thorough commercialization, common class interests and identities were supposed to completely dominate the politics of the new order, overshadowing parochial and mystical bases of social conflict.

In contrast to these theoretical expectations, the histories of many contemporary societies make evident that economic development and race divisions have been suitably accommodated. But there seems to have been no single pattern or template for a modernizing racial order. Extermination and assimilation have demarcated the most extreme "solutions" to the race question, with several patterns of subjugation and accommodation falling in between. Not surprisingly, given this situation, the literature of race and ethnic relations has yet to progress beyond the construction of various typologies of "outcomes."[5]

But patterns can be teased out of the seeming disorder. The study of the Texas border region is ideal in this sense, for its one striking feature has been the presence of great diversity in Mexican-Anglo relations at any one historical point. A symptom of this diversity has been the confusion, among both Mexicans and Anglos, on whether Mexicans constitute an ethnic group or a "race." This question, as the following history will make evident, has long been a contentious *political* issue in the region. The clarification of the race concept, in fact, must take into account its political nature, a point that has remained undeveloped in the sociological literature.

One of the better known axioms in the social sciences is that "races" are social definitions or creations. Although race situations generally involve people of color, it is not color that makes a situation a racial one. The biological differences, as Robert Redfield noted some forty years ago, are superficial; what is important are "the races that people see and recognize, or believe to exist," what Redfield called the "socially supposed races."[6] Generally missed in this type of discussion, however, has been the additional recognition that the race question, as a socially defined sign of privilege and honor, represents an arena of struggle and accommodation. The death or resurrection of race divisions is fundamentally a political question, a question of efforts, in George Fredrickson's words, "to make race or color a qualification for membership in the civil community."[7] To put it another way, the notion of race does not just consist of ideas and sentiments; it comes into being when these ideas and sentiments are publicly articulated and institutionalized. Stated more concisely, "race situations" exist when so defined by public policy.

Framing the race problem as a political question helps to clear the ambiguity concerning the sociological classification of Mexicans. The bonds of culture, language, and common historical experience make the Mexican people of the Southwest a distinct ethnic population. But Mexicans, following the above definition, were also a "race" whenever they were subjected to policies of discrimination or control.

This political definition of race enables us to sidestep a historical argument about the origins of Anglo-Saxon prejudice—whether these attitudes were imported and transferred to Mexicans or were the product of bitter warfare.[8] Both were important sources for anti-Mexican sentiments. Anglos who settled in the Southwest brought with them a long history of dealing with Indians and blacks, while the experience of the Alamo and the Mexican War served to crystallize and reaffirm anti-Mexican prejudice. Nonetheless, this psychological and attitudinal dimension, while interesting, is unable to explain variations and shifts in race situations. The important question is, Under which conditions were these sentiments and beliefs translated into public policy?

In this context, Texas independence and annexation acquire special significance as the events that laid the initial ground for invidious distinction and inequality between Anglos and Mexicans. In the "liberated" and annexed territories, Anglos and Mexicans stood as conquerors and conquered, as victors and vanquished, a distinction as fundamental as any sociological sign of privilege and rank. How could it have been otherwise after a war? For the Americans of Mexican extraction, the road from annexation to "integration," in the sense of becoming accepted as a legitimate citizenry, would be a long and uneasy one.

Concerning social change and development, ample work in historical sociology has explored the transformation of "precapitalist" agrarian societies into "modern" commercial orders. The importance of this literature for this study lay in the depiction of social change in class terms—in terms of the way landed elites and peasants responded to market impulses and to the emergence of a merchant class. According to the classic European version of this transition, a class of merchants emerged triumphantly over anticommercial obstacles of the landed elite, freeing land and labor of precapitalist restraints and transforming them into marketable commodities. The peasantry was uprooted and converted into a wage laboring class, while merchants and the commercialized segment of the landowning elite become a rural bourgeoisie.[9] Generally, however, these European case studies have emphasized internal sources of social change; the merchants were indigenous to the societies they ultimately transformed. The history of the Americas, on the other hand, pointed forcefully to a developmental path of plural societies formed through conquest and colonization.

While the European experience is an inappropriate model for a history characterized by war and "race" divisions, it nonetheless directed attention to familiar actors and to familiar events in the loosening of an elite's hold on land and labor. Instead of English gentry and merchants, there were the Mexican *hacendado* and the Anglo merchant-adventurer; instead of yeoman and peasant, the *ranchero* and indebted *peón*. And rather than wool, the enclosing of peasant holdings, Captain Swing and the Levellers, we had Longhorn cattle, the enclosing of the open range, and Juan Cortina and Mexican bandits.

In spite of the shortcomings mentioned earlier, then, a relaxed class analysis—one accepting of the political character of race situations— held considerable promise for outlining the structural basis of complex Mexican-Anglo relations. The relevance of the method emerged from the historical figures themselves, from actors who were "class conscious" as well as "race conscious." Whenever they were given the floor, their speech was punctuated with references to economic status, and their behavior was expressive of class-specific interests. Since these behavior patterns provided a context for Mexican-Anglo relations, understanding the diverse conditions along the border region proceeded through an examination of the divisions and relations between propertied and propertyless, of the way work was organized, of the pace and fluctuations of the market—in short, of the material features of particular societies across space and time.

This line of reasoning led eventually to a view of social change couched in terms of the displacement and formation of distinct class societies. I envisioned such change as a fundamentally uneven process that generally expressed itself through conflict and tension. In a typical sequence, an organic class society—one where social divisions and relations made sense to people—shattered and fell apart under the pressures of market development and the politics of new class groups. There followed a period of uncertainty as a new order was created and began to claim legitimacy from its constituents. The movement was toward the formation of a new class society, one where the ordering of people was again acceptable and appeared natural.

In concrete terms, this meant that the character of Mexican-Anglo relations would reflect the class composition of both the Mexican and Anglo communities and the manner in which this class structure was held together through work arrangements. To state the argument in a highly abbreviated form, Mexican landownership basically settled the question of whether or not Mexicans were defined and treated as racial inferiors. On the other hand, the character of work relations between owner and laborer—whether these were permanent, personalistic bonds or temporary, anonymous contracts—was refracted throughout the social order, shaping the manner in which politics, coercion, incentives, protocol—the stuff of social life—were organized. These work relations, for example, determined whether local politics would be organized through a political machine or through some exclusionary mechanism.

This type of microscopic analysis outlined the basis for explaining the variations in Mexican-Anglo relations in any one period. An underlying implication of this approach was that the arena for development consisted of a patchwork or mosaic of distinct local societies. These local societies were not vague entities but were bounded by administrative and political agencies with the authority to organize and regulate local social life—in the case of Texas, by county and city governments. Thus, whether or not Mexicans were "treated white" reflected the distinct class structure of Texas ranch and farm counties. The sociological patterns became more complex when the urban setting was considered; here the presence of Anglo merchants and an independent Mexican American middle class moderated the segregationist tenor evident in the farm areas. In view of these variations, it makes sense to say that Mexicans were more of a race in one place and less of a race in another.

Social or historical change in Mexican-Anglo relations was likewise made comprehensible through an analysis of the succession of dominant class orders, for these relations varied according to whether the dominant order was characterized by the paternalistic bonds between ranchers and cowboys, the impersonal divisions between growers and farm workers, or the flexible diplomacy between merchants and urban consumers. Briefly stated, the origins, growth, and demise of a racial order in the greater Texas border region corresponded roughly to a succession of ranch, farm, and urban-industrial class societies.

The complexity of race and ethnic relations in the development experience, then, does not signify an absence of order; it means only that the logical key or guide that can unravel the disorder has yet to be discovered. This work attempts to advance this process of discovery.

Organization of the History

If a straight line were teased from an entangled web of directions, Texas border history could be interpreted in terms of a succession of class societies, each with distinct ethnic relations: (a) a Spanish-Mexican *hacienda* society undermined by the Mexican War in the mid–nineteenth century; (b) an Anglo-Mexican ranch society undermined by an agricultural revolution at the turn of the century; (c) a segregated farm society undermined by world war and an urban-industrial revolution in the mid–twentieth century; and (d) a pluralistic urban-industrial society for the latter half of the twentieth century. This book is organized to describe this sequence of class orders and the corresponding change in Mexican-Anglo relations. Specifically, this history is divided into four periods, which I refer to as incorporation, reconstruction, segregation, and integration.

Part One discusses the experience of annexation and "incorporation." In the former Mexican territories, pogroms, expulsions, and subjugation of Mexicans were much in evidence where there was a sizable Anglo presence. Generally, however, the authorities of the new order sought to establish a "peace structure"—an accommodative arrangement between the leaders of the victors and those of the defeated—through which the commercial goals of Manifest Destiny could be pursued. In the nineteenth century, these efforts were centered on the creation of a land market. Where a peace structure existed, the old settlements retained their Mexican character. In short, at the time of independence in 1836 and annexation in 1848, one finds a landed Mexican elite, an ambitious Anglo mercantile clique, a class of independent but impoverished Mexican *rancheros*, and an indebted working class of Mexican *peones*. The new Anglo elite was generally Mexicanized and frequently intermarried or became *compadres* ("god-relatives") with landowning Mexican families. As one Texas scholar described the situation, the Anglo cattle barons established an "economic, social, and political feudalism" that was "natural" and not necessarily resented by those who submitted to it.[10] Annexation had merely changed the complexion of the landowning elite.

Part Two focuses on the agricultural developments that "reconstructed" the Anglo-Mexican ranch society, roughly the period from 1900 to 1920. At the turn of the century, when the "closing" of the frontier increased land values, and irrigation techniques, refrigerated railcars, and other innovations made farming in the arid Southwest possible and profitable, the second-generation American elite initiated an agricultural revolution. Within the space of ten years, much of the ranch country in South Texas was cleared to make room for farmers and a growing army of agricultural wage laborers. These farm developments did not implant themselves peacefully but provoked a violent reaction on the part of the old ranch settlers. In its most dramatic form, this conflict between new and old was expressed in the armed rebellion of Texas Mexicans and its thorough suppression by Texas Rangers. More commonly, the conflict expressed itself in bitter political contests between "old-timer" ranchers and "newcomer" farmers for control of county governments. The outcome of these political battles determined the path a local area followed.

Part Three describes the "modern" farm society of the 1920s and 1930s and examines the nature of race segregation. The large-scale immigration of farm settlers from the Midwest and the South and of farm laborers from Mexico overwhelmed the pioneer residents, both Anglo and Mexican, of the border region. Since farm labor requirements were satisfied by seasonal migrant labor and mediated through formal wage contracts, the paternalistic master-servant relationship of the ranch period became largely irrelevant. The decline of *patronismo*, however, did not signify that the experience of Mexican farm labor was that of free wage labor. A largely unexplored characteristic of this period consisted of the experimentation with various labor controls by growers.[11] Rather than being displaced from the land, the farm working class was firmly tied to the land through the use of "nonmarket" criteria and sanctions, including violence and coercion. Such labor controls set the context for a striking segregation of the races. In this period, the Mexicans became an "inferior" people, a community encircled and regulated by Jim Crow policies.

In Part Four, I discuss the demise of segregation and the rise of an urban-industrial order. This industrial period, unfolding roughly from World War II to the present, encapsulated the emergence of urban mercantile and consumer interests as a social and political force in Texas. Accompanying this emergence was a weakening of race segregation, reflecting a shift from a dominant class order of growers and farm laborers to one where merchants and urban consumers were prominent. The collapse of Jim Crow was accelerated by the Mexican American political activism of the 1960s and 1970s. Contemporary Mexican-Anglo relations, I suggest, represent a form of political integration, meaning that Texas Mexicans have been accepted as legitimate political actors and accorded a measure of influence.

The maps selected for the text illustrate key points in the transformation of a colonial Mexican society into a modern American order. The 1836 map of the Texas Republic emphasizes the importance of the Rio Grande in defining the shape of Texas; the map of cattle trails to Kansas points to the development of market connections for the Texas cattle industry; and the "Murder Map of the Texas-Mexican Border" highlights the bitter conflict between Mexican and Anglo during the 1910s. The remaining maps return to these themes. The map of county reorganization again points to the matter of redrawing political boundaries during the 1910s; the map of the migrant labor patterns (1939) illustrates the development of market routes for a labor market; and the map of political influence suggests the challenges and negotiation characteristic of Mexican-Anglo relations in the 1980s. In short, the maps display a certain symmetry in the development experience as they illustrate the themes of political boundary definition, market formation, and Mexican-Anglo relations.

The research materials for this work have been drawn from a variety of primary and secondary sources—they include cowboy diaries, travelers' accounts, land purchase records, old-timer recollections, congressional investigations, and the interview material collected by agricultural economist Paul S. Taylor in 1927–1930.[12] Since these materials lean heavily on Anglo sources, this is, in a sense, a history "from above." The Mexican side of the story surfaces throughout the discussion but still requires more research.

In the text, "Mexican" refers to both Texas Mexicans and Mexicans born in Mexico. "Texas Mexican" or "Mexican American" is used when it is important to stress the matter of group identity or American citizenship. The mention of "Mexican" and "Anglo" conforms with the everyday usage of the Southwest, although of course these labels conceal considerable diversity in the way both peoples have identified themselves. Texas Mexicans, for example, have called themselves Tejano, Mexicano, Indio, Castilian, Spanish, Latin American, Chicano, and Hispanic, with each identity reflecting a class character as well as the political climate of the time. Likewise, Anglo-Americans and European immigrants in Texas, including such "non-Anglo" subgroups as Irish, Italian, and Jewish, were referred to simply as "Anglos" or "whites."

Some aspects of this history may appear harsh. Such appearances stem, in part, from a common tendency to reject any effort that dwells too long on difficult memories or what appears to be the "bad side" of history. In the history of the "winning and developing" of the Southwest, however, the "bad" record is generally indistinguishable from the "good" accounts of victory over frontier hardships. There were many, as J. Frank Dobie described them, "rocky times in Texas" between Texicans and Mexicans.[13] The uneasy accommodation between Anglos and Mexicans, in fact, led me to emphasize the evidence pointing to paternalism and protection, the exchange of obligations and commitments, and the justice that was sometimes possible. This harshness can be further tempered by the fact, as argued in the concluding chapters, that the segregationist framework of southwestern society has been irreparably cracked.

The travelogues, diaries, and travelers' accounts could not help but stamp this work with the sense of a journey through communities across time. One source of inspiration was the "saddle-trip" that journalist Frederick Olmsted (writing for the *New York Times*) took through Texas in 1855–56.[14] The Texas trip, part of Olmsted's extensive travels through the South, was an effort to bring Northerner and Southerner into a dialogue on the slave issue. In a sense Olmsted was a "de Tocqueville" from the North traveling through the South. Although his travel notes and observations were keyed to the slave question, in Texas his commentaries touched on the significance of the Mexican War and annexation for the Mexican settlements. These commentaries served to kindle my interest in Texas history. Although a very different type of travelogue, this work, like Olmsted's, consists of observations whose intent is to promote a better understanding between two peoples.

PART ONE

Incorporation
1836–1900

Left: Mexican *charros* (courtesy Daughters of the Republic of Texas Library at the Alamo). *Above:* Cattle raid on the Texas border (*Harper's Weekly,* 1874; courtesy University of Texas Institute of Texan Cultures at San Antonio).

"The two races, the American distinctively so called, and the Spanish Americans or Mexicans, are now brought by the war into inseparable contact. No treaties can henceforth dissever them; and the inferior must give way before the superior race. . . . After the war, when the 40,000 soldiers now in Mexico shall be withdrawn, their places will be soon more than supplied by a still greater number of merchants, mechanics, physicians, lawyers, preachers, schoolmasters, and printers. In the towns of the valley of the Rio Grande, American stores are already established; the Mexicans themselves resort to these stores because they can there buy cheaper than of their own merchants; as for the American, we know him, he will never relinquish the right of trading, he would go to war again."

> Dr. Ashbel Smith
> Former Secretary of State, Texas Republic
> February 22, 1848

"There will be many coming. Choose from these newcomers men and women who are of your class. Make them your friends, and they will respond and be your friends."

> Advice of the old dons, circa 1870

On the Shape of Texas

*T*he American pioneers who helped to win and develop the Southwest came from widely varying backgrounds. There were the "GTT's," as the adventurers, petty speculators, and outlaws who had "gone to Texas" were known.[1] There were the European colonists, mainly farmers, mechanics, and craftsmen, which the Republic of Texas had settled to the west and south of the Austin–San Antonio road in order to establish a buffer between the Anglo-American colonies and the Indians and Mexicans. There were the pioneers who learned the Mexican way of riding horses and herding wild steers; these would eventually become known as "cowboys." And then, of course, there were the lawmen and rangers and bandits who waged sporadic warfare in the frontier. Although all these characters were part of the setting, I will focus on the least romantic and colorful, the merchants and land lawyers. I focus on them because I wish to explain the "making" of Texas, a history of market penetration and development that cannot be related without these characters. In fact, the "winning" of the West, of which the Mexican War was part, would be incomprehensible without merchants and lawyers.

This is not to argue that mercantile interests were the principal cause of the Mexican War. The causes were varied and complex—involving slaveholder interests, land-hungry frontiersmen, belief in Manifest Destiny, the Polk-Stockton intrigue, and so on—and have been discussed fully elsewhere.[2] It is clear, nonetheless, that the *comerciantes* were an essential element in this complex of causes, and clearer still that they were a major benefactor from the complex of results. The Mexican War assured the dominance of American mercantilism in the annexed territory as well as in what remained of Mexico. Therefore, to explain the particular development of Texas and of the Southwest in general, one must begin by looking at the region's principal architects, the capital-based and export-oriented element of the frontier folk, the merchants and land lawyers. To emphasize just how real and consequential mercantile "architecture" was, let us consider the huge, peculiar shape of the state of Texas.

In order to understand the far-flung boundaries of Texas, and the immediate cause of the Mexican War, we must forget the present condition of the Rio Grande and accept the fact that in the early nineteenth century the greatest expectations of the commercially minded settlers were pinned on that river. There was the intriguing possibility that the Rio Grande could connect the lucrative Chihuahua–Santa Fe trade with the Gulf of Mexico nearly two thousand miles downstream, and thus open up this trade to world markets.[3] The Spanish and Mexican governments had considered this a feasible project, and the earliest Anglo settlers often compared the Rio Grande's potential to that of the Mississippi or the Hudson. The original plan of Moses and Stephen Austin, in fact, called for establishing a colony in Texas that would serve as a base for linking the rich Santa Fe trade with Texas Gulf ports. Henry Austin, a cousin of Stephen, introduced the first steamboat on the Rio Grande in 1834, but the experiment did not get far. Mexican authorities, as Brownsville pioneer Edward Dougherty would later describe, constantly harassed and restricted the enterprise of American settlers, and this steamboat incident was a prime example. According to Dougherty, the Austins had secured the "navigation rights" from the Coahuila-Texas provincial government but the Tamaulipas provincial government, acceding to pressures from Mexican freighters and muleteers, refused to extend the same privilege and thus blocked any passageway to or from the Gulf. Speaking in 1867, at a time when steamboats had already worked a "miracle" in the Valley, Dougherty could not help but describe this episode sarcastically: "When in 1833 or '34, the enterprise of some Texans induced them to try a steamboat on the Rio Grande, it came as far as Matamoros . . . and instead of being welcomed as the harbinger of prosperity, as the dawn of a new era, every proprietor of an 'atajo' of pack-mules, saw destruction to that venerable institution, if the 'moving houses' of the Americans were to be permitted to do the carrying of merchandise. The pack-mule interest being backed by that of the 'burros,' carried the day. . . . The steamer, receiving no encouragement, abandoned the field."[4] The Mexican War, however, ended all such obstacles.

The commercial importance of the Rio Grande did not lie simply with the distant Santa Fe trade. What is usually overlooked but which proved to be as critical and more directly related to the outbreak of hostilities, was the port trade of Matamoros on the lower end of the Rio Grande. In the late 1820s, silver bullion, lead, wool, hides, and beef tallow from Monterrey, Saltillo, and San Luis Potosí were all passing through Matamoros, with silver constituting 90 percent or more of the value of the exports. By 1830 Matamoros, with a

Republic of Texas, 1836 (based on *Texas Almanac, 1986–1987*).

population of 7,000, was the largest town on the northern Mexican frontier and third in trade among all Mexican ports on the Gulf. Matamoros, in short, seemed destined to be the great entrepôt of northern Mexico. North American merchants recognized the strategic importance of this port city. David Willard Smith, a "Connecticut Yankee" merchant in Matamoros and also U.S. consul there, made it clear, in one dispatch sent to Washington in 1832, that the natural advantage of Matamoros gave it "a decided preponderance in a commercial and military point of view" to any other port on the Gulf of Mexico and that such important advantages had not "escaped the attention and enterprise of our citizens."[5] Perhaps the only disadvantage of Matamoros, a fatal weakness as it turned out, was that its harbor of Brazos Santiago was ten miles away—*north* of the mouth of the Rio Grande.

When the province of Texas declared its independence in 1836, the far-sighted men of the Austin and DeWitt colonies understood well the critical importance of the Rio Grande. The young republic, embarking on an ambitious and aggressive strategy, claimed the entire length of the river as its boundary with Mexico. It was a paper claim, of course, for the republic had no control or influence beyond the Nueces. Texan forces undertook two major military expeditions into Nuevo México (the Santa Fe Expedition) and Tamaulipas (the Mier Expedition) in order to assert these territorial claims, but the campaigns failed miserably. Defeat and capture, however, did not dampen the expansionist zeal of the Texians. The diary kept by Col. Thomas Jefferson Green contained the following spirited observation—written as he and the defeated Mier Expedition were marched through the lower Rio Grande settlements as prisoners: "The Rio Grande, from its head to its source, from the forty-second to the twenty-fifth degree of north latitude, is capable of maintaining many millions of population, with a variety of products which no river upon the north continent can boast. This river once settled with the enterprise and intelligence of the English race, will yearly send forth an export which it will require hundreds of steamers to transport to its delta, while its hides, wool, and metals may be increased to an estimate which would now appear chimerical."[6]

The strategic importance of the Rio Grande was well understood by the leaders of the Texas Republic. Here was a river that could link the rich commerce of northern Mexico, from Santa Fe to San Luis Potosí, with world markets; a river that could rival the Mississippi as the most important trade route of the continent. With the admission of Texas into the United States in 1845, the scene for the Mexi-

can American War was set, and the wildest hopes of the hawks
became possibilities. With American troops marching to claim the
Rio Grande as the new boundary between the United States and
Mexico, an armed confrontation was inevitable. But the confrontation was not, as many have argued, a matter of conflicting claims
over the "Nueces Strip." This stretch of land was practically worthless. Rather, the critical issue, as historian Leroy Graf makes clear,
concerned control of the harbor of Brazos Santiago, the only practical funnel through which northern Mexico could commerce with
world markets.[7]

With subsequent occupation of Mexico's northern provinces, Texas
pressed its claim to the length of the Rio Grande. In the south, it put
a quick end (in 1850) to what was seen as a northern-inspired "sepa-
ratist" movement of Brownsville merchants and lawyers to gain territorial status for the Nueces Strip. For its northwestern boundary, it
organized a Santa Fe County and appointed some county officials.
But these latter claims were so excessive that neither Congress nor
the president was willing to accept them. Bitter negotiations between the federal government and the former republic escalated into
threats of war, but a hard compromise was finally managed.[8] Texas,
whose treasury was virtually bankrupt, relinquished its claim to
Santa Fe in return for a compensation of ten million dollars. The
present shape of Texas attests, however, to the bargaining skill and
intransigent position of the Texan representatives. The western ex-
tremity of the huge state was pegged to include the important Paso
del Norte, through which the Santa Fe–Chihuahua trail and any
east-west routes had to pass.

Thus Texas emerged from the Mexican War with firm control of
both the Santa Fe–Chihuahua trade and, almost two thousand miles
downriver, the Matamoros-Saltillo trade. Such control proved to be
quite lucrative. The trade passing through American customs at "Brazos St. Jago"—the name became slightly Anglicized with annexation—in the boom period following the war was valued between ten
to fourteen million dollars annually.[9] By considering the Texan de-
signs on the commerce of northern Mexico, we come to a better
understanding of the rather huge and odd shape of Texas.

As far as navigating the length of the Rio Grande, the possibility that had first excited the hopes of many commercially minded
American pioneers, we might note that a U.S. Army steamer, in a
successful experiment, landed her cargo at Laredo in 1846 and that
an expeditionary patrol reached Presidio Rio Grande in 1850. The
expeditionary report, which concluded that the river could be im-

proved to make it navigable for steamboats to make the trip, was general knowledge by the time journalist Frederick Olmsted passed through Texas in 1855. His observations on the river sounded the common opinion of the time: "The river is regularly navigable for small steamboats, as far as Roma. Were there sufficient commercial inducement, it is probable that a class of boats might be constructed to ascend as high as the Pecos, the chief impediment, beside mere shifting shoals, being the Kingsbury Rapids, near Presidio. Through these it is thought a channel might be opened at an expense of one hundred thousand dollars."[10]

Such a recommendation was never followed, noted Edward Dougherty in an address before the Lone Star Literary Association of Brownsville, because the treaty specified that neither government could do anything on the River Bravo without the consent of the other. Several Mexican parties would object to any river project, even for the purpose of improving navigation, for "the masses have yet the same prejudices that their fathers had."[11] Dougherty saw no need for such opposition to dampen the "enlightened" spirit, for the commercial possibilities of the Valley were too great for advancement to stop. The enthusiastic Dougherty added that the Valley "has a greater producing capacity than that of any other stream in the United States of the same size, only needing labor to make the whole of it a perpetual garden," and that "nature designed it to be the outlet of the wealth of all this country." All that they needed to do was to give "Progress" a shove, as Dougherty exhorted the Brownsville literati: ". . . let us all willingly set our shoulders to the wheel and push ahead the 'car of Progress' in our noble valley, and when we get it started, let us take care and keep it marching on, marching on, and that we ourselves keep up with it."[12] Dougherty's words were prophetic. It would take another forty years, in the hands of another generation, but the "car of Progress" would transform the region.

The following chapters outline the connections between the Mexican War and the Anglo mercantile elite that directed the development of the Texas border region. The Mexican War secured the important port of Brazos Santiago for the United States, assured the commercial predominance of American merchants, and provided through the quartermaster system the critical infrastructure for the reorganization of marketing channels to northern Mexico.

The Mexican War, in other words, created the basis and organization for a powerful export-oriented upper class. There were, of course, other significant consequences of annexation. Not only had control of the Saltillo and San Luis Potosí markets been placed firmly in the hands of American merchants, but also a vast territory had been brought under new land and water laws. The effect was to "liberate" previously entailed property. Entailment had no status in Anglo-American jurisprudence; it was no protection against subdivision, as many land grant heirs who held "undivided interests" were to discover in court. Land was now a marketable commodity.

Ice cold beer and law West of the Pecos, Langtry, Texas, 1880s; white-bearded man is Judge Roy Bean (photo by H. Leslie Evans; courtesy University of Texas Institute of Texan Cultures at San Antonio).

RIVER NAVIGATION.

STEAMER ✳ "BESSIE"

–Makes Trips About Every Ten Days, From–

BROWNSVILLE TO

ALL UP-RIVER POINTS,

—:CARRYING FREIGHT AND PASSENGERS FOR:—

Santa Maria, Edinburg, Rio Grande City and

Roma, Texas;

Reynosa, Camargo and Meir, Mexico.

William Kelly,

Left: From Brownsville to all upriver points, 1893 (Chatfield, *Twin Cities of the Border*). *Above:* Brownsville steamboat landing, ca. 1865 (courtesy Barker Texas History Center, University of Texas at Austin).

2. The Rivalship of Peace

AMPLE HISTORICAL documents have described the Anglo-Saxon spirit that fueled the struggle for Texas independence in 1835–36 and the war with Mexico a decade later. Texas independence and subsequent annexation of the northern Mexican territory were essentially the reflection of a "manifest destiny." The Anglo-Saxon nation was bound to glory; the inferior, decadent Indian race and the half-breed Mexicans were to succumb before the inexorable march of the superior Anglo-Saxon people. In more defined terms, this destiny called for an expansion of the nation westward to the Pacific Ocean and southward to the Isthmus of Panama; and it called for the ports that would assure the nation's future as a mercantile empire.[1] The oratory of the former secretary of state of the Texas Republic, Dr. Ashbel Smith, before a Galveston audience in 1848 was characteristic of the language of Manifest Destiny. Describing the Mexican War as "part of a mission, of the destiny allotted to the Anglo-Saxon race . . . to civilize, to Americanize this continent," Dr. Smith believed that the "rude shocks" that Mexicans would experience would come not from "warlike hostilities" but from "the energy, industry and talents of the American population in peace." Indeed, Smith noted, "the war in which we are now engaged is comparatively a small matter, except as hastening and preluding to the rivalship of peace."[2]

At the time of Smith's address, there remained only the task of fulfilling the "grand, the important consequences of the Mexican War," of securing the "end of the institutions of Mexico" and carrying out the "substituting of new institutions."

Once annexation of Mexico's northern territories was formalized, the institutional transformation of which Smith spoke revolved fundamentally around the question of what was to be done with the annexed Mexican settlements. The Treaty of Guadalupe Hidalgo had outlined the general provisions for the protection of the Mexican person and property in the ceded territories. But in the immediate, day-to-day sense, there remained the matter of carrying forth the mission for land and trade; and there was the matter of dealing with the hatreds and prejudices created by war, and the question of establishing stable government.

This chapter explores the role of these basic elements—the sentiments of war, the need for stable governance, the desire for land and trade—in the immediate postwar period. The manner in which these elements mixed and separated along the Texas border region influenced the character of Mexican-Anglo relations in the latter half of the nineteenth century. These elements set the initial ground from which Mexican-Anglo relations would evolve.

Sentiments of War

War and annexation, so far as the survivors are concerned, generally raise the question of what to do with the defeated enemy. In theory and in practice, extermination and assimilation have defined the two extremes, with most outcomes falling in between. There are two major sequences, however. On the one hand, the occupying power may simply overwhelm the defeated people through immigration and settlement, so that within the space of a few years everything becomes completely transformed. Laws, public customs, authority, even the physical appearance of old settlements become foreign and alien to the native people.

The second sequence may have the same results but over a much longer stretch of time. There usually come first the merchants, who benignly and paternally serve as intermediaries between the natives and the new authorities. They may even intermarry and be seen as trusted protectors by the native people. There may be a period where a "bicultural" or "hybrid" generation exists, where the stamp of the native is still strong and vigorous. Nonetheless, the new rulers, however bicultural, plant the foundation for a complete transformation. They represent the seed of a new development, of an irrevocable change in evolution.

Both postwar sequences unfolded in Texas after its independence in 1836. The experience was determined mainly by previous settlement patterns, established travel routes, and, of course, economic incentives. There was no gold rush in Texas, but the land rush and the chaos of war overwhelmed the Mexican settlements above the Nueces River. Ten years later, in 1846, the Rio Grande settlements experienced the trauma of war and annexation. The fact that the land beyond the Nueces was seen as a "wild horse desert" spared these settlements the tragic experience of independence.[3] This semi-arid region west and south of the Nueces presented few opportunities beyond the commerce of El Paso, Laredo, and Matamoros. In these places, where Mexicans were the dominant population, an accommodative understanding between American merchants and the old Mexican elite worked to keep local matters under control.

Above the Nueces

The Tejanos, or Texas Mexicans, were, as historian James Crisp aptly put it, a "people of paradox."[4] José Antonio Navarro and others like Juan Seguin had believed it possible to be both a proud Mexicano and a loyal Tejano. During the rebellion against the Santa Anna dictatorship, such beliefs were not contradictory. Initially at least, the rebellion appeared to be another provincial revolt of liberal federalists against the conservative constitutionalists led by Santa Anna, a struggle similar to others then occurring throughout Mexico. The character of the Texas revolt changed, however, after 1836. The political alliance between Mexicans and Anglos in Texas, the alliance that made Lorenzo de Zavala the first vice-president of the republic for a few days, began unraveling soon after the rout of Santa Anna's army at San Jacinto. A spirit of revenge and abandon prevailed in the young republic, and many ex-soldiers carried out raids that claimed the land, stock, and lives of Mexicans, ally and foe alike. Many of the victims had fought alongside the Anglo colonists against the Santa Anna dictatorship. As a descendant of a loyalist Tejano family put it, "these men who had favored the independence, suffered from the very beginning. . . . Many lost their grants, and all lost their ideal— The Republic of Texas."[5]

The bitter aftermath of the Texan Revolution was felt most directly by the Mexican settlements along the Guadalupe and San Antonio rivers, those closest to the Anglo-American colonies of Austin and DeWitt. Here the Mexican communities were subjugated and in many cases expelled. In 1837 the Mexican communities of Victoria, San Patricio, La Bahía (Goliad), and Refugio were the first to feel the vengeance for the massacres at Goliad and the Alamo. The old Mexican town of La Bahía, once an important port with a thousand residents and the unlucky site of Fannin's massacre, was completely razed, and the fort and church destroyed. All that remained of this town when journalist Frederick Olmsted rode through in 1855 were extensive ruins and a "modern village . . . composed of about twenty jacales."[6] Even the aristocratic family of the empresario Don Martín de León was not spared recriminations. A. B. J. Hammett, biographer of the family, has sketched a vivid portrayal of the bitter experience of the Texas Mexicans loyal to the Texan cause: "This family like other loyal Mexican families were driven from their homes, their treasures, their cattle and horses and their lands, by an army of reckless, war-crazy people, who overran the town of Victoria. These new people distrusted and hated the Mexicans, simply because they were Mexican, regardless of the fact they were both on the same side of the fighting during the war."[7] During the brief tenure of the Texas Republic, Texas Mexicans suffered from forced marches, general dispossession, and random violence. In 1839 over a hundred Mexican families were forced to abandon their homes and lands in the old settlement of Nacogdoches in what is now East Texas.

In San Antonio, the old capital and stronghold of Texas, the life and property of Mexicans were hardly secure. Juan Seguin, captain in the Texas army, hero of San Jacinto, and (until recently) the last Mexican mayor of San Antonio, in 1840–42, noted that in those days "the American straggling adventurers . . . were already beginning to work their dark intrigues against the native families, whose only crime was, that they owned large tracts of land and desirable property." More eloquently,

> San Antonio claimed then, as it claims now, to be the first city of Texas; it was also the receptacle of the scum of society. My political and social situation brought me into continual contact with that class of people. At every hour of the day and night, my countrymen ran to me for protection against the assaults or exactions of these adventurers. Some times by persuasion, I prevailed on them to desist; some times also, force had to be resorted to. How could I have done otherwise? Were not the victims my own countrymen, friends, and associates? Could I leave them defenceless, exposed to the assaults of foreigners, who, on the pretext that they were Mexican, treated them worse than brutes?[8]

Due to murder threats against him and his family, Seguin was forced to flee to Mexico in 1842.

Other prominent families left, and by the 1840s, according to Canary Islander José María Rodríguez, "at least two hundred Old Spanish families" who had lived in San Antonio in the early 1800s were gone.[9] The machinations of Texan authorities and merchants against the landowning families were hardly disguised. Texan Army officer Thomas Jefferson Green, for example, was asked to use his military position to further his interest in Bexar County land by Edward Dwyer, a prosperous San Antonio merchant. In a letter to Green, dated October 4, 1836, Dwyer observed: " . . . the people [of San Antonio de Béxar] . . . are not sufficiently scared to make an advantageous sale of their lands. In case two or three hundred of our troops should be stationed there, I have no doubt but a man could make some good speculations with Gold and Silver. Bank notes will not do to purchase land from Mexicans."[10]

Even without the use of force or fraud, the great apprehension about the new Anglo-American rule compelled many Mexican landowners to sell and leave San Antonio. The erosion of the land base that formed the principal wealth of the Spanish-Mexican population began immediately after 1836. In the six years following the Texas Revolution, from 1837 to 1842, 13 of the most prominent "American buyers" purchased 1,368,574 acres from 358 Mexicans. Members of the Mexican elite were also actively involved in buying land, but the amount they accumulated—the 14 most prominent Mexican buyers purchased 278,769 acres from 67 Mexican owners—was hardly comparable with that amassed by the Anglo pioneers.[11]

Ten years later, in the aftermath of the Mexican War, another series of punitive expulsions occurred in Central and Southeast Texas. Entire communities were uprooted. Mexicans were driven from Austin in 1853 and again in 1855, from Seguin in 1854, from the counties of Matagorda and Colorado in 1856, and from Uvalde in 1857. Frederick Olmsted in his "saddle-trip" through Texas described these Mexicans as "lower-class" peons who were being expelled on charges of being horse thieves and consorters of slave insurrection. One newspaper item told the story of this period plainly:

> MATAGORDA.—The people of Matagorda county have held a meeting and ordered every Mexican to leave the county. To strangers this may seem wrong, but we hold it to be perfectly right and highly necessary; but a word of explanation should be given. In the first place, then, there are none but the lower class or "Peon" Mexicans in the county; secondly, they have no fixed domicile, but hang around the plantations, taking the likeliest negro girls for wives; and, thirdly, they often steal horses, and these girls, too, and endeavor to run them to Mexico. We should rather have anticipated an appeal to Lynch law, than the mild course which has been adopted.[12]

Even in San Antonio there was an attempt to drive away a large section of the Mexican population; but the plan failed because the Germans, who would have formed a major element of the proposed vigilante committee, refused to support these efforts. "They were of the opinion," observed Olmsted, "that this was not the right and republican way."[13]

By 1856, San Antonio had been half-deserted by its Mexican population. Of the town population of 10,500, 4,000 were Mexican, 3,000 were German, and the remaining 3,500 were American. The San Antonio of Olmsted was quite different from the San Antonio of Juan Seguin only twelve years before. The "money-capital" and government were in the hands of the Americans, while most of the mechanics and the smaller shopkeepers were German. The Mexicans appeared "to have almost no other business than that of carting goods." Nearly 60 percent of the Mexican work force were cartmen.[14]

The American settlers, in speaking of Mexicans, constantly distinguished themselves as "white folks." Newcomers were sometimes surprised at the rights of Mexicans. Olmsted overheard one newcomer informing another American that he had seen a Mexican with a revolver and stating that they shouldn't be allowed to carry firearms. The other replied that it would be difficult to prevent it— "they think themselves just as good as white men."[15] Around the Victoria area, Anglo-Americans had sharply distinct views of Germans and Mexicans: "They always employed German mechanics, and spoke well of them. Mexicans were regarded in a somewhat unchristian tone, not as heretics or heathen to be converted with flannel and tracts, but rather as vermin to be exterminated. The lady was particularly strong in her prejudices. White folks and Mexicans were never made to live together, anyhow, and the Mexicans had no business here. They were getting so impertinent, and were so well protected by the laws, that the Americans would just have to get together and drive them all out of the country."[16]

Not as fortunate were the Mexican teamsters who carted freight along the San Antonio–Goliad highway. During the summer and fall of 1857, Mexican teamsters were attacked by masked bands. The assailants were believed to be American teamsters who resented the competition with Mexicans. Despite seventy-five murders, civil authorities proved unwilling to arrest the attackers. As a result Mexicans began leaving San Antonio and prices increased 30 percent. After considerable pressure from San Antonio merchants, a troop of Rangers was detailed to patrol the trade routes in November. The raids ceased but no suspects were ever apprehended. The raids proved successful: Mexicans were effectively removed from the freight business between San Antonio and Gulf Coast ports.[17]

Thus, in the region where considerable numbers of Mexicans and

Anglos lived, the tragic aftermath one expects of war—recriminations, dispossession of land and belongings, violence, and revenge—was much in evidence.

Along the Rio Grande — Mexican remained in majority

Although the Rio Grande settlements south and west of San Antonio were not directly affected by the Texian struggles for independence, these wars depopulated the coastal areas close to the Nueces River, the boundary between the Mexican states of Texas and Tamaulipas. The livestock industry in this area was completely disrupted as Mexican settlers fled from their *ranchos* to the protected towns of the Rio Grande. As a measure of retribution, the Texas Republic had declared Mexican livestock to be public property, prompting many Texan veterans to conduct stock raids below the Nueces. These "reckless young fellows," according to one old-timer, were the first to be given the name of "cowboys."[18] In short, between 1836 and 1846 the strip between the Nueces and the Rio Grande constituted a veritable "no-man's land," claimed by the Republics of Texas and Mexico but actually controlled by Indian tribes.

Military occupation in 1846 and subsequent annexation replicated, in some respects, the experience above the Nueces after Texas independence. On the one hand, the fate of Mexican property rights was uncertain. Squatters and adventurers were everywhere; tales of fraud and chicanery were common; and deliberations in the Texas Legislature and in Texas courts all suggested an eventual confiscation of Mexican-owned property. The considerable expense of legal proceedings to defend old Spanish and Mexican titles, together with the uncertainty of the outcome, prompted many owners to sell to interested American parties at low prices.[19]

On the other hand, as had happened with the Texas Revolution, there was considerable repatriation after the Mexican War. Mexican refugees moved across the Rio Grande and settled among the old established towns of Paso del Norte, Guerrero, Mier, Camargo, Reynosa, and Matamoros. Other refugees established new towns, such as Nuevo Monterrey (now Nuevo Laredo) opposite Laredo and Mesilla and Guadalupe, both near El Paso del Norte.[20] Despite these refugee movements, Texas south and west of the Nueces River remained predominantly Mexican in population.

Unlike Texas above the Nueces, where the Mexican population had soon found itself outnumbered, the length of the Rio Grande region remained isolated until the turn of the century. Following the initial Anglo settlement after the Mexican War, there was no continued influx. The only exception was the Civil War period when another layer of ex-soldiers and merchant–camp followers was added to the communities of the Upper and Lower Rio Grande valleys. El Paso served as an important stop for travelers and merchants, but permanent Anglo settlement remained small until the arrival of the railroad in 1881. In South Texas, Laredo and Brownsville were completely away from the westward land movements and no free land existed. As in the case of El Paso, the few Anglo settlers who came were merchants, lawyers, or professionals whose occupation was tied with the northern Mexican trade or the new land business of the border region.[21]

The first U.S. Census, taken shortly after annexation, enumerated approximately 14,000 Mexicans in Texas, a serious undercount, which may be attributable to the personnel employed to collect the data—U.S. marshals, soldiers, and tax officials. The French clergyman Abbé Emanuel Domenech, for example, questioned the numbers, believing that "the Mexicans were then [in 1848] the most numerous, notwithstanding all that compilers of statistics have stated to the contrary; next the Anglo-Americans, and then the Germans." For the stretch of Texas the *abbé* was most familiar with, he was correct. Eighty to 90 percent of the population in a 300-mile-wide strip along the Texas-Mexico border was Mexican; and in some places the proportion of Mexican to Anglos reached about twenty-five to one.[22]

According to the best estimates Olmsted found, in 1850 there were 25,000 Mexicans in the state. Approximately 7,000 were concentrated in the region above the Nueces (around San Antonio and Goliad), 5,500 were below the Nueces (Laredo and the lower Rio Grande), 8,500 were in West Texas (El Paso and Presidio), and 4,000 were "floating about" the state. Comparable estimates for the Anglo population were 120,000 above the Nueces and 2,500 south and west of the Nueces. In other words, in 1850 the population beyond the Nueces consisted approximately of 2,500 Anglos and probably 18,000 Mexicans.[23]

In the immediate postwar period, this demographic mix made for an unstable situation. As had occurred earlier (in the 1830s) with the San Antonio and Victoria settlements, the Rio Grande settlements attracted the worst elements among the Anglo pioneers. In Laredo, as José María Rodríguez recalled in his memoirs, some Americans "began a movement to clean out the Mexicans. They would rant at public meetings and declare that this was an American country and the Mexicans ought to be run out."[24] In the Lower Valley, Abbé Emanuel Domenech, who ministered to the religious needs of the Brownsville area from 1849 to 1855, was blunt in his appraisal of the

Americans: "The Americans of the Texian frontiers are, for the most part, the very scum of society—bankrupts, escaped criminals, old volunteers, who after the Treaty of Guadalupe Hidalgo, came into a country protected by nothing that could be called a judicial authority, to seek adventure and illicit gains."[25] The *abbé* had especially harsh words about the Texas Rangers and ex-army volunteers in the area, describing them as "the very dregs of society, and the most degraded of human creatures." The Abbé Domenech was equally frank in his judgment of Mexicans: "I could never comprehend the Mexican's submission, supporting, as he did, at once the cruelty and the contempt of a nation which he sovereignly detested, had I not been so often the witness of his incredible *nonchalance* and imperturbable meekness. In these badly-organized regions, the Mexican might have an easy vengeance on his persecutors, who are quite the minority on the Texan frontiers; but vengeance is not in his heart; he would rather forget an injury than take the trouble of avenging it."[26] Notwithstanding the *abbé's* assessment, the situation along the Rio Grande proved to be extremely volatile. All that was lacking for the emergence of a movement of resistance and retribution was a precipitating gesture or act of defiance. The first Cortina War, which exploded a few years after Domenech had returned to France, had such origins.

According to the well-embossed story, Juan Nepomuceno Cortina, scion of a wealthy landowning family in the Lower Valley, came to the defense of a drunk *ranchero* and former servant from the beating of Brownsville Marshal Bob Shears.[27] Cortina shot the marshal in the arm in self-defense and carried the *ranchero* off to his ranch. Charges of attempted murder were filed, the Brownsville authorities refusing to compromise with Cortina. In response, Cortina and his supporters raided and captured Brownsville, the initial blow of a six-month-long war. Retiring to his Rancho del Carmen (in Cameron County), Cortina issued the following proclamation to the Mexicans of Texas (November 23, 1859): "Mexicans! When the State of Texas began to receive the new organization which its sovereignty required as a part of the United States, flocks of vampires, in the guise of men, came and scattered themselves in the settlements, without any capital except the corrupt heart and the most perverse intentions. . . . Many of you have been robbed of your property, incarcerated, chased, murdered, and hunted like wild beasts, because your labor was fruitful, and because your industry excited the vile avarice which led them."[28] Within a month, Cortina had organized an irregular force of five to six hundred men. Many of those involved in the Cortina War, according to a federal report on the matter, were *rancheros* who had been "driven away from the Nueces." Cortina defeated the Brownsville Rifles and Tobin's Rangers from San Antonio, maintaining control of the region until the U.S. Army sent troops in December 1859.[29]

The results of the Cortina War, according to the army commandant, were the depopulation and laying to waste of the whole country from Brownsville to Rio Grande City, 120 miles. Business as far up as Laredo, 240 miles, had been interrupted and suspended for five months. There remained no property belonging to Americans that had not been destroyed. And those *ranchos* spared by Cortina's men had been burned by the Texans.[30]

At the other end of Texas, attempts to assert ownership over several large salt deposits in the mid-1870s ignited a confrontation known as the "Salt War." Anglo merchants and politicians had shown interest in the salt lakes at the foot of the Guadalupe Mountains since annexation, and conflict over various schemes to tax the salt had constituted a volatile element in El Paso politics. For a hundred years or more the residents of Ysleta, San Elizario, and other towns along the Upper Rio Grande had hauled salt from the lakes freely. The lakes had created in these towns a group of merchants who plied salt throughout northern Mexico. In 1877 Judge Charles Howard attempted to make the lakes into "a money-making proposition," but his actions, including the public murder of Louis Cardis, the leader of the Mexican opposition, aroused a "mob" to seek revenge. Howard and two of his associates were killed, and the relief troop of Texas Rangers was defeated before order was restored.[31]

Thus, along the border, overt land dispossession, expulsions, and other repressive measures were not safe options. The Anglo pioneers were quite conscious of their small numbers in the region. After the Cortina rebellion, the threat of an uprising formed an important undercurrent in their psychology, a fear that perhaps motivated the practice of benevolent *patronismo* on their part. The "Cortina Wars" of 1859–60 and later of 1873–75 and the El Paso "Salt War" of 1877 were examples of what could happen. In all three episodes, competing claims to land or livestock precipitated a state of virtual warfare, with a mobilized Mexican element matching arms with the local constabulary and the Texas Rangers. The losers in these conflicts were usually the uninvolved civilian population, who bore the brunt of escalating and indiscriminate retaliation and counterretaliation. Indeed, the Nueces Strip of South Texas and the Trans-Pecos region of West Texas remained "untamed" for nearly fifty years after annexation. A frontier battalion of Texas Rangers, stationed in the border zone until 1920, represented the armed force of the Anglo-Texas order. A military unit during the Mexican War, the Texas

Rangers functioned as the military police of occupation, waging sporadic warfare whenever the need arose.[32]

Profits and stability, however, could not be maintained under such volatile circumstances. Peace and everyday governance required a more secure arrangement.

Structure of Peace : *accommodation between Anglos & elite Mexican*

The changes brought about by Texas independence and later American annexation were clear: a new political authority, new markets, and new land laws, to mention the most sweeping. A highly conspicuous elite of Anglo merchants, lawyers, army officers, and officeholders now controlled the trade and politics of the annexed Mexican settlements. Whether they lived together above San Pedro Springs in San Antonio, on the bluff overlooking the bay of Corpus Christi, or around Franklin's store opposite El Paso del Norte, the clique of Anglo merchants, military officers, and lawyer politicians constituted a self-conscious foreign enclave.[33] How did they govern?

In the case of the Texas-Mexican border region and generally in the annexed Southwest, the ability to govern in the immediate postwar period was secured through an accommodation between the victorious Anglos and the defeated Mexican elite, with the latter in command of the Mexican communities. In sociological terms, this accommodation was essentially a "peace structure."

By "peace structure" I refer to a general postwar arrangement that allows the victors to maintain law and order without the constant use of force. The concept focuses on the manner in which victors are able to exercise and establish authority over the defeated. In the Texas-Mexican region, such a peace structure was characterized by two major aspects: one, the subordination of Mexicans to Anglos in matters of politics and authority; and two, the accommodation between new and old elites.

The Fabric of Peace

Although the American presence generally represented a new class in an old Mexican society, it did not completely transform the traditional authority structure. On the contrary, the American merchants and lawyers merely affixed themselves atop the Mexican hierarchy. In some cases, they intermarried and became an extension of the old elite. For individual families of the Mexican elite, intermarriage was a convenient way of containing the effects of Anglo military victory on their status, authority, and class position. For the ambitious Anglo merchant and soldier with little capital, it was an easy way of acquiring land. The social basis for postwar governance, in other words, rested on the class character of the Mexican settlements.

These settlements were essentially a three-tiered society composed of landed elite, small landowners (*rancheros*) and *peones.* San Antonio in the 1830s, for example, was a highly structured class society. At the top were the prominent landed families, who lived in spacious flat-roofed stone houses; below them were the *rancheros,* who spent the greater part of their days working their cattle and horses and whose small adobe homes usually consisted of one sparsely furnished room; and at the the the bottom tier of the class order were the laborers, or *jornaleros,* who lived in *jacales,* which were nothing more than mud houses with thatched roofs.[34] A prominent contemporary of the period, José María Rodríguez, described the "great distinction between the east and west side of the [San Antonio] river" in the following manner: "The west side of the river was supposed to be the residence of the first families here, and the descendants of the Indians and Spanish soldiers settled on the east side of the river. . . . Most of the Canary Islanders who lived on this [west] side took great pride in preventing any marriage with mixed races and when one did mix he lost his caste with the rest."[35] Although frontier conditions made this caste system somewhat fluid, and families could in generations pass from one caste to another, the lines themselves were clearly drawn. Moreover, they were distinctions that the American pioneers were quick to recognize and accept. Ample evidence points to an early accommodation between old and new elites. Although initially outside this Spanish-Mexican structure, the Anglo-Saxon pioneers were accepted—depending on their class, of course—as equals by the "Spanish" elite.[36] By 1842, however, only six years after independence, the peaceful accommodation that had characterized Mexican-Anglo relations collapsed. The loss of land, the flight of the Mexican elite, and the Mexican War a few years later quickly eroded the influence of Mexicans.

In spite of this, San Antonio after the Civil War still had appearances, according to one resident, of a village "typical of Mexico then." The "early Americans" had become acclimated, had intermarried in many instances, "and in turn kept up many of the customs of this quaint old Spanish town." The town of about ten or twelve thousand inhabitants had a mingling of American, German, and French colonists with a large Mexican population. In the plaza could be heard "a babble of voices from three or four languages" but "almost everyone spoke Spanish and most of the business was conducted in this common language." The resident observer concluded that "the political border was at the Rio Grande, but Military Plaza was the commercial and social border between the countries."[37]

The Rio Grande settlements south and west of San Antonio differed little in their social structure. At the time of American occupation in the mid–nineteenth century, there were four major strata: the landed elite; the *arrimados*, or landless relatives of the elite; the *rancheros* and *vaqueros*; and the *pastores*. The society of the time has been described as a "patriarchal" one where the landlord acted as the head and the *vaqueros* and *pastores* acted as "faithful" subjects.[38]

Of the Rio Grande settlements, Laredo represented the peace structure at its best. Although Laredo had suffered from the depredations of "East Texas outlaws" and many families had resettled across the river (thus founding Nuevo Laredo), much of the strife prevailing in the Texas interior had been avoided. To a large extent, the confirmation of twenty land grant titles by the Texas Legislature in the 1850s was responsible for the peace. The wealth and power of landed elite were generally left undisturbed, and considerable intermarriage bound the old and new elites. Thus, in the postannexation politics of the area, ethnic divisions were secondary to those of class. Ordinances were published in both English and Spanish, American and Mexican holidays celebrated, and political offices divided equally; Mexicans ran the city while Anglos ran the county. Likewise, there was a tacit division of labor; Mexicans ranched and farmed while Anglos commerced.[39]

In the Lower Valley, the conservative upper class, fearful of outright confiscation of their property, was divided in their response to the Anglo presence. According to a well-informed source, some landed families "learned to get along with Americans by overlooking whatever misfortunes fell on the lower class of Mexicans." Retaining their property and benefiting from the American presence, the established families had little cause for complaint.[40] Their loyalties were subjected to a difficult test with Cortina's rebellion in 1859. Some lent the "war" quiet approval while others organized the repression of the "uprising." Unwavering support for the Anglo military forces—the Brownsville Rifles, the Texas Rangers, U.S. Army troops, and, later, Confederate troops—came from the Laredo elite in the form of a company of Mexican *rancheros* led by Santos Benavides, grandson of Don Tomás Sánchez, founder of Laredo.[41]

As in San Antonio and Laredo, the accommodation between the old and incoming elites in the Lower Valley manifested itself in tactical marriages. It was customary among the Mexican elite, as Jovita González has noted, that daughters were "married at an early age, and not for love, but for family connections and considerations."[42]

On the other hand, for the Anglo settler, marrying a Mexican with property interests made it possible to amass a good-sized stock ranch without considerable expense. The Americans and the European immigrants, most of whom were single men, married the daughters of the leading Spanish-Mexican families and made Rio Grande City "a cosmopolitan little town." Among those who claimed the Spanish language as their own were families with such surnames as Lacaze, Laborde, Lafargue, Decker, Marx, Block, Monroe, Nix, Stuart, and Ellert. As one Texas Mexican from this upper class recalled: "There were neither racial nor social distinctions between Americans and Mexicans, we were just one family. This was due to the fact that so many of us of that generation had a Mexican mother and an American or European father."[43]

Another way of securing political and economic alliances through kinship was through the sponsorship of baptisms, confirmations, or marriages. The sponsors then became *compadres* and *comadres* of the invitees. For the *ranchero* families whose daughters did not have enough status to qualify as marriage partners for the Anglo elite, the *compadrazgo* served as another manner of linking the future of their families with that of the new entrepreneurial and political upper class. Likewise for Anglo merchants and lawyers, this quasi-religious institution of the *compadrazgo* became a familiar vehicle for gaining recognition, status, and protection.[44]

For the Anglo settlers, some degree of "Mexicanization" was necessary for the most basic communication in this region, given the overwhelming number of Mexicans. But such acculturation meant far more than the learning of a language and a proper etiquette; it represented a way of acquiring influence and even a tenuous legitimacy in the annexed Mexican settlements. From participation in religious rituals and other communal activities to "becoming family" through godparenthood or marriage—such a range of ties served to create an effective everyday authority, a type that Ranger or army guns alone could not secure.

Occupation Politics

The military occupation established the pattern and climate for civilian rule. This meant that the interim military government of the Mexican settlements of the Upper and Lower Rio Grande valleys did not allow the defeated Mexicans to rule over the victorious American soldiers, however lowly in rank. This applied, by extension, to the American quartermaster employees and merchants accompanying the army of occupation. Mexican civilian leadership may have continued administrative functions but military personnel were under distinct military jurisdiction. Thus in 1850 a sizable fraction of the Anglo population in the Mexican settlements was essentially immune from the acts of civilian authorities. In San Antonio nearly half of the American population was part of the military presence, either as enlisted personnel or as wagon surveyors working for the military. Another 9 percent were merchants or clerks. In the occupied Lower Rio Grande Valley, nearly 40 percent of the American population were army personnel or employees and 15 percent were merchants or clerks.[45]

Once martial law was lifted and troops withdrawn or discharged, Americans and Mexicans, former enemies, maintained their distinct statuses in the courts, in the political parties, and in the town administrations of the old settlements. Two questions had to be settled. One concerned the status of Mexican property in the state. Since Texas had, under the terms of statehood in 1845, retained jurisdiction over all the land within its borders, it claimed to be exempted from the Treaty of Guadalupe Hidalgo. Thus the former republic carried out its own deliberations concerning the status of the annexed Mexicans and their land grants.

To adjudicate the matter of land grants, Governor Peter H. Bell appointed William Bourland and James Miller to investigate the validity of Spanish and Mexican titles. In Webb County, site of the first hearings, the Bourland-Miller Commission encountered opposition from Mexican landowners, who believed that the investigation was out to destroy rather than protect their rights. The impartiality of the proceedings and the prompt confirmation by the legislature of the commission's recommendations removed "this unfounded prejudice" and secured the loyalty of the landed elite of the Laredo area to the new order. Other landowners beyond the Nueces were not as fortunate and thus not as loyal as the Laredo grantees. In the Chihuahua Secession, only seven of the fourteen land grants were recognized. Of approximately 350 cases in the Tamaulipas and Coahuila secessions, "some two hundred" were confirmed by the legislature in 1852, and another 50 were subsequently confirmed by 1901. Of course, many of the grants confirmed were already owned, in part or whole, by Anglos.[46]

The second question requiring immediate attention was the political status of the Mexican in Texas. One of the liveliest debates in the Texas Constitutional Convention (1845) concerned whether or not the Mexican should be allowed the right to vote. The debate centered on whether the qualifying adjective "white" should be retained in the constitutional provisions that described the voters of the state.

The Harris County representative argued that the qualifier "white" should be kept, not because he feared the Spaniard; he welcomed them as he welcomed any portion of the Caucasian race that desired to settle in Texas. Rather he feared the mass immigration of "hordes of Mexican Indians": "Silently they will come moving in; they will come back in thousands to Bexar, in thousands to Goliad, perhaps to Nacogdoches, and what will be the consequence? Ten, twenty, thirty, forty, fifty thousand may come in here, and vanquish you at the ballot box though you are invincible in arms. This is no idle dream; no bugbear; it is the truth."[47] The proposal failed, however, because of opposition by several Anglo-Texan allies and protectors of the Texas Mexican elite (like Col. Henry Kinney of Corpus Christi). José Antonio Navarro of San Antonio, the only Texas Mexican (and the only native-born Texan) at the Constitutional Convention, argued eloquently against the proposal.

In spite of the formal defeat of disfranchisement at the convention, Mexicans in certain districts were denied the vote or allowed only limited participation. Corpus Christi merchant Henry Kinney observed that in several counties the practice immediately after independence had been to withhold the franchise from Mexicans, even though they may have fought against a people "of their own race." Traveler Frederick Olmsted observed that, if the Mexicans in San Antonio voted, they could elect a government of their own; "such a step would be followed, however, by a summary revolution."[48] Where Mexicans did have the right to vote, protests and threats from Anglo-Americans were constant reminders of a fragile franchise.

A typical protest was exemplifed by a hotly contested election for state representative from Nueces and Webb counties in 1863, where S. Kinney of Corpus Christi lost to Charles Callaghan of Laredo by a margin of thirty-five votes. The *Corpus Christi Ranchero* noted that Kinney was the choice of fifteen of sixteen voters where the English language was spoken and that "American men in an American country should have a fair showing in shaping the destinies of the country." The *Fort Brown Flag* of Brownsville joined in the protest, editorializing that "we are opposed to allowing an ignorant crowd of Mexicans to determine the political questions in this country, where a man is supposed to vote knowingly and thoughtfully."[49] Disfranchisement was the usual sentiment of disgruntled losers in electoral politics.

Where Texas Mexicans constituted a significant portion of the male vote, the politicians among the American settlers proceeded to instruct and organize the new voters. A common pattern was the controlled franchise, where Mexicans voted according to the dictates of the local *patrón*, or boss. Since these political machines delivered sizable blocs of votes in state and national elections, the Anglo *patrones* acquired influence far beyond that usually accorded "backwater" county politicians.

Generally, the lesser bosses were members of the wealthy Mexican families who had entered the political arena to maintain and defend their traditional status, as in the "subrings" of Brownsville, San Antonio, and El Paso.[50] But in all these instances, including places where Mexicans controlled most offices, as in Starr and Zapata counties, the figure of an Anglo boss legitimized Mexican political involvement. In the 1850s, the specific arrangements varied. Cameron County in the Lower Valley showed a nearly equal division of county commissioner positions. In Webb County, Anglos ran the county while Mexicans ran the city of Laredo. In El Paso County, the pattern was reversed, and Anglos ran the city while Mexicans ran the county.

The role of the Mexican elite as influential politicians was contingent, of course, on the presence of a large Mexican electorate. In San Antonio, where the Mexican population increasingly declined through the nineteenth century, Mexican representation on the city aldermanic council fell at an exponential rate after 1836. In 1837, for example, all but one of the forty-one candidates running for city elections were of Spanish-Mexican descent; a decade later there were only five. Between 1848 and 1866 each aldermanic council included one or two Mexican representatives; after 1866, however, even token representation was rare. Mexican political clubs remained active but constituted minor actors in the city's affairs. Through the early 1900s, the Mexican voice in city politics was symbolically represented by Anglo officials with familial ties to the Mexican upper class—the Lockwoods, Tobins, and Callaghans, for example.[51] The

Table 1. *San Antonio Aldermen by Ethnicity, 1837–1904*

Period	Non-Spanish-Surnamed	Spanish-Surnamed
1837–1847	31	57
1848–1857	82	17
1858–1866	82	11
1867–1874	55	4
1875–1884	67	2
1885–1894	72	1
1895–1904	60	0

Source: Based on listing in August Santleban, *A Texas Pioneer,* pp. 314–321.

tabulation in Table 1, with city administrations organized roughly in periods of seven to ten years, gives a clear indication of the decline in power of the Mexican elite in San Antonio during the late nineteenth century.[52]

The principle that in all matters of authority the Anglo stood over the Mexican was most evident in the area of law enforcement. After the 1840s, for example, there were no Mexican county sheriffs or city marshals in San Antonio but quite a few—again, generally members of the older wealthy families—were deputy sheriffs and assistant marshals. With some exceptions along the border counties, this division of authority was the pattern in the Mexican region of Texas.[53]

Pursuit of Trade

While the peace structure assured a degree of stability and continuity in the annexed settlements, the accommodation existed ultimately to serve the "right of trading" of the Anglo pioneer settlers. This signified the formation of an "export-oriented" elite whose activities would gradually dissolve the colonial character of the Mexican settlements, particularly the elite's hold on the land. Once the emotions of war and the "rule of cowboys" had subsided, the play of the market became a primary instrument of displacement in the annexed territories. This export-oriented elite, consisting of Anglo merchants and land lawyers with Mexican merchants as minor partners, was the basic catalytic agent in this transformative process.

The connection between the Mexican War and the origins of an Anglo-American mercantile elite was intimate and clear. Many merchants had been "camp followers" who were impressed by the trade potential with northern Mexico.[54] Another layer was added by Gen. Zachary Taylor's army and the citizen employees of the quartermaster. Many of the soldiers discharged at Camargo, for example, remained in the area following the declaration of peace. Henry Clay Davis, one of those released at Camargo, married the daughter of a landed Mexican family and built a *rancho* and a mercantile house across the river on land belonging to his father-in-law. The Davis Rancho formed the beginning of Rio Grande City. Other prominent pioneers came to the Valley as part of Taylor's quartermaster system. Cattlemen Mifflin Kenedy, who married the wealthy Petra Vela de Vidal, and Richard King were civilian pilots of the army's steamboats.[55]

The quartermaster system set up to supply Taylor's army of occupation in northern Mexico lay the groundwork for the merchants and entrepreneurs in the newly acquired region. Of San Antonio,

Olmsted noted that the capital owned there was "quite large. The principal accumulations date from the Mexican war, when no small part of the many millions expended by Government were disbursed here in payment to contractors. Some prime cuts were secured by residents, and no small portion of the lesser pickings remained in their hands."[56] In the Lower Rio Grande Valley, a significant new element in the local economy was the steamboat. When the government auctioned off its river craft as surplus material, it transferred the infrastructure it had developed over to the hands of the new capital-based elite. Charles Stillman in partnership with the river captains who had worked for the quartermaster—Mifflin Kenedy, Richard King, and James O'Donnell—purchased the craft and within a few years established a monopoly of all transportation on the river. This included a ferry from Brownsville to Matamoros, through which all goods to and from northern Mexico had to pass. Rates were high but there would be no competition in the freight business until after the Civil War.[57]

The Business of Merchants

Among the most prominent merchants of the annexed Southwest belongs Charles Stillman of Brownsville, a true "Connecticut Yankee." Stillman, the son of a wealthy Connecticut merchant, had settled in Matamoros in 1828 to handle the Mexican end of his father's shipping trade. By 1846 "Don Carlos," as he was known to his Mexican clients, had developed an annual business of $75,000 to $80,000, double that of any other American merchant with the exception of the U.S. consul, J. P. Schatzell, who claimed an annual business of $250,000. Trade of such magnitude, it should be noted, was not unusual for American consular officers at Matamoros. As historian Leroy Graf explained the matter, since Matamoros was not considered a "choice" assignment, the "most patently regrettable" individuals, adventurers who were anxious to accumulate a great financial return, were appointed.[58]

Much of Stillman's success in business stemmed not just from entrepreneurial talent but from the unusual political ability to maintain "good faith" with the warring sides during the Texian troubles, the Mexican War, and again during the American Civil War. In 1846, for example, Stillman was on hand to greet the columns of Taylor's army as they marched into Matamoros.

Stillman, as did probably most astute frontier merchants, fully understood the import of the Mexican War. Supported by the commerce accompanying the logistical support of Taylor's occupation of northern Mexico, Stillman built a dependable ferry service from Matamoros to Fort Brown and the new settlement forming on the communal lands of Matamoros. By the end of 1848, barely ten months after the ratification of the treaty, Stillman had already organized a land company to sell lots and develop the town of Brownsville on Matamoros' former ejidal lands. As a final demonstration of the meaning of annexation, Stillman purchased the government's war surplus river craft to control transportation and freighting around Matamoros-Brownsville. Tom Lea summed the matter well: "Peace or war, he used what he made to make more."[59]

Col. Henry Kinney was another frontier merchant with the rare political skill to maintain tacit Mexican support in spite of increasing tension with Anglo-Texan troops. In 1840 Kinney had set up, in company with an Alabama trader, a trading store on the Tamaulipas side of the Nueces River where it empties into Corpus Christi Bay. This store, which survived at the pleasure of both Texan and Mexican troops, became a principal conduit for the Mexican smuggling trade. When Taylor's army arrived at Corpus Christi Bay in 1846 to assert the Texan claim to the Nueces Strip, a claim that Kinney had done much to promote, Kinney was appointed quartermaster for the troops. In a few months, "Kinney's Ranch" became a boomtown of two thousand inhabitants, excluding troops. Kinney was in the enviable position of being merchant, quartermaster, and staff officer all at once. Col. Henry Kinney's good fortune was temporary, however. After the war, he attempted to develop the town of Corpus Christi, much like Stillman had done with Brownsville and Henry Clay Davis with Rio Grande City. Kinney's colonization schemes failed, however, and left him penniless.[60]

In sum, the successful frontier merchant was the one who learned to anticipate and adjust to shifting political allegiances. The art of business overrode patriotic idealism, affording merchants an aura of neutrality. Thus the wartime profits of the Civil War, like those of the Mexican War some fifteen years earlier, proved to be a boon for the most opportunistic entrepreneurs.[61]

The Practice of Lawyers

An integral member of the capital-based Anglo elite was the lawyer, who basically served to organize the land market in the new territories. For example, Stephen Powers of Brownsville, the best versed lawyer in Spanish and Mexican land law, cleared the titles to an immense portion of the grants lying between the Nueces and the Rio Grande. The building of the King and Kenedy ranches was essentially the legal handiwork of Powers and his junior associate, James B. Wells. In Laredo, Edwin A. Atlee, associated with the firm of Albert L. McLane, successfully represented many Mexican land grant heirs in establishing the legality of their land titles. In El Paso, Dale Evan Owens from Chicago established an important practice.[62]

Maverick

San Antonio's most prominent lawyer was Samuel Maverick, son of a wealthy Charleston merchant, graduate of Yale College, and owner of considerable holdings in the East and in Texas. Maverick, however, is best remembered for the business he never cared for. According to the well-known legend, Maverick was so busy with his land business that his unbranded cattle usually wandered loose around San Antonio. The residents, on seeing an unbranded stray, got used to saying, "There goes a Maverick," and in this fashion all strays and unbranded cattle came to be known as "mavericks."[63]

By virtue of their office, land lawyers were the critical intermediaries between the land-based Mexican elite and the capital-based Anglo merchants. Letters to Powers and Wells suggest the role. On the one hand, there were inquiries, mainly from prospective Anglo buyers, of the status of certain land claims and titles; on the other hand, there were powers of attorney, mainly from Mexican landowners, for representation in land litigation as well as last wills and testaments of deceased Mexican landowners; and, finally, another group of letters referred to land taxes and sales, settlements regarding claims, mortgage payments, and notices of land surveying.[64] Not surprisingly, as mediators of the land market, the land lawyers evolved into the most powerful political brokers of the new order. Brownsville lawyer Herbert Davenport described Powers' position pointedly: "He was almost the only public man of his day who understood the points of view of both the resident Mexicans who had owned land in that region before 1848, and the incoming Americans; and he rendered inestimable services to the border region by maintaining harmony among them."[65] According to Evan Anders, Powers built up influence among both the ranch owners and the Mexican population by "defending the land rights of certain Mexican families and by persuading others that they never really owned their land."[66]

On Powers' death in 1882, his pupil James B. Wells inherited the law practice and powerful political position. Wells continued to maintain close ties with the region's great landowners—he himself would accumulate over 44,000 acres—and, even more than Powers, he became known as the "friend and protector" of the impoverished Mexican masses. Much of his influence stemmed from his efforts to provide relief for Mexican *rancheros* and their families during the severe drought of 1893, as well as through his sponsorship of weddings,

Agents for large tracts of desirable land, 1893 (Chatfield, *Twin Cities of the Border*).

Alamo church and plaza, ca. 1855 (courtesy Daughters of the Republic of Texas Library at the Alamo).

baptisms, and funerals. As one commemorative account summed up the matter, Powers and Wells were brilliant politicians and talented courtroom lawyers with an extraordinary command of "simple, Anglo-Saxon English—which any English speaking ranchero, or the dumbest of jurors, could understand."[67]

The Interests of Mexican Entrepreneurs

Together the American merchant and the land lawyer provided the financial capital and legal work necessary to loosen Mexican ownership of land. Many of the Mexican elite who co-operated with the new authorities and merchants, on the other hand, shared in the prosperous trade of the postwar period. The new international boundary had given the river a strategic commercial significance. Wealthy Mexican families with branches on both sides of the river were in an excellent position for managing international trade. That this international trade consisted mainly of smuggled goods mattered little, for the trade had quickly acquired, in the minds of both Mexican and Anglo entrepreneurs, a legitimate status.

The smuggling trade flourished in the immediate postwar period. In the 1850s (and through the present decade of the 1980s) this trade consisted largely of manufactured goods flowing south into Mexico and agricultural goods flowing north into the United States. During the Civil War, Anglo and Mexican merchants of the river towns, from Brownsville through Laredo, gained small fortunes supplying the Confederate forces and transporting Confederate cotton down the Rio Grande for export. Mexican merchants established a line of freight boats to navigate the Rio Grande as far up as San Ygnacio in Zapata County. The Rio Grande, as an international river, represented the Confederacy's only market outlet not blockaded by Union forces.[68]

This commercial success was premised, of course, on the political and military support for the Confederacy by the landed Mexican elite. In South Texas the Mexican elite of Webb and Zapata counties, under the leadership of Santos Benavides of Laredo, protected the southwestern flank of the Confederacy from "renegade" Mexican leaders, such as the "brigand" Juan Cortina, who operated with federal support during the Civil War.[69]

But such political accommodation was not sufficient to account for continued land tenure. The strategic nature of the river was an important factor in the survival of old landed families in the lower border counties, as opposed to other families whose lands were located some distance from the border. The former's access to wealth based on trade, along with the right politics, accounted for their success. Santos Benavides, for example, who rose to the rank of colonel because of his loyalty to Texas and the Confederacy, and Antancio Vidaurri, a fellow Confederate officer with considerable landholdings, were in 1890 among the recognized "types of successful men in Texas." Benavides was known as the "merchant prince of the Rio Grande" and Vidaurri was engaged in extensive business projects, including mining, in Mexico. Among other positions, both had served as mayor of Laredo.[70]

The successful elite of the lower border counties combined large-scale ranching with an import-export business between Saltillo-Monterrey and either Brownsville, Corpus Christi, or San Antonio. They also engaged in farming, planting the first cotton and introducing the first modern plow and the corn planter.[71]

A Concluding Note

This brief description of the activities of the mercantile elite does not exhaust the number of adventures that this group concocted during the years following annexation. It is no exaggeration to say that there were hardly any major crises in which some merchants were not involved. This was a time when the spirit of Manifest Destiny was running high and even the wildest scheme seemed a worthwhile gamble. If one scheme turned sour, then there were others. Thus Col. Henry Kinney, representing the adventurous frontier merchant, left Texas after his "boom" of Corpus Christi fizzled to do some filibustering in Nicaragua.

In Texas, however, there was plenty for merchants to do. A campaign to create a new state separate from Texas, armed filibusters to establish a new republic in northern Mexico (the Republic of the Rio Grande), the politics of smuggling and tariffs—these suggest some of the political activities of the pioneer merchants during the ten years following the war. Even the first Cortina War of the late 1850s, according to some accounts of the time, was an exaggeration designed to get the soldiers, along with their business, back to the border.[72] Intrigue permeates the historical record. There is no need to claim that merchants were alone in all of these adventures and projects; by themselves they could hardly have done much. But merchants were central figures in molding the spirit of Manifest Destiny into concrete demands and proposals. As a class, merchants provided the stimulus and vision for many of the border difficulties during the postwar period. They were the architects of development.

The nature of the postwar order beyond the Nueces should be clear. The landed Mexican elite sought to protect their property through some form of accommodation and even subordination to the new authorities and merchants. Romance aside, marriage appeared to be mutually advantageous. As in so many historical situations where a defensive landed upper class and an ambitious mercantile group have met, marriage between representatives of the two seemed to be a classic resolution, a suspension, of the conflict between these two classes.

Nonetheless, there was a marked tension between the pursuit of commercial interests and the maintenance of peace. The "rivalship of peace" of which Ashbel Smith had spoken was inherently a contradictory proposition. Conflict over land claims, over access to water and natural resources, and over ownership of cattle and sheep constantly threatened the stability of the region's peace structure.

3. Cattle, Land, and Markets

MEXICANS IN TEXAS, especially above the Nueces, lost considerable land through outright confiscation and fraud. Below the Nueces, however, the experience of displacement was more complex. While fraud and coercion played an important part, the more systematic, more efficient mechanism of market competition also operated there. The accommodation between American mercantile groups and the Mexican upper class was, from a financial standpoint, inherently unequal; the former had "regenerative" wealth derived from trade while the latter had "fixed" wealth derived from land. The peace structure between the two elites, between "merchant capital" and "landed capital," saved some upper-class Mexicans, but it by no means forestalled the outcome of the competition between the two. By 1900 the Mexican upper class would become nonexistent except in a few border enclaves.

Before annexation the land tenure privileges of the elite had been effective restraints on a land market, and even after annexation land title difficulties discouraged any major growth of Anglo-American settlements in the Nueces Strip.[1] Not only did the first American settlers find that there was no free land, but they also found a land-ownership system of undivided *derechos,* or rights. Under Spanish and Mexican law, the true owners of these lands were not individuals but families and lineages. Under the new American legal system, however, the ancestral estate could be subdivided among heirs and sold without regard to family claims.

The freeing of the land from these patrimonial claims was accompanied by increasing linkages with national and world markets. Specifically, once the cattle trails to Kansas attracted the Anglo merchants to the prospects of ranching, it was a question of weathering the fluctuations of the market before the money-poor Mexican landowners lost their land. The Mexican upper class had only land and livestock, while the emerging Anglo elite generated its income through control of the lucrative trade of northern Mexico. Thus, the old Mexican upper class in the region, which had lost with the war whatever influence it had in controlling the marketplace, was locked into a losing contest with the pioneer merchants.

What heightened this competition between the old and new elites were their radically different views of landownership. The Mexican elite saw land as a family patrimony, as the basis for preserving a traditional life style, whereas the Anglo elite saw land mainly as an investment, as a basis for the business of ranching. In a fashion, this has been the common "history line" of Texan historians: that is, while borrowing heavily from Mexican tradition, the Anglo-Texans created the modern American version of ranching.[2] Richard King, to take a prime example, was a pioneer in such modernization: "Then to this basic Latin material for ranching, he added an Anglo-Saxon dynamic, a new thought. It was a financial enterprise, susceptible to an organized efficiency. It could be engaged in not merely for a way of life, but for a systematic yield of profit."[3]

A segment of the landed Mexican elite, as mentioned previously, successfully commercialized, assimilated a mercantile outlook, and retained a patrimony of land and workers. But, generally speaking, most Mexicans did not commercialize, either because they failed to acquire an export-related source of capital or because they retained a complacent attitude toward merchandising; they were eliminated in time. Eventually, taxes, drought, the disastrous fluctuations of the cattle market, the need to sink wells and improve the cattle stock, and the expense of surveying and defending land titles combined to displace the "unproductive" landowner.

This chapter explores the "play of the market" as it transformed landownership below the Nueces. The general argument I elaborate is a familiar one in comparative studies of agricultural development: namely, that the transition from subsistence cultivation to market production signified the displacement of a traditional landed elite by a new elite whose base was commercial capital. Rather than rubber, cotton, or sugar cane, however, the exportable item in this Texas case was the Mexican Longhorn.

The Matter of Displacement

The question of Mexican land displacement has been a topic of some controversy in Texas and southwestern history. Generally, the discussion has been framed in terms of whether the displacement was legal or fraudulent. This distinction, in my view, has limited value for explaining the record of land displacement.

Most Texan historians agree that intimidation and fraud played an important part in the dispossession of *rancheros* (or small ranchers). They hold the line, however, in the case of the Mexican elite, whom they say were protected from such spoliation. Historian John Mc-

Neely, for instance, points out that the property rights of the elite were generally recognized as valid by the Anglo-Texan authorities, that "it was remarkable how many Spanish and Mexican land grants were upheld in the border area of Texas, especially the Lower Valley." Likewise T. R. Fehrenbach argues that "what is usually ignored is the fact that the hacendado class, as a class, was stripped of property perfectly legally, according to the highest traditions of U.S. law." Such statements lose whatever force they have, however, because, as these and other Texan historians have recognized, not only did the new American law fail to protect the Mexicans but it also was used as the major instrument of their dispossession.[4]

One legal method characterized by considerable ambiguity, for example, was the so-called sheriff's sale ordered by county courts to settle tax arrears and outstanding private debts. These sales were formally auctions where the land was sold to the highest bidder, but the bids obtained were often so low that the entire court-ordered proceedings were suspect. Examples of this practice are plentiful. In June 1877, for instance, the Hidalgo County sheriff sold three thousand acres of the Hinajosa grant for a total cash price of $15.00 in order to cover tax arrears, and the following year an additional four thousand acres from the grant were auctioned for $17.15.[5] The question about legality, thus, was often an ambiguous and pointless matter.

The distinction between legal and illegal dispossession also appears somewhat irrelevant when the lives of many prominent pioneers make it clear that both types occurred. Court records indicate, for example, that the merchant-quartermaster Henry Kinney of Corpus Christi defrauded his friend Don Blas Falcón of El Chiltipín grant during the military occupation. The folklore of Kenedy Ranch workers includes an account of how Mifflin Kenedy fenced in the lake of his neighbor, Doña Eulalia Tijerina of La Atravesada grant, without authorization or compensation because "he wanted water." And critics of the King Ranch often alluded, as one anonymous newspaper commentator did in 1878, to the habit of King's neighbors to "mysteriously vanish whilst his territory extends over entire counties." The Texas Rangers, in fact, were known as "*los rinches de la Kineña*"—the King Ranch Rangers—to underscore the belief that they acted as King's strong-arm agents.[6]

While a legalistic approach cannot accommodate the ambiguous and contradictory nature of land displacement, a market-based explanation can identify clear patterns, especially after the immediate postwar period of weak authority and intense war sentiments, a time that might be described as the "rule of cowboys." Once authority and a market economy had been re-established in the new territories, land displacement of both a legal and a fraudulent character generally expressed a market-related logic. Even conflict and outright dispossession demonstrated a sensitivity to market demands.

A case in point was the so-called Skinning Wars (also known as the "second Cortina War") of the early 1870s. Because of a surplus of cattle, beef prices had dropped sharply, making the meat of the cow practically worthless. In 1869, the meat of a cow could be bought for 62.5¢ while hides brought $4.50 apiece. This market value of hides initiated an intense competition for mavericks (unbranded cattle) in the open range. Repeated disputes over the ownership of mavericks escalated into organized "skinning" raids and counterraids on both sides of the Texas-Mexican border. South Texas Anglos organized minute companies and vigilance committees whose actions were as reprehensible as those of the "cattle thieves." Anglo outlaws from Corpus Christi raided the Mexican ranches, killing every adult male, burning ranch buildings and stores, and driving the Mexican ranchers away from the Upper Nueces area.[7] Kenedy Ranch *vaquero* Faustino Morales, a witness of the raids, recalled that "there were many small ranches belonging to Mexicans, but then the Americans came in and drove the Mexicans out and took over the ranches . . . after that they fenced the ranches—it was the English, they fenced some land that wasn't theirs."[8] By the end of 1876, Texas Rangers under Capt. Leander McNelly had brought Mexican skinning raids and Anglo vigilance activities under control.

Under a peaceful and lawful climate, however, legal and quasi-legal mechanisms served to continue land displacement. In the best case, formally legal mechanisms—taxation, court-ordered surveys of land boundaries, time-consuming litigation, for example—burdened the money-poor elite with prohibitive expenses. In the worst case, these legal mechanisms constituted specific instruments of dispossession. Once the region had been integrated with the national market economy, there was little need for outright fraud on the part of the Anglo pioneer entrepreneurs. The natural course of free enterprise accomplished more or less the same result. The play of the market did the trick, triggering both voluntary sales and involuntary sheriff's sales.

Enclosing the Cattle Range

The effects of land dispossession in the region were not immediately apparent under the conditions of an open range. Since ownership of land and water sources could not be effectively enforced, life for the small *rancheros* and independent *vaqueros* continued much as before. As cattle increased in value, however, it was a matter of time, a matter of finding the appropriate fencing material, before the open range was enclosed. Essentially, these enclosures signified the assertion of property rights of the big ranchers and the decline of the marginal rancher and the independent cowboy. The barbed-wire fences made the facts of landownership and landlessness meaningful.

This is not the place to relate the story of the cattle industry, a development described fully elsewhere.[9] Although cattle from La Bahía (Goliad) and San Antonio had been driven to New Orleans as early as the 1780s, marketing cattle remained a difficult problem for another eighty years. Before annexation, only hides were exported, and tallow, horns, hooves, and meat were generally marketed locally. The meat was worthless as an exportable item. Following the Civil War, tallow or cow fat became for a brief period an important exportable item. The establishment of tallow factories quickly demonstrated the interest and advantage of the mercantile elite in the cattle trade. The *rancheros*, who had insufficient capital to set up the rendering establishments, had little choice but to sell their herds to King and Kenedy, who owned two of the four tallow factories in Nueces County. Along with handsome profits came control of the cattle trade of South Texas.[10]

Once the connection to northern markets had been secured and regularized, with the help of entrepreneurs like Joseph G. McCoy, who founded the Kansas "cow town" of Abilene, the cattle business "took off." Walter Prescott Webb has described graphically the experience of the first cattle drives to the North: " . . . they were groping, experimenting, trying this and that, until by the familiar system of trial and error . . . they came at length, and after great sacrifice, upon success. They beat out the trail . . . [and] reached the railroad, found buyers and a steady market, and heard once more the music made by real money rattling in the pocket."[11]

In fifteen years, from 1866 to 1880, slightly more than four million head of Texas cattle were driven north. The Chisholm Trail, whose tributaries originated in South Texas and passed through San Antonio on the way to Abilene, became so worn, according to one old trail driver, that dust was knee-deep to the cattle in some places. Beef prices soared to unheard-of heights, land became important, and investors from "out East" as well as from Britain began to capitalize the young but booming cattle industry.[12]

Thirty-five thousand men, of which one-third were blacks or Mexicans, drove cattle up the trails. One source argues that Mexicans were less likely to drive cattle north because they had a language

Cattle Trails, 1866–1895 (based on Jack Potter's Map of Cattle Trails;
courtesy of University of New Mexico Library, Special Collections).

handicap and were likely to experience considerable prejudice, while the black cowboy could expect some protection in the immediate post–Civil War period. Actually, these conditions worked to keep Mexican cattlemen from organizing their own drives north. Ample evidence indicates that Mexican *vaqueros* often drove cattle to Kansas, Nebraska, and Montana. Their trail driving was sanctioned by the organization of the outfit: Mexican cattle drovers worked for Anglo ranchers and Anglo trail bosses, an acceptable arrangement in Texas.[13]

Like the tallow trade, the cattle drives to Kansas were firmly in the hands of the wealthiest ranchers, for it cost a considerable sum to organize and finance a cattle drive to a railhead a thousand miles to the north. Economic historian T. J. Cauley notes that, once the experimenting was over, individual drovers gave way to partnerships and syndicates who managed drives as a business. By 1875 the "great bulk" of trail driving was handled by these concerns.[14]

Mexican cattlemen, then, did not drive their own cattle; it was expensive as well as dangerous. Instead, they sold their herds to Anglo middlemen or brokerage firms in San Antonio or in a South Texas substation for the cattle drives north. Alice was such a town; here Mexican *vaqueros* turned over their herds to Anglo cowboys for the drive north. Likewise the boomtown of Lagarto, located at the intersection of roads from San Antonio, Victoria, and Brownsville, was the trading place where Mexicans from South Texas and Anglo-Americans from East Texas sold and bought cattle and horses.[15]

Every innovation and capital improvement in ranching threatened the marginal rancher. So it was with the introduction of barbed wire in the 1870s. Before 1875 it had not been necessary to own land with ample water sources and pasture in order to be a cattleman; the frontier was still "open." Theoretically, all that was necessary was the rounding up and branding of mavericks with a registered cattle brand. The report of the U.S. commissioners to Texas, a report commissioned by Congress in 1872 to investigate the "depredations committed on the Texas frontier," provided an interesting view of the problems of Anglo and Mexican ranchers in South Texas.[16] The region, the commissioners discovered, was unfenced "save in a few isolated instances." This was not due to indifference or disinterest on the part of the ranchers. As the commissioners observed: "Where possible, stock-raisers inclose land as rapidly as their means will allow, and in one case, forty miles of fence, between two arms of Corpus Christi Bay, have been recently built, inclosing the vast herds of Mifflin Kenedy." Why, then, didn't more ranchmen fence their pasture land? According to the commissioners, in a statement that clearly suggested the particular problems facing Mexican *rancheros*, "the character of the occupation in which they are engaged, the present value of cattle in Texas, the scarcity of lumber, together with the peculiar features of land-tenure, prevent, as a rule, the fencing of their ranges, many of them being owned in common by various rancheros holding complicated titles."[17] The initiative of Kenedy, nonetheless, generated a broad movement, and by 1875 each cattleman on the South Texas coast had a fenced pasture of one thousand to five thousand acres. The *Corpus Christi Gazette* praised the practice as an important innovation: ". . . fencing will become the order of the day, and lands will cease to be almost worthless, as at present. Stock will be secure and safe from the depredations of Mexicans and robbers generally and an increase and sales [of cattle] will yield treble that now produced, while 'skinning and peeling' will cease to be a disturbing and demoralizing element."[18] By 1883 practically all the range land in South and Southwest Texas had been converted into enclosed ranches. "In fact," a range analyst noted, "all the country south of the Galveston, Harrisburg and San Antonio Railroad is now so fenced as to depend on rail shipments."[19]

Not all stockmen, however, benefited from the introduction of fencing. Because fencing shut off sources of water, it drove landless cattlemen and sheepmen toward the Rio Grande and the Pecos, to the rougher lands of less grazing capacity. The owners of arid lands, moreover, were compelled to drill wells or build water tanks, a necessity beyond the means of some. The result was a gradual but steady decline in the population of Corpus Christi, a decline whose effects were felt keenly by the town merchants. In 1885 trade losses forced a Corpus Christi merchant who had been in business for seventeen years to close his store. The *Corpus Christi Caller* commented on the event (May 31, 1885): "Much blame is attached to the large ranch owners who have fenced up the country to the exclusion of the small stockman and the farmer. But while they are censurable in a manner, we are partly to blame. Have the people of Corpus Christi ever united in an effort to get the large landowners to divide up portions of the lands for settlers?"[20]

The movement of landless cattlemen and sheepmen westward was a general one in the region. One old-timer by the name of Parsons moved to Uvalde in 1881 because Goliad was "taking on fence-lines. Cattlemen saw fences creep through their territory and they sought relief further west." Another old-timer by the name of Haby moved to Uvalde from Medina County when it began "getting fenced up." But these sparsely settled western counties were not themselves immune from the effects of fencing in other parts, for it increased competition for the remaining open range. This resulted in considerable conflict between sheepmen and cattlemen over grazing rights; much of this conflict assumed racial overtones.

There was some trouble between Anglo cattlemen and Mexican sheepmen around Uvalde. One Mexican sheepherder was killed for letting his sheep get on an Anglo's range. A sheepman-cattleman fight over a waterhole in San Diego left five men dead. A similar conflict in the Panhandle between Mexican sheepmen from New Mexico and Anglo cattlemen was settled peacefully when Don Casimiro Romero and Charles Goodnight agreed to divide the rangeland: sheepmen would have one side of the Canadian River valley, cattlemen the other. Generally, however, the situation was settled by forcing sheepmen to search for grazing pastures elsewhere, as happened in the Carrizo Springs area. Old-timer Bob Lemmons recalled the changes as follows: "The sheep disappeared and were displaced by the cattle for the reason that sheep and cattle won't run on the same range. There were fewer sheep after 1887 when the range was fenced. Cattlemen were in the majority and so there was no free range for sheep. Perhaps the price of wool was also responsible."[21]

When fences followed the landless cattlemen and sheepmen retreating westward, the closing of the frontier appeared imminent. In Frio County, this resulted in an intense fence-cutting conflict. There was no fence-cutting in nearby Dimmit County where fencing of the county had been completed by 1885. As Lemmons put it: "Those persons, Mexicans and Americans, without land but who had cattle were put out of business by the fencing."[22]

In sum, the enclosure movement during the 1870s and 1880s was one in a series of innovations that eliminated the landless cattlemen and sheepmen as well as those with land but with few financial resources. With no money to sink the needed wells, to buy additional pasturage, to buy rolls of the new barbed-wire fence, it was frequently the weather, quite literally, that determined whether a ranch remained in family hands, was mortgaged to a bank or Scottish syndicate, or was sold outright to a land lawyer or merchant.

Within twenty years after the first cattle trails to Kansas, the character of ranching had been completely transformed. The ranges were fenced with barbed wire, seeded with high-yield disease-resistant pasture grass; the cattle were cross-bred with imported strains and fed experimental grains and feeds; and special health preventive techniques were adopted—to cite a few of the innovations. Don Biggers in an interesting book, *From Cattle Range to Cotton Patch*, has described the changes of the cattle industry concisely. "In point of transformations and evolutions," noted Biggers, the cattle business was "without a counterpart. First there was the open range and free grass; then the overcrowded range and the contest for existence, followed by the lease law and the wire fence and disastrous drifts and die-ups; seasons of green pastures and big profits. It has progressed from the common scrub to the thoroughbred; from the wild speculative sphere to a scientific industry."[23]

The Play of the Market

Anglo and European immigrant stockmen left behind a clear appraisal of Mexican ranching in the region. The general portrayal was that of an unproductive enterprise, characterized by primitive methods, inefficiency, laziness, and even ignorance. Several accounts have described the water sources on these ranches as crude shallow mud trenches, the livestock as "scrub" cattle of little value, the land as being poorly utilized.[24] One Englishman, for example, while resting at the "Guinagato Ranche" between Laredo and Rio Grande City, observed that the place was typical of Mexican ranches: "They have no capital except a lot of land and some cattle which they occasionally sell. They seldom buy anything but coffee and tobacco, and their cash for this is what they receive from passers-by for corn and for leave to water at their well. The only work I have seen done since we have been here was by a party of six, one of whom was chiselling on a wooden plough and the other five were looking on!"[25]

These impoverished conditions were not the result of indifference or some traditional outlook; they were the result of a money-poor situation. The old settlements clung to their windmills rather than dig artesian wells, noted a resident, because of a lack of money. Mexican ranchers, according to another source, were receptive to technological innovation and improvements, believing that as soon as technological equality was attained, social equality would follow.[26] In attempts to keep pace with the new developments, some ranchers took the bold step of mortgaging their lands. In many cases, however, such a strategy only accelerated the loss of land and social status. Only a limited amount could be borrowed through a mortgage on land of little value. With liens on the land, as Mexican ranchers discoverd, the capital source they could tap was exhausted. Again, the occasional droughts and die-ups highlighted the precarious market situation of Mexican ranchers on unimproved land. With little money to improve water sources, droughts often proved to be the critical events that filtered out the poorly capitalized, inefficient ranches from the developing cattle industry.

As devastating as natural disasters like droughts were on Mexican land tenure, the invisible hand of market fluctuations at times proved more destructive. Integration with the national and international markets meant that ranching was now susceptible to the "booms" and "busts" of all market industries. The initial period following the founding of the trails to Kansas, from 1866 to 1872, was a boom period. In 1873 came the first sign of vulnerability; following a Wall Street crash, the beef market collapsed. Recovery in 1875 found a more mature ranch industry, with enclosed pastures and British capital for improvements of all sorts. From 1875 to 1885 the cattle industry enjoyed its greatest prosperity, with 1882 being the apex. Sane business judgment was overwhelmed by "spasms of enthusiasm," as Biggers put it, over the opportunities in ranching. In 1885 the market went "all to pieces in December, then came the collapse and prices went from bad to worse, reaching bed rock in 1887." Cattle prices tumbled from $35 a head in 1885 to $5 in 1887. The boom had ended, and no confidence was left in the industry. Then for nine years, beginning in 1886, "it seemed that every power of heaven and earth had combined against the cowmen. Droughts and die-ups followed and prices dragged along at starvation figures." In 1895 prices advanced again and by 1898 had risen to a boom level again, but they began to decline in 1900 and have dragged along since then, as Biggers put it 1905.[27]

Because the Mexican landowners were unable to secure the capital for the continuous improvements necessary in a developing and unpredictable cattle industry, their precarious market position became particularly clear during periods of a depressed cattle economy or a natural disaster. The fact that the landed Mexican classes sold only when they had to was a story repeatedly enacted in land offices and courthouses throughout the late nineteenth century. One common scene was set by the sheriff's sale ordered by county courts to settle tax arrears and private debts. Because titles could not be transferred to heirs until all tax matters as well as collection suits brought against the deceased had been settled, these sales generally followed the death of a landowner. Thus, when a money-poor clan lost its patriarch, it usually also lost its inheritance. Sometimes all that remained exempt from the sale ordered by a probate court, as in one 1879 case of a man ironically named Juan Rico, was the land "embraced in the homestead of the family of the said deceased."[28]

The case of the Miguel Gutiérrez family is an instructive example of how the Mexican upper class lost its land. According to the Nueces County land records, in 1878 Miguel Gutiérrez sold or gave Richard King 2,000 acres in return for unspecified "valuable considerations." Gutiérrez apparently died in 1879 or 1880, for in the latter year

17,872 acres of the Gutiérrez Santa Gertrudis grant were auctioned off to pay for tax arrears. King bought this sizable portion of Gutiérrez land for $240. The following year, in 1881, María Gutiérrez entered the picture (thus confirming the death of Miguel) and sold the remainder of the Gutiérrez Santa Gertrudis—24,354 acres—to King for $4,000. The laconic business entries in the Nueces County land records portray this drama of displacement plainly: within the space of four years, King had paid "valuable considerations" for 2,000 acres, $240 at a sheriff's sale for 17,872 acres, and $4,000 for the final 24,354 acres. King had added to his growing *rancho* the entire Gutiérrez Santa Gertrudis grant, comprising a total of 44,226 acres.[29]

Another case was provided by J. Frank Dobie, Texas historian and folklorist. Victoriano Chapa was of *la gente decente*, with a 10,000-acre ranch only twenty miles from the Dobie family ranch in the Lower Valley. During the terrible drought of the 1890s, Don Victoriano had all the old Spanish mares corralled and killed so that they would eat no more grass and drink no more water; these mares had no sales value. In 1901 Don Victoriano, then 89 years old, was persuaded to sell out the stock and lease the land, but as the time for delivering the ranch approached, Don Victoriano became depressed. According to Dobie, Don Victoriano said something like the following: "Why have we been talked into this evil trade? We belong here. My roots go deeper than those of any mesquite growing up and down this long arroyo. We do not need money. When a man belongs to a place and lives there, all the money in all the world cannot buy him anything else so good. *Válgame Dios*, why, why, why?"[30] Two days before the transfer, Don Victoriano committed suicide. Dobie's biographical sketch ended on a somewhat melodramatic note but it served to emphasize his point: like the old Spanish mares, the *gente decente* were also an old and dying breed.[31]

What was tragedy on one side was an epic tale of success on the other. The story of Edward C. Lasater, owner of the largest Jersey dairy farm in the world, is a case in point. Lasater began his business life in South Texas by operating in cattle on a large scale. Although very young at the time, he had fine personal credit because of his father's mercantile business in Goliad. Ever watchful of opportunity, Lasater invested heavily in Texas cattle during the money panic of 1893. A drought that year, however, razed the pastures, and Lasater found himself having to feed thirty thousand head through the winter. To make matters worse, the bottom dropped out of the cattle market and Lasater was a "$130,000 loser." Yet this financial disaster proved to be a boon for young Lasater. As the story goes: "Practically all the land was owned by Mexicans through grants from the Spanish and Mexican governments. In 1893, the great drouth year, the ranch-men lost all their cattle, and the cry for water went up everywhere. The Mexicans depended upon shallow wells which were no more than trenches; and while they were no worse off than Lasater who had lost all his cattle, he had one thing they did not have—credit, and confidence in his ability to provide an adequate water supply."[32] Lasater felt confident that he could better "the inefficient methods of the Mexicans" and obtain an abundant supply of water with deeper wells and pumps. But Lasater's confidence and survival did not rest on such intuition; it was based rather on his personal access to bankers "who knew his ability and honesty," and it was based on his knowledge "that the English companies which had been lending money to the Mexican grantees desired to have the land worked." Through such connections, Lasater received generous assistance, and while neighboring Mexican ranches were failing, he was able to purchase the huge landholdings of fifteen Mexican families at "give-away prices." According to the biographical account, "he began buy-ing up all the land he could get from the descendants of the Mexican grantees, making small cash payments, the balance on long time which was handled through loan companies. He had faith in the country."[33]

While Lasater pursued land, he had to be mindful of not being pur-sued himself, for market recessions and natural disasters were imper-sonal, "color-blind" events. Thus, in 1899 Lasater sought a $200,000 loan from the brokerage firm of Francis Smith in order to pay off his debts to Mrs. King and to expand his ranch. "It may be our insinuat-ing," reasoned the brokers in a letter to a potential investor, "that Mrs. King would be exceedingly glad to get the land on which she has a mortgage that made him feel that he would like to have the loan in the hands of someone else." Lasater received the loan, at the time one of the largest business deals handled by Francis Smith. The brokers had faith in Lasater, and so he was able to expand his holdings to 360,000 acres. The ranch was called the Lasater Ranch but was known as "La Mota" (meaning "hair knot") to the Mexicans.[34]

The role of British and Eastern investment capital in commercial-izing South Texas ranch land is largely an unknown story. Francis Smith and Company, for example, with offices in Indianapolis, Mem-phis, and San Antonio, had developed a speciality in managing in-vestments in southern plantations and South Texas ranches. Within a few years after opening the San Antonio office in the early 1880s, Smith had built a lucrative business in negotiating loans in the bor-der counties for several British mortgage companies. Lasater was one of Smith's successful clients. Another success story was that of

Mifflin Kenedy who, after more than twenty years at Los Laureles (242,000 acres), did not refuse an offer for $1,100,000 made in 1882 by a Scottish syndicate known as the Texas Land & Cattle Company, Ltd. Kenedy used the money to piece together a bigger ranch, La Parra, consisting of 325,000 acres in northern Cameron County. Such fragmentary evidence identifies British money as an element in the displacement of Mexican landowners.[35]

A View of King Ranch Expansion

If this economic argument is basically correct, then land records of the famous King Ranch should reveal the unfavorable competitive position of the Mexican landowner in the developing cattle economy. More specifically, Mexican and Anglo land sales to the King Ranch should express distinct responses to cattle market conditions. Sales to the ranch represent an excellent barometer of these distinct responses because the ranch pursued a consistent and aggressive land purchase policy. Here the record and legend are quite clear.

The legend can be related as follows. Late in her years, Henrietta King was quick to trace the key to the ranch's success to a bit of personal advice given to her husband in the late 1850s by then Lt. Col. Robert E. Lee, at that time in charge of protecting the frontier line of Texas from the likes of Juan Cortina and his guerrilla bands. The invaluable advice? "Buy land and never sell." Whether or not the expansionist bent of the ranch took root in such legendary soil is a moot point, for Richard King was quite capable of shaping his aspirations to fit the particular geography of South Texas. King's life endeavor, well known in Texas folklore, was to own all the land between the Nueces and the Rio Grande, to own, in other words, the disputed strip of land over which the United States and Mexico had begun a war. King never realized his life-long dream; at the time of his death in 1885 he held title to only 500,000 acres in South Texas.[36]

The phenomenal growth of the ranch, of course, was not based on determination alone. Alongside Robert E. Lee's wise advice and Richard King's ambitions were the profits of a steamboat monopoly, the capital with which to pursue wisdom and dreams. With secure profits from the river boats, especially those gained during the Civil War windfall, King and his life-long associate Mifflin Kenedy could well afford to purchase land, sink the needed wells, buy the miles of plank and wire fences, embark on a stock improvement program, and make the other improvements necessary to maintain a competitive advantage in the cattle industry. After the Rio Grande steamboat business was sold in 1874, the ranch already possessed the resources to continue its land purchase policy. Fluctuations in the cattle market did not affect the ranch because it had solid connections to credit to carry it through the bad years. Such ready access to credit, moreover, served to sustain ranch expansion precisely during periods when a depressed market or a natural disaster forced many South Texas ranches to become real estate bargains. Ready credit and strategic connections provided the undisputable momentum.[37]

On Richard King's death in 1885, his widow, Henrietta King, and the new *patrón*, son-in-law Robert J. Kleberg, continued the successful management of the ranch, demonstrating a business acumen not unlike the founder's. Robert Kleberg founded and developed the town of Kingsville, helped build two railroads through South Texas, helped realize the dredging project that made Corpus Christi a deep-water port, and expanded the ranch into "a kingdom of a million acres." By the time of Kleberg's death in 1932, the land books showed a total of nearly 1,250,000 acres.[38]

A close examination of a portion of these land books reveals the market-based character of King Ranch expansion. The ingredients for an ideal examination have been compiled by Sterling W. Bass, who researched county land records for ranch purchases in the southwestern portion of Nueces County (later organized as Kleberg County). In his master's thesis, Bass provided an appendix with detailed information concerning the year a purchase was made, the name of the seller, the location, the consideration or amount paid, the acreage involved, and occasional descriptive remarks—in short, sufficient raw material that could be organized into a "test."[39] Table 2 reproduces a section of Bass' appendix.

The purchases made from 1875 to 1904, a relatively tranquil period in the region, will be reviewed here. So far as policy and capability on the part of the ranch to purchase land were concerned, such factors were constant throughout the thirty-year period under consideration. The King Ranch had the financial resources to purchase at will if the landowner in question was willing to sell at a "standard price."[40] Over the following three decades, the ranch would buy 270,000 acres in 45 transactions involving both Anglo and Mexican landowners. These purchases were not random events, distributed equally or evenly between Anglo and Mexican landowners over the years. On the contrary, these land sales illustrate the connection between the particular market situation of these two ethnic classes and fluctuations in cattle market conditions.

By organizing the land purchase record of the ranch according to the fluctuations of the cattle market, the disadvantage of landed wealth before that of capital wealth can be demonstrated. On the one

Table 2. *King Ranch Purchases in Kleberg County Area,*[a] *1854–1904*

Year	Seller	Considerations	Acreage
1854	Elisondo, Manuel	$1,800	53,136
1854	Hinajosa, Pedro	$200	10,770
1862	Stillman, Charles	$20,000	95,272
1866	Graham, John	$250	28,000
1873	State of Texas	Certificate	640
1874	State of Texas	Certificate	258
1877	Edmondon, B. E.	$3,500	8,414
1877	Perez & Garcia	$1,000	4,428
1878	Gutierrez, Miguel	"Valuable considerations"	2,000
1878	State of Texas	Land scrip	1,920
1879	Benzon, Thomas	$3,300	3,160
1879	State of Texas	Land scrip	640
1880	Gutierrez, Miguel	$240	17,872
1881	Perceles, G.	$4,900	9,240
1881	Unknown	"Taxes"	6,085
1881	Irvine, Walter	Land scrip	1,280
1881	Cobb, W. A.	$600	14,700
1881	Morris, Nelson	$3,321	5,534
1881	Gutierrez, Maria	$4,000	24,354
1883	Edwards, L. E.	$495	4,900
1884	Collins, N. G.	Land scrip	4,000
1884	McCullough	Land scrip	1,280
1885	Collett, J. H.	Land scrip	2,476
1885	Russel, Nancy	Land scrip	1,280
1885	Abbey, Nancy	Land scrip	1,280
1885	Kleberg, R. J.	Land scrip	3,840
1885	King, R., Jr.	Land scrip	5,960
1885	King, Alice	Land scrip	4,200
1886	Fitch, John	$700	900
1886	McMahon, A. G.	$600	1,263
1887	State of Texas	Land scrip	3,000
1888	Hinojosa, Teodoro	"Sufficient"	1,400
1889	Woodhouse, H. E.	$7,000	26,568
1889	Garcia, Flores	"Sufficient"	53,136
1891	State of Texas	Land scrip	10,000
1891	State of Texas	Land scrip	4,700
1892	Canales, Albino	$600	1,280
1892	Ramnez, Francis	"Sufficient"	1,280
1892	Garcia, Andres	$1,100	2,200
1892	King, Alice G.	$980	3,200
1892	Lovenskiold, O. G.	$2,100	4,200

Table 2. *(cont.)*

Year	Seller	Considerations	Acreage
1893	Gussett, M.	"Sufficient"	1,280
1893	Gonzalez, A.	$1,100	2,100
1893	Villarreal, Manuel	"Indefinite"	4,000
1894	Gonzalez, A.	"Taxes"	2,260
1894	Kleberg, R. J.	Land scrip	2,169
1894	Gaza, Anna Maria	$1,800	9,000
1895	Canales, Andres	$1,200	4,000
1896	Canales, Andres	"Indefinite"	3,000
1899	Quintenitla, S. G.	$1,200	4,200
1900	Fitch, J.	$4,200	10,000
1901	Lopez, Juan	$1,200	3,000
1901	Jesen, E. R.	$1,700	4,000
1902	Gonzalez, E.	$900	4,200
1902	Kelley, William	$1,840	4,000
1902	Gonzalez, Lorenzo	Land scrip	4,280
1902	Holbien, Sarah	$1,920	1,920
1902	Caldwell	Land scrip	4,780
1902	Texas Land & Cattle Company	$6,000	6,000
1902	State of Texas	Land scrip	4,800
1903	King, Don	Land scrip	1,280
1903	Blucher, C. F. M.	Land scrip	1,280
1903	Cavazos, A.	"Taxes"	1,840
1903	Rodriguez, P.	$700	1,320

Source: Based on Stirling Wesley Bass, "The History of Kleberg County,"
pp. 246–250.

[a]Actually the southern part of Nueces County; it was organized as Kleberg County in 1913.

hand, land sales by Mexicans should follow the fluctuations or conditions of the cattle economy, increasing during hard times and decreasing during healthy periods. Since the land represented a form of ancestral birthright, there should have been little tendency on the part of Mexican landowners to speculate. Cattle ranching for Anglo landholders, on the other hand, was mainly a business proposition, not the basis for an inherited lifestyle. If the price was right, the *rancho* was sold. Anglo land sales should peak during inflationary, boom, periods and bottom out during depressed, bust, periods.

Based on the ample literature of the Texas cattle industry, the market fluctuations between 1875 and 1904 can be divided into five distinct periods: a cattle boom period (1875–1885), a market collapse and slow recovery (1886–1891), a severe drought period known as the "great die-up" (1892–1896), a strong resurgence in the cattle industry (1897–1901), and another drought period (1902–1904). Organizing the land record of the King Ranch according to each market period and ethnicity of seller provides a first approximation of patterned effects.

Table 3 shows more sales activity (number of transactions) and greater acreages sold by Mexicans relative to that by Anglos during poor market conditions. During 1886–1891, a period of collapse, Mexicans sold twice as much land to King as did Anglos, 54,536 acres as opposed to 28,731 acres. The sharpest contrast emerges during the great die-up of 1892–1896 when the King Ranch purchased

Table 3. *King Ranch Expansion in Kleberg County Area,[a] 1875–1904*

Market Condition	Anglo Sellers Acreage Purchased	Mexican Sellers Acreage Purchased	Totals
Cattle boom (1875–1885)	48,304 (11)[b]	57,894 (5)	106,198 (16)
Collapse & slow recovery (1886–1891)	28,731 (3)	54,536 (2)	83,267·(5)
Great die-up (1892–1896)	6,760 (3)	27,860 (8)	34,620 (11)
Strong resurgence (1897–1901)	14,000 (2)	7,200 (2)	21,200 (4)
Drought (1902–1904)	13,260 (5)	11,640 (4)	24,900 (9)
Total	111,055 (24)	159,130 (21)	270,185 (45)
	Other purchases, 1875–1904[c]		56,514 (13)
	Purchases, 1854–1874		188,076 (6)
	Total acreage, 1904		514,775 (64)

Source: Based on Table 2.

[a]Actually the southern part of Nueces County; it was organized as Kleberg County in 1913.

[b]Numbers within parentheses indicate the number of transactions involved.

[c]"Other purchases" include grants by the state for services, internal family transfers, a purchase from a land and cattle company, and a purchase at a sheriff's sale from an "unknown."

27,860 acres from Mexican landowners in eight transactions, while purchasing only 6,760 acres from Anglo owners in three transactions. The converse was true during the following period of resurgence of 1897–1901—Anglo owners sold 14,000 acres, nearly twice the acreage sold by Mexicans.

Looking only at Mexican sales activity over time, the same pattern appears. In general terms, more land was sold by Mexicans in times of poor market conditions and less sold in healthy times. During the ten-year boom of 1875–1885, the King Ranch purchased nearly 58,000 acres of Mexican-owned land, but the ranch would acquire nearly as much, 54,000 acres, in the following five years, a time of market collapse (1886–1891). Under depressed market conditions, in other words, the rate of acquiring Mexican-owned land had doubled. The next few years witnessed an infamous drought known as the "great die-up" (1892–1896), prompting eight sales totaling 27,860 acres. Ranch acquisition slowed considerably during the boom years of 1897–1901 (two purchases totaling 7,200 acres), but then accelerated during the three-year drought of 1902–1904 (four purchases totaling 11,640 acres). This kind of comparison across time is somewhat unwieldy because few tracts larger than 10,000 acres were left after 1890. Gradually, the ranch acquired all the land in the immediate area. By 1904 the holdings of the ranch amounted to approximately 514,775 acres. When Kleberg County was organized in 1913, only 20,000 acres of the county's 560,000 acres remained outside the private domain of the King Ranch.[41]

The relationship of market condition and sales with the King Ranch can be seen more clearly if the boom and bust periods, a total of sixteen and eighteen years respectively, are clustered and the differences in payment considered. Table 4 reveals, both in terms of acreage sold and in number of sales, that Mexican landowners generally parted with their land only when economic circumstances forced such a sale. While King Ranch purchases during boom times included almost equal acreages of Anglo- and Mexican-owned land (62,304 and 65,094 acres, respectively), this was not the case during periods of market depression or severe droughts. During these bust times the ranch purchased 94,036 acres from Mexican landowners, nearly *twice as much* as the 48,751 acres bought from Anglo landowners. To view the matter another way, of the 159,130 acres purchased from Mexicans over the thirty-year period, 94,036 acres, or nearly two-thirds of the total, were purchased during bust times.

The distinct market situation of the two ethnic classes becomes especially evident when the purchase price paid by the ranch is considered. The differences in prices paid to Anglo and Mexican land-

Table 4. *A Summary View of King Ranch Expansion*

	Anglo Sellers			Mexican Sellers		
	Cash Payment		Other[a]	Cash Payment		Other[a]
Market Condition	Acreage Purchased	Price per Acre		Acreage Purchased	Price per Acre	
"Boom times" (1875–1885, 1897–1901)	62,304 (13)[b]	34¢	—	45,222 (5)	27¢	19,872 (2)
"Bust times" (1886–1896, 1902–1904)	46,191 (9)	36¢	2,560 (2)	28,380 (8)	26¢	65,656 (6)
Total	108,495 (22)		2,560 (2)	73,602 (13)		85,528 (8)

Source: Based on Table 2.
[a]Entries in the Nueces County Land Record that do not indicate a cash payment.
[b]Numbers within parentheses indicate the number of transactions involved.

owners constitute a clear contrast, ranging from seven to ten cents more per acre for land of the former. The price variations may have been due to differences in quality and improvements in the land, but they nonetheless point again to the weak market position of Mexican landowners.

A more striking indication of the weak position of Mexicans is the ambiguous entries in the county land records. The land books did not list cash amounts for all transactions; in their place were entered brief but suggestive remarks—"sufficient", "taxes," "indefinite"— amounts that were likely well below most cash payments. The distribution of these entries is revealing, as Table 4 shows. Eight of twenty-one transactions with Mexican landowners involved unspecified payments: three entries of "taxes," two of "sufficient," two more of "indefinite," and one of "valuable contributions." Altogether these eight purchases constituted more than half of the acreage purchased from Mexicans: 85,000 acres of nearly 160,000. Moreover, the greater fraction of these purchases occurred, predictably, during the bust periods of the cattle industry.

The pattern of purchases from Anglo landowners, on the other hand, uncovers no clear correspondence between ranch expansion and market condition. Two factors complicate a direct relationship. First, there is no way of knowing from the purchase record alone whether the tract sold was a homestead, a form of savings or insurance, or a speculative investment. Land paper or scrip, for example, could represent either savings or speculation. Second, many Anglo landowners, whether ranchmen or not, remained connected with the mercantile activity where they had accumulated their capital in the first place. Their market situation was tied to market cycles independent of the cattle industry. In contrast, Mexican landowners, with ranching as their sole or primary livelihood, were highly sensitive to cattle market fluctuations.

In short, Mexicans parted with their land more easily under financial duress. The record of King Ranch expansion, once organized according to cattle market conditions and ethnicity of seller, directly reveals the marginal situation of many Mexican landowners in the late nineteenth century. While some Anglo landholders experienced similar circumstances, many sold their property not because they had to but because of an attractive purchase offer. The first generation of Anglo landholders, in particular, had little of the psychological attachment to land that Mexicans had. If they entered the world of ranching, they generally did so as a business venture.

A Concluding Note

The estate building of Anglo ranchers was a complex process that reflected the effects of market competition. Fraud and violence played a dramatic part in dispossession but their impact has not yet been ascertained. Perhaps matters may temporarily rest with the philosophical insight of one Mexican landowner, Catarino Lerma of the Lower Valley, who observed that "robbing" was a universal experience: "This robbing has always been in all countries. A man that could not rob could not be in society. When these people (King) got enough they put up laws against stealing. King took the land and Kleberg settled it. Martin Hinajosa used to question him about the existence of Mexican heirs."[42] Ambiguity characterizes the historical record, even in the land books, as the noncash payments of the King Ranch suggest. These ambiguous entries, nonetheless, underscored the tenuous situation of landed Mexicans during poor market conditions.

Other questions remain. Did the Mexican sheepmen experience a similar displacement due to market effects? Unlike the cattle industry where Anglo penetration as owners and workers (cowboys) was extensive by the 1870s, some evidence suggests that the sheep industry remained largely a Mexican affair. Anglo control of the cattle industry may even have prompted Mexican landowners to

The Klebergs and Los Kineños, 1935 (Toni Frissell Collection, Library of Congress).

shift from cattle to sheep. In the 1880s, the sheep industry began a long decline, and with it went an unknown number of Mexican fortunes; by 1890 only the counties bordering the Rio Grande had significant numbers of sheep; by 1910 the industry had almost vanished completely from South Texas.[43]

Another line of questioning concerns how Mexican landowners in a few border counties—Webb, Zapata, Starr, and Duval—were able to survive market competition and later make the transition to agriculture. In Duval County in the 1880s, for example, several Mexican *rancheros* were already experimenting with cotton cultivation and irrigation techniques. Such modernization had been motivated by the desire to attain political and social equality with the small but dominant Anglo community. While equality was not immediately forthcoming, continued Mexican landownership preserved the social basis for such an eventuality. At the turn of the century, three hundred Mexican American landowners, organized under a Mexicanized Anglo *patrón*, would lay the basis for the most enduring political machine in Texas.[44]

The accumulated evidence, however, does point to a general erosion of the Mexican land base. Lt. W. H. Chatfield, in an incisive description of Brownsville in 1893, compiled a listing of landowners with more than a thousand acres in Cameron County (1892), thus providing a record of landownership patterns forty-four years after annexation.[45] When organized according to ethnicity and size of landholding, the record tells us much about the erosion of the land base of the Matamoros grantees (see Table 5). By 1892 forty-six non-Spanish-surnamed owners owned over 1.2 million acres of land, nearly four times as much as the acreage owned by Spanish-surnamed owners. The presence of an Anglo elite was evident in the concentration of landownership: eighteen together owned more than a million acres, while the remaining twenty-eight had approximately 100,000 acres. In sharp contrast, landowning Mexicans by this time were predominantly small ranchers: only three of the sixty-nine Spanish-surnamed owners could be considered large ranchers, whereas forty-two owned less than 2,560 acres each. In neighboring Hidalgo County, a similar condition apparently existed. All recorded transactions in the 1848–1900 period occurred between Spanish-surnamed and non-Spanish-surnamed individuals, and in all cases the land passed from the former to the latter.[46]

A recent overview by historian Arnoldo De León underscores the general decline of landed Mexican classes in the nineteenth century. Through a sample survey of census manuscripts, De León has com-

Table 5. *Cameron County Landowners, 1892*

	Non-Spanish-Surnamed Average Acreage	Spanish-Surnamed Average Acreage
Large ranch (over 12,800 acres)	61,954 (18)[a]	37,615 (3)
Medium-sized ranch (2,560–12,800 acres)	6,303 (17)	5,756 (24)
Small ranch (1,000–2,560 acres)	1,503 (11)	1,621 (42)
Total	1,238,865 (46)	319,066 (69)

Source: Based on listing in W. H. Chatfield, *The Twin Cities of the Border and the Country of the Lower Rio Valley.*

[a]Numbers within parentheses indicate the number of ranches involved.

piled some telling statistics on the manner in which the Mexican class structure of South and West Texas changed during the period 1850–1900. At mid-century, the rural Mexican population was equally divided in thirds among ranch-farm owners (34%), skilled laborers (29%), and manual laborers (34%). By the turn of the century, the two top tiers had shrunk—ranch-farm owners comprised 16 percent of the Texas Mexican population, skilled laborers 12 percent— and the bottom tier of manual laborers had expanded, comprising 67 percent, or two of every three adult Mexicans. In contrast, the segment of the Anglo-American population that showed the greatest increase in the nineteenth century was the ranch-farm-owning class, from 2 percent in 1850 to 31 percent by 1900.[47]

In closing, it should be noted again that the same market forces that collapsed the Mexican class structure also worked their corrosive effects on the Anglo community. The King Ranch, as discussed earlier, acquired land in a "color blind" fashion. Technological innovations, such as barbed wire, for example, displaced both Mexican and Anglo ranchers with little land or money. The long-term effects were quite different, however. Market-based displacement within the Anglo community signified the replacement of one Anglo merchant-landowner with another Anglo merchant-landowner. Thus, market development for the Anglo community signified a "circulation of elites" as well as an elaboration of internal class differences. For the Mexican population, displacement of the landowning classes had more devastating and irreversible effects. The landed elite and the struggling *rancheros* were not replaced by their descendants or by other Mexicans. Thus, market development for the Mexican community signified a collapsing of the internal class structure. With few exceptions, the propertied classes of the Mexican settlements did not reproduce themselves.

4. Race, Labor, and the Frontier
(NW Texas plains)

THIS CHAPTER examines the process of nation building, or "incorporation," that took place in the annexed territories. We return, in other words, to the point raised by Ashbel Smith—that a greater task and challenge than war was the substituting of American institutions for Mexican ones. In brief, "incorporation," a complex phenomenon with political, economic, and social elements, refers to the assertion of national authority, the penetration of a national market, and, finally, the establishment of the national culture and settlement of citizens from the national core. In this context, the term "frontier" refers to the territorial fringe or periphery of an expanding nation-state or political entity; it is an area that has not been fully incorporated within the nation.

The incorporation of the annexed territories followed two general sequences. One sequence was the road of accommodation generally followed beyond the Nueces. The previous chapters have described the peace structure that obtained among the Rio Grande settlements and the systematic market displacement of landed Mexicans. Another question that figured prominently in the experience of annexation concerned the organization of work. For ranch labor, the Anglo landowners simply adopted the style of the Mexican dons and maintained the *patrón-peón* relations characteristic of the region. Beyond the ranch, however, the pioneer entrepreneurs found that there was a scarcity of labor. Or, to state it more concisely, few Mexicans were willing to work for "day wages."

The second sequence followed in Texas was the more traumatic and sweeping experience of completely uprooting the old order and transplanting a new one—of expelling Mexicans above the Nueces and removing Indians from the "great plains" north of San Antonio. In this context, the organization of the cattle industry on the Indian frontier offers an instructive contrast to that of the Texas border region. Beyond the Rio Grande settlements, there was free land—"free" once the Apaches and Comanches were finally removed in the 1870s. Nor was there a significant Mexican presence on the Llano Estacado (the "Staked Plains"), except for three hundred or so *comanchero* traders and sheepmen from the New Mexico settlements.[1]

Thus, there was no race issue that could immediately stratify the frontier order. In fact, at an early point in its history, the range life appeared to hold the promise of an egalitarian society. What emerged, however, on the free soil of the Panhandle were some of the biggest "cattle kings" of Texas. As was the case for the Rio Grande settlements, the development of the frontier basically entailed the claiming of the livestock, land, and water of the open range, an experience that created social divisions based on property and privilege. This assertion of property claims on all land and livestock, moreover, signaled the demise of the open range and the cowboy era.

Toward the late nineteenth century, two signs indicated that the new territories had become incorporated. One was evidence of an end to the problem of securing wage labor. On both the Mexican and Indian frontiers, the earlier forms of work arrangements—characterized by the paternalism of the border ranches and the egalitarianism of the Panhandle ranches—gradually gave way to formal wage-labor contracts. The second sign concerned the migration and formation of Anglo-American communities. Facilitated by an expanding railroad network, the new settlements basically Americanized the old Spanish-Mexican towns of the region: Spanish was displaced as the common language, intermarriages declined, and separate neighborhoods were formed.

Within this framework, then, this chapter will address three related questions about the incorporation of the frontier territories: (a) the questions of labor and race in the annexed Mexican settlements; (b) the development of the cattle business on the Indian frontier, an example of a different type of incorporation; and (c) the final phase of incorporation or what is often referred to as the "closing of the frontier."

On the Mexican Frontier

For several decades after annexation, life along the border continued in much the same way as before. Even as the American mercantile elite displaced Mexican *rancheros* and money-poor landed elite from their land, the life of the landless Mexicans, the *peones* and the *vaqueros*, remained generally unaffected. The cattle *hacienda* remained the dominant social and economic institution of the border region, and the work relations that linked Anglo *patrón* and Mexican worker remained paternalistic and patriarchal. The development of a cattle industry required no fundamental changes in traditional labor relations. The longevity of the *hacienda* as a social institution was due to its resiliency: finding a market, it would respond and produce; lacking one, it would turn inward and become self-sustaining.[2]

Beyond the ranch economy, however, Anglo and European pioneers who wished to experiment with such money crops as cotton or cane were severely limited by the scarcity of day laborers. Mexican workers were viewed as unreliable because many still owned small tracts of land and worked only to supplement their meager incomes. Mexican *rancheros* devoted themselves to cultivating corn, the most important subsistence crop in their diet. Once subsistence needs were met, Mexican *rancheros* turned to raising cattle, which was more profitable than farming. The Abbé Domenech never could understand how a *ranchero* of the lower border lived, "for he labours little or none; the very shadow of labor overpowers him, and he comprehends not activity, save in pleasures." The wonderment was largely rhetorical, however, for the *abbé* provided the answer to his own question. The *ranchero*'s work in tending to "herds of oxen, horses, goats, and sheep" required very little labor, "and therefore does he like it so much."[3] Thus, few Mexicans were willing to pick cotton or cut cane.

On the other hand, the masterless, ex-*peón* population present in Texas may have refused to have anything to do with plantation labor. These ex-*peones* were not just those left behind by the refugee elite of Texas, but comprised also those who fled peonage in northern Mexico. Escape to Texas at times reached such critical proportions that cotton cultivation in the neighboring state of Tamaulipas was threatened. The possibility of escape weakened debt peonage on the Mexican side, much as it had weakened American slavery on the American side. During the fifteen-year period (1845–1860) between the Mexican War and the American Civil War, the Texas-Mexican border was the boundary sought by both escaping Mexican *peones* and black slaves. The boundary was also the working zone for slave and *peón* "catchers."[4]

Given these circumstances, far less cotton was cultivated in the Lower Rio Grande Valley in the decade after the Mexican War than in the preceding period under Mexican rule. American expansionist interests, as historian Graf noted, argued that the Mexican laborer was unreliable because he was "accustomed to compulsory labor in his own country if he did not have his own little piece of ground." Large-scale planting was impossible because under the "free labor conditions of Texas" Mexicans worked only to satisfy their needs, which were few. According to this reasoning, there were two ways in which a permanent labor supply could be secured in the Lower Valley: (*a*) if the United States controlled both sides of the Rio Grande, black slave labor could be introduced with safety and large-scale plantations begun, or (*b*) if there was a *"peón* law" for western Texas, local authorities would have the power to compel the Mexicans to work and "thereby ensure the farmer a steady labor supply, as well as reduce vagrancy."[5] The Civil War, which followed shortly after these proposals were offered, made these questions moot.

Throughout much of the late nineteenth century, Mexican labor, according to employers' accounts, remained an unstable and unpredictable element. Two factors may be offered in explanation. One, Mexican laborers, ex-cowboys and ex-*peones*, were being taught the discipline of commercial life. Perhaps the most common complaint by employers concerned the Mexicans' fondness of leisure time. One farmer who had moved to San Antonio from East Texas after the Civil War "had been accustomed to negro labor; but, as there were few negroes in the town, he was forced to employ Mexican laborers." Mexicans worked, until the 1880s, for fifty cents a day, and then for seventy-five cents. Laborers were able to live on this wage because "they had few expenses, food was cheap, and clothing scant." Farmers understood that "to get a week's work out of a man it was necessary to hold his pay until Saturday. If you paid him Wednesday, you would not see him until Monday, and sometimes, he stayed away until need sent him to work again. At that time, no one ever thought of the farm hand buying ground or building more than a thatched hut on a squatter's site."[6] The early commercial enterprises of the border region had to make allowances for an incompletely trained wage labor force.

The second factor points to the lack of daily work, which may account for the much observed slow, listless work style of the Mexican laborer. Unattached ex-*peones* had a difficult time surviving on wage labor in the late nineteenth century. In Mexico, for example, day laborers who were given work worked as slowly as possible for fear that there would not be any more work. As one observer put it, the day laborer is "suspicious if he is offered money, for that seems to mean that he is going to lose his job, which is far more of an insurance to him than such an uncertain and unproductive commodity as money." A debt that guaranteed a job was preferable to money. Available evidence suggests this situation may have obtained in the Texas border region, especially once the "open range" had been enclosed. During the severe drought and depression of the 1890s, for example, "with unemployment everywhere, day laborers in gangs sought jobs at the Santa Gertrudis and were put to work clearing brush."[7]

While Mexicans proved reluctant to perform farm labor, work on the ranches continued to be meditated by the old practice of debt peonage. Although peonage was formally illegal, most men and women on Texas ranches nonetheless looked to a *patrón* to provide them with the necessities of life, to give them work, to pay them wages, and, finally, to donate a *jacal* and provisions when they grew too old. In return, there was a loyalty to the ranch and its owners that acknowledged and repaid a *patrón*'s sense of noblesse oblige.[8]

Peonage and Ranch Life

The country of the lower Rio Grande was characterized by large self-sufficient ranches. The Randado Ranch of the lower border was a typical large Mexican ranch—80,000 acres and 25,000 head of cattle, with a store, chapel, water tank, twenty or more adobe houses with thatched roofs, a little graveyard, a post office, and a school "where very pretty little Mexicans recited proudly in English words of four letters." The Anglo-owned ranches were similar but usually bigger. The Kenedy Ranch of "La Parra," 325,000 acres, had three hundred employees with a church and a school of 125 pupils. The King Ranch, atypical only because of its size, was a *hacienda* of 500,000 acres during Richard King's lifetime, with a commissary and store, stables, corrals, carriage and wagon sheds, blacksmith's shop, and houses for five hundred workers and their families.[9]

According to Jovita González, the "servant class" of the ranch was divided into two distinct groups: the *"peón* proper" and the cowboy. While the cowboy tended cattle and horses, the *peón* tended goats and sheep, worked the fields, and performed all the menial and personal labor around the ranch. The *peón* was "submissive to his master's desires, obeyed blindly, and had no will of his own." Debts for medical necessity, debts inherited from the father, food debts from the ranch commissary, and so on tied the *peón* securely to the ranch owner.[10]

In contrast, "the master had no control" over the *vaquero*, or cowboy, who was usually the son of a small landowner or sometimes a rancher himself. There were no regular paydays and years might pass before a cowhand would have a wage settlement with his employer. In the interim, clothing, ammunition, tobacco, and other necessities were purchased and sent to the cowboys by their employer. While generally more independent than the *peón*, *vaqueros* could also fall into debt for years. Catarino Lerma, in a 1928 interview with Paul Taylor, recalled how life was in the 1860s: "In the '60s the vaqueros got $10 a month and board. The pastores got $3 to $4 a month. They used to be in debt from $300 to $400. Ramirez, the Mexican rancher, wanted them in debt like slaves."[11] At these wages, a debt of three to four hundred dollars meant for a *vaquero* nearly three years of work owed, and for a *pastor* at least nine years owed. *Pastores* were especially vulnerable to indebtedness. In the late 1870s and early 1880s there was hardly a shepherd who was not in debt from one hundred to five hundred dollars. This did not signify that a *pastor* never changed employers. Debts were a "certificate of character," which new employers were expected to assume.[12]

In the absence of a "*peón* law," the character of peonage was expectedly inconsistent on the Texas Mexican frontier. Domenech believed that the *peones* were "reduced to slavery by misery, idleness, or gambling" and that their condition was not hereditary and seldom lasted a lifetime.[13] Sometimes peonage appeared to be the desire of the employer, sometimes that of the employee; and sometimes only the paternalistic shell of peonage remained in practice. This work tradition continued in force long after the mechanism of debt had been effectively discarded.

The Anglo pioneer ranchers, as noted previously, were Mexicanized to some degree. In the most extreme form, these ranchers acquired the traits of a *hacendado*—a paternalistic bond with the *vaqueros*, an identification with the ranch, an obsession to expand one's land holdings. Ex-steamboat captain Richard King was an exemplary case of the new *hacendado*. In the words of Tom Lea, King with his Irish-accented Spanish was a curious blend of "pilothouse commander and hacienda patriarch."[14] A newspaper account published in Corpus Christi described Richard King as "eccentrically baronial," as one who fluctuated between fits of temperance (when he would "screw down his expenditures to the lowest cent") and the "wildest excesses of semi-barbaric hospitality." The article also noted that "as is King so is Kenedy, saving that he has always lacked hospitality, King's saving clause."[15]

Like the Spanish dons of the eighteenth century, King had solved his labor problem by leading an *entrada* (literally, "entrance") of settlers to his new Santa Gertrudis ranch. In 1854, after King had bought the herds of a drought-stricken Mexican village, he extended an offer to the village: he would resettle the entire community on his ranch where they could have homes and work. The village accepted the offer, and the resulting *entrada* consisted of more than a hundred men, women, and children with their belongings. The *vaqueros* and their families came to be known as Los Kineños, the people of the King Ranch. They became recognized for their skill and loyalty to the King family, providing the critical armed guard during the "troubled times" of the region. Among the Kineños, it was common to find three generations of ranch hands—son, father, grandfather—working alongside one another.[16]

In less dramatic fashion, other Anglo ranchers obtained loyal, permanent workers by hiring the *vaqueros* of the grantees and *rancheros* they displaced. The core of Kenedy Ranch cowboys, for instance, consisted of the descendants of the families who had worked on La Atravesada before Kenedy purchased the grant in 1882.[17] Likewise, on the Mellon Creek Ranch of Texas pioneer Thomas O'Connor, the majority of hands were Mexicans, most of whom had been born and raised on the ranch. Included were descendants of the De la Garzas, who once owned a large ranch on the San Antonio River before the Texas Revolution. Many of the Mexican families had never left the ranch for any considerable length of time. They had "no idea of the value of money," noted the ranch biographer, "nor do they wish to have it. One of them refused a check for his wages saying that he did not want anymore of that paper because the rats always ate it up." Each of the O'Connor ranch divisions had several pensioners, for "every man who proves himself a faithful worker never need have any fears about his later years." Jesús Gonzales—"Old Casus"—had worked on the Mellon "for thirty-five years at least"; he was kept as a pensioner with the nominal employment of chicken raising until his death. The bond of paternalism was strengthened by the Catholic religion shared by both ranch owners and workers. The chapel built for the Mexican colony by this Irish Catholic family was cared for by "Antonio Rodríguez, a faithful Mexican," whose son "inherited his father's charge, and jealously guards the little church and keeps it neat and clean."[18]

The general success of Anglo ranches along the Texas border rested on the ability of the owners to assimilate the ways of the *patrón*. In the smooth transition from Richard King to son-in-law Robert Kleberg, a critical factor was the latter's understanding that the necessary ingredients for labor relations at the Santa Gertrudis consisted of the "personal regard and responsibility of the *patrón*" and the "personal faith and loyalty of the *gente*."[19] So effective were such paternalistic work arrangements that they survived as a feature of South Texas ranch life well into the twentieth century.

In places where peonage continued into the twentieth century, a certain evolution had taken place. Debt probably no longer constituted its underlying mechanism. Despite wages, perhaps the power of precedent, of sedimented tradition, was sufficient to keep the character of *patrón-peón* relations—essentially, labor relations circumscribed by paternalism, reciprocal obligations, and permanency—in place. The sense of belonging to a ranch was another important feature of this relationship.

The scarcity of work may also have been a major factor supporting the practice of peonage. Especially after the mid-1880s when the number of hands needed for ranching had declined, permanent ranch work under a benevolent *patrón* may have been a better situation than the alternative—migratory cotton picking. If the *patrón* fulfilled his obligations, there was little impulse on the part of the "free" *peón* to leave.

The chronic lawlessness of the region may have also reinforced the importance of the *patrón-peón* relationship. For the Anglo *patrón*, it was a question of being protected from the "treacherous" element of the Mexican population. For the *vaquero* and his family, it was a matter of being protected from the violence of Anglo lawmen, vigilantes, and outlaws. Both *hacendado* and *vaquero* required the services of the other. Several suggestive statements regarding this protective character of the *patrón-peón* relationship have come from the work of ranch folklorist J. Frank Dobie. Defending Mexicans from the charge of treachery, Dobie noted that the ranch Mexican "will take the side of his *amo* ["master"], if he likes him, against any Mexican that tries to do his *amo* an injustice." On another occasion, Dobie complimented the Mexican ranch hand as follows—"For uncomplaining loyalty, he is probably an equal to the 'befo de wah' darky and as trustworthy."[20]

The Matter of Race

Mexican-Anglo relations in the late nineteenth century were inconsistent and contradictory, but the general direction pointed to the formation of a "race situation," a situation where ethnic or national prejudice provided a basis for separation and control. The paternalism of the Anglo *patrones* and the loyalty of their Mexican workers did not obscure the anti-Mexican and anti-Anglo sentiments and divisions of the ranch world.

In the late nineteenth century, these race sentiments, which drew heavily from the legacy of the Alamo and the Mexican War, were maintained and sharpened by market competition and property disputes. Every conflict provided an opportunity for a vicarious re-creation of previous battles. The Mexican cattle "thieves" of the 1870s, for example, claimed they were only taking "Nana's cattle"—Grandma's cattle—and that "the gringos" were merely raising cows for the Mexicans. Texas ranchman William Hale presented the other point of view: "Killing a Mexican was like killing an enemy in the independence war." Since this was a conflict "with historic scores to settle [Goliad and the Alamo] the killing carried a sort of immunity with it."[21] The English lady Mary Jaques, who spent two years on a Central Texas ranch in the late 1880s, noted in her journal that it was difficult to convince Texans that Mexicans were human. The Mexican "seems to be the Texan's natural enemy; he is treated like a dog, or, perhaps, not so well." What especially upset Lady Jaques, however, was the assimilation of such instincts by educated Englishmen who had settled in Texas. Describing the commotion over plans to lynch a Mexican, Jaques remarked: "It seems scarcely credible that even a fairly educated Englishman, holding a good position in Junction City, an influential member of the Episcopalian Church, should have become so imbued with these ideas that he . . . gleefully boasted that he had the promise of the rope on which the 'beast' swung, and also of his scalp as a trophy. 'I have one Mexican scalp already,' he exclaimed."[22] For both Anglos and Mexicans, the power of assimilation made actual participation in the Texas Revolution or Mexican War an irrelevant point. These shared memories simply provided a context for the ongoing conflict of the day.

The basic rules regarding Mexicans on many ranches called for a separation of Mexican and Anglo cowboys and a general authority structure in which Anglo stood over Mexican. As Jaques noted in 1889, the Texans ate in the ranch dining room and "would have declined to take their meals with the Mexicans." The Mexicans, for their part, "camped out with their herds" and cooked their weekly ration of flour, beans, and other groceries.[23] Likewise, underneath the much-discussed paternalism of the King Ranch and the loyalty of the *vaqueros* was a clear hierarchy of authority along race lines. Trail driver Jeff Connolly of Lockhart, Texas, recalled the days of herding King Ranch cattle to the Red River: "The only white men with the herd were Coleman and myself, the balance of the bunch being Mexicans. All the old-timers know how King handled the Mexicans—he had them do the work and let the white men do the bossing."[24] Nor were these bosses ordinary "white men." The ranch foremen and subordinate bosses were, as a rule, former Texas Rangers. An apparent exception to this pattern was Lauro Cavazos, descendant of the San Juan Carricitos grantees. Cavazos worked as foreman of the ranch's Norias Division, which comprised the old San Juan Carricitos grant.[25] Cavazos, however, was not actually an exception to the postwar authority structure, for there was no problem with Mexicans bossing other Mexicans.

This understanding about authority was carried well into the

twentieth century. Again, J. Frank Dobie provides the clearest statement of the practice: on the smaller ranches and stock farms in the
Lower Valley, the Mexicans were managed by Anglo owners or bosses;
on the larger ranches, the *mayordomo* (overseer) was usually Anglo,
but the *caporales* (straw bosses) were often Mexican. However, if
"white hands" worked alongside Mexicans, then the *caporal* was
"nearly always white."[26]

Landed Mexicans represented the complicating factor in the Mexican-Anglo relations of the frontier period. Even during the worst
times of Mexican banditry, the permanent Mexican residents who
were landowners were seen as "good citizens" while the large "floating" population temporarily employed on ranches were seen as sympathizers of the raiders.[27] Similar distinctions were made in the less
dramatic, daily encounters. For example, in her first trip to Corpus
Christi in 1870, Mrs. Susan Miller of Louisiana stopped at the State
Hotel and "was horrified to see Mexicans seated at the tables with
Americans. I told my husband I had never eaten with Mexicans or
negroes, and refused to do so. He said: 'Mexicans are different to
negroes and are recognized as Americans. However, I will speak to
the manager and see if he will not put a small table in one corner of
the room for you.' He did so and we enjoyed our meal."[28] Evidence of
inconsistent patterns at times comes from ironic sources. They indicate, nonetheless, that not all Mexicans were seen or treated as inferior. In fact, most pioneers, especially merchants and officials,
were quite adept at drawing the distinction between the landed
"Castilian" elite and the landless Mexican. Thus, L. E. Daniell, author of *Successful Men in Texas* (1890), described the physical appearance of prominent "Canary Islander" José María Rodríguez as
"five feet nine inches in height, complexion dark, but not a drop of
Indian blood in his veins." As if to emphasize this point, Daniell
added that Rodríguez had "in his veins the blood of the most chiv-
alric Knights that made the Olive of Spain respected wherever a
Knightly name was known."[29]

The well-known aphorism about color and class explains the
situation on the Mexican frontier—"money whitens." The only
problem for upper-class Mexicans was that this principle offered neither consistent nor permanent security in the border region. Certainly it did not protect them from the racial opinion of many Anglos. One descendant of this upper class described their reaction as
follows: "Now that a new country has been established south of the
Rio Grande they call our people *Mexicans*. They are the same people
who were called Spaniards only a short time ago. Some say the word
in such a bitter way that it sounds as if it were a crime to be a *Mexi-*

can. My master says he is one, and is proud to be one. That he is a member of the white race, whether he be called Mexican or not."[30]

On the Indian Frontier

An interpretation of the nineteenth-century Southwest can hardly ignore the notion of the "frontier," one of the most popular and ambiguous themes in American history and politics. One popular image is that the frontier was a country of free land and resources, a place where the most humble folk could stake a homestead and the young and ambitious had a chance to engage in trade. Another popular notion is that the western experience was basically democratic and egalitarian, a theme identified with historian Frederick Turner. Basically, Turner attributed the formation of American democracy to the frontier, where the hardy pioneer spirit of individualism dominated and overcame established tradition. Following Turner, Texas historians have emphasized the "fair play" and fundamental equality of frontier life.[31]

Western historians have often demonstrated the limited validity of these ideas. Despite the legendary fortunes of a few, the West was no "promised land," and many who went west left or died without bettering their condition. In similar fashion, the hardships of frontier survival and the necessities of frontier business—protection against Indians and Mexican bandits, the construction of irrigation systems, the annual cattle roundups, for example—were communal undertakings that imparted a basic sense of equality. But once law and order were established, the communal spirit and sense of equality among the American frontier communities tended to evaporate.[32]

The settlement of the Central and North Texas plains illustrates the manner of development on the open frontier. Settlement beyond the "tree line" of East and Central Texas followed the line of army forts and the removal of Indian tribes in 1870 to reservations in New Mexico and the Indian Territory. Unlike South and West Texas, there was no significant Mexican presence in the Staked Plains. The first Anglo settlers were cattlemen and the cowboys who worked for them. Initially there was no significant status difference between the two since every cowboy could theoretically become a cattleman. Range life between 1867 and 1880, as Walter Prescott Webb described it, was "idyllic"—"the land had no value, the grass was free, the water belonged to the first comer." Mavericks, or unbranded cattle, presented an unparalleled opportunity to get into business, as another source put it, "without cash, capital, or scruple."[33]

Ten years of trail driving to northern markets, however, completely changed the situation. Success and failure, good and bad luck, the judicious investment and the foolish one combined to separate cowboys into two groups: those who owned cattle and fenced pastures and those who hired themselves out to tend the cattle and fences. The distinction became especially pronounced once the cattle boom attracted investors from "back East" and from London. English syndicates as well as American concerns made cattle and range investments representing millions of dollars. By the late 1880s British ranching interests controlled one of every four or five acres in the Panhandle.[34]

These investors had two ways of guarding their ranch interests. One was to buy out the ranch entirely at a handsome price and assign a manager to run the place. Thus, in the late nineteenth century, some of the largest Panhandle ranches were managed by British-accented administrators who reported to a home office in London or New York. The other safe avenue for investors who knew nothing about ranching (except from the exaggerated reports they read) was to work through cowboy partners in Texas. Such partnerships account for the making of the legendary "cattle kings." The accumulation of fortunes within a single lifetime came to those cowboys who were financed through the backing of English and American capitalists. Trail driver Henry Campbell, for example, had found financial backing with a Colonel Britton, a Chicago banker, and established the Matador Ranch, in which he had a one-fifth share. Charles Goodnight, hired cowboy, entered a partnership with the Englishman John Adair and organized the JA Ranch in the Panhandle. Shanghai Pierce, once a hired hand, amassed more than a million acres because of a profitable agreement with the Kountze Brothers' banking firm.[35] In brief, the entry of outside capital accelerated the differentiation of pioneers into "cattle kings" and "cow hands."

As the cattle industry came to represent huge investments of capital, the questions of water rights, grazing rights, and cattle ownership acquired a new significance. Ranches increased, herds became numerous, range rights became more precarious, and grass and water became scarcer. Cattlemen with land organized to assert their property rights as well as to extend their control over the public domain. They formed associations to control grazing and water rights, to organize roundups, to supervise branding, and to combat cattle diseases and thieves. In the process, they acted also to discourage the homesteader and the independent cowboy.[36]

Mavericking, once a common practice, became a dangerous activity in parts where established cattlemen desired to retain complete control of the range. Even the meaning of frontier terminology changed. "Rustler," for example, used to designate cowboys paid a commission for every maverick found and branded with the employer's brand. Once the big ranch owners agreed that no more maverick commissions would be paid, rustlers began to be looked on as thieves and outlaws, and in some places "rustler" was used as a derisive label for homesteader and small rancher.[37]

Partly as an effort to stop rustlers and homesteaders or "nesters," the large cattlemen began to enclose their ranges with wire fences. These enclosures set off a fence-cutting war across the range lands, from the Panhandle to South Texas. The fence cutters, according to a Ranger undercover agent, were "what I would call cowboys, or small cow men that own . . . . from 15 head all the way up to perhaps 200 head of cattle and a few cow ponies, etc." Fence cutting to these cowboys, added the Ranger agent, was a communal activity endowed with a sense of righteousness. By 1884 the fence wars had become so serious that a special session of the legislature passed a law making it a penitentiary offense to cut an enclosure. It was a great loss for the cowboy. "They finally got it stopped," recalled an old-time Frio County fence cutter, "but it cost them lots of money."[38]

With the enclosed range, the cowboy witnessed the rapid disappearance of those features that had given him some personal satisfaction. The chances of becoming a rancher through mavericking and squatting on public land no longer existed. Whatever else the cowboy may have been, the cowboy was now a casual wage laborer. This was accompanied, moreover, by critical changes in personal relations between workers and owners. The boss who was both owner and cattleman, of humble origins, had vanished from the Panhandle country by the late 1870s. In marked contrast to the personal rule of these cattlemen was the formal rule of the big cattle companies who hired accountants and managers. A Panhandle county sheriff described the contrast: "They [the cattlemen] got right out with the boys on the trail; did just as much work as the boys, ate the same kind of food. Their cowboys would have died in the saddle rather than have complained. See what we have now; a bunch of organized companies. Some of them are foreign and have costly managers and bookkeepers who live on and drink the best stuff money can buy and call their help cow servants."[39] Specific cowboy grievances stemmed from the rigid control by the Panhandle Cattlemen's Association of the branding of mavericks, plus the association's opposition to cowboys owning small herds and taking up small parcels of public domain. In April 1883, led by the foremen of three large ranches, the cowboys of the Panhandle went on "strike" over the unsettled grievances. The Texas Rangers were brought in to break the strike, culminating in a pitched battle involving cowboys, small herd owners, and Rangers at Tascosa. This show of strength by the big landowners was all that was necessary to crush the strike, but resentment lingered for years. A few of the more embittered men formed the Get Even Cattle Company, which stole cattle from the different company ranches and drove them to New Mexico.[40]

Thus, the promise of the frontier civilization disappeared as old social divisions based on wealth and property resurfaced, although in distinctively western garb. Forty years after annexation, the appearance of rustic democracy and free land had largely evaporated. In sociological terms, the Panhandle frontier represented what might be called a social order with "open resources."[41] Because conditions were fluid and opportunities abundant, the social classes of the frontier society had not assumed a fixed character. Once the frontier was settled and its commercial opportunities monopolized by a distinct group, a society with closed resources and fixed, visible class lines appeared.

A Comparison with the Texas Border Region

In the late nineteenth century, the contrast between the cattle kingdoms of the Panhandle and those of the Texas border was a striking one. The Panhandle ranch was managed strictly as a business enterprise by corporate accountants or ranchmen turned businessmen. The wage contract, stripped of the camaraderie that once characterized the relationship between ranch owner and cowboys, mediated openly and formally the obligations and exchanges between owner and worker. Cowhands worked for wages, lived in bunkhouses, sometimes "struck" for better wages and working conditions, and were hired and let off according to the seasonal needs of the ranch. For the cowboy of the Panhandle, the contractual relations with the rancher made the class lines of the ranch world quite clear.

In contrast, the South Texas ranch, while a business, was operated by Mexican or Mexicanized Anglo *patrones*, who maintained paternalistic relations with permanent *vaquero* workers. It was commonplace to find ranches with generations of workers on the ranch. Here the class distinctions between ranch owner and worker were clearly drawn, but these actors were bound to each other in a manner that tended to produce a sentiment of kinship. Such a bond tied the fate of the two classes and races together, making the ranch a self-sufficient and insular social world.

Despite the differences between the ranches of the Panhandle and of South Texas, the incorporation of these frontiers illustrates that a central element of the western experience concerned the monopolization of rights and privileges by big ranchers at the expense of the small cattlemen and independent cowboys. To put it another way, development entailed the elimination of the "unproductive" user of land (whether owner or nester), an experience characterized by market competition as well as by fraud and violence. Along the border this conflict assumed a racial character whereas in the Panhandle it had a nascent class character.

The basic regional differences can be summarized as follows. In the Panhandle area, the cattle and land stock companies of New York and London reorganized the open frontier and sharpened the class lines of the ranch world. Along the Texas border, the mercantile elite modernized the cattle *hacienda*, maintained old work arrangements, and eliminated the marginal ranchers.

End of the Frontier

The Catarino Garza affair of the early 1890s, a Texas-based rebellion against Mexican President Porfirio Díaz, briefly shifted national attention to the lower Rio Grande border. As was the general case with newcomers and passing travelers in the border region, the descriptions generated by the Garza incident were colored with a mixture of disbelief and jaundice. Journalist Jonathan Speed, writing for *Harper's Weekly*, described the Rio Grande frontier then as "an overlapping of Mexico into the United States, and the people, though they have been American citizens for more than forty years, are almost as much an alien race as the Chinese, and have shown no disposition to amalgamate with the other Americans." Soldier Richard Harding Davis, part of the troop assigned to track down Garza, wrote in his journal that the country was "America's only in its possession" and "Mexican in its people, its language, and its mode of life." Davis, describing the country as the "backyard of the world," recalled that General Sheridan once said "that we should go to war with Mexico again, and force her to take it back."[42]

By the time of Garza's aborted invasion of Mexico, the economic and social repercussions set off by the extension of railroads into South and West Texas and northern Mexico had been at work for fifteen years. In the late 1870s and 1880s, the railroads had opened the greater Texas-Mexican border region to more extensive American economic penetration and population shifts. Thus the Americanization of the cities and the railway-inspired economic boom went hand in hand. San Antonio in 1891 was symptomatic of the new era. The town was being "boomed," as Mary Jaques noted on a return visit, by

"Eastern capitalists" who had faith in the future of Mexico. Moreover, the handsome residences of merchant millionaires, cattle kings, and "real estate princes" were replacing the old adobe houses and *jacales*, with the Mexicans "being gradually driven out of the place."[43] In the rural areas, also, there were signs of an impending collapse of the old social order. The most telling of these signs was the appearance of wage laborers.

Securing Wage Labor

By the 1880s the work of the cowboy in Texas was increasingly irrelevant. One, the task of fencing was over and fewer men were needed to handle cattle; two, the railroad had brought shipping points much closer, rendering trail driving an inefficient way of shipping cattle to market. The number of cowboy laborers needed for ranching was reduced by a third, according to one estimate. The work of cowboys, moreover, was becoming specialized: on the large ranches, fence-mending teams, construction teams, and roundup teams all handled their respective tasks. In general, cowboys had to devote less time to working with cattle and more time to mending fences and greasing windmills. As a result of such changes, Theodore J. McMinn of St. Louis, a cattle range expert, remarked on February 16, 1885, that the cowboy was becoming a "comparatively infrequent personage" in the ranch business: "Leasing, fencing, and the management of great herds by companies on strictly business principles have gradually eliminated the old-time cowboy." McMinn opined that, although fewer cowboys were needed, "a better class" of employees was the positive result.[44]

On the ranches with Anglo and Mexican hands, this meant the dismissal of the Anglo cowboys and the retention of the Mexicans, primarily because the latter received one-half to two-thirds the wages paid "any white man," as one report put it, a differential that remained fairly consistent from the 1880s through the 1920s. Thus, large ranches in West Texas favored the Mexican cowboy by a ratio of two to one over the Anglo hand. Likewise on the coastal plains in San Patricio County, the reorganization of the Coleman-Fulton Pasture Company to emphasize experiments in agriculture called for "replacing white cowboys with Mexicans, who would undoubtedly work for less, and for reducing the work year to nine months."[45]

The general result, however, was displacement from ranch work for both Anglo and Mexican cowboys. There were few alternatives for the ex-cowboy. Left to his own desires, the cowboy was not likely to leave the ranch and take up farm work. To advice that he give up herding, one *vaquero* from Ysleta in West Texas recalled saying that "I was a woolly Texan from Spanish America and did not believe in doing any more work with plow or shovel than I could help." Nonetheless, in the latter quarter of the nineteenth century, *vaqueros* and *rancheros* from the Rio Grande settlements began to supplement their subsistence through seasonal agricultural labor, "which expanded or contracted as needed." In his own fashion, Dobie explained the predicament well when, in describing a Mexican ranch hand who had spent fifty years with one master, he noted that "had his *amo* not lost his fine ranch in the recent downfall of the cattle business, old Juan would yet be living on it with plenty of goat meat and *tortillas* as long as he could chew."[46]

For a period of time, the railroad provided work for the trail drivers it had displaced. Cowboys as well as former *peones* extended the instrument of their final displacement throughout South and West Texas. One track camp, in J. L. Allhands' description, was in essence a "rolling village" composed of "about four hundred men, a most conglomerate and strange population, white, negro, and for a short while a few Greeks, with the slow plodding Mexican predominating."[47]

The railway network also provided an impetus for cotton production in the subhumid sections of the state, and this further accelerated the displacement of cowboys as ranchers turned their pastures into sharecropper plots.[48] In the 1870s Central Texas pastures were the first to be converted to cotton fields. Seasonal migrations from the Lower Valley to the cotton fields around San Marcos and Seguin began in earnest in the 1880s and before the end of the century had repopulated the area with significant Mexican settlement. Catarino Lerma recalled that "Mexicans used to walk to cotton picking or ride with burros" in the 1890s: "They went as far as Guadalupe and Austin and the Sabine River and never returned. The railroads here were all built by the Mexicans. Some Mexicans went to sugar cane in Louisiana, in the 1890s."[49]

In the Coastal Bend area of South Texas, the shift from cattle to cotton took place in the late 1880s. Newspaper editors, cotton farmers, and merchants discussed their views of the suitability of Mexican labor frankly, in public print. One such observation by S. G. Borden, who had been growing cotton for three years, suggested that the problem of securing trained wage laborers had been solved: "I have employed in cultivation almost entirely Mexican laborers, who I find work well, and readily learn to use our improved tools. Such labor is abundant along the Nueces River and can be secured at 75 cents a day, boarding themselves, and paying only for days of actual work. I have as yet had no difficulty getting cotton picked by the same labor, by contract at seventy five cents per hundred pounds, furnishing only sacks for picking."[50]

Americanizing the Cities

When the national rail system tied the old cities of the region—El Paso, San Antonio, Laredo—to the rest of the American union, all sorts of Americanizing influences began to be implanted immediately. The railroad prompted other changes, for it brought enough of the new American stock to enable them to form their own exclusive society. Intermarriages, which had been common from 1835 to 1880 throughout the region, gradually declined. Distinctions between Mexican and Anglo were drawn in sharp racial terms: the train's passenger car, according to one passenger, was "equally divided, 'For Whites' and 'For Negroes'—which in the south-west of Texas reads 'Mexicans.'"[51] As the Mexican elite declined as an important presence in the border region, the "peace structure" became irrelevant and was discarded.

San Antonio, the old capital of Texas, was the first city with a major Mexican community to experience the modernization introduced by the railroad. Speaking of his boyhood in San Antonio in the 1860s, William J. Knox remembered "about a rich and proud class of Mexicans who owned the center of town, living in the best houses, and also owning the hundreds of irrigated acres lying in this well-watered valley." Rapid changes followed when the Southern Pacific Railroad reached San Antonio in 1875. The commercial lots around the plazas were sold by their Mexican proprietors, either because they had fallen into debt or because they thought it best to move. By the early 1880s almost all Mexicans had left Alamo Plaza and had moved across the San Antonio River to the areas west of Main and Military plazas. New businesses sprang up with new business methods, and banks appeared. Money could not be borrowed in long, loose loans. Mortgages were drawn with time limits, and "the Anglo-Saxon, by peaceful penetration gradually acquired the choice business sites and best farms." Concluded Knox: "Old San Antonio of brilliant court and docile peasant was no more."[52]

The pushing west of the Southern Pacific in 1878 from San Antonio to Eagle Pass and the building of the International and Great Northern in 1883 toward Laredo brought ruin to the freighters. In Knox's words: "The old 'freight trains' were manned, bossed, and in

Mexican sheep shearers near Fort McKavett, 1892 (U.S. Department of Agriculture, *Special Report*, 1892; courtesy University of Texas Institute of Texan Cultures at San Antonio).

some cases, owned by Mexicans. Their place was taken by the iron horse managed by a different race." The fate of the Mexican teamsters was illustrated by the case of a Mexican teamster boss Knox knew by sight. In Knox's description, the Mexican boss rode a beautiful black stallion with the bearing of a Napoleon as he led his train out of the town amidst applause: "Years passed, changes came, and the discarded 'schooners' rotted away. The writer, years afterward, discovered the same old-time boss working for the city with pick and shovel; he still wore high-topped boots, and, as of old, retained the leather hat string beneath his chin."[53]

The technological changes affected everyone, Anglo and Mexican, in the frontier society. One Anglo freighter who did "runs" between San Antonio, Uvalde, Del Rio, and Eagle Pass, noted that "in 1881, with the coming of the Southern Pacific railroad, our trade went 'blooe.'" The freighter then became a ranch foreman.[54] But despite the color-blind nature of technological displacement, preliminary research suggests that Mexicans experienced a greater degree of "downward mobility." According to Allwyn Barr's study of nonmanual workers (or white-collar workers), in a thirty-year period from 1870 to 1900, "native whites" (meaning "Anglos") showed a 2 percent rate of downward mobility, European immigrants a 5 percent decline, Mexicans 14 percent, and blacks 17 percent.[55]

In May 1881, the Southern Pacific entered El Paso from San Diego, California. The following month the Atchison, Topeka, and Santa Fe had reached the town from the north. Two more railroads—the Texas and Pacific and the Galveston, Harrisburg, and San Antonio—reached El Paso by January 1883. Until then the population of El Paso, in the words of historian William Holden, consisted of "only Mexicans, old Texans, and a few hardy adventurers from other states." Added Holden: "Within a short time El Paso began to throw off the lethargy of an isolated Mexican village and take on the aspect of a growing American town." The four railroads that converged on El Paso transformed the town into a major railroad, mining, ranching, and labor center. As important were the political changes associated with these developments. The railroads had attracted merchants and professionals, who in 1882 initiated a reform movement against the established political ring. By 1883, these reformers had won a special election transferring the county seat from Ysleta to El Paso, where Anglo businessmen and lawyers could better manage the political and economic affairs of the area.[56]

In Laredo, where the "peace structure" was in its best form, everything began to change with the arrival of the Texas-Mexican Railway from Corpus Christi in 1881 and the International and Great Northern from San Antonio in 1883. According to a promotional booklet, the railroads "infused new life into the old fashioned sleepy town." Buildings of modern American design were built and modern conveniences introduced. In 1882 the principal streets were graded and graveled and a handsome courthouse and city hall were built. In 1883 a water works company laid mains under streets and a telephone exchange was installed. The first English-language newspaper was established in 1884, and Laredo saloons began posting their prices in U.S. currency. In 1886 and 1887 smelting and sampling works were built by the Kansas City Ore Company and the Guadalupe Mining Company of Philadelphia. In 1888 the "Edison Incandescent system" was installed. In short, within a few years after the International had reached Laredo, the town had "blossomed" into modernity.[57]

Such modernity invariably signified important political shifts. In Laredo, electoral politics appeared to assume a distinct class character as two parties, one called *botas* (meaning boots) and the other *guaraches* (meaning sandals), organized the contending sides in 1885. The contest involved a class antagonism but not in the "rich versus poor" manner suggested by the party labels. Rather, the *bota* leadership represented the new merchants who had arrived with the railroad and the *guarache* leadership stood for the older aristocratic element of Laredo. Both sides had a loyal Texas Mexican following. In 1886 the *botas* won a clean sweep of city and county government, resulting in a riot between supporters of the two sides. The *guaraches* declined and thereafter the old Mexican elite settled for a minor role in a bipartisan coalition, formed at the turn of the century, called the Independent Club.[58]

In sum, the result of rapid growth after the arrival of the railroad was the formation of two societies, one Anglo and the other Mexican. San Pedro Creek, according to a visiting correspondent, had come to be "the dividing line between American San Antonio and Mexican San Antonio." "The aggressive, pushing" Anglo called "his San Antonio the San Antonio" and recognized "the Mexican San Antonio as only 'over the San Pedro.'" In Laredo the transition reduced the influence of the old guard but did not uproot the social order as in other places. According to Judge José María Rodríguez, there were several attempts by "land boomers to wreck that town and load it down with taxes." But Rodríguez had hope that the old families would "not sell out their land to the stranger and then rent from him."[59]

The Car of Progress

The Rio Grande region below Laredo was spared the trauma of railway-related modernization for another two decades. Brownsville, in fact, had declined since the boom days of the mid-nineteenth century. The "car of Progress," of which Brownsville entrepreneur Edward Dougherty had spoken so eloquently in 1867, had somewhere taken a wrong turn.

As single-minded as Dougherty and other merchants may have been about their commercial plans, economic development was not made of whole cloth, the result of a grand design agreed to by an export-oriented elite. Rather, it was an undetermined process influenced by various political and economic circumstances. One significant circumstance consisted of the competition that characterized the internal relations of the capital-based elite itself. The reward for "winners" was essentially the opportunity to implement a favored blueprint of development.

The mercantile elite, in other words, was by no means a unified class, a class filled with solidarity.[60] The same market forces—access to capital, control of technological innovations, skillful reinvestment of profits—that operated to the great disadvantage of the landed elite and the landless cowboys also exerted their influence within the mercantile community. The commercial fortunes of Brownsville in the late nineteenth century may serve as a case in point.

Within a few years after annexation, merchants had found themselves splitting up into strata with various degrees of status and privilege. Those who had moved quickly and gained control of some aspect of the Mexican trade found themselves becoming wealthier. The small merchants, on the other hand, were increasingly forced out of the northern Mexican trade for lack of sufficient capital. The small merchants resented the "monopolists," with much of their resentment centering on the high freight charges of the steamboat monopoly of Stillman, King, and Kenedy. The "antimonopolists" had plans to build a twenty-two-mile rail line from Port Isabel to Brownsville, but not much came of this talk until after the Civil War. In 1870 the Reconstruction state legislature, reminded of King's and Kenedy's "short loyalty" to the Union, granted the antimonopolists the required charter. By 1871 a narrow-gauge railroad was operating, and three years later King and Kenedy sold the steamboat company to Capt. William Kelly, a supporter of the antimonopolists. The twenty-year reign of the steamboat monopoly had been broken, one

Mexican family outside their *jacal*, San Antonio, 1877 (courtesy Daughters of the Republic of Texas Library at the Alamo).

of the few times that King and Kenedy found themselves on the losing side. But this victory of the antimonopolists, complete as it seemed, was short-lived.[61]

In 1880 King and Kenedy joined with Corpus Christi merchant Uriah Lott to build a railroad from Corpus Christi to Laredo where it would connect with the Mexican National Railway to Monterrey. In the world of commerce, this was an unquestionable tour de force. King and Kenedy had outflanked their Brownsville rivals, for the cart and wagon trade between Brownsville and the Mexican interior could not compete with the railway route between Corpus Christi, Laredo, and Monterrey. By 1882 the new trade route had channeled the Mexican trade away from Matamoros-Brownsville to Laredo–Corpus Christi, two hundred miles north. Laredo grew from 3,521 in 1880 to 11,319 in 1890, a phenomenal increase. Meanwhile the Brownsville area receded into isolation, its population remaining roughly between 5,000 and 6,000 people for the last twenty years of the nineteenth century. The days of the big merchant had passed for the Brownsville area. The fleet of steamboats steadily dwindled until 1903 when the last riverboat stopped its runs. The King Ranch land books suggest that the financial collapse of Captain Kelly came earlier, in 1902, when he sold Henrietta King four thousand acres of land.[62]

Thus the Lower Valley, as Army Lt. W. H. Chatfield observed in a promotional booklet in the early 1890s, remained isolated from the great American population centers. This remoteness ("without the means of rapid transit"), together with its Mexican influence, had retarded its growth and the development of its natural advantages. "The sociology of this people," Chatfield added, was "particularly remarkable" and bordered on "the romantic," filled with a life of "pastoral ease," "urban success," intermarriages, and "freedom from crime." The subject was "a tempting one," but Chatfield's explicit mission was not sociological but commercial; he wished to advance "the awakening of this people from their long period of somnolence" through his description of business opportunities in the area.[63]

The politics of the Lower Valley retained a distinctive insular character. In Brownsville, the Anglos who had settled in the immediate postwar years had intermarried with each other and the elite Mexicans and for the next fifty years ran "the county, the city, and the Mexicans almost as a feudal family system." The first generation ruled until the 1870s and 1880s; the second generation offspring governed through the 1910s and 1920s. The tenure of this pioneer elite would not be broken until the early twentieth century with the immigration of Anglo farmers from the Midwest and the South. As one Valley resident noted: "The onrush of the new Americans, eager to make a fortune, anxious to accumulate wealth as soon as possible, changed the placid, easy-going life which had existed in the border counties."[64]

PART TWO

Reconstruction

1900–1920

Left: "Typical Revolutionist" of northern Mexico, ca. 1915 (courtesy Hornaday Collection, Archives Division, Texas State Library). *Above:* Army patrol squad outside its thatched hut *(choza)* headquarters, ca. 1915 (courtesy Hornaday Collection, Archives Division, Texas State Library).

"O bury me not on the lone praire-ee
  where the wild coyotes will howl o'er me!
In a narrow grave just six by three
  where all the Mexkins ought to be-ee!"

—Texas Ranger Patrol Song, circa 1900

"Come on, you cowardly Rangers;
No baby is up again you.
You want to meet your daddy?
I am Jacinto Treviño!

Come on, you treacherous Rangers;
Come get a taste of my lead.
Or did you think it was ham
between two slices of bread."

—Ballad of Jacinto Treviño, circa 1912

A Great Transformation :

[handwritten annotation: farmer upland rancher, capitalism upland patron-peon hacienda, (paternalism)]

At its height in the nineteenth century, the cattle kingdom represented, in Walter Prescott Webb's words, "the best single bit of evidence that here in the West were the basis and promise of a new civilization unlike anything previously known to the Anglo European-American experience." Barely fifty years after the annexation of the West, however, the ranch society collapsed before the rush of farm settlers. "The life of one man," noted Webb, "spanned the rise and fall of the cattle kingdom."[1] What brought about the fall of this ranch society?

The setting for the farm transformation can be described briefly. Toward the end of the nineteenth century, the cattle industry had begun to show signs of a serious collapse. Already by the late 1880s the Texas livestock industry had felt the harmful effects of world overproduction, overgrazing, droughts, quarantine laws in the northern states, and the closing of the cattle trails; all contributed to the demise of the regional industry.[2] The more business-oriented stratum of ranch owners, particularly the land and cattle companies of the Panhandle, began to search for ways to shed their unproductive property. By the turn of the century, the conditions making for a "new era," according to a contemporary, had come into place. The homesteads of Kansas and Nebraska had been exhausted, fertile Indian land had already been overrun, and thousands of midwestern farmers were seeking large tracts of land they could not possibly buy at home. The technological advances of the day—dry farming techniques, irrigation systems, the refrigerated rail car, for example—had now made the successful pursuit of intensive farming in the semiarid Southwest possible. Here were millions of acres in grazing land that could be converted to agriculture. With ranch lands, which originally had cost as little as twenty-five cents an acre, selling for six dollars an acre to a high of twenty dollars, the idea of farm colonization seemed like an answered prayer to the hard-pressed rancher. The irony of the situation did not go unnoticed. "The once-despised homesteader," historian Gene Gressley has pointed out, "became the courted settler."[3]

[handwritten annotation: needing money due to cattle market decline, ranchers sold to farmers (who had necessary techniques to farm sw)]

The farm colonies recruited by ranchers and developers made their presence felt throughout the Southwest, and nearly everywhere one can find incidents and episodes of tension between old and new residents. While this meeting between cowboys and farmers played itself out throughout the state, nowhere did it reverberate with such dramatic and explosive force as among the Mexican settlements of the border region. Here the ranch society was older than the American cowboy world; its roots and traditions in the area dated back to Spanish colonization in the early eighteenth century. American annexation in the mid–nineteenth century had introduced a new elite stratum of Anglo pioneer merchants, officials, and ranchers, but essentially the Mexican ranch society had remained intact. During the late nineteenth century, in fact, the Mexican settlements in the region had expanded.[4]

A great transformation began, however, with the introduction of commercial agriculture in the early 1900s. The transformation was not the result of some logic or imperative intrinsic to commercial farming, for Mexican *rancheros* and some Anglo old-timers proved themselves capable of shifting from livestock to farming while maintaining intact the character of the local order. It was the introduction not of farming but of ready-made farm communities, transplanted societies from the Midwest and the North, that produced the sweeping, dramatic changes in the region. In the midst of a ranch society based on paternalistic work arrangements, there emerged and grew a farm society based on contract wage labor and business rationality. Everything that held the ranch society together—shared interests, shared world views, conceptions of what was proper and just, rules concerning the use of force, in short, the substance of culture—was pulled apart. This particular experience reflected the effects of what Eric Wolf calls "North Atlantic capitalism," which everywhere destroyed "unproductive" societies, broke apart old communal ties, and replaced them with new material and social structures, with new social relations, new solidarities, and new metaphors.[5]

In the context of the Texas border, this transformation assumed a sharp racial character with generally tragic consequences for both Mexican and Anglo. It undermined the accommodative "peace structure," which for two generations had contained the sentiments and politics of race antagonism. Thus, this conflict represented much more than just a rancher-farmer confrontation. It was a conflict between two distinct societies; it was, in the portrayal given by Jovita González in 1930, a "struggle between the New World and the Old" that at the same time was a "race struggle."[6]

The two chapters that follow describe the manner in which the farm projects developed within the matrix of the old ranch society and outline the conflict that resulted between new and old settlers. Although this conflict surfaced along the entire length of the Texas-Mexican border region, I will focus primarily on the densely settled Lower Rio Grande Valley, where the conflict was most acute. In this context, I examine two important movements of this period—on the one hand, an irredentist guerrilla war waged by Texas Mexicans and the repression carried out by Texas Rangers; on the other, the conventional politics that pitted old-timer against newcomer for control of local government.

Each of these responses, the revolutionary and the conventional, has been noted and discussed by a few southwestern historians, but these interpretations remain fragmented and present a very different emphasis from that which I present here. The border troubles have generally been explained as Mexican banditry or as revolutionary activity that "spilled over" from neighboring Mexico. The sudden formation of counties during this time, mentioned by a separate group of historians, has been seen as a demographic phenomenon: that with increased population there was a need for more efficient and accessible government. The following argument weaves together these explanations of two ostensibly distinct phenomena and shows how they were both basically a reflection of the struggle between newcomer farmers and old ranch settlers.

Although the warfare and the conventional political battles were simultaneous responses to the expansion of commercial agriculture, for the sake of preserving the order of historical explanation, I will discuss the failed revolution first. Then with this revolutionary impulse checked and the plans of the *sediciosos* removed from the historical agenda, I will turn in the companion chapter to the political struggles centering on control of local governments. The outcome of these conventional politics was a reorganization of the region in order to effect a separation between ranch and farm.

5. The Coming of the Commercial Farmers

TOWARD THE end of the nineteenth century, the entrepreneurial element of the South Texas elite was quite mindful of the great discoveries and experiments taking place in the state and the Southwest. Against a backdrop of fluctuating and discouraging cattle prices were hopeful signs of new possibilities. In 1898, Robert Kleberg had discovered, by digging deep wells on his Santa Gertrudis ranch, a great aquifer, an underground lake "three times the size of Connecticut"; the discovery earned Kleberg the title "Modern Moses." The same year, a hundred miles to the northwest in Dimmit County, farmer T. C. Nye netted over one thousand dollars per acre on his experimental crop of Bermuda onions; to local farmers accustomed to cotton profits of ten to fifteen dollars per acre, the new crop appeared to be a "godsend." Another unexpected gift—the Spindletop discovery of oil in East Texas in 1901—created considerable excitement in South Texas and a few preliminary explorations in the region were begun before the first decade of the twentieth century had passed. These successful experiments in cultivating cash crops, digging artesian wells, and boring for oil portended great changes, at least in the minds of a few farsighted merchants and ranchers. As James Tiller, economic historian of the Winter Garden region in South Texas, described the times: "Land speculators and men of vision saw that all the ingredients necessary for a successful farming area were present." Tom Lea says the same in more lyrical fashion: "Artesian wells came in, flowing strong, bringing visions, changing the economic prospect of the isolated area."[1]

Vision was essential. The area was still sparsely settled brush country. The railheads, a day or two away over dirt trails, were the only connection to domestic markets—fine for cattle and horses but impossible for vegetables and fruit. Influential residents of the area had repeatedly petitioned the Southern Pacific to build a rail extension into South Texas, but these efforts were ignored. The region was so undeveloped that the Southern Pacific saw no profits in the proposed road. Impatient with the situation, the leading ranchers and businessmen of the region—Kleberg, Richard King II, John Kenedy,

Jim Wells, John Armstrong, Robert Driscoll, Sr. and Jr., and the "Spaniard banker" Francisco Yturria, among others—pooled their capital and resources and financed the railroad themselves.[2]

Planting the Seed

Completed on July 4, 1904, the St. Louis, Brownsville, and Mexico Railway was a 160-mile-long road that connected Brownsville with the Corpus Christi terminal of the Missouri-Pacific railroad system. The railway was unusual, as Valley resident Dellos Buckner observed, because it preceded commercial and population growth—"it had to create its own traffic and commerce." The gamble paid off quickly and handsomely. The rancher-investors formed real estate and irrigation companies, sliced their ranches into farm tracts, and boomed towns on their property. With the railroad came farmers, and behind them came land developers, irrigation engineers, and northern produce brokers. By 1907, the three-year-old railway was hauling about five hundred carloads of farm products from the Valley. So successful were the initial colonization projects that, four years after the railway's inauguration, the *Houston Chronicle* (July 12, 1908) chided those who had predicted failure:

> The superficial observer who saw conditions as they were then, and who thought only in days and minutes and not in weeks, years, and generations, as big men think, was ready to pronounce the whole conception of a railroad through that section as chimerical, and saw visions of failure, bankruptcy, and blasted hopes. . . . The man behind the road paid no heed to pessimistic predictions, but drove his lines over every obstacle . . . through the range of the longhorn, across the ranches, over the dominion of the rattler and the horned frog, went the new road, the avant courier of a marvelous development.[4]

Success in the "Magic Valley," as it was now advertised, spurred colonization efforts throughout the greater South Texas region. In Zavala and Dimmit counties, farm development had begun as early as 1901 but did not "take off" until rail trunk lines connected the area to San Antonio in 1909. The results were as expected: "With access to outside markets assured, settlement of the area proceeded at an ever-increasing rate. Ranchers, sensing tremendous profits, began breaking up their holdings into smaller tracts and selling them to eager northern colonists."[5] The Seven D, Cross S, and Catarina ranches were divided into farms; towns sprang up almost overnight; and the subregion was christened the "Winter Garden."

Elsewhere in South Texas the farm developments proceeded in similar fashion. Rising land values, inflated by the prospect of colonization, drew ranchers and outside land promoters into local projects and speculative schemes. The biographical sketches of old-timers contain many stories of the success built on farm development. J. A. McFaddin of Victoria, for example, converted his 42,000-acre ranch into cotton and corn fields around 1905, when land in his section went from ten cents an acre to seventy-five dollars an acre. In La Salle County, William Irving sold 10,000 acres of his 60,000-acre ranch for cultivation and "perhaps in due time the ranch will be subdivided into farms" because the land had become "too valuable" to hold as pasture land. In Duval County, C. W. Hahl advertised land as "Rosita Valley" and sold acres for fifteen dollars per with 7 percent interest. And Col. Dillard Fant, owner of 225,000 acres in Hidalgo County and 60,000 acres in Live Oak County, sold out to farmers and retired to San Antonio. In fact, the common success story in "San Antone," according to Charles Harger's review in 1911, was "rich rancher—bought land for a trifle and sold to farmers—worth half a million."[6]

Ranchers not wishing to bother with the details sold entire sections of their land to developers. The sales strategy of these land promoters was nearly everywhere the same. Ranches were renamed with titles suggesting prosperity, advertisement was pushed vigorously in the old farming sections of the Midwest and the South, and prospective colonists were promised "an almost Eden-like existence."[7] According to a historical account of Nueces County, these promoters worked to convert pastures to plowed fields: "The promoters' glowing descriptions of the soil's fertility were matched only by the ponderous titles of their developments. They acquired large blocks of ranch lands and in naming their tracts memorialized both themselves and the former owners with names such as 'the George H. Paul Subdivision of the Driscoll Ranch'; the 'F. Z. Bishop Subdivision of the Weil Ranch'; and 'the Roberts and White Subdivision of the Hoffman Ranch.'"[8]

The net result of these various efforts was one of the most phenomenal land movements in the history of the United States. Frank Putnam, in a feature article for *Collier's Magazine*, described this movement with a slight touch of literary license: "We are witnessing the largest migration of human beings that has ever taken place since history began to be recorded. It is, moreover, the most impressive human migration in another respect, it being the first that has taken place in Pullman cars."[9] Charles Harger, in a slightly more restrained review of the situation, likewise described the rush as "the greatest land movement known in the history of the West"—"It was thoroughly planned. Tons of 'literature' were scattered through the agriculture states of the Mississippi Valley. Special rates were made for homeseekers' excursions."[10] Between 1905 and 1910, on the first and third Tuesday of each month, special excursion trains took prospective homeseekers—some old-timers called them "home-suckers"—to investigate the possibilities of the "Magic Valley" and other irrigable areas of South Texas.[11] They bought land, settled in communities planned by the ranchers or land developers, chose the most profitable cash crop that could be cultivated, and began to recruit Mexican day laborers. An agricultural "revolution" had begun.

The farm revolution basically unfolded between 1900 and 1910. A second surge of agricultural expansion would come between 1920 and 1930, but by then the basis for the new society of commercial farmers had been laid. The census classification of ranches as "farms" and changes in county boundaries make straightforward comparison difficult, but the aggregate data nonetheless suggest the rapid shift in the regional economy.[12] With farm colonization, the number of "farms" increased dramatically and the average "farm" size decreased, an indication of the division of ranches into farms as well as the reclamation of unused, semiarid land. In Cameron County in 1910, for example, there were 709 farms with an average size of 770.1 acres; by 1920 there were 1,507 farms averaging 198.6 acres; and by 1930, 2,936 farms averaging 45.6 acres. The economic face of Hidalgo County was changed in similar fashion—from 677 farms averaging 969.5 acres in 1910 to 4,327 farms averaging 126.9 acres in 1930. Conversely, the number of cattle fell significantly. In the area bounded by Starr, Hidalgo, and Cameron counties in 1910, the number declined to almost half by 1920, from 174,513 head to 99,597.

The rapid growth in the region's population also suggests the intensity of the agricultural developments. At the turn of the century, the deep South Texas region had a total population of 79,934.[13] By 1920, this had doubled to 159,842 and by 1930 had doubled again to 322,845—of which the lion's share (216,822) was concentrated in Cameron, Hidalgo, Willacy, and Nueces counties, the four farm counties of the region. Just north of the region, in the Winter Garden counties of Dimmit, Zavala, Frio, and La Salle, the increase in farms and people likewise suggests the dramatic character of farm colonization. Between 1900 and 1930, the Winter Garden area experienced a threefold increase in population, from 8,401 to 36,816.

These figures suggest how quickly the Texas Mexican and Anglo frontier settlers were overrun by *fuereños* from the Mexican interior and newcomers from the Midwest and the South. Not until the 1930 Census, however, when Mexicans and "whites" were counted separately, was there a statistical indication of the ethnic composition of the new farm order. Then one sees that the four farm counties of the Valley had Anglo "minorities"—Willacy was 41.9 percent "native white," Cameron 47.5 percent, Hidalgo 43.6 percent, and Nueces 48 percent. The Winter Garden counties also had Anglo minorities— Dimmit was only 25 percent "native white," Frio 38 percent, Zavala 27 percent, and so on. In the new era of commercial agriculture, in other words, South Texas remained basically Mexican. The society of the farm counties, however, would be quite unlike that of the ranch counties.

Confrontation between New and Old

When the first farm seekers from the Midwest arrived in South Texas in the early 1900s, the world they found still had much of its centuries-old Mexican character. Cattle ranching still dominated the regional economy, as it had since the Mexican settlements had been established in the mid–eighteenth century. Huge ranches were enclosed by barbed wire, but these retained the features of *haciendas.* Even the patriarchal and paternalistic relations between *patrón* and *peón* remained basically unchanged. The *patrón* was still protector, counselor, judge, and dispenser of favors and material rewards; the *peones,* for their part, still constituted the loyal work force and, in time of danger, the loyal private army of the *patrón.*[14] Politics were run by a handful of Mexicanized Anglo bosses supported by a loyal Texas Mexican electorate, with contested elections generally the result of internal divisions among machine politicians. Such was the "feudal world" that many amazed farm seekers discovered in the region.

Many other aspects of this frontier society fascinated the new settlers, but their amazement stemmed basically from discovering a "half-civilized" world in the remote reaches of a highly advanced twentieth-century nation. Their fascination with these survivals from the past, however, would be no hindrance to the imperatives of progress. In this the newcomers were confident to the point of arrogance: they would be the builders of a modern civilized society.

The fledgling farm communities, however, did not enjoy a peaceful infancy. As the demands and expectations of the newcomers increasingly called into question the interests and sentiments of those tied to the old order, a wall of tension and antagonism between the two began to build. Every aggressive move by the farming communities brought forth a negative response from the old. The conflict was expressed in various oppositions—not only as newcomers versus old-timers or farmers versus ranchers, but also as northerners versus southerners, Anglos versus Mexicans, good government leaguers versus machine politicians, and progressives versus conservatives. The particulars were complex, but in general the labels "newcomers" and "old-timers" describe well the opposing alignments that coalesced during this period.

At the center of the rising antagonism were opposed views of economic development. The newcomers wanted publicly financed improvements—paved roads, marketing facilities, irrigation projects, schools, and so on—which they felt were necessary for the survival and expansion of their communities. The ranchers, especially those who had had no part in promoting colonization in the first place, were unequivocally opposed to any newcomer initiatives that would raise tax rates or clear away additional pasture land for farming. Mexican landowners, in particular, were quite conservative about any change, about selling land or encouraging settlement, and thus generally acted to obstruct any venture that threatened to disrupt their way of life. In Zapata County, for example, "the people continued living their placid existence becoming only aroused when Americans try to buy or lease their land."[15]

Even the sponsors of the farm colonies quickly abandoned whatever sanguine expectations they had. The ruling pioneer families had not anticipated a challenge to their long-standing reign by the newcomers; relinquishing absolute control over local matters—elections, land assessment, taxation, and so on—had not been part of the plans they had for the region. One segment of the farm sponsors, as noted earlier, was apparently content to sell out and withdraw to a wealthy retirement in the region's cities. Some influential families, however, had never thought of retiring; they expected to service and direct the farm towns they had created as bankers, merchants, and political officials.

A representative and well-documented case is that of Kingsville in Kleberg County. Not only had this town been placed in the middle of the King Ranch, but the town also was serviced completely by companies owned by the King-Kleberg family. The Kingsville Company, the Kleberg Bank, the King's Inn (the town hotel), the Kingsville Ice and Milling Company, the Kingsville Publishing Company, the Kingsville Power Company, the Algodon Land and Irrigation Company, the Gulf Coast Gin Company (for ginning cotton)—all were financed solely or primarily by the King-Kleberg family. Bob Kleberg, to note

Tom Lea's understatement, meant to keep the development of the town firmly in hand: "If citizens accustomed to wider latitudes came to resent the tight monopolistic rein Kleberg maintained over the community he created, they must have been aware of that rein the day they arrived and chose to stay."[16] But the farm settlers in Kingsville demonstrated early a staunch refusal to be "bossed." The King Ranch lost the first election of Kleberg County in 1913, and subsequent maneuvering by the ranch required considerable tact.

Everywhere in South Texas where they settled in large numbers, as O. Douglas Weeks observed in 1930, the newcomers challenged the old order. The settlers from the Midwest carried with them definite ideas about government and politics. The political conditions they found in their new home, in Weeks' vivid description, "at first dazed them, and then, as misfortunes multiplied, disgusted them. They began to talk about county rings and to condemn the Mexican-Americans as ignorant tools in the hands of bosses, who thereby were able to perpetuate their tyranny."[17] To the sponsors of the farm projects, who had not figured on relaxing their accustomed control and position in the region, the situation was somewhat ironic. Lea captured the sense of irony when he noted that the developments which Kleberg had brought about "involved the Santa Gertrudis with a myriad of ventures beyond its pasture fences, and planted a briar patch of politics within the front gate." The sponsors of progress had made a serious miscalculation. Except for a few skeptics wary of all innovation, it had never occurred to the prodevelopment ranchers and politicians that the farm settlers might not like the way everything was arranged. Whatever reservations the old-time leaders may have developed about the farm boom, however, were overcome by the prospects of speculative profits.[18]

Thus, the struggle between newcomer and old settlers became centered on control of county governments that possessed the power of tax assessment and collection and the provision of public services. So long as the political machines maintained their dominance, conservative Anglo and Mexican ranchers were able to block further farm development. Where farmers were successful in wresting control from the old-timers, the consequences for the ranchers were clear. As C. C. Richardson, secretary of the Brownsville Chamber of Commerce, put it in 1929, "The high taxes on roads, water, etc. compel owners to clear the land." A Nueces County rancher likewise complained that "they tax unimproved land equal to improved and taxes will eat up the unimproved land."[19]

The duel between farmer and rancher was an economic conflict only in a narrow sense. Interwoven in this conflict between rancher and farmer was the race question, a matter that had been somewhat domesticated by the politics of accommodation or "peace structure" of the previous fifty years.

Collapse of the Mexican Ranch Society

The impact of the farm developments on the Texas Mexican people was profound. In this period the border counties finally felt the full weight of Mexican displacement from the land, replicating a process long before experienced in the upper counties around San Antonio and Corpus Christi. Taxes, mortgage debts, legal battles, the effects of the erratic cattle and sheep market, outright coercion and fraud, as well as the cash offer of land speculators, all combined once more to reduce the number of Mexican landowners. The magnitude of this displacement remains unknown. Census data, as noted before, suggest the rapid demise of the ranch society. Although these statistics indicate the fate of Mexican ranchers indirectly, the primary sources leave little doubt on this point—the dispossession of landed Mexicans was a sweeping one.

The Laredo newspaper *La Crónica* noted in its April 9, 1910, edition that a rapid transfer of land was taking place in the area: "The Mexicans have sold the great share of their landholdings and some work as day laborers on what once belonged to them. How sad this truth!"[20] According to Jovita González, a perceptive witness of the period, the farm developments signified an "American invasion" of the border towns. The arrival of "hordes of money-making Americans . . . proved to be a rude awakening to the Latin Americans," but particularly to the "landed aristocracy," which, "impregnable in its racial pride, lived in a world of its own, sincerely believing in its rural greatness."[21] As González described the reaction of these landed Mexicans, "It was a blow to see these new arrivals ruthlessly appropriate all that had been theirs, even the desert plains. They saw all political power slipping from their hands; they saw themselves segregated into their own quarters."[22]

The force of the farming projects was felt not only by the land-owning Mexicans; its weight pressed equally hard on the merchants and artisans of the Texas Mexican towns. These classes of small shopkeepers and craftsmen, noted González, "resent the invasion of the Americans. The introduction of new and improved methods, the chain stores and Piggly Wigglies have driven the middle class grocers out of business. The same thing has happened with owners of dry goods stores, drug stores, etc. . . . "[23]

Even the landless Mexicans who worked the cattle ranches were not spared the effects of the farm transformation. As ranches were sold and converted to farms, both Mexican *vaquero* and *peón* found themselves displaced, free to search for new employers. The choices were few. The skilled *vaquero* looked down on the farm laborer with "mingled contempt and pity," observed folklorist and old-time rancher J. Frank Dobie in the 1920s, but nonetheless "more and more of the *vaqueros* in the lower country are turning to cotton picking each fall."[24] What else could they have done? Cattle ranching was no longer the unchallenged way of life and work on the South Texas plains. In the new world of commercial farming, the Mexican cowboy, the artisan of the ranch, quickly discovered that his skills were increasingly irrelevant.

From a broad historical view, the agrarian development of this period can be seen as the last in a series of crises that eroded the centuries-old class structure of the Mexican ranch settlements. By 1920, the Texas Mexican people had generally been reduced, except in a few border counties, to the status of landless and dependent wage laborers. To fill the great demand for farm labor, displaced *peones* and *rancheros* from Mexico were recruited to work in Texas. Thus the budding South Texas towns of this period—Donna, McAllen, Asherton, Kingsville, to name a few—were populated by two major racial classes, Anglo farmers and Mexican laborers. There were, of course, other class groups among Anglos and Mexicans, but these paled before the sharp division that separated Anglo and Mexican in this reconstructed rural society. In the transition from stock raising to farming, as Paul Taylor put it, the "American whites" had become the farmers while the Mexicans had become the laborers who cleared the land of brush and tended the crops.[25]

As might be expected, these events resulted in a dramatic change in Mexican-Anglo relations. González described the consequences for the Mexican people: "The farther one gets away from the River the worse conditions are. In the towns along the boundary-line, where the descendants of the old grantees live, Mexicans have more or less demanded certain privileges, which they still retain. But segregation of the two races is practiced in every town north of the counties bordering the River."[26] The result everywhere was the same: where commercial agriculture made significant headway, the previous understanding between Mexican and Anglo was undermined. Mexicans now found themselves treated as an inferior race, segregated into their own town quarters and refused admittance at restaurants, picture shows, bathing beaches, and so on. "The friendly feeling which had slowly developed between the old American and

Mexican families," González observed, "had been replaced by a feeling of hate, distrust and jealousy on the part of the Mexicans." The old Mexican elite was bitter about the changes, as one prominent member made clear:

> We, Texas-Mexicans of the border, although we hold on to our traditions, and are proud of our race, are loyal to the United States, in spite of the treatment we receive by some of the new Americans. Before their arrival, there were no racial or social distinctions between us. Their children married ours, ours married theirs, and both were glad and proud of the fact. But since the coming of the "white trash" from the north and middle west we felt the change. They made us feel for the first time that we were Mexicans and that they considered themselves our superiors.[27]

A sharp distinction was now made between Mexicans, which included *peones* as well as landowners, and Anglos, most of whom were newcomer farmers. The newly arrived American did not distinguish between the aristocratic and laboring classes—"to Americans both types are the same—Mexicans." In Nueces County one Anglo old-timer noted to Paul Taylor that "a newcomer here did not distinguish between an old Spanish family and other Mexicans; it was embarrassing to them and to me." Likewise, in Dimmit County an old cattleman felt "sorry for these high class Mexicans who are sometimes refused service at hotels. They are really Spanish and white, but the laborers are Indian." The collapse of the Mexican ranch country in the expanding farm areas, however, had carried with it most traces of these internal distinctions, at least as far as the Anglo farmer was concerned. Even among former *vaqueros* and *peones*, the displaced elite, which had prided itself as being Castilian, was now commonly referred to as *"los tuvos"*—"the has-beens."[28] In the rural society these commercial farmers were creating, there were no longer any significant differences between the displaced "Spanish" elite and the landless "Mexican." Now a Mexican was simply a Mexican.

The duel between farmer and rancher, then, was no insignificant conflict. On the outcome hinged the destiny of the old oligarchy and with it the fortunes of the landed Mexicans and the old way of doing things. Integrally woven into this struggle was the character of relations between Mexican and Anglo. The Anglo old-timers, according to one observer of the time, had often treated Mexicans harshly, but it was generally an order tempered by paternalism and patronage. The new settlers, on the other hand, did not understand Mexicans and frequently subjected them to indignities and discriminations that the older Anglo-American would never think of doing. Old-timer Emilio Forto, Cameron County sheriff, attributed the tension and conflict to the "unwillingness of American newcomers to the valley to accept the Mexican." Ninety percent of the newcomers, noted the sheriff, do not understand or "care to learn the customs or to respect the ideals of the Mexicans." Such, then, was the volatile setting created by the new farm communities. Not only did opposed economic interests separate the American newcomer from the Texas Mexican but so did, as Forto put it, "a lack of sympathetic understanding between the two races."[29]

Misunderstanding, not surprisingly, showed up in the most physical way. As old-timer attorney Frank Pierce noted in his recollections, the conflict between Americans and Mexicans increased with the arrival of newcomers from the northern states: "Several Americans were killed at different times, and some Mexicans. As precaution, and to forestall any attempts to kill, rangers were brought to and stationed at convenient points along the Lower Valley."[30] Between 1907 and 1912 sixteen Mexicans were killed by Rangers and peace officers in Hidalgo and Cameron counties. In Pierce's words: "Most of the killings, it was alleged, occurred while the officer would be attempting to make an arrest, the Mexican resisting and showing a disposition to injure." Sheriff Forto was more direct—a large share of the border troubles could be explained by "the reckless manner in which undisciplined 'pistol toters,' Rangers and other civil officers, have been permitted to act as trial judge, jury and executioners."[31]

Perhaps because of a deep-seated fear of the Mexican, the old-time Anglo bosses and ranchers of the region did not move to curtail the anti-Mexican activities of the newcomers or the Rangers. For Jim Wells and his allies, strong support for the Rangers had always represented the ultimate defense in case paternalistic accommodation with Mexicans ever failed. Such appeared increasingly to be the situation as the old-timers were swept up by the racial hysteria of the newcomers.[32]

With the situation for the Mexican deteriorating rapidly, approximately four hundred Texas Mexican leaders—journalists, schoolteachers, and mutual aid society representatives—gathered in Laredo in 1911 to draft some plan of action. The Congreso Mexicanista, as the assembly was called, called for an end to educational discrimination, denounced the pattern of officially sanctioned lynchings of Mexicans, and urged Texas Mexicans not to sell their land.[33] In the face of violence, however, the resolutions of the *congreso* proved to be ineffectual rhetoric. The voices of moderation were overtaken by the increasing polarization between Mexican and Anglo in South Texas.

Insurrection and Suppression :   *conflict between Anglos (Rangers) + Mex*

In the context of this ranch-farm struggle occurred one of the most dramatic episodes in the history of the Southwest, the armed insurrection of Texas Mexicans and its brutal suppression by Texas Rangers. The conflict turned the Valley into a virtual war zone during 1915–1917.[34]

Hundreds of incidents were recorded, with the peak of the troubles occurring between July and November of 1915. An area "only slightly less than that of Connecticut," as historian Charles Cumberland described the affected region, was halted in its economic development, hundreds of people were killed, thousands were dislocated, and property worth millions of dollars was destroyed. Although the troubles were generally seen as outlaw banditry—it is rare to read reports of this time that did not speak of "Mexican bandits"—almost all of the serious raiding stemmed from an irredentist program known as the Plan de San Diego (so named because the plan was signed in San Diego, Texas). The major provisions of the plan proclaimed independence from "Yankee tyranny"; called for an uprising on February 20, 1915, by the "Liberating Army for Races and People" (to be composed of Mexicans, blacks, Japanese, and Indians); and proposed the creation of an independent republic to consist of Texas, New Mexico, Arizona, Colorado, and California. During most of 1915, the "bandits" operated within the general framework of this program. Groups of from twenty-five to a hundred men, organized in quasi-military companies, raided the Valley over widely separated points, in actions that included train derailments, bridge burnings, and sabotage of irrigation pumping plants.[35]

Plan de San Diego = anti-Anglo revolt + nativism

Most Texans saw these disturbances as pure and simple Mexican banditry whose origins lay in revolutionary Mexico. The very discovery of a master plan was seen as evidence of "foreign" influence. Some claimed that Mexican revolutionary leaders—either Victoriano Huerta or Venustiano Carranza—had authored the plan to pressure Woodrow Wilson into recognizing their claims to the Mexican presidency. And almost all sources pointed to German inspiration and support. Judge Harbert Davenport of Brownsville, for example, believed that the Germans were successful in stirring up the Mexicans because they "had a more realistic appreciation of the psychology of the old, Southwestern Mexican ranchero; a breed that already was

Anglos blamed Mex Rev + Germans

dying out by World War One."[36] To a large extent, these explanations about outside influence were based on the common belief among Texans that "their Mexicans" would never organize such an uprising.

The argument presented here, in contrast, places primary emphasis on the domestic situation in the Texas border region. Clearly the border raids from Carranza-held territory into South Texas served Carranza's political interests. The first phase of raids, from June through October of 1915, took place while Carranza sought American diplomatic recognition; and the second phase, from March through July of 1916, occurred while Carranza sought to expel Pershing's Punitive Expedition from northern Mexico. Yet, in spite of Carranza's manipulation of the Plan de San Diego and the German interest in it, the plan was "grounded solidly," as James Sandos has argued, in the bitter character of Anglo-Mexican relations of the time; it was "an authentic product of the border region."[37]

In other words, the international situation—revolution in Mexico and war in Europe—was a critical context for the rebellion that took place in the region. What made these outside events and influences meaningful, however, were local conditions. Most U.S. military observers stationed in Texas recognized that a basic condition making for the rebellion was the prejudice and contempt that Mexicans in the region were subjected to. The dire and pressing situation of the Texas Mexican was clear. The sense of urgency appears in various pieces of evidence: in the call to not sell the land; in the bitterness of the old elite; in the displacement of *rancheros, vaqueros,* tenants, and artisans; in the racism of the newcomers; and in vigilante lynchings and police executions. As in many revolutionary situations, vengeance for specific wrongs (usually the killing of a relative) rather than commitment to a radical ideology was the prime catalyst behind the Texas Mexican insurrection.[38]

More historical work is needed to fit these pieces into a rigorous description, but the principal theme of this portrayal can already be stated. The old Mexican frontier was being made "safe" for farmers. The border troubles essentially represented the armed conflict between an old ranch society and an aggressively expanding farm society. In this context, the Texas Mexican insurrectionists and the Texas Rangers constituted the opposed military forces. Before proceeding further, the border troubles and armed confrontations should be described in more detail.

Even though the increase in "bandit activity" from across the river had been noted as early as January 1915, it was March before the situation caused concern among Texas officials. An organizer of the insurrection had been arrested in mid-January, and a copy of the

Plan de San Diego seized, but during the spring and summer months the connection between the visionary plan and the Valley raids was never seriously considered. Anglo-Texans remained incredulous that a "bunch of Mexicans" could even think of such an insurrection. Old-time rancher Lon C. Hill recalled later for the U.S. Senate investigating committee (in 1919) the bewilderment of Texans when they heard that the Mexicans "were going to run all of the Gringos out": "Well, to my mind and to the other fellows', that was absolutely inconceivable, you know, how a bunch of Mexicans would take a fool idea in their heads that they were going to kill all those Americans and take all that country, you know; it was just laughable to us, you know, that they really meant to do it. But they were coming."[39] The old-timers could feel that something terrible was threatening. Mexicans with whom they had lived in close harmony for years avoided contact. Mexicans who had always been tractable and friendly became sullen. The mystery deepened when the old-timers learned that some of their "honorable, high-class Mexicans, that we all had confidence in and whom we believed to be good citizens," were involved in seditious activities. "The inside dope" was never obtained from the leaders but, as Hill testified, "we would get hold of some fellow . . . and ask them what in the name of goodness is the matter with you Mexicans; are you all going crazy here?"[40]

By July, the raids began to receive widespread attention and create considerable fear. Attacks occurred weekly and increased in frequency until by mid-August the news of death or serious injury to Anglo citizens became a daily occurrence. Confronted with raids they could not understand and that threatened their lives, the Anglo residents of South Texas became panic-stricken. They formed vigilante committees, which administered "summary justice" to Mexican suspects. As the raiding intensified, these border residents began to realize, in Webb's words, "that the disturbances had behind them a purpose, an intelligence greater than that of the bandit leader or of his ignorant followers."[41]

Whatever doubts may have remained about a "greater intelligence" were quickly dispelled on August 8 with an attack on the Las Norias Division of the King Ranch. The attack was carried out by a well-organized party of sixty Mexican raiders who carried a red flag with the inscription "*igualdad e independencia.*" The American response was swift and determined. After the raid on Las Norias, according to Pierce's account, the Rangers began a systematic manhunt and killed 102 Mexicans; citizens and army officers who saw the bodies, however, estimated that at least 300 Mexicans were killed.[42]

The Americans, Webb explained, found sufficient cause for this

Above left: Cowboy recruits for service against bandits, 1915 (courtesy
Hornaday Collection, Archives Division, Texas State Library). *Above right:*
Texas Rangers with Mexican bandits killed at Norias, 1915 (courtesy Texas

Department of Public Safety). *Center:* Homeseekers feasting on water-melons in midwinter, ca. 1910 (courtesy Hornaday Collection, Archives Division, Texas State Library).

"reign of terror against the Mexicans" when they learned that the Germans and Japanese were supplying the raiders with arms and bombs, that the IWW (Industrial Workers of the World) and Mexican radicals were providing them with "incendiary literature," and that the Mexicans were plotting to retake Texas and other southwestern states. Executions and lynchings of Mexicans became so commonplace the *San Antonio Express* (September 11, 1915) reported that the "finding of dead bodies of Mexicans, suspected for various reasons of being connected with the troubles, has reached a point where it creates little or no interest. It is only when a raid is reported, or an American is killed, that the ire of the people is aroused."[43] A few days after this report, the *Express* (September 15) described the typical manner in which executions were carried out: "Three Mexicans among six prisoners taken on suspicion after the Los Indios fight yesterday were killed today near San Benito. It was stated that they escaped from the San Benito jail during the night, and that their bodies were found some distance from town today with bullet holes in their backs."[44] Executions of "escaped" suspects were not the only evidence of Anglo retribution. Posses burned homes of suspected raiders and sympathizers, disarmed all Mexicans, and forced them to move into towns where they could be better controlled.[45]

With the conflict intensifying and spreading, the region's economy ground to a halt. An exodus of Texas Mexicans created a severe labor shortage, leading the mayors of six Valley towns to call for the protection of "good Mexicans" on the American side of the river. Nonetheless, "thousands of Mexicans and Mexican-Texans," as Pierce described the movement, "crossed from the Texas side to Mexico seeking safety and refuge. Many of these joined the raiders and bandits and organization along the Mexican river front was constant and open."[46] While Texas Mexicans fled to Mexico, Anglo-Americans left their farms and ranches and moved to Corpus Christi or San Antonio. The region was half-deserted as more than thirty thousand Valley residents left the area.

Toward the end of October 1915, the raiding and attacks tapered off, bringing an uneasy quiet to the Lower Rio Grande Valley. American diplomatic recognition of Carranza had brought the raids from Carranza-held territory to a stop. On the other hand, Pancho Villa, angered at this recognition of Carranza, began attacking Americans in northern Mexico and in the Upper Rio Grande Valley around El Paso. The massacre of American mine employees in Chihuahua by Villista raiders on January 10, 1916, sparked off a series of attacks on Mexicans and Mexican Americans in El Paso; only the interven-

Pancho Villa

tion of regular army troops from Fort Bliss prevented a full-scale riot. Prominent Villista sympathizers were arrested, and many were simply run out of town. In nearby Fort Hancock, local citizens were reported to be "cleaning out" the local Mexican population. Two months later, five hundred Villistas burned and looted Columbus, New Mexico, an act that prompted Pershing's Punitive Expedition through northern Mexico. Carranza demanded that the expedition be withdrawn from Mexican territory and ordered his troops to resist Pershing's advance. Clashes in Mexico between Pershing's troops and both Villista and Carrancista forces nearly sparked a full-fledged war between Mexico and the United States. These clashes, however, did lead to an immediate revival of raids across the length of the border.

The tempo of hostilities picked up rapidly in May 1916. On May 5, eighty raiders struck at Glenn Springs and Boquillas in the Big Bend area. On June 11, 14, and 15, Mexican raiders were again reported crossing into Texas close to Laredo and Brownsville. In response, state militia from Virginia, Iowa, Illinois, the Dakotas, Minnesota, Indiana, Nebraska, Louisiana, and Oklahoma were ordered to the Valley. By the end of June, practically all the American armed forces available for combat duty, approximately fifty thousand men, were stationed along the Lower Rio Grande.[48]

After June 1916, the raids ceased altogether, although antagonism and suspicion between Mexican and Anglo remained volatile for a considerable period. In Kingsville, two former Villista generals—arrested and executed "while escaping"—had reportedly planned to destroy railroad lines and carry out bombings in several cities, with San Antonio as the principal target. Arrests of suspected Mexican insurrectionists in Corpus Christi, San Antonio, and San Angelo continued through October of 1916. Throughout the greater border region, Anglos feared a general uprising of Mexicans. The Coleman-Fulton Pasture Company in San Patricio County, for example, purchased weapons, organized a home guard, and was investigating the possibility of purchasing a "rapid-fire gun" because, in the words of the company superintendent, "if we should get a cotton crop and have a thousand or two Mexican pickers here, then there might be some danger of some one trying to get them to make an uprising of some sort." In many ways, the Zimmerman Note of 1917—the German proposal of an alliance with Mexico—was somewhat anticlimactic. But the note served to confirm, despite Mexico's rejection of the offer, the suspicions that Anglos had of Mexicans in Texas as a potential internal enemy.[49]

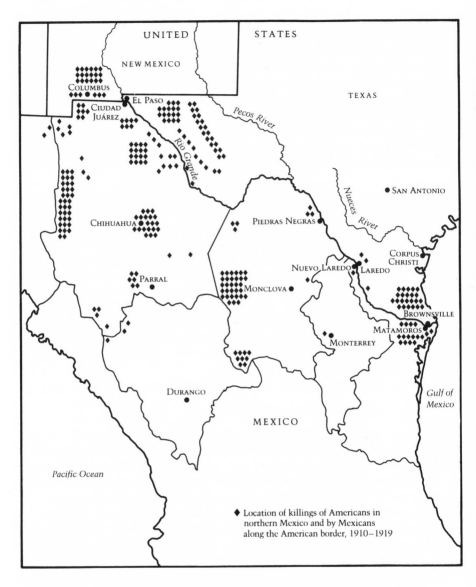

UNITED STATES

NEW MEXICO

COLUMBUS

TEXAS

CIUDAD
JUÁREZ

EL PASO

Pecos River

Rio Grande

CHIHUAHUA

Nueces River

PIEDRAS NEGRAS

SAN ANTONIO

PARRAL

NUEVO LAREDO LAREDO

CORPUS
CHRISTI

MONCLOVA

MONTERREY

BROWNSVILLE

MATAMOROS

DURANGO

Gulf of
Mexico

MEXICO

Pacific Ocean

◆ Location of killings of Americans in
  northern Mexico and by Mexicans
  along the American border, 1910–1919

Murder Map of the Texas-Mexico Border (based on Murder Map of Mexico in
U.S. Congress, Senate, *Investigation of Mexican Affairs*, 1 : 845).

Peace was reestablished, in the opinion of many Valley residents, because of the "elimination of note-writing protests" and the threat of an American attack and bombardment of Matamoros, acts that showed the Mexican authorities the American troops were there to stop the raiding. The thorough suppression of Texas Mexicans by Rangers also contributed to peace. According to Webb, between five hundred and five thousand Mexicans were killed in the Valley during the troubles compared to sixty-two American civilians and sixty-four soldiers.[50]

Yet the cessation of hostilities did not come because of military victories or threats. Historians have simplified events considerably by saying the raids ended once Carranza took a personal interest in controlling them; but they are correct when they argue that the raids were brought to an end through action by Mexican army and civil officials rather than through action by American forces.[51] Much had to do with the resolution of the Mexican Revolution itself, for this signified the removal of Mexico as a staging area for Texas Mexican guerrillas.

The question of how the *sediciosos* were defeated, however interesting, is not important for this discussion. What is more central is the question of representation or significance—that is, what did the raids and repression mean?

Making the Frontier Safe for Farming

The raids, simply stated, were a response on the part of Texas Mexicans to the new farm developments. The leadership and soldiery of the insurrectionists were drawn heavily from the Texas Mexican community. Between a thousand to three thousand men had reportedly pledged to the Plan de San Diego. According to historians Emilio Zamora and Rodolfo Rocha, the rebels drew their strength from the classes of the Texas Mexican ranch society threatened by the farm developments—*rancheros* and *vaqueros*, shopkeepers and artisans, and some sharecroppers. Many of the raiders had joined the plan in order to regain land lost by their parents and grandparents. Most of the guerrilla activity took place in the four counties where commercial agriculture had made the greatest inroads—Starr, Hidalgo, Cameron, and Willacy.[52] Jovita González, speaking of Zapata County, suggested the connection between the farm developments and the raids: "The same sentiment which has kept these people from selling their land to Americans came into view . . . when a number of Zapata people joined the Carrancista troops in retaliation for the punitive Pershing expedition."[53] More directly, the wife of rebel leader Aniceto Pizaña stated that *"los americanos"* simply wanted to drive them off their land.[54]

There was, of course, a segment of the Texas Mexicans that fought against the *sediciosos*. Established leaders, such as attorney J. T. Canales of Brownsville and Deodoro Guerra, a Hidalgo County boss, led posses and intelligence units in combatting the raiders.[55] Mexican *vaqueros* tied to the ranch remained loyal to their *patrón*, whether Anglo or Mexican. The most prominent example was the loyalty displayed by Los Kineños (King Ranch cowboys) during the bandit raids, for which they have been eulogized. Old-timer Maude Gilliland, speaking of the troubles of 1915, felt compelled to make the following qualification about Mexicans: "I do not wish to convey the impression that all Mexicans are bad. There were good Mexicans as well as bad Americans. Ranchers along the border depended almost exclusively upon Mexican vaqueros for their labor; and these vaqueros, generally speaking, were reliable, loyal and trustworthy. Strong ties of friendship existed between many American and Mexican families. No better friends were to be had than these faithful ranch Mexicans."[56]

Nonetheless, the farm developments threatened the "good" Mexicans. It became increasingly clear to *ranchero* and *vaquero* that the Anglo *patrón* no longer desired to guarantee their security or could no longer do so. The old-time leaders found themselves unable or unwilling to moderate the indiscriminate actions of the newcomers and Rangers against Texas Mexicans. In fact, the major ranchers of the region—Robert and Caesar Kleberg, Ed Lasater, John Kenedy, George Parr, Lon C. Hill, among others—were among the most adamant in urging an immediate and thorough suppression; they petitioned state and federal authorities for permission to follow raiders into Mexico, requested the imposition of martial law, and recommended the creation of a security zone along the Rio Grande. Thus, as old-timer Emilio Forto explained to the commanding officer of the American forces, the conflict escalated because "many lives of good Mexicans were sacrificed by Rangers and other civil officers, and the more ignorant and illiterate Mexicans were induced to be revengeful against Americans."[57]

To see the Rangers as simply a band of "pistol toters," however, would minimize their significant partisan role in the Valley during this period of farm development. The Rangers were not merely suppressing seditious Mexican bandits; in the larger picture, they played the critical part in paving the way for the newcomer farmers. Forto made this point emphatically in his statement to the American commandant: "From all reports (some from army officers whose testimony is probably available) a campaign of extermination seemed to have begun in those days. The cry was often heard, 'we have to make this a white man's country!!' It would not be difficult to establish the fact that many well-to-do natives of Texas, of Mexican origin, were driven away by Rangers, who told them 'If you are found here in the next five days you will be dead.' They were in this way forced to abandon their property, which they sold at almost any price."[58]

Likewise attorney Frank Pierce, who did not hesitate to urge the use of force to end the Mexican raids, described the Ranger record during this time in tentative terms—"supposedly," "it is alleged," and so on—and distinguished them sharply from the service performed by the U.S. and state militia. Pierce concluded his guarded discussion of the Rangers by saying: "The author cannot let pass this opportunity to say that during the bandit raids of 1915 many evil influences were brought to bear to clear the country of Mexicans. To his knowledge more than one was forced to flee and to convey his chattels before going."[59] The repression, in the straightforward interpretation of Emma Tenayuca, could only be understood in the context of land development then taking place: "Texas Rangers, in cooperation with land speculators, came into small Mexican villages in the border country, massacred hundreds of unarmed, peaceful Mexican villagers and seized their lands. Sometimes the seizures were accompanied by the formality of signing bills of sale—at the point of a gun."[60] Even Webb, the Ranger historian, acknowledged that "many innocent Mexicans were made to suffer" and that "many members of the force have been heartily ashamed" of their part in "the orgy of bloodshed."[61] Yet this "orgy of bloodshed" was what was necessary to make the region secure and safe for newcomer farmers. In this, the Rangers played the critical military role on the side of the farmers.

What made this partisanship clear was the involvement of the Texas Rangers in the electoral politics on the side of the newcomers. Once the Rangers sided with the newcomers against the old-timers, they overstepped the bounds that influential politicians like Jim Wells and Archie Parr were willing to tolerate. Because of their partisan activities, the Rangers were reorganized by the legislature and reduced to a company of special investigators in 1919.[62]

In short, the insurrection and suppression, while fueled by international tensions and the threat of war with Mexico, must be placed in the context of a struggle between a modern farm society and an old ranch order. With the defeat of the *sediciosos*, peace returned to the Valley and whatever alternative they may have dared dream was removed from the historical agenda. Mexican Texas proceeded to develop along two paths: one led directly to the world of commercial agriculture; the other pointed still to the feudal-like world of ranch life. Which path a particular area took depended on who won the conventional political battles for control of local government. Again the opposing alignments suggest the contest between the new and the old.

6. The Politics of Reconstruction

new farmers vs. old-time machines (rancher/merchant cliques)

BEFORE THE arrival of the farm settlers, South Texas politics were generally characteristic of "manorial societies" governed by a landed elite. Politics consisted essentially of "in-house" fights between cliques of merchants, lawyers, and big landowners. The strength of competing cliques was based on the allegiance of landowners, who in turn commanded the loyalty of poor relatives and dependent workers. Republican and Democrat, in this context, meant little more than an organizational name for the contending elite factions. In places where Mexican *rancheros* and townspeople constituted an organized force, as in Webb and Duval counties during the late nineteenth century, local politics assumed an apparent class character, with the merchant party known as *botas* (boots) and that of the *rancheros* and townspeople as *guaraches* (sandals). But in the absence of class distinctions, where the political arena was dominated by organizations of competing elites, colored cloth and banners sufficed to distinguish the major parties. Red versus blue: red for Republican, blue for Democrat. A landowner indicated his preference, for the sake of the commoner, by his choice of colors. Ideological matters were unimportant; landowners joined one party or the other, Jovita González noted in reference to Starr County politics, "not for political convictions but for personal enmity and hatred." Likewise, observed another student of the region, associates of Jim Wells generally broke with the Democratic machine simply to establish their own rival organizations. The charge of "bossism" under these circumstances held little meaning as a partisan issue.[1]

A Matter of Good Citizenship

With farm colonization, the character of regional politics became increasingly complex and diversified. The newcomers added to the Republican and Democratic rolls, but these loyalties proved to be unimportant. Frustrated in their desire to develop the area, the newcomers discovered that they had more in common with each other than with their red and blue compatriots. Thoroughly disgusted with the situation they found, they began to organize in Democrat-

Republican coalitions, called themselves good citizen leagues, and challenged the old-line Democratic politicians. Local politics became transformed from a contest between competing cliques of landowners and merchants to one between distinct landowning groups—ranchers versus farmers. The color scheme became irrelevant; now it was the "old ticket" versus the "new ticket," the ring versus the antiring, the machine versus the good government league. Established Democratic officials were accused of bossism, and their tactics described as "corralling" and "herding Mexicans"—derisive imagery fashioned by farmers against the ranchers. Through investigations instigated by the newcomers, the old-time politicians were forced to defend their organizational power. Thus, Archie Parr, according to his loquacious lawyer, was a leader who "leads simply by the power of love that the people who follow have for him."[2] And the King Ranch, according to Jim Wells' testimony, directed five hundred Mexican votes "through friendship and love": "The King people always protected their servants and helped them when they were sick and never let them go hungry, and they always feel grateful, and it naturally don't need any buying, or selling or any coercion—they went to those that helped them when they needed help." Moreover, explained Wells, this type of guidance was a natural idea among Mexicans: "The Mexican naturally inherited from his ancestors from Spanish rule, the idea of looking to the head of the ranch—the place where he lived and got his living—for guidance and direction. It came legitimately and naturally from that Spanish rule—that idea did."[3]

Such tradition and friendship, of course, were meaningless to the farm settlers. The situation in the Lower Valley "shocked the sensibilities" of the newcomers and led them to condemn "the Mexican-Americans as ignorant people who were unfit to have a vote."[4] Every political practice and norm that helped keep the old-timers in power was seen as illegal or corrupt. Thus, speaking Spanish at the polls and having Texas Mexican election judges were un-American, the difference between Texas Mexican and Mexican "alien" was a matter of semantics, and political rallies of Texas Mexicans were held to be illegal. One unsuccessful newcomer challenger of John Nance Garner charged, in a common episode of this period, that 10,000 of the 27,000 votes cast in the primary were those of Mexican aliens and that one illegal method used "in preparing the Mexicans . . . was that of feasting them by the thousands at 'goat barbecues.'"[5]

The condemnation of the Texas Mexican voter did not come simply because the newcomers found their attempts to develop the country frustrated by the old-time machines. The opposed interests of farmers and ranchers fueled the confrontation, but the differences were greater in scope than just a question of economic concerns. The farmers were not just demanding a supportive county government; they insisted also on a new morality, a new code of social relations. Exemplary of the new code was the prohibitionist spirit of the newcomers. As historian Dan Kilgore notes of Corpus Christi during this period, "the transition from a frontier cowtown to a city with the standards of morality demanded by the new farmers did not come without trauma. There were numerous conflicts, but the climax developed when the town became bitterly divided over prohibition."[6] On March 10, 1916, a countywide referendum settled the issue, by a bare 218 votes, in favor of the "drys"; the heavy vote in the small farming towns had carried the question.

An integral component of this new morality concerned the proper place of the Mexican. The newcomers generally described their campaigns as "uplift" movements meant to purify the ballot, develop the country, and make Americanism supreme. What gave these claims substance was a view of Mexicans as racial inferiors. Texas Mexicans, in the eyes of the farmers, did not merit the rights and privileges of Americans; they were American citizens in name only. As the *Carrizo Springs Javelin* (August 5, 1911) put it, these Mexicans belonged to that "class of foreigners who claim American citizenship but who are as ignorant of things American as the mule." In a similar vein, University of Texas economist William Leonard, in a 1916 article entitled "Where Both Bullets and Ballots Are Dangerous," characterized the Mexican voters as a "political menace," for they "retain vestiges of the primitive man's willingness to attach themselves as followers to any one who may have shown them a kindness." The occasion for the comment was election fraud in Corpus Christi, a conspiracy in which a "supporting company" of "ignorant, unnaturalized Mexicans" had supplied the critical votes. What Leonard, a newcomer from Iowa, took as evidence of ignorance was the fact that of the twenty to thirty Mexicans who testified in federal court—"no one had any conception of the Democratic or any other ticket. The only ticket of which they had any notion was the so-called 'Old Ticket.'" Leonard's portrayal of Mexican voters, in an ironic sense, revealed the limited understanding newcomers had of the region and pointed as well to the conflict between new and old then unfolding. The "Old Ticket" that the Mexicans were supporting was the party of old-line politicians who were wrestling with newcomers like Leonard.[7]

In this contest between new and old politicians, the Texas Mexican was left with little choice. The Mexican American supported

Table 6. Major Political Events in South Texas, 1910–1930

Place	Year	Event
Cameron	1910	Old-timer Judge Jim Wells loses Brownsville to "independent" Democrats and Republicans.
Starr & Hidalgo	1911	Republican Ed C. Lasater carves new county of Brooks from "Mexican County" of Starr.
Starr, Duval, & Zapata	1913	Independent Democrat D. W. Glasscock carves new county of Jim Hogg to "get away from Mexican domination."
Kleberg	1913	King Ranch loses first county election to newcomers.
Dimmit	1914	Newcomer farmers establish the White Man's Primary Association.
Nueces	1915	Election scandal in Corpus Christi results in federal convictions of old-line politicians.
Duval	1911–1915	Independents and Republicans defeat old-timer Archie Parr's attempts to divide Duval into two counties.
"Valley"	1919	State investigation of Senate race between Parr and Glasscock.
Cameron	1920	Jim Wells loses control of county.
Hidalgo	1928	"Hidalgo County Rebellion" results in federal investigation and conviction of machine politicians.

the old bosses, as one Mexican American civic leader explained, because "this crowd understands the Mexican-American psychology far better. What may the Mexican-American expect from the new Anglo-Saxon settler? He doesn't understand him; he has scarcely visited his little old towns; he looks upon him as ignorant—perhaps *Mexican*. In fact, he fails to distinguish between Mexican citizens and Mexican-American citizens on the one hand, and also between classes of Mexicans."[8]

The conflict exploded into several major political scandals and controversies. During the 1910s and 1920s the old-timer Anglo elite, allied with remnants of the landed Mexican upper class, found itself embattled by newcomer farmers who demanded public improvements, higher property taxes, an end to dictatorship, and the beginning of American decency. The newcomers charged the old-timers with fraud, with mismanagement of funds, with voting Mexican aliens, with bossism, with selling out Americanism. The old-timers responded by saying that the newcomers were mistreating and intimidating American citizens of Mexican extraction and that the newcomers were fanning the flames of a potential "race war." This war, as discussed in the previous chapter, did take place, effectively disrupting the region for most of 1915 and 1916. Alongside the violence of these times, the struggle between new and old also found expression in conventional politics. A digest of the major challenges and defeats weathered by the old-timers suggests the intensity of this conflict geographically (see Table 6).

The result of this political struggle was twofold: on the one hand, the number of counties in the region nearly doubled, from seven to thirteen, as ranch and farm areas were separated into distinct jurisdictional zones; on the other hand, where the farmers were victorious over the rancher, the Texas Mexican was disfranchised or eliminated as an important political factor.

In order to describe the course of this political struggle and its various outcomes, the discussion is organized around a string of case studies. First the reorganization of the region will be considered. Then the discussion will focus on the manner in which the political struggle between the newcomers and the old-time machine politicians unfolded, with serious consequences for the voting rights of Texas Mexicans.

The Reorganization of County Government

In many respects county government was the most important policy-making unit of the national government at this time. The powers of

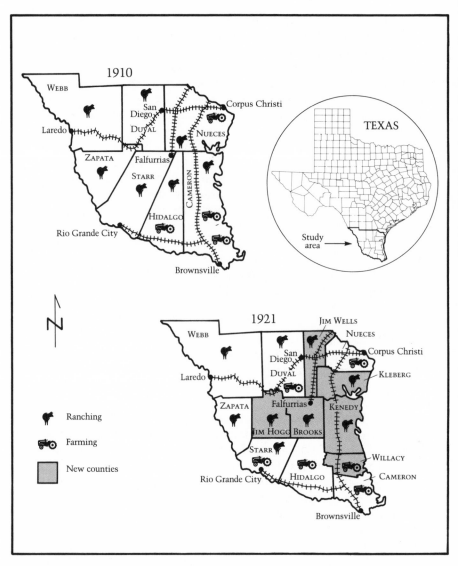

County Reorganization in South Texas (based on data from U.S. Bureau of the Census, Thirteenth, Fourteenth, and Fifteenth Census of the United States: 1910, 1920, 1930).

tax assessment and collection, supervision of elections, and provision of public services were firmly in the hands of county officials. Their power rested on the fact that through the 1930s the county was the *sole administrative body of government.* The federal government and the state of Texas exercised little administrative control over county functions. Not until 1931, for example, were counties required to file a copy of their annual budget with the state comptroller of public accounts. Typical of the times, however, the law did not provide for any enforcement mechanism.[9]

It is not surprising, then, that the struggle between newcomer and old-timer should center on control of county governments. The bitter and often violent elections represented key battles for the power to direct local development. In this political warfare, both sides devised various strategies. The most ingenious perhaps was the idea of creating new counties. Neither side monopolized the tack. Once the strategy of dividing counties to separate ranch from farm areas was introduced—by the master politician Jim Wells, according to one source[10]—both ranchers and farmers led movements to create new local governments. The intensity of these movements, and of the antagonism underlying them, can be seen by what happened to county boundaries at this time. Within the space of ten years, between 1911 and 1921, the seven-county area of deep South Texas was divided into thirteen counties (see map).

The common explanation of South Texas historians attributes the creation of new counties to the population increases and to the subsequent need for more effective and accessible public services.[11] Contrary to this argument, however, the new counties were sparsely settled ranch areas. Closer examination reveals that the pressure for new counties stemmed from the fundamental conflict between newcomer farmers and old-timer ranchers and their Mexican allies. The argument about the need for efficient and accessible government constituted part of the political rhetoric in which this battle was expressed.

A survey of various movements to create counties will suggest how complex the actual battle between newcomer and old-timer was. Before those movements that were successful are considered, it may be well to first consider one that failed.

The Case of Dunn County

Duval County, whose population was overwhelmingly Mexican, was the archetype of the Texas Mexican hybrid society of the late nineteenth century. While most Mexicans were ranch and farm workers, as many as three hundred families still owned land. The Mexican class order was complex, and those of "comfortable means" were to be distinguished from the commoners. Anglos and European immigrants, although less than 10 percent of the population, controlled the trade and politics of the county, a situation that fostered a lingering resentment among the landowning Mexicans. Both the *bota* and the *guarache* political factions had a record of offering only token concessions to the wealthier Mexican classes. At the turn of the century, Archie Parr, a Spanish-speaking *patrón* with a loyal following, capitalized on the tension and was able to forge an alliance between Mexican landowners and some Anglo landowners; in the process he created the foundation for a potent political machine.[12] The machine organization, headed by Archie Parr and later by his son George, not only protected Mexicans from Anglo racism but also ensured a more "balanced" distribution of political offices and patronage among Anglos and Mexicans.

In 1911, Archie Parr, at that time state senator, proposed the creation of Dunn County from the southern half of Duval. Unlike other reorganization attempts, the Dunn County proposal was not a response to threatening farm developments; rather, Parr had simply recognized a method that could increase the local revenues and patronage at his disposal. The legislature approved the bill but the new county was never organized because of concerted efforts and protests on the part of Republicans and Independents in Duval. The protestors identified themselves as the "progressive" element in the county and were composed primarily of Anglo stock owners and farmers, with token support from Mexican townspeople in service occupations. Farmers had the prominent leadership role in the coalition.

The anti-Parr arguments were presented in a forty-page pamphlet entitled *Remarkable Conditions in Duval County,* which the protestors sent to the Texas Legislature in 1915. The purpose of the protest pamphlet was to make the legislators realize "the conditions surrounding those who are attempting to develop that section of the State. The County at the present time is beginning to be settled by a high class of citizens, and to divide the county would mean to retard its settlement and development, increase the taxation without any corresponding benefit. The people will simply have to support two county governments instead of one, and it must be conceded that from the records in this matter that one of the kind is about all any community can reasonably stand."[13]

According to the protestors, the new county was "the result of a political trade," that the Parr faction would surrender all offices in Duval County to another faction while "taking control of the pro-

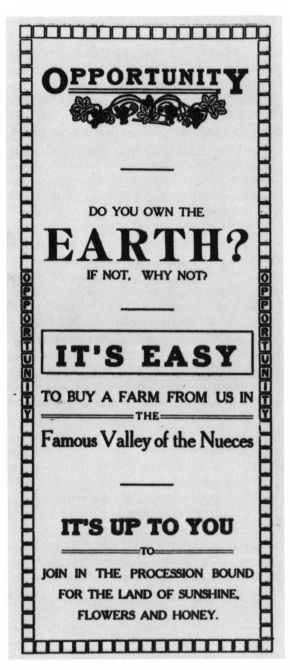

Pryor Ranch prospectus, ca. 1915 (courtesy Daughters of the Republic of Texas Library at the Alamo).

posed Dunn County." The strategy of the progressives was simple—present an unending series of lawsuits to block any actions by Duval County officials. Thus, as soon as the Duval County commissioners had drawn the precinct boundaries of the new county and called for elections, T. M. DuBose, a farmer, filed a suit charging that the precinct division was "arbitrary, unfair, unjust and unlawful." Citing the acreage, population, and mileage of public roads in each of the four precincts of the proposed county, the DuBose suit pointed out that the division had no rational basis, had not been established with any regard to the convenience of residents, and was contrary to the legislative act creating Dunn County, which stated that "an imperative public necessity exists . . . because of the great inconvenience to which the people are subjected."[14]

The Duval County Commissioners Court, in an attempt to undermine the DuBose suit, divided the county a second time. Again a farmer, Charles H. Williams, filed suit seeking a permanent injunction against the proposed division on the basis of "irrational" precinct boundaries. There was, of course, a rational basis underlying the subdivision of Dunn by Duval County officials; it touched on the "race" question, on the need to balance representation in the new county. According to the brief submitted by the officials, the commissioners court subdivided the new county in order "to give to the Americans as nearly equal representation in the Government of the County as was given to the Mexicans" and so that neither Americans nor Mexicans "would absolutely dominate in the governmental affairs of the County." The testimony of Archie Parr was explicit on this point: "Precinct No. 1 . . . has not always been in that shape, but the Commissioners' Court figured we wanted to give the Mexicans an equal division of the Court with the Americans and we ran that line across there. Then we cut Precinct No. 2 below there and there is not an American in it, and we are running a Mexican there for Commissioner. In Precinct No. 3 there are 50 Americans living there and we wanted to give them the Commissioner so we are running an American in there."[15] This justification, however, only served the cause of the plaintiffs. The Court of Civil Appeals ruled that a division based on racial lines was in "utter disregard" of the "convenience and rights" of voters; and the second attempt to organize Dunn County was enjoined by the court. Afterward it was discovered that the north line of Dunn County was more than one-half mile too near the county seat of Duval County, in violation of the Texas Constitution, and the act was declared unconstitutional.[16]

Despite Parr's legislative and legal setbacks, he remained entrenched as the political boss of Duval County. After 1910 the new-comers' in-migration declined and by 1920 many of them, demoralized and disgusted, had sold their land and moved from the county.[17]

Brooks and Jim Hogg: A "Progressive" Initiative

While the progressive element in Duval prevented a subdivision of the county by the Parr machine, it led a campaign to create two new counties from the machine-dominated counties of Hidalgo, Starr, and Zapata. Again the issue, although shrouded in arguments about convenience, revolved around the related questions of development and Mexican political influence. Mexicans owned most of the land in these border counties and, represented by tightly run political organizations, they provided those in favor of development with little latitude for maneuvering. Carving new counties from the conservative machine counties offered a possible solution.

In the case of Brooks County, Ed C. Lasater, a prominent old-time Republican in the area, had challenged the control of the Manuel Guerra family in Starr County for years. After the bitter election of 1900, Lasater began a campaign to have a new county created out of the northern Falfurrias portion of Starr, but the bill expectedly failed in two or three legislatures due to opposition from South Texas Democrats. The persistent and increasing challenges directed at the county machines, however, wore down the old-timer politicos. After witnessing the dramatic loss of Brownsville to newcomers in 1910, Manuel Guerra panicked and withdrew his opposition to the new county in order to safeguard his political tenure. In 1911 "Brooks county was created and Starr County was deprived of its best soils for grazing, pasturing and farming purposes."[18] The separation, however, restored the homogeneous character of Starr County as a Mexican ranch society; it secured the rule of the Guerra family through the 1940s.

Jim Hogg County has a similar, if unexplored, history. D. W. Glasscock, a newcomer in his first term as state representative, passed legislation creating Jim Hogg in order for his constituents "to get out from under the domination of the Mexican vote at the other end of the county that rested upon the Rio Grande"—meaning apparently Zapata County.[19] This coincided with protests from Brooks County residents who accused Lasater of manipulating the Mexican American vote. In fact, the proponents of Jim Hogg County used the same arguments that Lasater allies had made two years prior when they had called for the formation of Brooks. In 1913 Jim Hogg County was carved out of portions of Zapata, Duval, and Brooks counties. The secession had its intended effect: although 75 percent of the land remained in the hands of Mexicans, the new county government was controlled completely by Anglos.[20] The basis for development was thus set.

Disgust with Mexican politics, in short, was a platform that newcomers and old-timer independents found easy to stand on as they campaigned against established machine politicians. The issue of Mexican domination, although expressing the fundamental racial tension surfacing in South Texas, was intimately associated with the question of local development. Mexican landowners and Anglo independents had diametrically opposed views on the matter of progress. The differences can be seen in the paths taken by the old and new counties. Both Starr and Zapata rejected the irrigation developments and were consequently spared the "invasion" of newcomer farmers. While Starr and Zapata remained, according to contemporaries, "untouched by progress and development," Lasater was busy selling farm tracts in the new county of Brooks. The impact was evident. At the time of the Southern Pacific's arrival in 1906, Falfurrias was a cattle ranch with fewer than 200 people occupying a spread of over 400,000 acres. By 1920, according to a biographical sketch of Lasater, he had sold 60,000 acres of his 360,000-acre ranch and had built Falfurrias into a town of 2,500 people—"thrifty and industrious farmers from Iowa, Kansas, Texas, Nebraska, Indiana, and other states."[21]

The Retreat of the Ranchers

The second movement behind the sudden pace of the county reorganization was a defensive strategy on the part of the old-timers. Four new counties—Willacy (1911), Jim Wells (1911), Kleberg (1913), and Kenedy (1921)—were carved away from the old counties of Cameron, Hidalgo, and Nueces, areas where farming had developed and expanded the most.

If "parent" and "offspring" counties are clustered according to a few suggestive categories—number of farms, average farm acreage, population density, and assessed valuation per acre—the contrast between farm and ranch areas becomes clear.[22] In every instance, with the exception of Starr County, the parent counties had the greatest number of farms or ranches, the smallest average acreage, the greatest population densities, the highest assessed valuation on land; these were, in other words, the areas undergoing intensive farm development. The new offspring were actually the old ranch areas of the region (see Table 7).

Table 7. *South Texas Counties According to "Parent-Offspring"*
Clusters

County & Year Organized	Land Area (sq. mi.)	No. Farms	Average Acreage	Popula-tion Den-sity (per sq. mi.)	Assess-ment (per acre)[a]
Nueces (1846)	775	1,969	(192.4)	66.8	$61.64
Jim Wells (1911)	791	1,302	(3,115.9)	17.0	24.28
Kleberg (1913)	698	548	(932.2)	17.8	13.64
Cameron (1848)	840	2,936	(45.6)	92.3	65.56
Willacy (1911)	574	814	(319.1)	18.3	5.50
Kenedy (1921)	1,335	13	(61,547.7)	.5	—
Hidalgo (1852)	1,555	4,321	(126.9)	49.5	98.96
Starr (1848)	1,348	1,349	(181.9)	8.5	7.41
Brooks (1911)	974	513	(1,087.4)	6.1	15.24
Jim Hogg (1913)	1,140	312	(1,706.6)	4.3	18.16
Undivided counties:					
Zapata (1858)[b]	1,040	338	(854.1)	2.8	3.32
Duval (1876)[b]	1,703	1,241	(578.7)	7.2	19.29
Webb (1848)	3,219	522	(2,529.7)	13.1	8.59

Source: Based on U.S. Dept. of Commerce, Bureau of the Census, *Fifteenth Census of the United States: 1930, Population,* vol. III, part 2, and *Agriculture,* vol. III, part 2; *Texas Almanac & State Industrial Guide,* 1925.

[a] 1924 county assessors' valuations.

[b] Partial division with Jim Hogg County in 1913.

Willacy County, organized in 1911 and reorganized in 1921, provides the best example of the process. In 1911, the northern range lands of Cameron County were severed from the "Magic Valley" developments and organized as Willacy. Due to the modest success of the Raymond Town and Improvement Company, however, commercial farming spread northward from Cameron and into the new county. In 1921 Willacy was reorganized to account for this expansion. The greater part of the county, still solidly ranch area, became the new county of Kenedy and what remained—the farm area of Raymondville—became the new reconstituted Willacy. The census figures tell the story plainly: in 1930 reorganized Willacy County had a population density of 18.3 and 814 farms with an average size of 319 acres; the new county of Kenedy, meanwhile, had a population density of 0.5 and 13 "farms" with an average size of 61,500 acres.

Ranchers, then, pulled their lands away from the counties inundated by waves of newcomer farmers. This type of strategic retreat, however, was not a completely successful maneuver. Some ranchers invariably succumbed to the lure of selling farm land, and thus agriculture had a tendency to "spill over" and reintroduce the very conflict that ranchers had attempted to circumvent.[23] Even the carefully paced development of Kleberg County was not free of tension between farmer and rancher.

Convenience was a factor behind the making of Kleberg, noted Ben F. Wilson, Jr., in his economic history of the county. But the primary justification was to separate from Nueces County, which "had voted several large bond issues and was prepared to vote even more issues." Since the western portion of Nueces would receive little benefit from the proposed issues and taxes, the formation of a new county "became much more than an idea."[24]

While the economic interests of all individuals concerned led to the creation of a new county, the distinct needs of the King Ranch and the newcomers soon broke apart whatever unity in purpose had existed. In the first county election, the King Ranch lost control of Kleberg, and "Judge Wells was then called in and it required all of his acumen to get the situation in hand," according to Wells' law partner, Harbert Davenport. The ranch's political worries were only beginning, however. The new settlers were demanding bond issues for public improvements, which meant, since such revenues came from taxable property, that the Santa Gertrudis stood to bear the greater share of local government expenses. According to the official ranch biographer, Tom Lea, the ranch saw it had a proper obligation, but "its predominance on the tax rolls went unmatched by any predominance at the voting polls: the interests represented by the ranch could be subject to a punishing tax rate created by the voting majority who would pay very little of the tax."[25] In this context, every proposed improvement—paved roads, hospital construction, courthouse expansion, and so on—became embroiled in intense political debates. Indicative of the changes taking place, the county commissioners passed in 1919 a stock law prohibiting livestock from running at large.[26] Thus, one finds in Kleberg County, despite the efforts of Robert Kleberg to regulate local development, a repetition of what was happening generally in the region.

In short, the reorganization of the region represented the result of various local movements to resolve the stalemate between those favoring development and those opposed to it. The common arguments used to argue for or against new counties were the question of accessible, convenient government and the problem of Mexican corruption in politics. Having discussed the former, I can now turn to the latter.

Disfranchising Texas Mexicans

The political movements of the newcomers centered on the question of Texas Mexican political rights. Several cases—the 1914 White Man's Primary Association established in Dimmit County, the 1919 investigation of Valley politics, the 1928 "Hidalgo County Rebellion," to mention a few—illustrate the tendency of newcomer farmers to focus their challenge on the weakest link of the old-time machines, their overwhelming Mexican American constituency. Where the newcomer was victorious, the result was the general disfranchisement of the Texas Mexican.

In South Texas the predicament of the newcomer farmers was clearly outlined: they were locked in a political battle with Anglo old-timers kept in power by Mexican American voters. The way to defeat the machines, and to assure their complete defeat, was to disfranchise their base of support, the Texas Mexican electorate. To a considerable extent, the state legislature and the state Democratic Party, responding to the changing demographic composition of the population, paved the way by providing a legal context for a variety of measures that made it difficult, if not impossible, for the Mexican American to vote. In 1902, the poll tax requirement was passed, and in 1903 the Terrell Election Law establishing a direct primary system and requiring that poll taxes be paid between October and February was enacted. Terrell himself was explicit about the intent of the law; it would prevent opening "the flood gates for illegal voting as one person could buy up the Mexican and Negro votes." Proponents of the Terrell legislation also noted that Mexicans and blacks would either fail to pay so far in advance or lose their receipts when election time came around. In 1904 the State Democratic Executive Committee approved the practice of the White Man's Primary Association by suggesting that county committees require primary voters to affirm that "I am a white person and a Democrat." And in 1918, the legislature passed a law eliminating the interpreter at the voting polls and stipulating, moreover, that no naturalized citizens could receive assistance from the election judge unless they had been citizens for twenty-one years.[27] The intent of this act was meant to discourage Texas Mexican voters who, with the potential "naturalization" of the Mexican immigrant, constituted a decisive bloc of voters in the state. While these laws and policies sanctioned control of the Mexican American voter, the county officials were the critical actors here; they, as noted before, had the authority to administer and thus to interpret federal and state election codes the way they saw fit.

White Man's Politics: Dimmit County, 1914

The case of Dimmit County, just north of Webb County and part of the Winter Garden district, illustrates well the steps and rationale the newcomer farmers took in their attempts to control the Texas Mexican voter.

Although the Winter Garden district was spared some of the more dramatic confrontations characteristic of the Valley, some signs of tension between old-time ranchers and newcomer farmers were evident. Two railroads entered the region in 1910 or 1911, and in a few years it changed composition from a sparsely settled ranch area to a mixed ranch-farm economy. Dimmit County, as one Asherton old-timer recalled, was settled by poor farmers, most of whom came without the twenty-five dollars per acre that rancher B. Richardson was asking. In response to the farm projects, more and more Mexicans made Dimmit their home, so that by 1915 they constituted slightly more than half of the county population. Coincident with this change was the establishment of the White Man's Primary Association (WMPA) in 1914, a move that effectively disfranchised Mexican Americans in local elections. The White Man's Primary, in the words of the *Carrizo Springs Javelin* (June 12, 1914), "absolutely eliminates the Mexican vote as a factor in nominating county candidates, though we graciously grant the Mexican the privilege of voting for them afterwards."[28]

Between 1911 and 1914, and for several years afterward, when justifying the WMPA the *Javelin* regularly editorialized on the subject of Mexican voters, citing corruption, ignorance, the right to a decent "white man's election," and the purity of Anglo women. An editorial of October 4, 1913, for example, after describing the manipulation of the Mexican vote, posed two key questions of its readership—"Who is going to cast the vote of Dimmit County, White men or Mexicans?" and "Are you a white man standing with white men, or are you—well, something else?"[29] The *Javelin*'s rallying cry of race control, while indicating the supremacist sentiments of the Anglo population, also reflected the changing composition of the region from a ranch area to a mixed ranch-farm economy. Underneath the eloquent, biting rhetoric about Anglo women's purity lay a conflict between rancher and farmer.

Not much is known about the machine politics of the county or about the established figures like rancher Richardson. The political practices of the area, however, were no different than those characteristic of the border ranch region. The *Javelin* editorialized regularly, as it did on July 26, 1913, that "we want to get rid of the unnecessary and disgusting traffic in Mexican votes."[30] One resident interviewed by Taylor recalled that "before the white man's primary the candidates would buy up the Mexican votes with whiskey, money, clothes, dances, etc., and corral them. The night before the election they would guard them and then march them up to the polls like cattle."[31] What was feared by "whites"—that is, the small farmers—was that a moneyed person, especially a big rancher, would assume control by favoring and protecting Mexicans. They were concerned, in particular, about a Catarina rancher who was "sympathetic" to Mexicans.[32]

The newcomer farmers in Dimmit County, as everywhere in South Texas, wanted to create an environment favorable to commercial farming, and to do this they needed to uproot the old *patrón* system of politics. The WMPA, by forcing candidates to limit their appeal to the Anglo community, guaranteed that no paternalistic alliance between large landowners and Mexican workers would disturb or restrain the influence of the small farmer. The WMPA also provided the farmers the political base by which they could control the wages and movement of the migratory work force, a motive discussed in later chapters. Campaign expenses also figured noticeably in the *Javelin's* repertoire of arguments for defending the WMPA. Under the previous system, noted an editorial of October 22, 1915, a candidate could spend up to $5,000 for a county office that did not pay that much for an entire term. Under the White Man's Primary system, on the other hand, a candidate's expenses need not "exceed one hundred dollars."[33]

In short, the WMPA was the mechanism by which small farmers assured their control over the development of the region. The significance of the WMPA as a victory for the small farmer was expressed in the *Javelin's* editorials about "race control" and the campaign expenses saved by the system. The *Javelin* made the point clear in a February 10, 1928, editorial when, in lamenting the conditions in Hidalgo County, it praised the WMPA as a mechanism for "clean and economical politics" and for making "candidacy possible to a man of small means."[34]

Glasscock versus Parr, 1919

In early 1919 a Texas legislative committee investigated the state senatorial race between challenger D. W. Glasscock and incumbent Archie Parr. The political controversy concerned the certification of the Democratic primary elections as well as the conduct of the general election in 1918. After a heated primary election for the Senate seat between Glasscock and Parr, again basically a contest between independent newcomers and old-timers, Glasscock appeared to have edged Parr by a small margin. At the state party convention, however, the Parr forces led by Jim Wells outwitted the Glasscock forces by having the convention nullify returns from some Glasscock boxes, thus certifying Parr as the official Democratic candidate. Glasscock supporters were outraged by the convention action and began a write-in campaign for Glasscock for the general election. Parr won handily and Glasscock's supporters persuaded the state legislature to investigate the situation.[35]

Glasscock supporters, many of whom had been fighting Archie Parr over the attempt to subdivide Duval County, testified that the Glasscock campaign represented an "onward and upward movement" for the purity of the ballot and decency in politics on the Rio Grande. It was "a great movement in that country to try to get the Anglo-Saxon on top." Attorney Claude Pollard, representing the Glasscock people, noted that Glasscock had carried every American county and "every American box in every mixed county in the district" in the primary election and that in the general election "he carried every American County except Nueces and every American box in every mixed county except Mission, Pharr and Mercedes." Pollard noted that the campaign was not against Mexicans "as such." In Pollard's words, "this thing of these illiterate Mexicans voting down here is not the fault of the Mexicans, don't ever get that into your head. If you will let those Mexicans alone, they would be just as indifferent to the elections held in that country as the Negroes are in East Texas now. But it is the politician, the bosses, the white men who seek to control the offices and the policies of that country, and who pay the poll taxes for them, and drag them to the election and vote them as . . . they have been voted here."[37]

The Parr supporters, led by an able lawyer by the name of Marshall Hicks, ripped apart the claims of the Glasscock people about fighting for a noble cause. Hicks argued that this was "a bitter political fight by the enemies of Senator Parr cloaked under the guise of an 'uplift movement.'" The Glasscock people, noted Hicks, had used every means at their disposal to defeat Parr. They "got in touch with the ranger force of the State" and "investigated every county which was carried by Senator Parr and not a single county which was carried by Glasscock." Asked Hicks rhetorically: "Were they hunting evidence in order to purify the ballot? Were they hunting evidence on the Rio Grande to try to change those conditions?" The result of the Ranger interrogation was the spreading of "a spirit of terrorism among those Mexican people." At Corpus Christi the Rangers told the Mexicans "that, if they could not read, write and speak the English language and they voted, they would be put in the penitentiary."[38] Thus, noted Hicks, Mexicans who "were born in Corpus Christi and reared in Corpus Christi and had business there" stayed away from the polls "because this thing had been pulled, they were scared, they did not know what to do, and they would not vote"; consequently, "only about sixty-odd Mexicans" voted in Nueces County.

Hicks' strategy was to demonstrate that Glasscock had no moral standing in a basically soiled election. The strategy worked. The majority report of the investigative committee sustained the result of the general election, and this majority report was accepted—narrowly—by the Texas Senate. By a vote of sixteen to fourteen in favor, Archie Parr was recognized as the state senator from the Valley.

Hidalgo County Rebellion, 1928

A late replay of the conflict between old-timer and newcomer occurred with the famous "Hidalgo County Rebellion" of 1928. Again there was an "uplift" movement, known as the Good Government League (GGL) and composed of Republicans and independent Democrats, aggressively challenging the old political machine led by A. Y. Baker, ex-Ranger and sheriff of Hidalgo. At the center of the controversy lay the rejection of the Weslaco box, a newcomer stronghold, by the incumbent machine officials, thus denying the GGL candidate for county judge a close victory. At the request of Citizens Republican Committee of Hidalgo, a U.S. congressional committee investigated the situation.[39] The testimony it collected uncovered details of the familiar political conflict between old-timer and newcomer, with Mexican American voters caught in the middle.

Judge A. W. Cameron, the incumbent official whose victory was questioned, testified that the Weslaco box was thrown out because of the "troubles" surrounding voting there.[40] According to Cameron, the Citizens Republican Committee and others had intimidated Mexican Americans, that "something like 200 to 300 Mexican-American voters did not show up at all," and that on election day a crowd of three thousand to four thousand people near the Weslaco polling place were calling out, "Don't let those Mexicans in to vote. Throw them out." Moreover, added Cameron, across the street from the polling place were "men with shotguns" to see that the crowd was not interfered with. The Republicans called Cameron's charges a pretext to throw out the Welaco box; but many did not disguise their opinion of the Mexican voter. Under questioning by B. O. Kimbrough, attorney for the Citizens Republican Committee, Mrs. H. O. Schaleben testified, as evidence of machine tactics to control the

"American vote" in Edinburg, that they "were compelled to go across the track into the middle of the Mexican town and vote in an old Mexican quarter":

> Mr. Kimbrough. Did you ever make any effort to have your polling place moved into the white section of town?
> Mrs. Schaleben. Yes; we requested that it be moved, and this year we took a petition . . . with some 498 signatures . . . to the precinct judge and the county judge and requested that the polling place be moved; but it was not moved. It is in the old Mexican quarter and it is surrounded by Mexican stores and residences.[41]

The result of this investigation was very different from the one that had preceded it nine years before. The Select Committee recommended that the U.S. attorney-general take proper action in prosecuting Hidalgo County officials for fraudulent practices. The tide had clearly turned in favor of the newcomers. Hidalgo County boss A. Y. Baker was found guilty of throwing out ballot boxes. Baker disappeared before he was sentenced. Some say he was murdered, some that he committed suicide, others that he escaped into Mexico.[42]

The New Political Landscape

In many ways, these political battles and county divisions signaled the triumph of a new age over the old. The population in the farm counties, like that of the ranch, was mainly Mexican, but these societies were so dissimilar that a sharp line must be drawn between the two. Where the pioneer elite was successful in defending the old order, relations between Mexican and Anglo continued in more or less the same accommodative pattern as before. Where the newcomer farmers defeated the old oligarchy, Mexican-Anglo relations changed dramatically to a manner better suited to the demands and interests of commercial farming. Not unexpectedly, where the farmers wrested control from the ranchers, one of their first measures was the disfranchisement of Texas Mexicans, as through the White Man's Primary Association in Dimmit or simply through intimidation and other "informal" means. Who won the battle between the newcomers and old-timers, in other words, affected the local social order in fundamental ways.

Election results from South Texas counties reveal a graphic view of the distinct organizational politics of the old and new social orders. For the purpose of illustration, it suffices to consider two

Democratic primary elections (Democratic primaries, as in other southern states, were the "real" elections at this time)—the 1912 U.S. senatorial contest between Morris Shepard and J. F. Wolters and the 1924 gubernatorial race between Miriam "Ma" Ferguson and Felix Robertson.[43] By organizing the county tabulations from South Texas according to whether or not they returned a "machine vote"— that is, 75 percent or more majority for a particular candidate—the contours of the old and new political structures can be outlined. The returns point to the effectiveness of local machines—complete in the ranch counties and weak in the farm (see Table 8).

The 1912 senatorial primary demonstrates the muscle of Jim Wells' political organization, perhaps represented best by the vote of his home county of Cameron. In Cameron, J. F. Wolters received 1,411 of the 1,617 votes cast. Duval and Starr counties also performed impressively, giving Wolters a combined vote of 1,223 and allowing Morris Shepard only 6 votes. Despite this powerful support from South Texas, Wolters did poorly in other areas of the state, receiving 39.1 percent of the state vote compared to Shepard's 48.9 percent.

By the time of the 1924 gubernatorial primary, which "Ma" Ferguson won with 56.7 percent of the state vote, the decline of machine politics was evident. Several counties still had a potent machine organization; Duval and Starr counties, for example, gave Ferguson 1,927 votes to Robertson's 10. But the number of "independent" counties had increased dramatically, and their share of the South Texas vote was four times greater than that of the remaining machine-dominated counties. The vote tabulations, however, reveal an interesting irony, the key to the lingering influence of the machine counties: voters in the nonmachine counties, despite their greater numbers, rarely gave candidates conclusive majorities.[44] Thus the highly organized parties of the ranch counties still possessed the critical swing votes. In 1924, despite the greater strength of the "good government" counties, the candidate of the machine counties carried the region by almost a 3,000-vote margin, not much different from what favored politicians received during the days of Jim Wells.

By 1930, nonetheless, the influential place of commercial farming in the region was unquestioned. The farm population, allied with prodevelopment ranchers, had seriously crippled the power of the South Texas machine. In the guise of good government leagues, the newcomers had seized control over several counties from the old-timers. Of the thirteen counties in deep South Texas, farmers thoroughly dominated the politics and economy of four (Willacy, Cameron, Hidalgo, Nueces) and challenged the rule of ranchers in

Table 8. Election Returns from South Texas, 1912 and 1924

Type of Vote	1912 U.S. Senatorial Primary			1924 Gubernatorial Primary		
	County	Wolters	Shepard	County	Ferguson	Robertson
Machine Vote	Webb	364	36	Webb	852	175
	Duval	688	5	Duval	1,260	5
	Starr	535	1	Starr	667	5
	Willacy	73	0	Kenedy[a]	88	4
	Brooks	254	55	Zapata	128	13
	Cameron	1,411	206	Jim Hogg	17	116
	Zapata	(not reported)				
Subtotal		3,325	303		3,012	318
Nonmachine Vote	Jim Wells	123	135	Jim Wells	640	380
	Hidalgo	571	312	Hidalgo	747	1,423
	Nueces	491	312	Nueces	2,625	2,839
				Kleberg	467	751
				Willacy[a]	80	40
				Brooks	92	92
				Cameron	1,526	1,521
Subtotal		1,185	759		6,177	7,046
Total		4,510	1,062		9,189	7,364

Source: Based on *Texas Almanac & State Industrial Guide*, 1914, pp. 45–49; *Texas Almanac*, 1925, pp. 83–89.
[a] Kenedy County is basically Willacy County of 1912; Willacy of 1924 is a new county.

another two (Jim Wells, Kleberg). The ranch life remained uncontested in five counties (Kenedy, Webb, Brooks, Jim Hogg, Zapata); and in two counties (Duval and Starr) Mexican *rancheros* had made a transition to farming.

Peace and Gradual Development

The meeting between the old and new did not result in an explosive combination everywhere in South Texas. Along the Nueces valley, there occurred a "peaceful" transition or accommodation between rancher and farmer. This seemed related to two general factors. On the one hand, the ranch society along the Nueces valley consisted largely of Anglo landowners and Mexican *vaqueros* or *pastores*. In Dimmit, Jim Wells, Kleberg, and Nueces counties, Mexican landowners had been completely bought or forced out by the 1880s, although a few of their descendants remained in the vicinity. In contrast to the Lower Valley, a conservative ranch-owning class opposed to farming was largely absent.

The other key factor concerns the intensity of the farm colonization. In areas where farming developed peacefully alongside ranching, colonization did not occur in the "boom" style apparent in the Lower Valley. In Dimmit County, according to Asherton banker R. W. Taylor, there was "no general selling off of land by advertisements" and rancher B. Richardson "wasn't able to develop the country from outsiders as he had hoped."[45] The same applied to neighboring Frio County, where the transition to a mixed ranch-farm economy was made smoothly. And in Kleberg County, Kingsville grew in "an atmosphere of order" because Robert Kleberg kept the development of the area well in hand—"controlling sales, discouraging speculators." There was, nonetheless, some tension between newcomers and old-timers in Kleberg and in the other mixed farm-ranch counties as well, but this was contained or never serious enough to produce bitter political divisions.[46]

The result of such stability—owing to slow development and the absence of rancher opposition—was that the newcomers were able to become assimilated to the ways and beliefs of the ranch old-timers. In the Winter Garden, farmers referred to their farms as "ranchos," adopted the practice of having permanent Mexican sharecroppers, learned Spanish, and "ate tortillas and beans in the houses of the workers." "These traditional American farmers and individualistic ranchers," as one account of Frio County put it, "were also landlords and *patrones* in ways different from Midwestern farmers of this era."[47] The *patronismo* of Winter Garden farmers was based ultimately, of course, "on the economic needs of the *rancho*" and thus would disappear once migratory wage labor displaced croppers in the 1920s. The point, however, is that farm colonization did not everywhere produce a race war or bitter duel between Anglo old-timers and newcomers. Some form of assimilation, some blending of old and new, was a possible intermediate step between ranching based on *patronismo* and peonage and farming based on business rationality and wage labor. Slow development favored such intermediate cultural change.

The development of deep South Texas showed the converse to be also true. The rapid pace of farm colonization within the well-developed Mexican ranch society of the region afforded little latitude for adjustment on either side. The result was a polarization between the new and the old and a conflict highlighted by rebellion and repression. Accommodation between the rancher and the farmer came only through the clear separation between their respective societies.

Obituaries of an Era

A carefully read map of the region reveals the symbolic imprint of the great farm projects. Many of the new towns, like Palm in Dimmit county, Riviera in Kleberg, and Orange Grove in Jim Wells, bear the advertising line selected by the land promoters; even the street names memorialize the relatives and friends of the developers. The old guard, of course, assured themselves a due recognition in the changing topography of the region. Kingsville was named after the King family; Robstown after cattleman-businessman Robert Driscoll of Corpus Christi; George West after George West, rancher, entrepreneur, townbuilder, philanthropist, and owner of the 60,000 acres of land that surrounded the town.[48] The names of the new counties—Kenedy, Kleberg, Jim Wells, Brooks, Willacy—likewise paid tribute to the leading pioneers of the area. Engraved on courthouse plaques were the appropriate eulogies, such as the one placed in the Jim Wells courthouse: "By force of character, intellect, and winning personality, he became a recognized leader of South Texas, and for 40 years he remained a mighty influence for good, in the affairs of his state and nation, living to assist in the transition of this half-Mexican borderland into the splendid American wonderland today."[49]

The frontier days were gone, and old-timers and *viejos* sensed that they were the last of a distinct generation. The basis of the "horse culture" no longer existed as before. There was still talk of branding and roundups but, as Webb noted, "the oldster understood that the meaning of these terms had changed."[50] In the Texas Mexican com-

Top: Joy ride on Tex-Mex border, Rio Grande City, 1915 (courtesy Roy W. Aldrich Collection, Barker Texas History Center, University of Texas at Austin). *Bottom:* Brownsville's water system, ca. 1910 (courtesy Hornaday Collection, Archives Division, Texas State Library).

A Nuestros Compatriotas
Los Mexicanos en Texas

Un grito de verdadera indignación y de ira, ha brotado de lo mas profundo de nuestras almas, al ver los crímenes y atropellos que a diario se están cometiendo en indefensas mujeres, ancianos y niños de nuestra raza, por los bandidos y miserables rangers que vigilan las riberas del Río Bravo.

Indignación justa y santa, que hace enardecer la sangre que circula por nuestras venas y que nos impulsa, nos ordena, a que castiguemos con toda la energía de que somos capaces, a esa turba de salvajes, que avergonzarían, al tigre hambriento y a la nauseabunda hiena.

¿Cómo permanecer indiferentes y tranquilos ante semejantes atentados? ¿Cómo permitir semejantes ofensas inferidas a nuestra raza? ¿Acaso ya se acabó en nosotros el sentimiento de humanidad y de patriotismo? ¡No! estará adormecido pero es fácil despertarlo.

Basta ya de tolerancia, basta ya de sufrir insultos y desprecios, somos hombres conscientes de nuestros actos, que sabemos pensar lo mismo que ellos "los gringos"; que podemos ser libres y lo seremos y que estamos suficientemente instruídos y fuertes para elegir nuestras autoridades y así lo haremos.

El momento ha llegado, es necesario que todos los buenos mexicanos, los patriotas, todos aquellos que aún les quede el resto de vergüenza y de amor propio, es necesario, lo repito, acudamos a las armas, y al grito de "Viva la Independencia de los Estados de Texas, Nuevo México, California, Arizona, parte del Estado de Missisipi y Oklahoma que de hoy en adelante se llamará "República de Texas", nos unamos a nuestros compañeros de armas, que ya iniciaron el combate, dando pruebas de valor y patriotismo.

¡Viva la Independencia!
TIERRA Y LIBERTAD.

CUARTEL GRAL. EN SAN ANTONIO TEXAS.

Primer Jefe de las operaciones,

2o. Jefe de Estado Mayor,

Luis de la Rosa.

Aniceto Pizaña

Land and liberty: recruiting handbill for the Plan de San Diego, 1915 (National Archives).

munities, observed González, the once abundant folklore was "fast disappearing": "The goat herds, the source of nature's lore, are almost a thing of the past, the old type of *vaquero* is fast becoming extinct, and the younger generation look down with disdain on the old stories and traditions of its people."[51]

Concern with preserving a record of the ranch life led one group of Anglo old-timers, organized as the Old Time Trail Drivers' Association, to assemble a collection of stories and testimonies. Many of these commentaries were poignant farewells—poignant not just because death was only a few steps away, but because their entire world faced death, because with them the last representatives of a distinct culture would pass away. The eloquent testimony of John C. Jacobs of San Antonio was not uncommon:

> It seems now as though it was all in some other world and under fairer skies. The cowboy as he was then is gone from the earth. The railroads and wire fences have got his job. His old sorebacked cow pony is aged and wobbly. The automobile has got his job and his old three-quarter rigged saddle, with its busted rawhide cover, hangs out in the old rickety shed—a relic of former days—and soon the last of his tribe will sack his saddle, roll and light his last shuck as he bares his breast to the winding trail out over the Great Divide where, we trust, vast herds of long-horned cattle roam over fertile plains and slake their thirst from crystal streams.[52]

Several old-timers waxed nostalgically for the good times, and many—including those who had helped bring about the new age—felt that understanding between people had eroded. A common view was that of rancher–town builder–banker George Hindes of Pearsall, who believed that "the milk of human kindness is drying up, and the latchstring is being pulled inside."[53]

In contrast to the nostalgia and regret of the old-timers, the spirit of the new farm towns, in Harger's words, was that of "young men, filled with enthusiasm and enterprise . . . who believe that they will in the end be the financial leaders of a rich country." Added Harger, "The day when a top hat and a dress suit meant ribald jeering and perhaps a few revolver shots as a mark of disapproval, has departed— as has the typical cowboy."[54]

PART THREE

Segregation
1920–1940

Left: Texas Ranger on patrol outside Austin, 1946 (courtesy Texas Department of Public Safety). *Above:* U.S. Border Patrol officials outside Del Rio, 1926 (photo by Eugene O. Goldbeck; courtesy Ed Goldbeck).

"American society has no social technique for handling partly colored races. We have a place for the Negro and a place for the white man: the Mexican is not a Negro, and the white man refuses him an equal status."

—Max Handman, 1930

"The Mexico-Texan, he's one fonny man
Who lives in the region that's north of the Gran';
Of Mexican father, he born in thees part.
For the Mexico-Texan, he no gotta lan';
And sometimes he rues it, deep down in hees
    heart.
He stomped on da neck on both sides of the Gran';
The dam gringo lingo he no cannot spick,
It twista da tong and it maka heem sik;
A cit'zen of Texas they say that he ees!
But then,—why they call heem da Mexican
    Grease?
Soft talk and hard action, he can't understan',
The Mexico-Texan, he no gotta' lan'."

—Américo Paredes Manzano
"The Mexico-Texan," 1939

A Sign of Modernity

*T*exas entered "modern economic life" in the early twentieth century, according to Elmer Johnson, industrial geographer of the University of Texas. An essential element of this entry was the agricultural revolution in the humid Texas plains, which "added vast quantities of foodstuffs and raw materials to domestic and international trade." The growth and dominance of regional specialization in farm production, moreover, indicated "tremendous strides towards a completely commercialized agriculture." Along with widespread urbanization and the growth of manufacturing, such specialized farming constituted "major movements" in the commercial and industrial development of Texas.[1]

Along the Texas borderlands, this movement in commercial agriculture radically transformed the Mexican ranch country. The nature of this transformation can be framed boldly—in terms of a demise of a world of cattle *hacendados* and *vaqueros* and the rise of a world of commercial farmers and migrant laborers. Having cleared the area of chaparral, mesquite, and conservative ranchers, the newcomer farmers were essentially free to build a new society. The trappings of development were dramatic signs of the new order. Introduced rapidly in the 1920s, automobiles, highways, libraries, movie houses, drugstores, and so on soon distinguished modern farm areas from the horse and cow country of the ranch counties. So impressive were the changes that many newcomers saw themselves as the "first settlers" of the region.

A more significant sign of modernity than physical trappings was the social arrangements of the farm order. These arrangements owed much to the business standards and market practices that the newcomers introduced. The innovations are familiar ones in the story of development. In contrast to the permanent workers, paternalistic service, and complacent patriarchal attitudes of before, the modern society was characterized by wage laborers, impersonal contracts, and a rational market orientation. Workers themselves were assessed in terms of market costs; they were measurable items of production known as the "labor market." Relations between farmers and laborers, in short, were thoroughly commercialized.

But the most striking aspect about the new social arrangements was its obvious racial character. The modern order framed Mexican-Anglo relations in stark "Jim Crow" segregation. Separate quarters for Mexican and Anglo were to be found in the farm towns. Specific rules defined the proper place of Mexicans and regulated interracial contact. The separation was so complete and seemingly absolute that several observers have described the farm society as "caste-like."[2] The notion of caste, borrowed from a very different social context, applies poorly to Jim Crow segregation in the United States; it suggests, nonetheless, the degree to which race consciousness and privileges permeated social life in the farm order.

The emergence of a Mexican school system suggests definite patterns. The first "Mexican school" was established in 1902 in Central Texas (in Seguin) and the practice continued unabated until Mexican ward schools existed throughout the state. By 1930, 90 percent of South Texas schools were segregated. By the early 1940s, separate schools for Mexicans existed in at least 122 school districts in 59 representative counties.[3]

How can the segregation of Mexicans at this time be explained? What connection did it have with the development of commercial agriculture? Three general points, explored in detail in the following chapters, help explain the connection.

The first point emphasizes the extent to which Mexican-Anglo relations were a reflection of basic labor problems. The major concerns of Anglo farmers during the 1920s were the organizing and disciplining of a Mexican labor force, which they attempted to accomplish through numerous controls. This web of controls can be thought of, following the suggestion of Barrington Moore, Jr., in terms of "labor-repressive" commercial agriculture.[4] In this type of economy, agricultural production is based on a work force tied to the land through nonmarket means—through violence, coercion, and law. This condition requires strong, undemocratic political measures to contain the response of the working population. Viewed in this manner, many aspects of segregation can be seen as a functional extension of the need to organize and control Mexican labor.

The second point concerns the manner in which wage contracts mediated Mexican-Anglo relations and social life generally. In contrast to the master-servant bond of ranch life, the temporary impersonal contracts meant that relations between the two were generally anonymous, formal affairs. Or in the straightforward language of a noted authority on "border Mexicans," the racial mistrust of the time was due to a lack of "shoulder rubbing," to the fact that "we touch the Mexican at but a single point of contact—the industrial.

And it is just there that all the hatreds and misunderstandings and the wars have arisen since time began."[5] This element of anonymity and mistrust was evident in the anxious public discussion concerning the place of the Mexican in the Southwest. Physical separation, in this sense, was necessary to control the Mexican stranger; elaborate social rules were necessary to ensure that Mexicans knew their inferior position in the developing order.

The third point concerns the culture of "race-thinking." Such beliefs and sentiments concerning Mexican inferiority antedated the construction of the farm order, but in this modern context they acquired new importance. Texan history and folklore, previous experience with other races, biological and medical theories, Anglo-Saxon nationalism—all furnished important themes for the farm settlers in their dealings with Mexicans. Whether indigenous or imported in content, the culture of race-thinking made the segregated world a reasonable and natural order.

Influential as the farm world was, however, it was not an isolated economy. Despite the attempts of farmers to immobilize their work force, migration to the cities and to other states by Mexican workers was a major characteristic of the social order. There remained, moreover, a tier of Mexican ranch counties where the social order was quite different from that found in the Anglo farm counties. The final chapter in this section examines the contrast between the Mexican ranch and the Anglo farm societies.

7. The Structure of the New Order

WITH THE triumph of commercial agriculture over cattle ranching and family farming came the striking development of towns with separate Mexican and Anglo sections. In many cases, the new towns were divided into Mexican and Anglo quarters by the railroad tracks that had brought the farmers, "boomed" the towns, and linked the region to a national and international market. In some newcomer towns, a tripartite division existed, as in Kingsville, between Anglo, black, and Mexican, or, as the Anglo settlers put it, between "Kingsville, Africa, and Mexico."[1] The division cut across all spheres of rural life; "separation in domicile, separation in politics, and separation in education," as Taylor described the situation in the Winter Garden, was characteristic of the new order.

In seeking to explain the emergence of such divisions at this time, two general arguments immediately come to mind. One is that segregation—meaning specific policies of exclusion—was a natural outgrowth of the significant immigration from the South and the Midwest. The Anglo settlers formed their own neighborhoods, built their own schools and churches, married with their own, and ensured that their political interests were attended to. Ethnocentricism, in this view, provided the basic impulse for segregation. A related argument is that the context for separation was set by old-timer prejudices and actions, a legacy that the newcomers accepted and assimilated. With the Anglo farm settlements, the incoherent character of Mexican-Anglo relations of the previous century had finally gained a sense of consistency.

Both lines of reasoning contain valid points, for newcomer ethnocentricism and old-time Texan prejudices were powerful influences in shaping the contours of the farm order. These views, however, understate the extent to which the segregated society was a new order, a point I wish to develop in this chapter. Segregation, in other words, was not merely a natural unfolding of previous foundations or legacies—not just an immigration of more prejudiced Anglos or an assimilation of the old. This was a new society, with new class groups and class relations, with the capacity to generate an "indigenous" rationale for the ordering of people. While demographic movements and the notion of race privilege were a basic part of the twentieth-century story, the specific mechanisms of separation can be better understood in terms of the division of labor in the farm order. Since the farmers were Anglo and the laborers were Mexican, the construction of the farm society essentially proceeded on the basis of simple racial exclusions.

This chapter introduces the "modern" farm world of the Texas border region. This introduction consists of two tasks. The first is to describe the population movements, settlement patterns, and occupational placements that made for a new class order. The second is to describe the class structure and relations of the farm order.

The Cultural Mosaic

The farm developments introduced considerable diversity in the border region. The agricultural developments brought together Anglo old-timers and newcomers, southerners and northerners, Protestants and Catholics, Texas Mexicans and (in Taylor's words) "Old Mexicans." Although the demographic mix was complex and seemed unordered, an underlying logic can be discerned if the colonization projects are dissected into their constituent bits and pieces. Underneath the great population movements and settlements of Anglos and Mexicans during this period were the plans and strategies of land development companies and labor agencies.

Several county histories have suggested the influence of promotional land campaigns in patterning newcomer settlement. In Kleberg County, the towns founded by Chicago banker Theodore Koch and his Koch Land Company—Vattmannville, Riviera, and Riviera Beach—were composed of Illinois Catholics. And in Dimmit County, according to a local banker, the newcomers who "came from Louisiana, Illinois, Virginia, and Montana" were settled in two distinct waves. The first wave consisted of southerners too poor to pay rancher-developer Richardson the twenty-five dollars an acre he was asking, and the second wave consisted of northerners recruited by well-organized land companies. Thus, Asherton, settled around 1906, was a southern town and Catarina, founded in 1926, was a northern town. Even in the Lower Valley, where the cultural diversity of the new settlers was most pronounced, the imprint of land development can be outlined.[2] Those who settled before 1920 had farm backgrounds and those who settled afterward came from business and urban backgrounds, a distinction due to a shift in the sales strategies pursued by land companies. The secretary of the Brownsville Chamber of Commerce explained that "at first we used to get the poor farmers from the north; then the successful farmers. Now we go after the successful commercial and salaried people who let the companies take care of their land and trees for three years or more and plan to come down here later on."[3]

The Mexican side of the new farm towns and hamlets likewise reflected the recruiting practices of private employment agencies and labor agents. Since these activities, according to the Texas State Employment Service, were "practically unchecked," the settlement patterns of Mexican laborers are less evident than those of the Anglo farmers.[4] One general pattern suggested by the local sample surveys of the period is that the proportion of native-born and foreign-born depended on proximity to the Mexican border. In Dimmit County, less than fifty miles from the border, 36 percent of the Mexican population were Texas natives; in Kingsville, a hundred miles or so from the border, 56 percent had been born in Texas; and eighty miles farther north, in Karnes County, 64 percent of Mexican farm laborers interviewed by the U.S. Farm Security Administration were Texas-born. San Antonio, a major staging area for casual Mexican labor, was an understandable exception; here a one-eighth sample survey of Mexican heads of households consisted of 35 percent Texas natives.[5]

In the new society and economy, the "Texas-born Mexican" functioned as an intermediary between Anglo employers and Mexican laborers. As Knox noted of the San Antonio community, where the "floating Mexican type" worked, one found "the young American-Mexicans, the interpreters, bosses, timekeepers, or holders of higher positions." The "foreign-born Mexicans" (as Knox called Mexicans born in Mexico!), although they may have been skilled laborers in Mexico, were forced to take the lowest form of labor because they knew little English.[6] In the rural areas, the situation was similar. Migratory laborers were comprised of both Texas Mexicans and Mexican nationals, with the latter dominating. Most intermediary positions, especially small labor contractors, crew foremen, and sharecroppers with supervisory duties over seasonal labor, were occupied by Texas Mexicans.

In short, the farm developments introduced considerable diversity in the region. In certain places, as in the Winter Garden, the class configuration of the farm society revealed distinct cultural groupings: working farmers and tenants were southerners, absentee farmers northerners, migratory workers Mexican nationals, and labor contractors and foremen Texas Mexicans. Generally, the situation was more complex, as the recent arrivals assimilated the identities and language of Texans and *tejanos* and the old settlers learned the new ways of the modern farm world.

For the Anglo newcomers, not knowing Mexicans was as likely to create suspicion and uneasiness as it was curiosity. Local histories of the period, which generally mention the building of the first church, the first bank, and so on, contain several examples of awkward and tense "first meetings" between the new settlers and the Mexicans. One amusing encounter was described by one of the first settlers of Riviera, a Mrs. J. B. Womack, in a letter to a midwestern friend: "Not very long after Mr. Womack and Mr. Horstman had gone, I observed several Mexicans, mounted on prancing ponies, approaching. I closed the doors and windows and then hid myself. They rode around the building calling and knocking. I could understand only the word 'carta.' I supposed they wanted a cart—maybe wanted to put me in the cart. Anyway I finally came out and talked to them and found they wanted their mail out of the post office. One of the boys could speak a few words in English."[7] Mrs. Womack noted, by way of explanation, that "all I knew of Mexicans was from reading History and war stories. I had the impression that all Mexicans were cruel and treacherous like those I had read of."

Adjustment to the region was difficult enough to force some newcomers to make major changes in their plans. Thus, the superintendent of the Benavides Independent School District, J. M. Momeny, temporarily left teaching when he first arrived in Duval County because "not understanding the people of this locality, I was a little fearful of my understanding and ability to work with them, and so decided to become manager of C. W. Hahl's Real Estate Office in San Diego."[8]

Such moments were temporary; they reflected the initial period of acclimation, when newcomers were beginning to make sense of their new environment. After fifteen years or so, social distinctions between newcomers and Texan natives, while not altogether gone, carried only symbolic meaning. According to a former easterner, whenever around natives the newcomer "speaks softly of such matters as the Alamo, the Republic, and Longhorn cattle. They were before his time, and older Texans are liable to be touchy about them."[9] Despite the affected sensitivities of Texan natives, newcomers proved themselves capable of assimilating Texas history and Texan ways.

In the Mexican communities, as in the case of the Anglo towns, the new arrivals gradually became indistinguishable from the old within a generation. The Kingsville survey suggests this type of "amalgamation": of the 352 families, 38 percent (133) were headed

Mexican cotton pickers' house, 1929 (Taylor, *American-Mexican Frontier*, p. 128).

by parents born in Texas, 26 percent (91) by parents born in Mexico, and the remaining 36 percent (128) by parents, one of whom had been born in Texas and the other in Mexico. The play of acculturation, however, was confined—"sectioned" may be a better word—by the fundamental division between Anglo and Mexican communities. Mexicans, as Anglos often noted, could not assimilate Americanism as the Italians or Germans could.[10]

Demography of Segregation

The feature that imparted the greatest semblance of coherent planning in the new age was the separation of the Mexican and Anglo communities. Segregated residential sections had been planned by ranchers and town developers and maintained through sales policies. In San Patricio County, the Taft Ranch, the model pasture company, paid meticulous attention to these social questions. The ranch in 1910 had built a hospital with separate structures for each of the three ethnic groups on its property. There were Christmas handouts of candy sacks to the "Anglo-Americans, Latin Americans, and Negroes, each group meeting in separate places." And in 1912 the ranch had erected a separate building to provide schooling for Spanish-speaking children. Thus, the custom of social separation was already established by the 1920s when the ranch subdivided its land into the farm tracts and town lots of Taft and Sinton. Likewise, in the Winter Garden, the "Mexican town" of Asherton had been laid out by rancher-entrepreneur Richardson. An Asherton banker noted that "one or two Mexicans tried to buy in the American town but when they found they were not wanted, they left." Along the coastal plains in Kingsville, separate quarters for Mexicans were included in the meticulous preparation of the Kleberg Town and Improvement Company. Mexicans were "entirely segregated in the northwestern section of the town" where they had "their own dry goods stores, grocery stores, meat markets, tailor shops and a number of other shops and businesses." In the Valley town of Weslaco, segregation was instituted in 1921, the town's inaugural year. A municipal ordinance allocated the area north of the Missouri Pacific Railroad tracks to industrial complexes and Mexican residences and business establishments while that to the south was reserved for the residences and businesses of Anglos. In nearby McAllen, a similar separation of Mexican and Anglo was ensured by the sales policies of the McAllen Real Estate Board and the Delta Development Company.[11]

Residential separation demarcated, in a highly visible way, the distinct social standing of Anglo and Mexican in the new order. The physical appearance of the two towns expressed the social hierarchy dramatically. American neighborhoods of handsome wood frame houses, paved streets, and enclosed sewers stood in sharp contrast with Mexican towns of corrugated tin shacks, dirt roads, and outdoor privies. On the social plane, the rules of etiquette served to acknowledge Anglo superiority before the Mexican. Mexicans were expected, according to a historical account of a Winter Garden county, to have "a deferential body posture and respectful voice tone" whenever in the presence of Anglos. All contact between American and Mexican followed rather explicit rules. Movie houses, drugstores, restaurants, retail stores, banks, schools, and so on—the institutions of "modernity"—had brought with them definitions of the "proper place" of Mexicans. Public buildings were seen as "Anglo territories"; Mexican women were "only supposed to shop on the Anglo side of town on Saturdays, preferably during the early hours when Anglos were not shopping"; Mexicans were allowed only counter and carry-out service at Anglo cafés; and all Mexicans were expected to be back in Mexican town by sunset. So completely segregated were the two towns that, in effect, "there was an Anglo world and a Mexicano world" whose main point of contact was the "dusty fields."[12]

Segregated schools were a straightforward reflection of the racial divisions of the farm towns. In the Lower Valley, the towns of Edinburg, Harlingen, and San Benito segregated their Mexican school children through the fourth and fifth grades. And along the dense string of newcomer towns of Highway 83—the "longest mile" of McAllen, Mercedes, Mission, Pharr–San Juan, and Weslaco—Mexican school segregation was an unbroken policy. On the Gulf Coast plains, Raymondville, Kingsville, Robstown, Kenedy, and Taft were among the new towns where segregation was practiced. And in the Winter Garden area, Mexicans were segregated through the fifth grade in Crystal City, Carrizo Springs, Palm, Valley Wells, Asherton, and Frio Town. There was no need for segregation beyond the fifth or sixth grade, as many school authorities and growers noted, because Mexicans rarely "get that far." Once sufficient numbers began passing the sixth grade in the late 1920s, the segregated system was expanded and Mexican junior and senior high schools began to appear.[13]

Because school segregation was associated with newcomer settlement, the concentration of the Anglo population in South Texas outlines rather clearly the complex situation in the region. Professor Herschel Manuel's exacting breakdown of the Texas Scholastic Census of 1928–29 according to ethnicity, combined with various evi-

Table 9. *School Segregation in South Texas Counties, 1928*

Integrated	% Anglo[a]	Segregated	% Anglo[a]
Zapata	1.0	Cameron	34.3
Jim Hogg	14.8	Hidalgo	29.0
Brooks	17.2	Kleberg	44.4
Webb	10.6	Jim Wells	42.5
Duval	8.4	Willacy	37.7
Starr	3.6	Nueces	49.9
		Dimmit	24.7
		Zavala	30.3

Source: Based on Herschel T. Manuel, *The Education of Mexican and Spanish-Speaking Children in Texas*, pp. 70–75, 160–165.
[a]Ages 7–17.

dence of local conditions, shows a suggestive correspondence between segregation and Anglo settlement.[14]

Surveying school conditions in a "representative sampling" of twenty-four counties in South and West Texas, Manuel found a varied situation. In *rural* common-school districts, there was no segregation of Mexican children in eleven border or near-border counties included in the survey, with a tendency among towns having large Mexican populations "to maintain a separate Mexican school" in at least four of the eleven border counties. In the remaining thirteen counties farther "back from the border," there was a noticeable tendency toward "at least partial segregation" in rural as well as in city schools. In the counties where segregation was institutionalized, the percentage of Anglos on the scholastic rolls generally ranged from 30 to 50 percent. In contrast, the percentage of Anglos in the integrated counties clustered around 10 percent and never exeeded 20 percent. Table 9 illustrates the pattern.

What do these demographic patterns mean? To understand the *structural* foundation for this rigid division, the class structure and class relations that tied and separated the two communities must be examined. To see how the class structure in the farm counties followed race lines, it will be adequate to consider three general class groupings—farm owners, tenant farmers, and farm laborers.

The Rural Class Structure

An efficient way of presenting this material is by organizing the information according to the distinct farm zones that emerged in

South Texas. Such specialization represented the selection, after some initial experimenting, of the cash crop that could be cultivated most profitably under local conditions. In the Winter Garden area above Laredo, the "fertile soil, mild climate, and abundance of pure water" from artesian wells favored onion and spinach cultivation. The Lower Rio Grande Valley district "with its rich soil area and its subtropical climate" was ideal for growing a variety of crops, of which the most lucrative specialty was citrus fruit. And along the Gulf Coast plains, where developers had claimed that soil was "adapted to all semitropical fruits, vegetables, and farm crops," the farm settlers quickly discovered that an inadequate supply of well water as well as its magnesium content made extensive irrigated farming impossible. The only practical alternative left to the disappointed settlers was dry-farming of cotton. Thus, out of the possibilities afforded by natural and market conditions developed three distinct zones—the Winter Garden vegetable district, the Valley citrus area, and the Gulf Coast cotton belt.[15]

The population of these Texas farm areas can be classified according to the three general categories of farm owners, tenant farmers, and farm laborers. Farm owners were not a homogeneous class. There was a basic distinction between rich growers and poor working farmers. Some farmers, in the eyes of many local residents, were actually commodity speculators; they belonged, as one college-educated man put it, to the "leisure class." Thus, in the Winter Garden, most of the land was in the hands, according to a local critic, of a dozen "onion speculators"; and another resident figured that only about forty to fifty big landowners in the area needed the Mexicans. In the Nueces cotton district, 60 percent of the land, according to a well-informed source, was in the hands of absentee growers. And among Valley citrus growers, the division between the two types of landowners was drawn in sharp relief in a 1940 report: 45 percent of the owners were absentee landowners and not dependent on income from the land; the remainder were small growers dependent on landed income and were perhaps in debt.[16]

Among the tenant farm population, significant variations in contractual agreements with landlords, in the freedom to cultivate and market a crop, and in ownership of the "basic requirements of production," to use a phrase of the U.S. Department of Agriculture, separated the market situation of regular tenant farmers from that of sharecroppers.[17] A basic distinction must be drawn between these two groups.

Those on thirds and fourths, commonly known as "tenant farmers" or "share tenants," were essentially cultivators renting land and a house from a landlord. The tenant farmer provided the rest—the seed, equipment, a team of horses or mules, his own labor, and usually the labor of his wife and children as well. At the end of the harvest season, the tenant farmer would pay the landlord one-third of the grain and one-fourth of the cotton he and his family had cultivated during the year. Sometimes the landlord exacted a cash rent instead of payment in kind.

In contrast to these "regular" tenant farmers were those cultivators on halves, commonly known as "sharecroppers"; these were basically laborers who were compensated by payments in kind in lieu of cash wages. Under a halves agreement, the sharecropper furnished only his labor (and that of his family), for which he could keep one-half of the cotton cultivated on the acreage assigned him by the landlord. Generally, sharecroppers received considerably less land to cultivate than did tenants on thirds and fourths. Landlords usually provided about thirty acres, enough land for one team of horses or mules, per plow-hand. Mexican sharecroppers, on the other hand, were rarely given more than fifteen acres per plow-hand. According to one prominent cotton grower, landlords had an explicit idea of what was "too much" for the Mexican.[18]

While a picture of a local order divided into landowners and tenants can be visualized, it is somewhat more difficult to conceive of a society whose work force was constantly roving. Carey McWilliams provided a suggestive image—think of an "army of cotton pickers" that gathers strength as it travels to pick maturing cotton. In McWilliams' description: "From the lower valley, where the season starts, comes the initial vanguard of about 25,000 Mexican migratory workers. As the army marches through the Robstown–Corpus Christi area, an additional 25,000 recruits join the procession. By the time the army has reached central Texas, it has probably grown to about 250,000 to 300,000 workers. Recruits join the army, follow it through a county or two, and then drop out, to be replaced with new families from the next county."[19] McWilliams estimated that more than half of this migratory Mexican army made a round trip of nearly two thousand miles, all within the state, in an annual procession to find work.

In terms of "cheapness," there was very little difference between the actual earnings of Mexican sharecroppers and migrant laborers. Nonetheless, because croppers were under less supervision than wage hands, perhaps because they had a different relationship to the land and workplace, croppers were generally regarded as a higher class than wage laborers.[20]

The census data of this period do not allow a racial breakdown of the various farm classes. A rather evident pattern of segmentation along racial lines, nonetheless, suggests the composition of these classes. Abundant descriptive evidence, for example, discounts Mexican landowners as a significant class group in South Texas agricultural counties. In 1929, there were twenty-nine Mexican landowners in Nueces County, most of whom owned less than a hundred acres of land. In Dimmit County, there was a similar pattern.[21]

A close look at the historical record also uncovers a common tendency for Anglo landlords to contract Mexicans on halves and Anglos on thirds and fourths (or on a cash rent basis). In Nueces County, according to one local farmer, there were a few Mexicans on thirds and fourths, but very few—"not 5 percent of the county." In Frio County, on the edge of the Winter Garden, only 30 to 40 of the 397 *cuarteros* (share tenants) were Mexican while the 218 *medieros* (sharecroppers) were Mexican. Even in Central Texas, this pattern held. In Caldwell County, the county agent for the U.S. Farm Service estimated that, of the 2,300 tenants, 200 were Anglo, 450 were black, and the remaining 1,650 were Mexican. Ninety-five percent of the Mexican tenants were half in rents.[22]

Finally, there is little question about the identity of migratory farm labor. Approximately 96 percent of the 5,500 Mexicans in Crystal City were migratory. In Nueces County, where only 45 percent of the 52,000 residents were Mexican, they nonetheless constituted 97 percent of the local cotton supply; blacks made up the remaining 3 percent. The migratory labor force in the state, in fact, was overwhelmingly Mexican. In 1940 the Texas State Employment Service estimated on the basis of its experience and records that, of the 200,000 to 300,000 "full time" migrant laborers in Texas, 85 percent were Mexican, 10 percent were Anglo, and 5 percent were black.[23]

This type of segmentation among the rural classes allows a recasting of the census data within the social context of the Texas border region. Table 10, by considering the number of farm operators and laborers per 100 farms, highlights several points about the race-class structure in South Texas farm zones.[24]

Basically, the higher classes of owner-operator and share tenant (on thirds and fourths) were Anglo in composition, and the lower classes of sharecropper and farm laborers were Mexican. But interesting variations in the social structure according to farm zone are evident. There were wide differences in the number of tenants and laborers in the three farm zones, differences that suggest tenancy and migratory wage labor were alternative labor systems. The cotton belt, for example, had the highest concentration of tenants (69 of every 100

Table 10. *Farmers and Laborers in South Texas Farm Zones, 1930*

	Cotton[a]		Citrus[a]		Vegetables[a]	
	Per 100 Farms	Average Acreage	Per 100 Farms	Average Acreage	Per 100 Farms	Average Acreage
Owner-operators (Anglo)	31	253.2	53	73.2	67	1,685.3[b]
Share tenants (Anglo)	44	181.6	40	51.3	25	135.7
Sharecroppers (Mexican)	25	95.1	7	53.2	8	73.9
Farm laborers (Mexican)	172		239		1,430	
Total						
All operators	4,442		6,834		446[b]	
All laborers	7,620		16,316		6,363	

Source: Based on U.S. Department of Commerce, Bureau of the Census, Fifteenth Census of the United States: 1930, *Agriculture*, vol. III, part 2.
[a]Cotton: Nueces, Jim Wells, Kleberg, and Willacy counties; citrus: Cameron and Hidalgo counties; vegetables: Dimmit and Zavala counties.
[b]Includes 89 stock ranches.

farms were operated by share tenants or croppers) and the lowest concentration of farm laborers (172 for every 100 farms). In contrast, the Winter Garden counties of Dimmit and Zavala had the highest number of laborers (1,430 per 100 farms) and the lowest of tenants (33 per 100 farms). The citrus counties occupied an intermediate position.

The three zones had, to put it in another way, class structures of differing shapes. The cotton belt counties had a "middle sector" of tenants, of which Mexicans were a sizable number. The vegetable counties, on the other hand, were divided into two polar classes of Anglo farm owners and Mexican farm laborers. The citrus counties, with a middle sector composed mainly of Anglo tenants, displayed another variation in the way race and class were combined in the rural areas.

This, then, completes a composite description of the farm order of South Texas. From one-third to two-thirds of all farms were tended by Anglo owner-operators; the remainder were in the hands of non-propertied cultivators, who in turn were sharply divided between Anglo tenants on thirds and fourths and Mexican tenants on halves. During the picking season, a large transient Mexican labor force worked the farms, including those held by tenants.

Given these work arrangements, it is no surprise that South Texas farmers had a reputation as "drugstore farmers" who sat around town and let the "Mex" do the farming. The farmer, for his turn, believed the Anglo tenant depended too much on Mexican croppers and laborers. For Anglo tenants who subcontracted their rented land to Mexican sharecroppers, such dependency on Mexican labor was more often seen as a privilege, an advantage of living in South Texas, rather than a matter for derision.[25]

This local scenario could be drawn repeatedly for the agricultural counties of Texas; it represents the "mold" for South Texas as well as for Central and West Texas. In the greater border region, migrant work and sharecropping were essentially labor arrangements for Mexicans. Having described these arrangements in some detail, I can now discuss their significance for social relations between Anglo farmers and Mexican workers.

The Freedom of Wage Laborers

When South Texas entered the world of commercial agriculture the settlement patterns were shaped by land companies and labor agencies; the cultivation of specialty crops was largely determined by market demand. No other feature, however, points as dramatically to the commercialization of rural society than does the formation of a migratory Mexican labor force. In sharp contrast to the ranch counties, where labor needs were still satisfied through relatively stable, long-term arrangements, the requirements of commercial farming were met through temporary wage labor. Such seasonal contracts essentially made for impersonal, anonymous contacts between Anglo and Mexican. The words of a Dimmit County resident were directly to the point: "Many Americans come across the Mexicans only when they [Mexicans] are working for them, and then they [Americans] deal only with the [Mexican] contractor. Only twice a year do they have anything to do with them, at harvest and at transplanting. There is no occasion for social intercourse."[26]

Sharecropping, once an adequate way of anchoring labor to the land, was also no longer economically sound. Texas cotton farmers, as the Rural Land Owners Association declared, simply could not "support 12 months in the year the large amount of labor required for a few weeks only." Likewise, vegetable growers could "make more money by working the Mexicans than by leasing to them."[27] Ruth Allen, in her 1931 study of women in cotton production, reasoned that the future belongs to the hired farm laborer: "The opportunity to get rid of the overhead cost connected with the keeping of 'croppers' on the farm can be transferred to the social group, especially the town, by the use of hired labor." A survey conducted by the U.S. Farm Security Administration in 1936 in Karnes County likewise noted "the prevalence of sharecroppers as a source of wage labor." Of the 285 Mexican farm laborers interviewed, 99 were also cropping at the time, 42 had quit cropping within the previous year, and another 35 had cropping experience. Altogether, three-fifths of the Mexican farm workers were or had been sharecroppers.[28]

The decline of sharecropping in the region took place unevenly. In the cotton-growing counties, contracting sharecroppers on small parcels adjoining the landlord's farm was viewed as an excellent way of ensuring the availability of cheap resident labor throughout the year. Some landlord-farmers even calculated a ratio for the number of sharecroppers one needed according to the size of the farm. Nueces County farmers, for instance, figured that one Mexican cropper on 15 acres was "about right" for every 160 acres on their farms. Debt-peonage was not unknown. The mobility of some Mexican share-croppers was predicated on the willingness of a new landlord to assume the cropper's previous debt. One Dimmit County farmer described the practice in 1929: "They are generally always in debt; mine are always in debt. We pay them out when we take them over from somebody else to get them free. I paid $250 debt to get one Mexican, but this man has teams and is high class. I would not do it for a common *pelado*."[29] The more benevolent landlords arranged credit for their tenants, gave them "extra fruit from the orchard, a loaf of bread, or . . . children's old clothes." In return, the cropper family was expected to perform various chores and services for the landlord's family—keep house, do the laundry, tend to the farm animals, as well as undertake farm labor.[30]

In spite of such paternal exchanges, the sharecropper of the 1920s and 1930s was basically an adjunct to the emerging system of migratory wage labor. From the farmer's viewpoint, the Mexican tenant was expected to protect the landlord in dealings with migratory laborers. As one ex-northerner put it: "I put Pancho over my transient Mexicans in cotton picking. He knows them and I don't. He protects my interests. . . . Once he's attached to you, you never need worry; he'll defend you against all his kin."[31] The "permanent" sharecroppers served as the critical intermediaries between the Anglo *amo* (master) and an anonymous body of mobile Mexican workers.

The signs that paternalism was a dying element were present in the 1920s. Social relations between Anglo farmers and Mexican laborers in the new farm towns made this rather evident. When Mexican sharecroppers and other "regulars" ventured, as one historical account of Frio County puts it, "into the more impersonal, segregated towns of sheriffs, merchants, and *ricos* they apparently experienced more mistreatment than on their *ranchos.*"[32] Even on the *rancho*-farm, the paternal relationship between Anglo *patrones* and Mexican sharecroppers was a fragile one. As one Mexican tenant in Frio County described the situation: " . . . we were never close, not truly *compañeros* [close companions]. The *gringos* were only nice so we would work harder and stay with them until they no longer needed us. No, Mexicanos did not really like their *patrones*. And the *patrones* did not really like us. We were not bonded together like *la familia*. If we could have left we would. If the *gringos* didn't need us, they would have sent us away."[33] In the 1920s, in fact, it became commonplace to find sharecroppers expelled forcibly at the end of each harvest season. With the rise of a mobile work force, permanent sharecroppers became a liability, dispensable workers. The numerous cases of expulsion in the late 1920s presaged the impending collapse of sharecropping during the Great Depression.

The newcomer farmers were inclined to see the changes in labor arrangements as progressive ones. Contractual obligations, they noted in their favor, had replaced the "feudal" obligations of peonage. One cotton farmer in Nueces County described the matter eloquently to Paul Taylor:

> You can come down here and talk of subjection, but he's as free as a bird of the air. Don't come down here from the north and describe the poverty of the Mexicans at the back door of the white man's high civilization. Don't forget that he's an independent individual. There never lived a person in such freedom. All his work is by contract, no one drives him, he can stop any time and roll his shuck cigarette and Lobo tobacco, and his pay is by the weight at the scales. There's no arrogance, there's no oppression. The normal battle of supply and demand takes place every year.[34]

In the course of this normal battle, landless Mexicans now followed the brief seasons of various crops, exercising their newly granted "freedom" to negotiate. In the 1930s, for example, Crystal City families cut spinach from November through April, worked onions from April through May, and then topped beets or picked cotton from May through November, when the whole cycle would start over again. The importance of the contract surfaces clearly when one looks closely at the work activity of Mexicans in any one period of this migrant cycle. The nature of winter garden farming, as in the spinach area of Crystal City, required a large surplus labor force that could be rushed to the fields one day and withdrawn or transferred to other fields the next. In the course of a single day, Mexican field crews might find themselves working for three or more employers. Such contract labor was ideally suited to meet the needs of a seasonal labor-intensive agricultural economy.[35]

Frequently, these needs were not directly related to the harvest season but were the result of market price fluctuations. Either peak market prices or rapidly declining prices could prompt growers to rush the harvest of their crops. Such market considerations, in fact, were responsible for one of the more perplexing themes in the region's agricultural history—the fear of "labor shortages." There were conflicting reports on this point in the 1920s, primarily because farmers and local authorities regularly claimed evidence of "labor shortages." Ample information concerning cotton cultivation in this period allows one to construct hypothetical estimates that illustrate the nature of the problem.[36]

Nueces County, one of the leading cotton counties in Texas, provides a good model for calculating the size of the migratory work force required for a harvest. In the 1920s good cotton land yielded approximately 170 pounds of cotton per acre and a "good picker" could pick about 200 pounds of seed cotton (*algodón limpio*) per day. At this rate, an average-sized farm (269 acres) in Nueces could be worked by a crew of 25 "good Mexican pickers" in about two weeks, not counting Saturdays and Sundays. Over a ten-week picking season, five farms could be worked by one crew of 25 good pickers. Theoretically, then, the 500 owner-operated farms of Nueces required 100 crews, each with 25 workers, or approximately 2,500 laborers altogether. This figure, however, greatly underestimates the actual number of Mexican laborers who worked in Nueces County, because as a rule most cotton growers wanted their cotton picked immediately. Particularly when the timing of market sales was important, a situation might arise where all 500 farm owners desired to have their cotton picked in the same week of the season. Such a situation, a common one in a speculative year, would require a force of 25,000 laborers.

These hypothetical estimates provide an approximate idea of the great size of the seasonal labor force needed to work one Texas cotton county. The great range between these two estimates, moreover, suggests that "labor shortages" were quite relative matters. These were indications not so much of the actual number of laborers in the area but of market conditions that moved farmers to have their cotton picked at a certain time. The possibility of a shortage at a critical point in the season was a source of considerable anxiety for the commercial farmer. It was sufficiently bothersome, as we will see, to move him to devise ways that could immobilize the Mexican worker.

In the farm counties, the peonage of the ranch variety was rare, but other forms of control and coercion more appropriate to a system of migratory wage labor emerged. These practices and conditions, sometimes also described as "peonage" by contemporaries of the period, had a distinct seasonal character. In some places in Texas, to cite one example, it was customary to invoke vagrancy laws at the beginning of cotton picking season.[37] Especially in times of feared labor "shortages," the mechanism of arrest served to force laborers to work for wages for the two weeks or so necessary to pick the farmers' cotton. This practice in one South Texas county went so far as to assume the characteristics of a pass system. Thus, the controls of commercial agriculture had a very different character from those of cattle ranch areas; in the farm areas, they were basically a means for regulating the movement of wage laborers.

A Concluding Note

In the formation of the segregated farm society, the ethnocentric and prejudiced sentiments of the Anglo newcomers played a highly visible role, as a later chapter will discuss. As an analytical point of departure, however, considerable attention must be given the class structure and relations of the farm order. In this context, Mexicans were primarily a ready supply of laborers and Mexican towns were fundamentally "labor camps."

The place of Mexicans as farm labor surfaced clearly in the opinion and explanation surrounding two central issues of the time—the matter of Mexican immigration and the question of Mexican schooling. By reviewing this opinion and explanation closely, the interests that directed the segregation of Anglos and Mexicans will become clear. The design of segregationist policies in the farm counties, from educational programs to residential codes, drew its force from the need to regulate and maintain a reservoir of cheap Mexican labor.

8. The Mexican Problem

the solution: Mexicas kept in agric labor, out of industry [handwritten annotation]

IN THE midst of the confident and ambitious mood that accompanied the sweeping agricultural transformation of Texas and the greater Southwest lingered a somber realization—a hesitant, reluctant acknowledgment of a significant Mexican presence. The recognition was necessarily ambivalent: the rapid development of the region was dependent on Mexican labor, yet this type of labor brought with it unknown and potentially troublesome social costs. Politicians, educators, and concerned citizens warned that Mexicans were the cause of political corruption and fraud, the destruction of homogeneous rural communities, labor problems, crime, and disease, among other social problems.[1] What was to be done with the Mexican?

There were opposing views on the question. Growers argued that the feared social costs of Mexican immigration could be regulated; small farmers and workers, on the other hand, predicted the "undoing" of America. The end result, after a decade of frequently bitter discussion, was a compromise—Mexicans were to be kept in the fields and out of industry. The proper place for Mexicans in modern Texas was that of farm laborers.

No Place for Mexicans?

The discussion of the Mexican question was not exactly new. A similar discussion, carried publicly in national magazines and major newspapers, had occurred immediately in the aftermath of annexation. The solution of the period lay in the optimistic faith that the backward Mexican race would disappear before the energetic Anglo-Saxon. Labor economist Victor Clark, for example, referring to physicians who believed that the Mexican race had "low powers of resistance" to disease, noted in 1908 that "the impression of Americans here [Los Angeles] and in the Territories [Arizona and New Mexico] accords with the opinions given from Colorado, that the American-born Mexicans are a decadent race, yielding before the physically more vigorous immigrants from Europe and the East."[2] The prediction never came to pass, although it was widely held among Anglo-

Americans in the Southwest. The great increase in Mexican immigration, in any case, made such beliefs irrelevant. In 1910–1919,
173,663 Mexicans immigrated to the United States, compared to
only 23,991 for the previous decade. In 1920–1929, the number
of Mexicans crossing into the United States rose dramatically to
487,775.[3] The Mexican presence again commanded the attention of
the Anglo.

Warnings about the dire consequences of Mexican immigration
appeared rather regularly in the popular and academic literature of
the early twentieth century. University professors, ministers, social
workers, politicians, and eugenicists warned of grave social problems; some even envisioned an ominous clash between blacks and
Mexicans for "second place" in Anglo-American society. In a 1921
issue of the *Annals of the American Academy,* Congressman James
Slayden of San Antonio criticized growers and businessmen for failing to look "beyond the next cotton crop or the betterment of railway
lines."[4] As Slayden put it, "large planters short of labor . . . welcome
the Mexican immigrants as they would welcome fresh arrivals from
the Congo, without a thought of the social and political embarrass-
ment to their country." Substituting the Mexican for the black,
moreover, was "jumping from the frying pan into the fire." What this
might mean, Slayden concluded, "no one can tell. Probably our
safety and peace lie in the fact that as yet so few of them, comparatively, are coming."

Slayden's assessment of the situation, however, came before the
"deluge" of Mexican immigrants in the 1920s. As they kept coming,
and in increasing numbers, the outcry about social decay reached
near-hysterical levels. Eugenicists pointed out with alarm that Mexicans were not only intellectually inferior—they were also quite
"fecund." Imaginative calculations were formulated to drive home
the point. C. M. Goethe, president of the Immigration Study Commission, speaking of a Los Angeles Mexican with thirty-three children, figured that "it would take 14,641 American fathers . . . at a
three-child rate, to equal the descendants of this one Mexican father
four generations hence."[5] One journalist who traveled through
the midwestern and Rocky Mountain states in 1926 reported that
this type of hysteria—what he called "statistical terrorism"—had
gripped the region. "Nearly every streetcorner nativist could prove,"
wrote the journalist tongue in cheek, that "the last Nordic family in
the republic will have to choose between starvation and emigration
to Greenland on or about October 17, 2077 A.D."[6]

The same message was presented in the popular literature by other
"experts" on the subject of Mexicans. The Reverend Robert McLean,

for example, in a highly recommended "first-hand account" of life among Mexicans in the Southwest, conveyed his reservations about the "average Juan Garcia" through a colorful homily: "But this *chili con carne!!* Always it seems to give Uncle Sam the heart-burn; and the older he gets, the less he seems to be able to assimilate it. Indeed it is a question whether *chili* is not a condiment to be taken in small quantities rather than a regular article of diet."[7] All the law and prophets, concluded the Reverend McLean, ought to hang on this dietary lesson so far as Mexican immigration was concerned. Uncle Sam simply had no stomach for Juan García.

In short, the Mexican problem had nothing to do with integration or assimilation; rather, it was a question of locating another inferior race in American society. There was general agreement, in Texas and elsewhere, that Mexicans were not a legitimate citizenry of the United States. They were outside the civic order, and references to American national integrity and Texas history were often ill-disguised claims of Anglo supremacy. A comparison with the "Negro problem" seemed natural.

In Texas, where most Mexican immigrants went, the discussion about Mexicans was especially sharp and intense. As early as 1916, University of Texas Professor William Leonard had predicted that the coming of Mexicans would have disastrous effects for rural Texas. Already community life was dying "a lingering death" and whole neighborhoods were "slowly passing into decay." Leonard, a newcomer from the Midwest, described the nature of the problem as follows: "Society in the Southwest cannot easily adapt itself to the handling of a second racial problem . . . for Mexican immigrants, there is no congenial social group to welcome them. . . . They are not Negroes. . . . They are not accepted as white men, and between the two, the white and the black, there seems to be no midway position."[8] The same position was argued by Texas sociologist Max Handman in a 1930 issue of the *American Journal of Sociology.* American society simply had no place for "partly colored races." What might result from this, Handman conceded, he was not sure—"but I know that it may mean trouble."[9] Texas labor historian Ruth Allen, in another commentary of the period, voiced a similar concern eloquently: "When the Negro had begun to rise out of the semi-peonage of the one-crop farm and a vicious credit system, we brought across the Rio Grande horde after horde of Mexican peons even more ignorant and helpless than the Negro. One can only marvel at the temerity of a people who, faced with the gravest race question of all time, have injected into their civilization a second group, alien in background and language, and not readily assimilable."[10] Allen ended her rather grim assessment by saying that Anglo-Saxons must face the race problem or "let the Negro and the Mexican take upon us a terrible vengeance for years of exploitation, deprivation, and oppression."

If Mexicans were a racial menace, an unassimilable alien presence, why increase their ranks by encouraging immigration? Class interests divided the Anglo population into opposed positions on the issue.

The Debate over Mexican Immigration

There were major disagreements among Anglos on the course that economic development should take and what social costs were acceptable. Generally speaking, growers and their business allies held that Mexican labor was necessary for continued growth and thus favored an "open border" with Mexico. The other side, composed of working farmers and urban workers, claimed that Anglo labor and small farmers could develop the area and called for a closed border and for repatriation of those Mexicans already in the Southwest. The stand of merchants and businessmen in this debate depended on the composition of their clientele. Most bankers and big businessmen saw their fortunes tied with the success of commercial farming and thus usually aligned themselves behind the growers. A minority opinion, however, apparently the view of retailers and others dependent on the local domestic trade, held that agribusiness threatened to ruin the country and that small, diversified farming should be the model to pursue. These opposed views of development provided the framework for approaching most major political and social issues, including those dealing with the Mexican presence.

Indispensable Laborers

Through the 1920s national policy making was decidedly in favor of agribusiness interests in the Southwest. Although the restrictionist immigration acts of 1917, 1921, and 1924 had effectively barred immigration from certain sections of Europe and Asia, growers and other southwestern employers had successfully lobbied to have Mexico (under the guise of the "Western Hemisphere") exempted or excluded. The results for working farmers in Texas were disastrous. In Central Texas, tenant farming was on the point of total collapse, and tenant farmers in South and West Texas recognized that the same fate was in store for them.[11]

Not surprisingly, many Texans were quite conscious of "a gulf between classes" on the issue of Mexican immigration. Sociologist Charles Hufford, in a 1929 survey of West Texas ranchers, farmers, and tenant farmers, provided some measure of the class-related differences. Of the forty-four ranchers and farmers interviewed, thirty-three believed their business to be favorably affected by Mexican labor and thirty-five thought Mexican labor to be satisfactory. Tenant farmers thought otherwise. Of the twenty-two surveyed, fifteen believed Mexican laborers to be an unfavorable influence, and eighteen believed them to be inefficient.[12] In South Texas the division of opinion ran along similar lines. Anglo working farmers and wage laborers did not hesitate to place the blame for the Mexican problem on the grower: "The small farmer and laboring man wishes the Mexicans were out of the country. The big grafting man fancies them; they work cheaper." Small cotton farmers and Anglo cotton pickers were unanimously against further immigration of Mexican laborers, denied that Anglo laborers would not pick cotton, and emphasized the prevailing low wages—"Mexican wages"—of the area.[13] Even the working farmers, however, were compelled to hire Mexicans because, as another tenant explained, they could only afford to pay Mexican wages: "A lot of white men would come down from the north and set onions, but they can't do it at Mexican prices, and we can't afford to pay more at the present prices of onions. At smaller acreages and better prices we could pay white men's wages. Nearly any working man would do any of this work if he got a white man's price. Millionaires are ruining the working man."[14] One Anglo laborer in Nueces County expressed the common sentiment of his class when he told Taylor he wished the Mexicans could be put back in their own country. "Of course," added the laborer, "it is to the interest of the wealthy to have them here, and they run the government."[15]

The growers, of course, disagreed. "Without the Mexican," one West Texas grower noted, "the laboring class of white people, what there is, would demand their own wages and without doing half the labor the Mexican does." Or as one Nueces County grower put the familiar argument, "We big farmers can produce cheaper than the family on 100 acres."[16] Mexicans, in any case, were well suited to perform the task of agricultural labor. Nueces County cotton growers were lavish in their praise of the Mexican's qualities as field labor: "You can't beat them as labor." "I prefer Mexican labor to other classes of labor. It is more humble and you get more for your money." "The Mexicans have a sense of duty and loyalty, and the qualities that go to make a good servant." "They are the best labor

Mexican cotton pickers bound for Corpus Christi, 1929 (Taylor, *American-Mexican Frontier*, p. 102).

we have." "No other class we could bring to Texas could take his place. He's a natural farm laborer." [17]

The position of businessmen on the question of Mexican immigration depended on whether they were tied in some way with agribusiness or were "independent." Those merchants with grower connections understood that a low-wage, mobile labor force was necessary to continue farm development in the region and thus supported unrestricted immigration. When confronted with the negative consequences of unrestricted immigration, such as the presence of large, conspicuous Mexican settlements, these progrower merchants were quick to defend the Mexicans and to point out their positive qualities. Much like the growers who praised the Mexicans for their qualities as laborers, merchants were likely to comment on the positive qualities of Mexican buying habits. One merchant in South Texas, for example, explained to Taylor why he preferred Mexican immigration over that of European stock: "Let me tell you that the Mexicans buy out of the stores of South Texas more John B. Stetson hats than the whites; they don't think anything of paying $16 for a hat. I don't want the damn Sicilians to come in." [18]

In contrast, most independent retailers sensitive to the buying habits and spending power of their Mexican clientele were well aware that farm development placed critical limits on the growth of a domestic market. It was not difficult to see, when Mexicans constituted a significant portion of the retail trade, that unrestricted immigration had serious consequences for the store. Thus, independent retailers generally opposed continued Mexican immigration, advocated the diversification of the farm economy, and even proposed the paying of higher wages to the present work force. A controversial statement circulated by the Laredo Chamber of Commerce spoke to the point: "We have got about as far as we can with cheap labor. . . . Our merchants have no trading territory. Labor with $1.25 wages can't buy." After characterizing South Texas farmers as "onion speculators" who live in hotels, the statement went on to call for an alternative to big agribusiness: "What we need is more white farmers and more capital, and we can't go ahead until we get them. We don't need more cheap labor. We should not drive out our own labor in the North to provide ourselves with cheap labor here." [19] The Laredo chamber was somewhat of a "maverick" business organization in South Texas, a characteristic that can be attributed, in part, to the powerful position of merchants in that border city. In border counties with no major trading center, however, only the Anglo merchants serving the Mexican trade, Anglos who were already marginal in any case, would openly espouse the Laredo position. In areas where growers had both the money and the power, most businessmen supported the dominant line.[20] Thus, the Laredo statement was quickly repudiated by other South Texas businessmen. The president of the Del Rio Chamber of Commerce said that the Laredo chamber president did not understand the situation in the farm counties because he was an oil man who used high-priced labor and not "this cheap labor." Thus, concluded the Del Rio businessman, "he does not represent us." To stress the point, the Del Rioan added that the secretary of the Laredo chamber, the apparent author of the statement, was married to a Mexican woman.[21]

As the 1920s wore on, the line between the opposing sides was drawn fairly clearly. Restrictionists counted small farmers, progressives, labor unionists, and eugenicists among their ranks; the antirestrictionists, meanwhile, were spearheaded by large-scale growers, railroad executives, and businessmen.[22] The conflicting economic interests of the two sides were quite evident, but the immigration question also raised the question of "national integrity" so far as race was concerned.

The Social Costs of Immigration

What gave the national and regional discussion of Mexican immigration its highly charged, controversial character stemmed from the social and political implications involved. European and Asian immigration had been barred in large part for such nationalist reasons, and the same reasoning dictated that Mexican immigration be stopped.

Those opposed to Mexican immigration repeatedly emphasized, with great effect, the moral and political dangers presented by Mexicans. In the 1920 congressional debates over immigration policy, Representative John C. Box from East Texas, then still a stronghold for small Anglo farmers, warned the House about the perils of "de-Americanization" and of a "hyphenated citizenship," as well as the dangers of political unrest, for the people who were coming from Mexico and Europe "have not been trained in the schools of order but have stewed in disorder." Importing this type of labor, moreover, would change the "relationship and spirit of American industrial life . . . to the undoing of America." "We want no peasant or peon or coolie class nor caste system," added Box, "dividing us into an upper and lower world."[23]

Those who defended the policy of unrestricted Mexican immigration, the antirestrictionists, understood well the talk about the social ills presented by the Mexican race. When it came to assessing

the Mexican, in fact, Texas growers outdid the Anglo nativists supporting the Box Bill. The president of the Ysleta Farm Bureau in West
Texas, for example, was curt but straightforward when asked for his
opinion of Mexicans: "The Chilis are creatures somewhere in between a burro and a human being."[24] But, added the agribusinessman,
"We would hate to lose this junk we've got now." The Ysleta bureau
accordingly had passed a resolution against the Box Bill. Growers
throughout Texas generally found themselves in the same dilemma—
not fond of Mexicans but heavily dependent on them for labor.
"More Mexicans are not best for the country," one Nueces cotton
grower told Taylor; "it isn't good for the country because we expect
to live here." Paul Taylor, sensing the irony of the grower's position,
asked why he wanted unrestricted immigration if he did not want to
associate with Mexicans. Because, answered the grower, "We can
never get the whites to live and work as we have it here. The whites
who would work on halves would not be any good. You could not
handle them as easily." One Dimmit County resident, nonplussed
by Taylor's probing questions, failed to see any contradiction in his
position: "We don't want them to be associated with us, we want
them for labor. I don't know how we would get along without Mexican labor."[25] Another Dimmit County resident said that they "would
be blowed up" if Mexicans were stopped from coming, and that they
could keep things under control; but still he was worried: "They
don't vote, but they increase like rats. If something is not done we
will soon be shoved out of the picture. There ought to be a law
passed that every (white) married couple should have so many children and if they don't, they ought to find out why."[26]

Such considerations had moved a few growers to support restrictionist legislation and to encourage diversification, but economic interests generally outweighed social principles. One farmer summed
up the situation nicely. His principles, as he explained to Taylor,
ruled out Mexican immigration because Mexicans "haven't the mentality" of Anglos and "are an inferior race." But principles are one
thing and interests another, noted the farmer: "My principles rule
my selfishness, but I am kind of weak on that. We need them and
they need us."[27]

The antirestrictionists, then, were quite mindful of the possible
social consequences of continued Mexican immigration. As a rule,
however, they felt confident that they could control the situation—
and in a manner that would satisfy both social principles and economic needs. Agribusinessmen, after all, only wanted laborers, not
neighbors or fellow citizens. To those who warned of dire consequences, the progrower politicians presented the familiar argument

that strict measures could be taken to guarantee that Mexican agricultural laborers would not "wander off" into other work or stay beyond the term of the harvest.[28] In one memorable exchange before a congressional committee in 1926, for example, restrictionist Robert L. Bacon of New York pointed out to the progrower witness from Corpus Christi, S. Matson Nixon, that nearly half his district was Mexican and that a high proportion of these were voters. The New York congressman then asked Mr. Nixon for his opinion of that type of situation. Nixon handled the delicate question rather well:

> Mr. Nixon: I think that they [the Mexicans] offer excellent material for American citizenship. . . . I believe I can truthfully say that American civilization and American ideals are as high in Texas as any state in the United States.
> Mr. Bacon: That is what I am in favor of. I am in favor of keeping Texas white.
> Mr. Nixon: That is all right. But I think Texans who are thoroughly familiar with Mexican influence feel satisfied that they are fully capable of maintaining their superiority over the Mexican.[29]

There was no contradiction in having Mexican American citizens and in safeguarding the Anglo-Saxon character of Texas and the United States. One distinguished professional man from Corpus Christi explained to Taylor how the two were reconcilable: "If the Mexicans came in and demanded social equality the case would be entirely different. But the Mexicans have sense, and innate courtesy, and they don't demand social equality like the Negro. There never will be any race question with the Mexicans."[30] A cotton grower from the same county appraised the Mexicans in similar terms: "They are docile and law-abiding. They are the sweetest people in this position that I ever saw."[31] Unlike the alarmist nativists, then, growers and their allies were not overly worried about any Mexican menace. Their modest proposals, which were essential for the continued development of the region, would not jeopardize Anglo-American society.

A Compromise: Keeping Mexicans in Agriculture

By 1930 the decay that so many had predicted had progressed beyond hope, and the social commentaries about the Mexican in Texas were no longer warnings but eulogies and resigned statements of fact.

Writing in 1930 University of Texas Professor Robert Montgomery described the changes in rural life as "a sad chapter in the history of the state." Speaking of a typical Central Texas town, fictitiously named Keglar Hill, Montgomery portrayed its fate after the coming of Mexicans as follows: "Keglar Hill, as a way of life, was one with Carthage and Thebes. The Nordic-American tenants, who for twenty years had tilled the farms, . . . had educated their children in school and church, and had contributed fairly to the building of a healthy and pleasant community, were uprooted utterly."[32] Through the early twentieth century, this story of Keglar Hill, a story about the displacement of Anglo tenant farmers by Mexican sharecroppers and laborers, repeated itself throughout Central, West, and South Texas. Anglo tenant farmers and laborers, of course, understood what was happening. With the matter of land tenure completely in the hands of the landlord, it was only a question of time before the switch to the "cheaper" Mexicans came. One West Texas tenant summed up the situation in 1928 as follows: "Mexican labor forces our farm boys to the cities. Mexicans take their work at a rate lower than American boys can live at. A few more years will give it all over to the Mexicans."[33]

Away from the fields, the situation of the Anglo nonfarm worker was not much different. The position of most Anglo workers, if one judges from the statements and actions of organized labor, was completely unsympathetic to Mexicans. Not only were more Mexicans coming every year, reported one worried labor official to the AFL Executive Council in 1919, but they also were now moving out of agriculture and accepting employment in "different lines of efforts" to the detriment of labor standards and the best interests of the country. In Texas, the state chapter of the AFL refused to recognize the existence of a wage-earning class in agriculture, and its various affiliates made it clear that they would not work alongside Mexicans and that they opposed the hiring of unskilled Mexican workers.[34] Texas oil workers, many of them ex-cowboys and ex-tenants, were likewise quite upset about the "immigrant increase" in the industry. At the convention of the International Oil Workers in 1920, the oil unions passed a resolution asking for "an investigation of the situation, the sending back to Mexico of immigrants illegally in the United States, and return to agricultural work of those remaining." In some oil fields, the tense situation exploded into riots against Mexicans. In 1921, oil workers in the Ranger and Island Oil fields in Mexia (North Central Texas) clubbed and threatened Mexican workers and their families with death unless they left within twelve hours. Governor Pat Neff imposed martial law in Mexia and sent eighty state troopers to end the brutalities. The Rangers arrived too late, however, to save several women and children from dying of exposure.[35] This was no isolated incident; similar episodes occurred in mines and manufacturing plants through the 1940s.

The overwhelming sentiment among nonfarm workers, organized and unorganized, was for the expulsion or regulation of Mexican workers. Already by the early 1920s, many unions in the Southwest had formulated "gentlemen's agreements" to blackball all Mexican workers. Texas unions handled Mexican workers in much the same way that they dealt with blacks: through outright exclusion, through segregated locals, and through racial quotas in employment. As the decade wore on, these exclusionary proposals became more strident as organized labor joined eugenicist associations in decrying the "alien" danger that Mexicans posed for the nation. The political direction provided by the American labor movement pointed clearly toward maintaining skilled work as a preserve for Anglo workers. Especially in Texas, Anglo workers saw the "color bar" as an important concession to be won from employers.[36]

And so on went the regional and national debates on Mexican immigration through the 1920s. The progrower interests, with their considerable influence in Congress, were able to defeat the restrictionist efforts repeatedly. By the end of the decade, however, the restrictionists had built a strong national movement and had found an unexpected ally in President Herbert Hoover. In 1928 executive orders to enforce existing immigration law effectively closed the border, and the president and Congress appeared stalemated, at least momentarily, on the Mexican issue.

It was perhaps fitting that a compromise solution to this stalemate should come from Texas in the form of a proposal to "restrain" the movement of its Mexican workers to state boundaries. This proposal, embodied in the Emigrant Labor Agency Laws of 1929, received the endorsement of both the AFL and the chambers of commerce of the state.[37] Such significant consensus was not difficult to understand; the labor agency laws represented the first step to deal with the mutual interests of Anglo workers and growers. Organized labor in the state was ready to concede agriculture to Mexicans—an already accomplished fact by this time—if it could work out some arrangement that would protect the status of nonfarm workers. Texas growers, for their part, found themselves competing with major out-of-state interests for Mexican labor and were amenable to a plan that would keep Mexicans in the fields and out of industry.

For the farm counties, the end result was that agricultural labor became defined as "Mexican work." One Dimmit County resident put the matter clearly: "Onion transplanting is distinctly the work of Mexicans. There are quite a few whites who would do it and who need the work, but they are too proud to do it because it classes them as onion setters."[38] A ranch manager in the same county agreed and provided an example: "The Americans can usually get something better, for example, filling station work. My brother took $1 a day there rather than $1.50 from my father on the farm." A Nueces County farmer remarked similarly that "when some whites see Mexicans doing farm work, they don't want to do it." And in West Texas, according to one tenant farmer, tenants opposed Mexican labor "because you have to work with them."[39] Other reports from farmers and workers throughout the state repeatedly point to the sensitivity of Anglos to these matters of race and class.

Separate and Subordinate

Keep Mexicans ignorant;

Nowhere was the intent of farm settlers to build separate institutions for the races clearer than in the "Mexican school" system they constructed. The farm settlers understood well the potentially corrosive force of "educating Mexicans" for the maintenance of their divided world. The divisions of the racial order made little sense if Mexicans were "better educated" than some Anglos or if both were "mixed" in school. Educating the Mexican also raised the danger that Mexicans might seek "social equality"—a possibility, according to many well-placed sources, feared by lower-class Anglos but discounted by the "higher-ups" who knew better. But again, as in the discussion about Mexican immigration, the key element in Mexican school policy was the concern of farmers in securing and controlling farm labor. If farmers were to keep this labor reservoir, Mexicans had to be kept ignorant. On this point, in the late 1920s, there was no need for school officials and farmers to be less than explicit.

While there was no comprehensive plan that made for a Mexican school system, the various efforts of farm settlers in effect accomplished the same results. Where local districts first allowed a few Mexicans to attend public schools with Anglo children, the opposition of Anglo parents soon overturned such ill-considered policy. The protest of Anglo parents of Pharr–San Juan in Hidalgo County in 1919, for example, led the Pharr board to transfer its Mexican school children to a nearby "Mexican church"; the Anglo citizens had arranged to have the Catholic church used as a Mexican school.

And in Valley Wells (Dimmit County), where they first admitted Mexicans, the "antagonism of the older generation" stopped the practice. Similar protests in other communities likewise influenced school trustees to create a Mexican school or, better yet, to avoid any public expenditures on Mexican schooling. In some districts, local policy restricted Mexican children to an elementary education. In the West Texas school districts of Pecos and Sonora, for example, there was a standing policy of not allowing Mexicans beyond the sixth grade. In the Bishop district of South Texas, Mexicans who wished to attend high school had to do so in neighboring districts.[40]

The results for Mexican schooling, that which existed, were evident. Mexican schools were substandard, with inadequate supplies and poor facilities. Their Anglo teachers, who frequently shared the common Anglo belief about Mexican biological and intellectual inferiority, received lower salaries than teachers at the "American schools." School enrollment and attendance were never encouraged. Although state aid was determined on the number of school-age children in the district (thus assuring that all districts would count their Mexican school-age children), school boards had developed a practice of spending the overwhelming share of these monies on the "American schools." Although these local practices and policies were violations of Texas law, state officials generally did not intervene because, as one local school official explained, they understood quite well that the counties were dealing with "the lower element."[41]

In the absence of a statutory plan, the segregationist policy manifested itself in acts ranging from everyday administrative staff decisions to the informal opinions and formal decisions of school trustees.[42] Those entrusted with administering the separate schools had few difficulties in creating appropriate policies and explanations for the handling of the Mexican problem. School authorities usually relied on a combination of pedagogical and popular sociological explanations to justify the Mexican school situation—mental retardation, language problems, poor hygiene, health reasons, failure to appreciate education, inherent inferiority, and so on. But all of these "scientific explanations," in the rather frank opinion of one school trustee, were beside the point: "It isn't a matter of what is the best way to handle the education here to make citizens of them. It is politics. That is the way we excuse what we do." And politics in the farm counties, the trustee explained, meant that the Mexican school policy was influenced by the needs of local growers: "We don't need skilled or white-collared Mexicans. . . . The farmers are not interested in educating the Mexicans. They know that then they can get better wages and conditions. There isn't a concerted effort against them but the white-collar man is not a common laborer."[43]

School administrators had to be conscious of the position of the school board with respect to Mexicans. As one Nueces County superintendent sympathetic to Mexican education noted, his board "won't let me enforce compulsory attendance": "When I come to a new school I always ask the board if they want the Mexicans in school. Here they told me to leave them alone. If I tried to enforce the compulsory attendance law here the board would get sore at me and maybe cause us to lose our places, so I don't say anything. If I got 150 Mexicans ready for school I would be out of a job."[44] Generally, however, school superintendents needed little prodding to establish an appropriate Mexican policy. Some sounded much like onion growers themselves. One superintendent of a segregated school district, for example, explained the situation in the following manner: "You have doubtless heard that ignorance is bliss; it seems that it is so when one has to transplant onions. . . . If a man has very much sense or education either, he is not going to stick to this kind of work. So you see it is up to the white population to keep the Mexican on his knees in an onion patch or in new ground. This does not mix very well with education."[45]

The growers, of course, were quite straightforward about their educational philosophy regarding Mexicans. The sentiment of a Dimmit County grower was representative: "Educating the Mexicans is educating them away from the job, away from the dirt. He learns English and wants to be a boss. He doesn't want to grub."[46] Another Winter Garden farmer expressed the same opinion in more elaborate fashion. "They should be taught something, yes. But the more ignorant they are, the better laborers they are. The law which keeps them out if they can't read [the literary test] keeps out the best laborers and lets in the worst. If these get educated, we'll have to get more from Mexico."[47] Another onion grower was worried about the farm labor situation because "there is a movement of our Mexican north, and education of Mexicans takes them out of manual labor." Conditions were becoming critical. "We have got to have a class of people who will do this kind of labor," the grower emphasized to Taylor; "if we can't have the Mexicans, it will stop all this development."[48]

Unlike the immigration issue that revealed the class tensions within the Anglo community, the Mexican school question evoked no significant dissent or controversy. Anglo workers, for their part, were not troubled by the fact that growers wanted to keep Mexicans ignorant and in the fields; such policies limited competition with Mexican laborers. There was also the touchy question of equality, a question that made lower-class Anglos feel uneasy. Unlike the confident growers and businessmen, the Anglo workers were quite conscious of having to assert their superiority over the Mexicans. The blunt statement of an American sharecropper was representative: "Why don't we let the Mexicans come to the white school? Because a damned greaser is not fit to sit side of a white girl."[49] Anglos from higher classes, aware of the uneasiness of the poor Anglos, frequently commented on the tension. A Dimmit County education officer noted in this regard: "The lower down the white man is the more he will object to the Mexicans. The higher class whites object less. The lower class white feels that the Mexican who is educated will try to be equal to him. The higher class American knows that going to the same school doesn't imply equality."[50] A "high class" Anglo in Nueces County corroborated this kind of observation, pointing out that the failure of Mexicans to progress in schools was due to the prejudice that came "chiefly from ignorant Americans who are not sure of their footing."[51]

The only segment of the Anglo community to be affected adversely by the growers' education philosophy was the merchants serving the Mexican trade. Again, it was the Laredo Chamber of Commerce, speaking for this group, that took a solitary position and advocated schooling for Mexicans: "We got to educate the children. They are now holding back the progress of our children in the schools."[52] Pragmatic grounds for Mexican schooling existed. William J. Knox, a San Antonio educator (and well-known old-timer), outlined the arguments in 1915: the current approach to Mexican schooling—where you count them for the scholastic census, but refuse to educate them—was a short-sighted policy as a "business proposition." The Mexican who finds himself and his family in communities where they are not wanted, and where the children are not provided schooling, "packs up his little wagon, takes his little fund and goes to the town or city where he and his are given a fair chance. Many a little town had lost good, steady labor and quite a good cash trade in that they have failed to see the business advantage of a neat, up-to-date school for its Mexican ward."[53] Knox had made precisely that point to the businessmen of a small town some years before and, after some reflection on the matter, they "built a splendid school for their Mexican ward."

Unfortunately for Mexicans, Knox's reasoning contained serious flaws. The business proposition, as noted earlier, generally led growers and their town associates to oppose Mexican education. "As long as the attitude of the people who control Mexican labor controls the schools," concluded one superintendent, "little will be done, not until a few generations come and then demand it."[54]

A Concluding Note

As the immigration and school questions make clear, the construction of a segregated farm society did not consist of a single set of policies; nor did it follow a unilinear and determined course. On the contrary, the discussion of the Mexican problem among Anglos suggests different tendencies and points to different directions, even within the context of race supremacy. There were, in other words, various strategies for handling inferior races; which strategy was favored depended on the particular economic interests of class segments within the Anglo community. For growers and their allies, development meant importation and repression of Mexican laborers; for Anglo working farmers and wage laborers, development meant containment and exclusion of Mexicans. Although merchants generally sided with one of these two positions, a third tendency emerges if the situation of the retailer dependent on the Mexican trade is considered. Such businessmen were concerned about developing an internal market, an interest that sometimes led them to challenge both plans of separate development. This mercantile concern often gave Anglo merchants in the Texas border region a "progressive" outlook on race relations but, as will be discussed later, this was by no means a consistent outcome. Merchants always followed their best interests when it came to political matters.

This sheds light on one aspect of the complex social order. The diversity in local conditions owed much to these class-related divisions within the Anglo community. Put another way, whether Mexicans could vote, go to school, eat in restaurants, and so on depended to a considerable degree on the class composition of the Anglo community. Where Anglo merchants had a powerful independent voice, as in Laredo and other urban areas, the racial order tended to be less abrasive. Working farmers and laborers, on the other hand, made clear that they wished Mexicans could be put back into their own country, a sentiment that sometimes exploded in pogroms and expulsions of Mexicans in local areas. But in the 1920s and 1930s, the growers were in command. The new farm society that emerged was their world, constructed according to their social principles and economic needs. The duality of the farm society, in this sense, not only reflected the superiority of the Anglo-American but also served to preserve a cheap Mexican labor force. This, then, was the proper place of Mexicans in Texas. Outside the social order but a necessary part of it, Mexicans were attached to the new agricultural society through the construction of separate and subordinate institutions that rigidly defined their position as farm laborers.

9. *The Web of Labor Controls*

THE HARSH conditions experienced by the Mexican in Texas farm counties appear as a matter of fact to the most casual historian of the region. Mexican consular reports, accounts in Mexican and U.S. newspapers, the interviews that Taylor had with Anglo farmers, sheriffs, and other officials—all attest to the brutal and volatile character of Mexican-Anglo relations in the farm areas.[1] The foundation for these "rocky times," as J. Frank Dobie would have called them, consisted of the labor controls and discipline imposed by Anglo farmers on Mexican farm workers. Immobilization of sharecroppers and pickers through debt was an obvious type of control. The dismissal or removal of wage laborers for the purpose of avoiding payment was another type. Under this latter category fell a number of specific examples: shotgun settlements, the cancellation of credit at the local store, the timely leak to the Border Patrol. Somewhat more sophisticated were the efforts of county and state officials to restrict the movement of wage laborers. These various types of controls, then, suggest the wide-ranging circumstances encountered by Mexican workers in the modern farm order.

This chapter outlines the logic underlying these coercive labor relations, a logic I refer to as "labor repression." A key but neglected notion in development studies, labor repression imparts a sense of coherence to the wide-ranging controls of the period. In my use of the term, labor repression refers basically to the use of compulsion for organizing the recruitment, work activity, and compensation of wage labor. In the following discussion, I examine the connections between this repressive experience and the demands and fortunes of commercial agriculture. The discussion first considers the market situation of commercial farmers that moved them to devise labor controls; then the logic that wove these instances and expressions of control into an integrated web is presented.

The Dilemma of Commercial Farmers

The farmers of South Texas shared two basic concerns: one, they wanted cheap labor; two, they wanted it at the right time and in suf-

ficient numbers. These concerns did not distinguish the South Texas
farmer from his counterpart elsewhere, for these interests essentially reflected a common class position. By the close of the nineteenth century, according to one economic historian, the American
farmer had become a businessman "as tightly enmeshed in the web
of a world market as a Boston banker or a New York merchant."[2]
Farmers now devoted their time and energy to the cultivation of a
commodity for profit. What makes the story of the commercial
farmers in South Texas interesting, however, lies in the manner in
which they seized upon the racial character of the work force to improve their market situation. In competition with foreign crop im-
ports as well as with domestic production, South Texas commercial
farmers sought to minimize their overhead by cutting costs in the
one area most amenable to their control—wages. In order to eliminate the possibility of competitive bidding for labor, local farm organizations would meet before the season opened to determine the prevailing rates that all growers of a particular crop or in a certain
locality were expected to follow.[3] Wage-fixing, however, could not be
an effective measure unless the movement of laborers to workplaces
with higher wage scales was constrained. In an unfettered labor market, the commercial farmer or urban industrialist who offered relatively attractive wages, whether the workplace was within the same
county, in a neighboring county, or in a distant state, tended to upset any local wage-fixing. In order to maintain a low wage scale in
South Texas, then, the mobility of the agricultural worker had to be
restricted.

There was no question among Anglo settlers in South Texas that a
major asset of the region consisted of its cheap labor pool. Agribusinessmen, their chambers of commerce, and local county newspapers constantly emphasized this great advantage of the area. One
land prospectus in the Winter Garden region, for example, pushed
the "sell" in a succinct statement: "The cheapest farm labor in the
United States is to be had in this section."[4] Newspapers like the
Galveston News and the *Corpus Christi Caller* likewise invited prospective agribusinessmen and industrialists to invest in South Texas,
citing the presence of ample cheap labor. So cheap was Mexican labor, in fact, that the introduction of mechanization on commercial
farms was effectively retarded by the higher costs and less profitable
returns from machines.[5] The degree to which these wages were depressed surfaces clearly when the Mexican wage scale in Texas is
compared with those in neighboring states. According to the information compiled in a 1926–1927 study of Mexicans in the United
States, the average wage of Mexican laborers working cotton in the

southern and southwestern states was lowest in Texas.[6] A Mexican picker working Texas cotton received a daily wage of $1.75. In Arizona the Mexican cotton picker received $2.75; in California, $3.25; in Arkansas, Louisiana, and Mississippi, $4.00.

There was, of course, a sharp distinction between "white wages" and "Mexican wages." In the eyes of most farmers, the differences between the two were basically adjustments to the minimum living standards of Mexicans and Anglos. The lifestyle of the Mexican, in fact, framed a common argument that farmers used in justifying their preference for Mexican labor over that of Anglos. One land development agent put it this way: "The white people won't do the work and they won't live as the Mexicans do on beans and tortillas and in one room shacks."[7] Likewise, the same commercial prospectuses that invited agribusiness and industrial investors to South Texas discouraged the settlement of any Anglos who did not have capital or some skill or profession to offer. In the Winter Garden district, the Carrizo Springs Chamber of Commerce cautioned through its pamphlet, appropriately entitled "Your Opportunity May Be Waiting in Carrizo Springs, Texas," that "American laborers" should stay away because of the unequal competition with the living standards of Mexican labor. In Nueces County one farmer explained the matter to Taylor in this way: "The Mexicans are the only class of labor we can handle. The others won't do this work; the white pickers want screens and ice-water. To white pickers I say, 'If you will accept the houses we have for the Mexicans, you can work.' They said they were broke and they had to."[8]

Exceptions to the racial-class boundaries in South Texas might occur, and a farmer might contract Anglos as sharecroppers or pickers. But generally Anglos were denied work as pickers or sharecroppers. Anglo men who could not finance a crop, that is, go on thirds and fourths, were considered unfit as far as most farmers were concerned. A prominent Nueces County landowner echoed the sentiment of Anglo farmers in the area: "I prefer any Mexican to a sorry white man." These preferences not only were based on considerations of wages and lifestyles but also fundamentally involved the question of tractability and powerlessness. A landlord-farmer could determine the character of the work relationship much more readily with Mexicans than with Anglos. One cotton farmer summed it up compactly: "Whites cannot be as easily domineered, led, or directed as the Mexicans."[9]

South Texas farmers, then, had the low wage labor they wanted. As a second basic interest, farmers only wanted this labor for temporary work during the critical picking and harvesting seasons. This desire for cheap but temporary labor, however, entailed an internal tension. Temporary wage labor meant that laborers had to be mobile. Mobility for the laborer, in turn, meant that Mexicans could work for the highest bidder for their labor. Such competitiveness in the labor market, of course, would undermine the low wage scale of the area. As it was, large commercial farmers in many South Texas counties were often concerned about "labor theft." In times of acute labor shortages, many stood guard over their Mexican cotton pickers with shotguns to ward off labor agents or other farmers. Such accusations of theft were regularly leveled at the small farmer who, wishing his crop picked quickly, was willing to offer slightly higher wages than the fixed local norm.[10] The problem of labor theft, however, was not one limited to the intracounty movement of Mexicans. Why not travel to a neighboring county where they were offering ten cents a hundred pounds more? Or why not emigrate to Arkansas where they paid $4.00 a day in picking wages as opposed to $1.75 in Texas? This, then, framed the basic dilemma confronting the commercial farmers of South Texas. Wishing to preserve their labor resource, they had to restrict the movement of Mexican farm workers in some way.

Nowhere was there a clearer expression of this overriding concern to restrict labor mobility than in the attitude of farmers toward road building programs and ownership of cars by Mexican laborers.[11] Cars and roads, the much heralded symbols and carriers of the new world, had penetrated the old cattle country of frontier Texas, but their introduction resulted in no automatic freedom of movement for the landless Mexican. Large landowners in particular were expressedly against the "good roads" program and the ownership of cars by Mexicans. One large cotton farmer said he had Mexicans on halves "but never more" because they would spend their earnings on old cars. "The Mexicans stay better on halves." But car ownership had apparently spoiled the transient Mexican as well. The auto had ruined the Mexicans, according to one farmer, because now they would say, "All right, if you don't give me what I want I will go where I can get it." One prominent Nueces County cotton grower informed Taylor that it was best to get the Mexican in trucks. "If they have their own cars, they travel every week to see where the cotton is. If they have no way to move about, it is better." Another cotton grower expressed the sentiments of his counterparts in the area: "The majority of farmers prefer Mexicans without transportation. They are going to stay with you then until they are through." In fact, this dislike among landlords and farmers of Mexican car ownership frequently expressed itself in attempts to "attach" cars in order to satisfy debts at the end of the season. The comments of one Corpus Christi judge in reference to peonage laws suggest what must have been a common practice among Nueces County farmers: "You can't attach a Mexican's auto; it has been decided that an auto is a 'wagon and team,' and so protected by the laws from attachment. You might get them under the laws against swindling. I think they (the Mexicans) ought to believe it that they can be put in jail for leaving when in debt." [12]

The difficulty with Mexican labor, then, centered on its mobility. How did the Texas farmer resolve this problem? Debt constituted one common basis for the immobilization of labor, but it was ill-suited for a migratory labor system. Other measures had to be developed.

The Logic of Repression

A survey of the controls that farmers experimented with uncovers a puzzling complexity. Some restrictions appeared as individual attempts with an ad hoc character; others were collective efforts with more formal features. Horsewhipping, chains, armed guards, near-starvation diets, to name a few of the props involved, portray the more brutal side of labor coercion. Vagrancy laws, local pass systems, and labor taxes point to a more institutionalized dimension. The variety—even ingenuity—of these practices suggests a complex patchwork of exploitation. Clearly these diverse responses to the problem of Mexican mobility all point in the same direction—toward regulation of movement. Nonetheless, on the surface such diversity appears to weaken the central idea of labor repression. In what sense can one say that these various forms of control composed an integrated pattern?

The variety in controls can be attributed to three sources. In the first place, these measures were tailored to the labor arrangement; different sets of restrictions, in other words, were associated with sharecropping and migratory labor. Second, the number of controls represent the experimentation of newcomer farmers with various methods for immobilizing Mexican labor. In many ways, such experimentation involved a search for a political solution that would assure them a low-wage labor reservoir; at each step, farmers turned to political agencies with increasingly broader jurisdiction and power. The various controls, then, can be placed on an ascending scale according to their sponsorship: individual farmer or agricultural company, local agribusiness organization, county government, and state government. Finally, the restrictions were related to the condition of the labor market—which measure might be imposed depended on whether a labor shortage or surplus existed.

In the following discussion, I will first describe the most common controls associated with sharecropping; then I will proceed to describe those associated with migratory labor. The ascending scale of political sponsorship that farmers obtained in their efforts to create an effective repressive apparatus will become evident. In a final section, I will discuss how the condition of the labor market and other market factors shaped the form of repression.

Debts and Shotguns: Regulating the Sharecropper

In reviewing the cases of coercion associated with Mexican share-croppers, two distinct trends surfaced. On the one hand, large land-owners attempted to immobilize the cropper through debt. The frank words of a San Antonio official of the U.S. Employment Service should suffice to reiterate this point: "Some of the farmers here advance from $250 to $500 a year to the Mexican families. They use the debt as a club to keep them on the place. They bluff the Mexicans through fear of the law and personal violence. This is more prevalent with the big landowners."[13]

On the other hand, there were cases throughout the length of Mexican Texas where the landlord would terminate the contract of the sharecropper in order to appropriate the cropper's cotton.[14] The Mexican consul in El Paso, drawing on his experience with conditions in West Texas as well as throughout the state, told Taylor that landlords often terminated the contracts of croppers on the pretext that they failed to follow some instruction. "They may be then ordered off the place by a deputy sheriff and probably the horses and chickens are attached to pay the debts." In Central Texas, a U.S. Farm Service official noted that some landlords cut the tenants' store allowance in June or July when the crop looked good. By cutting their allowance, the landlords were able to run the Mexicans off the place. The Mexican consul in Corpus Christi described the difficulties of the local Mexican population in this Gulf Coast region in similar terms: "Almost all of the difficulties we encounter are because the farmers tell the Mexicans working on halves to leave without their pay or share of the crop. Almost all of these difficulties are arranged. There isn't much difficulty over payment of the pickers."[15]

Finally, the Mexican vice-consul in McAllen reported similar experiences in deep South Texas in the 1930s. In a letter addressed to an inquiring Mexican congressional deputy, the vice-consul noted that in his region the landlord "*rentistas*" have studied innumerable ways of legally breaking their contract with their Mexican croppers and, with this in mind, look for some difficulty so they can remove

him from his work—"por supuesto, cuando éste ya está terminado."[16]
These legal maneuvers were at least a bit more sophisticated than
another common method of breaking sharecropping contracts—the
so-called shotgun settlement, a tactic whereby an armed farmer
drove off his cropper or laborer in lieu of payment of wages.

At first sight, expulsion of a sharecropper may seem to be an ironic
form of labor control. The irony consists only of semantics, however,
for shotgun settlements and other methods used to terminate work
contracts were fundamentally a means of securing subsistence labor.
During the tenure of the contract, the expelled worker, either a regular wage hand or a sharecropper, had basically worked for subsistence wages, that is, for the monthly advances given to feed his family. If his horses, chickens, or automobile had been attached to pay
for the farmer's advances, then the expelled laborer had, in fact,
worked for much less than subsistence. He had actually *borrowed* in
order to live and work. Expulsion, then, appears to be an inverted
form of peonage. It was one, however, suited to the labor arrangement. To put it another way, controls geared to *resident labor*, from
debt peonage to shotgun settlements, revolved around the question
of retention or expulsion—for lack of a better word, on the "exit"
side of a labor contract. In contrast, the emphasis of controls associated with *seasonal labor* lay in recruitment.

A word might be said about the circumstances facing the farmer
that made for the use of debts and shotguns. Farmers with extensive
holdings, those most concerned with having stable resident labor
throughout the year, were the ones most likely to immobilize sharecroppers and the ones least likely to run them off.[17] Conversely, the
small farmer or tenant farmer on thirds and fourths would be the one
most susceptible to running his croppers and pickers off. In a more
marginal market situation than the agribusinessman, the small
farmer might be tempted, in a good crop year, to settle his contractual agreements with a shotgun; in a bad year, he might be forced to.
In short, the controls associated with resident Mexican labor were
appropriate for the labor arrangement. The other way of obtaining labor, through a system of migratory wage labor, also had its set of appropriate restrictions.

Promises and Passes: Recruiting Seasonal Labor

Farmers dependent on seasonal Mexican labor were concerned with
immobilizing the workers at the proper time. There were several
ways of accomplishing this objective, but perhaps the most common
method was through recruitment of contract laborers under false

pretenses. Labor recruitment and contracting constituted the only manner in which the migratory labor system was organized in Texas until the mid-1930s. With little state supervision or regulation, such organization of the work force was susceptible to considerable manipulation on the part of commercial farmers and labor contractors.[18] Emilio Flores, secretary of the Mexican Protective Association in San Antonio, explained to the fact-finding Federal Commission on Industrial Relations (1915) how such manipulation was arranged. Employment agencies and labor contractors would go down to the border and recruit Mexicans by making attractive but false offers. The contract laborers, however, would not discover the actual terms of the contract and conditions of their work situation until they arrived at their destination. The result? As Flores testified before the commission: "When they [the Mexican laborers] sometimes refuse to comply, because of the promises of the employment agency at the border or at San Antonio, they are guarded until they work out what they owe. I have known a number of Mexicans to be chained in Gonzales County and guarded by armed men with shotguns and made to work these moneys out. This was officially reported and is of record."[19] Flores then named a score of Central Texas and South Texas counties and towns where Mexican workers had been subjected to brutal force, including instances of whipping and murder. Such episodes of coercion were an integral element of the work experience of the Mexican contract laborer during this period of rapid development. One Mexican interviewed by the sociologist Manuel Gamio in 1930 recalled his personal experience with Texas farmers and authorities about the year 1912. The passing of the years had done little to erase the bitterness:

> In San Antonio, we were under contract to go and pick cotton in a camp in the Valley of the Rio Grande. A group of countrymen and my wife and I went to pick. When we arrived at the camp, the planter gave us an old hovel which had been used as a chicken house before, to live in, out in the open. I didn't want to live there and told him that if he didn't give us a little house which was a little better we would go. He told us to go, and my wife and I and my children were leaving when the sheriff fell upon us. He took me to the jail and there the planter told them that I wanted to leave without paying him for my passage. He charged me twice the cost of transportation, and though I tried first not to pay him, and then to pay him for what it cost, I couldn't do anything. The authorities would only pay attention to him, and as they were in

league with him they told me that if I didn't pay they would take my wife and my little children to work. Then I paid them.[20]

This incident was no isolated or exceptional case. It was only a reflection of a system of controls that local farmers and authorities had instituted in order to have the cotton picked.

Another common practice used to immobilize seasonal Mexican labor occurred through the timely enforcement of vagrancy laws. It seems to have been customary in Texas for vagrancy laws to be applied at the beginning of each cotton picking season, especially if there was a labor shortage or, more accurately, if laborers refused to work for the wages offered by local farmers.[21] Vagrancy laws, in fact, provided the legal basis for one of the more elaborate local arrangements used to regulate Mexican labor in South Texas—the "hiring and pass systems" of the Lower Rio Grande Valley. In 1927 court testimony in the "Raymondville Peonage Cases" uncovered a compact in Willacy County between local cotton farmers, the county justice of the peace, the county attorney, and the county sheriff and his deputies.[22] During times when labor was needed, local farmers would recruit contract laborers who discovered, upon arrival, that the terms they had agreed to were misrepresentations. Any who then refused to work were picked up by the local deputies, found guilty of vagrancy, and fined double the amount owed the farmer for transportation or food. The convicted were then given the option of working off the fines by picking cotton for the farmer who had recruited them. Any laborers passing through the county during the picking season also experienced the same fate: convicted of vagrancy, they were informed that the fines should be worked off in the cotton fields. Naturally such "convict labor" was routinely guarded by armed deputies while working cotton. To complement this method of recruiting labor, a "pass system" was instituted to prevent unauthorized pickers from leaving the county. Laborers leaving the area had to have passes signed by one of the local farmers involved in the compact.

In this deep South Texas district, generally only Mexicans ended up being "hired" through the Willacy County system. This system, however, apparently could operate in a color-blind fashion whenever Anglo vagrants wandered into Willacy County. In fact, this color-blindness appears to have been partly responsible for the downfall of the Willacy pact, which occurred shortly after two young Anglo men had stumbled into the hiring net. These Anglo pickers provided, for a local attorney who was "politically hostile" to the sheriff, the necessary ingredient for removing the sheriff from office: in these Anglo vagrants, the attorney had unimpeachable victims and witnesses, traits that Mexican and black laborers lacked before Anglo juries. The court proceedings resulted in convictions, and five officials, including the sheriff and the justice of the peace, were sentenced to terms ranging from one month to eighteen months.

The convictions were a shocking and unexpected blow to the Texas farmer. Many observers, Anglo and Mexican alike, commented that the trial and convictions had occurred because Raymondville officers had involved two young Anglos. In Nueces County some farmers had an "aggrieved feeling" that the law had left them helpless. Considerable sympathy was extended to those convicted: the sheriff, in fact, was given a celebration in his honor upon his release from imprisonment. An official from the U.S. Department of Justice defended the convicted authorities: "They ought to be able to make the Mexicans work out their debt. The peonage cases were extreme. There was a labor shortage in 1926. They don't generally do that (that is, guard the pickers with guns)."[23] The Justice official was making the popular but circular argument of many farmers and politicians of the day. Naturally, fear of labor shortages moved commercial farmers to devise ways to immobilize labor; this condition, after all, provided the motive for repression.

In sum, the repression of transient Mexican workers focused on some aspect of labor recruitment, and two common methods of recruitment centered on misrepresented contracts and vagrancy laws. "Entrapment" is an accurate description of this type of control. The frequent companion of such entrapment was physical force, for the effectiveness of this method lay in the quick and emphatic suppression of any initial resistance by the Mexican workers. Likewise, the supervision of entrapped labor generally carried with it the threat of physical discipline. This corresponds to one suggestive observation in the testimony of Emilio Flores regarding contract laborers. "Many cases of outrages committed with these unfortunates," Flores noted, have been "traced back to the manner in which said labor is secured."[24] Again this points to an interesting relationship between labor arrangements and certain types of coercion. Mexican sharecroppers and other resident laborers, although often threatened with physical force, were generally spared such brutality because of the farmer's need for stable, year-long labor. At least for the duration of the contract, paternalism tended to characterize the farmer's relationship with the Mexican "regulars." In contrast, the temporary character of seasonal labor undermined any need for paternalism and emphasized the instrumental nature of the work relationship. Thus, where the oppressive features of this relationship were transparent, as for entrapped migrant labor, force and discipline had to play the necessary lead role.

Licenses and Taxes: Protecting the Migrant Stream

The character of racial exploitation during the early twentieth century, then, was largely a response to the imperatives of commercial agriculture. A straightforward economic interpretation, however, does not explain the quiltlike quality of repression in rural Texas, for whether or not labor controls might surface depended in large part on what was possible locally. Where consensus among local farmers and authorities could be negotiated, some measure along the lines of the Willacy County system might be attempted. Internal dissent, however, threatened any plan, as was evident in the frequent complaints about farmers who engaged in "labor theft" and exceeded fixed wage levels. Given the varying political conditions in South Texas, the techniques and strategies established to regulate Mexican labor were expectedly different from county to county. There was no uniform response to the problem of Mexican mobility.

The county, in any case, constituted a particularly inadequate base for regulating the movement of Mexican migratory labor. The cotton circuit alone stretched from the southern tip of Texas to the northwestern edge of the Panhandle, a round trip of nearly two thousand miles. Thus, even where the farmers of a county were in agreement concerning wages and the form of labor recruitment, the lack of a regulatory agency that could coordinate the movement of Mexican labor within the state jeopardized the efforts. North Texas and Central Texas farmers, for instance, depended heavily on the Mexican labor of South Texas and regularly commissioned labor contractors to recruit for them in that area. In this manner, competing farmers from various counties could upset any local arrangement to immobilize Mexican labor.

Here, then, one finds a basis for the intricate web of labor controls in rural Texas: a varied county response to the Mexican labor problem and the absence of an intercounty organization that could coordinate the movement of Mexican labor. Thus, labor repression in Texas consisted of a set of ineffective and inefficient controls. This was quite evident in the contradictory behavior of farmers. On the one hand, they hampered the movement of Mexican labor; on the other, they competed with each other for this labor. These dual conflicting features were major characteristics of South Texas agriculture.[25] In fact, the element of competition between farmers was undoubtedly responsible for the "freedom" that Mexican farm workers did have at this time.

This competition for labor, actually the underlying source of dissension within the ranks of the Anglo commercial farmers, points to the *internal* circumstances that made for a fragmented repressive web. One must ask, however, why farmers were unable to organize behind a common program that would circumvent the need to compete for Mexican labor. Why were farmers, recognizing the general ineffectiveness of their controls, unable to go beyond their "labor thieving" ways? Undoubtedly, this failure to formulate a common labor policy has much to do with the peculiar difficulties that beset organizations of commercial farmers. Farm communities as a rule have been characterized as divided by individualism, competition, and suspicion.[26] One point of consensus, however, is quite clear. Texas farmers, confronted with the possible loss of their Mexican labor pool in the late 1920s, rallied and proposed a solution to the problem of Mexican labor mobility. A set of bills designed to restrain Mexicans from leaving the state was introduced and passed in 1929 by the Texas Legislature.[27] In these Emigrant Labor Agency Laws, one finds the initial impulse to create a formal repressive labor policy. Again competition between employers for the same labor source would cause these efforts to fail; this time, however, the competitors would be agricultural and industrial concerns in the Midwest and the North. In order to understand, then, why labor repression in Texas remained a patchwork of individual and localized efforts, one must also look at the *external* political and economic interests that blocked the development of restrictive labor policies on the state level.

So long as additional Mexican labor could be recruited from across the border, Texas farmers were apparently not overly disturbed by the overall ineptness of their controls. Toward the late 1920s, however, a number of events moved farmers to search for a legal and more effective basis for regulating the movement of Mexican labor. Perhaps the most significant event was the discovery of Mexicans by midwestern and northern industry in the late 1910s and early 1920s. In a 1929 interview, the passenger agent for the Missouri, Kansas, and Texas Railway in San Antonio described the intense recruitment activity of those days.[28] The Pittsburgh Plate Glass Company shipped about 600 Mexicans from San Antonio in 1923 and about 1,800 the following year; Inland Steel was shipping Mexicans out of North and South Texas, and United States Steel was shipping Mexicans mainly out of North Texas; in 1925 alone the Missouri, Kansas, and Texas Railway shipped about 4,200 Mexicans out of San Antonio; and so on. Naturally, at the receiving end of these labor shipments, the increase in number of Mexican workers was quite apparent (and in some cases provoked protests by Anglo workers). On sixteen railroads in the Chicago-Gary region, for instance, the number of Mexicans employed in "maintenance of way" work was insignificant in the 1910s. This number, however, increased rapidly in 1920 and 1922. By 1923 Mexicans comprised 22 percent of the 10,000 workers in "maintenance of way"; by 1928 they comprised 42 percent of this work force (3,963 of 9,228 employees). In fifteen industrial plants in the Chicago-Gary area—five meat packing plants, seven metal and steel plants, a cement plant, a railroad-car repair plant, and a rug factory— the increase in Mexican workers followed a similar pattern. Their number during the 1910s was insignificant; 1920 and 1922 registered increases; a steady growth followed so that by 1928 Mexicans constituted nearly 11 percent of the work force in these industrial plants, or 7,050 employees of the total of 65,682.[29]

The circumstances that stimulated the interest of these distant companies in the Mexican population of the Southwest and of Mexico were, quite simply, the restrictionist quotas placed on European immigration in the early 1920s. At least for one business, the Michigan sugar beet industry, the shift to Mexicans as its labor source was nearly complete. The result was a thorough ethnic transformation of the Michigan agricultural work force from "Slavs" to Mexicans. Plainly sensitive to the mounting criticism from northern labor as well as from Texas farmers, the San Antonio–based labor agent for a Michigan sugar company blamed the immigration laws for these adverse effects. Before the restrictionist laws, Michigan farmers had shipped German and Russian immigrants out of Cleveland and Chicago for sugar beet work. "The biggest crime of the quota law," noted the agent, "was to keep that class of people out."[30] This was, of course, the familiar lament of midwestern and northern agribusinessmen and industrialists toward restrictionist immigration legislation. By the end of the 1920s, Texas farmers had joined in such complaints and protests. By this time, the continuing efforts of American restrictionists, including organized labor in the North, had led to a partial closing of the Mexican border. In the eyes of the Texas farmer, the people necessary for the development of the country, the Mexican laborers, were being kept out. As one Dimmit County farmer put it: "We have got to have a class of people who will do this kind of labor."[31]

In the 1920s, then, the Texas farmer saw his labor supply jeopardized in two ways. On the one hand, the enforcement of immigration laws endangered his inexhaustible source in nearby Mexico. On the other, the activities of these distant "outside" employers threatened to siphon off his domestic labor source—the Texas Mexican—as well. Increasingly, the Texas farmer found himself competing with agricultural and industrial concerns with considerable capital. As if this were not enough, in 1927 the Raymondville convictions served to discourage any local initiative in responding to this challenge. The situation for the commercial farmer was critical; his advantage in the competitive agricultural market was based in large part on the restricted Mexican labor he had. Under these pressing circumstances, the Texas farmer reacted.

In 1929, with the support of the South Texas Chamber of Commerce, the Winter Garden Chamber of Commerce, and the West Texas Chamber of Commerce, A. P. Johnson, the state representative from Carrizo Springs (Dimmit County), introduced legislation explicitly designed to "protect" the Mexican labor reservoir in Texas.[32] Through occupation taxes, variable county tax surcharges, and the posting of a return transportation bond in each county where laborers were recruited, the Emigrant Labor Agency Laws directly aimed to restrict the recruitment of Texas Mexican labor by outside industrial and agricultural interests. The Texas State Employment Division expressed the intent in plain language: "The occupation taxes were established to discourage invasions from outside on the State's labor and mobile workers."[33] State Representative Johnson, the author of the Labor Agency Laws, explained to Taylor how they were basically a response to the restriction of Mexican immigration: "It is the same situation as where you have had a stream of water running through your ranch. If someone turns its source off you want to put up a dam to hold what you have got." Johnson continued his explanation, saying that this state law could open the way for federal immigration laws to be amended in order to permit seasonal labor along the border. In Johnson's words: "If other parts of the country could feel free (from) having Mexican seasonal labor dumped on them, they would not object to a seasonal supply here."[34] This "theory of restraint," as the lawmaker called it, was proposed as a compromise to demands from organized labor for restrictive immigration legislation. As one Dimmit County resident argued, immigration authorities could stop Mexicans "from going out of the four border states; they could stop them there as well as they can on the river here."[35] In this vein, the Labor Agency Laws were seen as protecting Anglo workers in the North from competition with Mexican labor. Thus the Texas AFL, moved by a spirit of solidarity with their northern brethren, joined with the chambers of commerce in supporting the labor bills. Organized labor in Texas, of course, was no disinterested party—some unions wanted Mexican immigrants put back in Mexico and Texas Mexicans kept in agriculture.[36] The political situation for the Mexican in Texas, then, appeared quite ominous. With 85 percent of the state's migratory labor force composed of Mexicans, the thrust of these labor laws was clear: they were in essence a set of racial labor laws.

The particular outside employers that Texas farmers and politicians had in mind when they drafted the Emigrant Labor Agency Laws were the northern sugar beet companies. Together these various companies formed one of the most formidable competitors for seasonal labor, annually recruiting approximately ten thousand Texas Mexicans to work the beet fields of Michigan and northern Ohio.[37] It comes as little surprise, then, that Texas farmers frequently explained the need for the labor laws in terms of the recruiting activity of these beet companies. One group of Nueces County farmers put it succinctly: "We got a law passed to keep the Mexican in Texas and out of the beets. The border states need a temporary passport for Mexicans; put a boundary on Texas." Another group of Nueces County farmers interpreted the labor laws similarly, adding that the legislation constituted only a first step: "We wish to prevent the transportation of Mexicans where they don't belong. Through employment agencies he gets to where he has no business, where he gets in competition with union labor. Congress does not care so much if we keep them so our first step was to make it as hard as possible for the agents of the beet sugar companies to get labor . . . We propose a deadline, beyond which the Mexicans could not go North."[38]

Such a proposal apparently never proceeded beyond the point of being resolutions endorsed by local farm organizations, for the beet companies, recognizing the intent of the Labor Agency Laws, immediately responded to these initial measures. The first state bill, which levied an occupation tax of $7,500 on out-of-state labor recruiters, was enjoined by a federal court upon the petition of a Michigan sugar beet company.[39] The response of the state legislature was equally determined and swift. "There was the danger of its being declared unconstitutional because of the prohibitive fee," explained Carrizo Springs Representative Johnson, "so we repealed it and then passed the second law." The second law required only an annual occupation tax of $1,000 and variable county surcharges, from $100 to $300, depending on the condition of the local labor market. Supervision of the Emigrant Labor Agency Laws was placed, appropriately, in the hands of the state commissioner of labor statistics.[40]

In addition to this emergency legislation, a third bill was passed in order to satisfy the "imperative public necessity." This law, which the legislator from Carrizo Springs described as "a police power measure," required the labor agent to post a $5,000 bond in order to "protect" the return of the recruited laborers. This return transportation bond was to be posted in each county where the agent recruited. A provision in the law, however, allowed for a "dispensation" if the recruited laborers waived their "rights" before the county judge. The bond provision was subsequently ruled unconstitutional by a federal court, again upon legal action pursued by Michigan sugar beet companies.

Considering the defeats of such legislation in the federal courts, it is difficult to assess how successful these labor laws were in their diluted form. Certainly they pointed to an effective strategy, for the migratory labor system at the time was primarily organized through the labor contract method. Approximately 60 percent of the cotton picking in Texas was handled through labor contractors.[41] Thus, legal restrictions on the activity of labor contractors—licensing and taxation being the primary vehicles—appeared to be a most promising manner by which to regulate the movement of Mexican migratory labor. Future legislation could readily have extended the principles of the Emigrant Labor Agency Laws to include domestic labor contractors and, in this fashion, have regulated the movement of Mexican labor within the state as well.

To some degree, this result was achieved through the legislature's formation of the Texas Farm Placement Service (TFPS) in 1934. The stated purpose of the TFPS was to regulate the movement of farm labor in order to eliminate "aimless wandering" of migrants, to reduce the recruitment fees of farmers, and to make the entire farming enterprise more efficient.[42] Basically, the farm placement system worked to bring "demand and supply" together during the peak seasons of various sections of the state. Farmers placed their orders for laborers with the local TFPS office and workers were accordingly directed to the farmers. This need for market efficiency did not require a color-blind operation of the program. The standard request form used by the TFPS asked farmers whether they preferred "white," "Negro," or "other" laborers, and whether this was an "open" or "closed" specification. As the TFPS Annual Report of 1939 noted, "particular care had to be exercised in selecting the groups because some farmers preferred whites, some Mexicans, and others negroes."[43]

Armed with these orders for labor, uniformed TFPS agents manned highway checkpoints to direct migratory workers to local farmers who had requested a specified number and type of laborers. While such placement appeared harmless on the surface, the agents in fact had the police power to enforce the Emigrant Labor Agency Laws requiring that labor contractors pay occupational taxes and various security bonds. In this manner, the TFPS exercised some control over the Texas Mexican contractor. As a TFPS document stated, such regulation served to discourage the "loss of husky boys and men to sugar beet States."[44]

How effective the Texas Farm Placement Service was and might have become is a matter that requires more research. By the early 1940s, the war emergency and the urgent defense needs for soldiers and workers basically made such labor regulation a secondary concern.

Shortages and Surpluses

Having described how the complex array of controls reflected different labor arrangements and different levels of political jurisdiction, I can now turn to one last factor that helps us comprehend the market dynamic underlying labor repression—the condition of the labor market. The relationship was a straightforward commonsensical one. During times of abundant labor the farmer did not have to be concerned about the consequences of running his Mexicans off. Replacements could be readily obtained. Conversely, in periods of expected shortages, farmers tended to hold their Mexican labor. The various restrictions not only corresponded to the two principal types of agricultural labor, sharecroppers and migratory wage workers, but also reflected the condition of the local labor market as assessed by the commercial farmer. This assessment was not actually a measure of the supply of workers so much as an indication of the market situation of the farmer. Shortages and surpluses were summary references of the labor costs the grower was willing to incur, the urgency with which he wanted the crop marketed, and the willingness of Mexicans to work under those conditions. Or as a Dimmit ranch manager put it, those farmers who yelled labor shortages were those who wanted their crop picked immediately: "If they can't start the same day they want to, they say they can't get enough labor. We are overrun with hands."[45] Table 11 represents the connections among labor controls, labor arrangements, and market situation of commercial farmers.

In short, whenever the farmer could not obtain a sufficiently cheap or tractable labor force through the normal play of the market, repressive measures provided the logical alternative. Thus migratory labor controls—vagrancy laws, misrepresented contracts, and so on—expectedly followed a seasonal pattern and were invoked when-

Table 11. *A Web of Labor Controls*

| | Labor Arrangement | |
Market Situation	Sharecropping	Migratory Labor
Labor shortage	Debt peonage	Vagrancy laws Local "pass" systems Recruitment through misrepresentation Labor agency laws
Labor surplus	Shotgun settlements Breach of contract (appropriating the cropper's share)	Breach of contract (nonpayment)

ever farmers and growers could not get local laborers to work for the fixed wage scale. Likewise, shotgun settlements were apparently indications of the vulnerable market position of the small commercial farmer. In this context, then, one can examine more closely the market circumstances that created shortages and moved farmers to repress Mexican wage labor.

Shortages: Competing in a World Market

A survey of the labor needs cited by South Texas farmers readily suggests that shortages were relative matters. As mentioned before, much depended on how quickly the farmer wished the crop picked and marketed. This decision, in turn, depended on extralocal conditions, such as the market trend in crop prices, crop production regionally and nationally, competition with foreign producers, and so on. Onion growers around Carrizo Springs and Laredo, for instance, were sensitive to competition with Egyptian onions; they were vigilant in following "the daily fluctuations in the market price of Bermuda onions in New York"; and consequently they were quite aware of the importance of moving their crop to market at the right time.[46] For the Winter Garden area, these worldwide market linkages generated an interest in having a large disposable labor force that could be rushed into the fields one day and withdrawn or transferred to other fields the next.

Like onion growers, cotton farmers had discovered that they could reduce the cotton harvest from a matter of weeks to a matter of days by using a large migratory labor force. In the hypothetical case presented earlier, I explained how a force of 2,250 laborers would be sufficient to work Nueces County cotton farms over a span of ten weeks, the duration of the picking season. However, if a sharp rise or decline in cotton prices prompted these farmers to have their cotton picked within the same week, a migratory army of 22,500 laborers would be needed. Within the context of these extralocal market circumstances, a commercial farmer could claim a shortage of labor. This apparently was the setting for the Willacy pass system of 1926.

Texas cotton farmers found 1926 to be a particularly bad year for them; cotton prices declined sharply from previous years, apparently as a result of overproduction: 5,623,000 bales were produced in 1926 compared to 4,163,000 bales produced the year before, an amazing increase in production of 35 percent.[47] At the same time that cotton production was at record levels, cotton prices in 1926 declined to their lowest point in a decade. From 20.33 cents per pound in 1925, Texas cotton prices plummeted to a low of 12.73 cents in 1926. These market conditions, then, were the concrete features behind the triggering of labor controls. Depressed price levels and a bleak outlook meant that farmers had to reduce labor costs while they scrambled to have their cotton picked and marketed before prices dropped even lower. How was it possible to secure such a temporary low-wage work force quickly? Entrapment of migratory Mexican laborers was one sure way of accomplishing this end, as the Willacy "hiring and pass systems" illustrate. This type of peonage, at least before the 1927 federal convictions of the Willacy authorities, was a common practice in South Texas. The point that should be emphasized is that this practice was a market-conditioned response.

Another example of market-conditioned controls consists of the 1929 Winter Garden injunctions against Mexican contractors.[48] Again, this was a situation where growers had misread the market and had overcommitted their farms to a poorly priced crop. One frustrated grower, assessing the 1929 season, told Taylor that "the country is bankrupt and driven to hell; the whole thing is uneconomic." To make matters worse, the inexperienced newcomers of Catarina—the town was only four years old—had raised wages in order to attract more Mexican labor. Upset at this high wage offer, the growers of neighboring Asherton filed a set of injunctions accusing the Mexican labor contractors (who were handling the recruitment for Catarina) with not having the necessary labor agency licenses. The temporary injunctions were subsequently overruled, but in the meantime they had intimidated the Mexican contractors and thus accomplished their purpose.

The Asherton growers justified the action simply enough: "There's

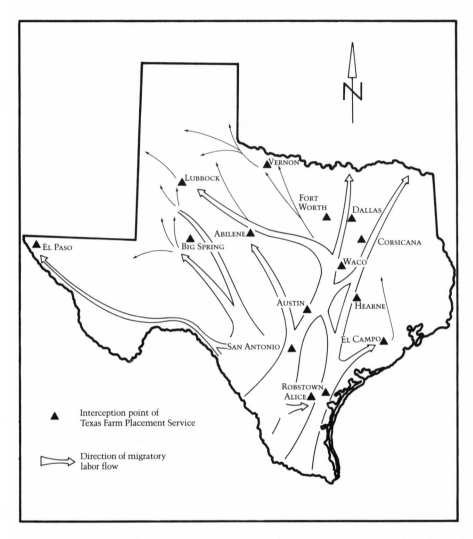

Migratory Labor Patterns, 1939 (based on Texas State Employment Service, *Annual Report of the Farm Placement Service*, 1939).

a law in Texas against taking labor out of a community when there's a shortage there." But in 1929 there was no shortage in Dimmit County. A market report of the Department of Agriculture, in fact, commented on the plentiful labor the county had that year. The troubles of the growers, as the report made clear, lay in the depressed market prices for the bumper crop they had planted. One local settler caught the irony of the situation: "The farmers would get better prices and would not glut the market if they could not get so many Mexicans." [49]

In short, labor shortages were not related in any simple or direct way to the size of the available labor force. Rather, they were more directly the product of extralocal market conditions that moved farmers to desire a disposable work force at critical moments. At least for the coercive side of this experience—I describe Anglo protection of the Mexican in a following chapter—the treatment of the Mexican laborer by the Anglo farmer was in large measure related to the fluctuations of commercial agriculture itself. Whether to increase profits or minimize losses, Anglo farmers sought to accomplish this by fixing local wages and restricting the movement of their local Mexican labor force.

Shortages: The Flight of Mexican Labor

On the other hand, a basic dimension of this farm problem lay in the emigration of the rural Texas Mexican population to Texas cities and to places outside the state. The importance of such emigration, as we saw, was explicitly recognized by farmers concerned about the loss of their Mexican labor. It was this concern that compelled them to attempt a more effective organization of the labor market in a repressive manner. The other side of the labor shortage issue, in other words, lay in the fact that Mexicans were exercising their fragile legal right to sell their labor. I have already indicated the extent to which Texas Mexicans were willing to travel in their search for better working and living conditions. During the 1920s, the agricultural and industrial Midwest witnessed the introduction of Mexicans as a significant addition to the working population. In the 1930s, over 66,000 Texas Mexicans were leaving the state annually to find work. [50] The fact that Mexicans searched for higher-paying work and were sensitive to workplace conditions is an obvious but critical point—one largely obscured by a romantic literature that has portrayed the Mexican as passive. The obvious should be emphasized: Mexicans were conscious of the world they lived and worked in. In their search for work in Texas, Mexicans were sensitive to rumors about bad treatment and poor working conditions at particular farms; for them, it was a matter of protection. Anglo farmers acquired favorable and unfavorable reputations that circulated among the local and migratory Mexican population. One disliked grower in Dimmit County, for example, had to bring in Mexicans from San Antonio, over a hundred miles away, because local Mexicans would not work for him.[51] Even then another landlord had to "front" for him in the hiring and supervising of these imported workers. One Nueces County grower felt frustrated by the networks that existed among Mexican workers: "The Mexicans always strike. Every Monday morning they want to know if . . . [the farmers] aren't going to raise the prices. They have anarchists—agitators—who go round and tell them what price to pick for."[52]

Mexican workers who found themselves in intolerable situations often took the only recourse open to them—escape. In fact, debt peonage and escape were commonplace events in the life of Mexican sharecroppers and pickers. The massive emigrations to other states present no less dramatic evidence of the Mexican response to their world in Texas. There were, of course, other responses—abortive strikes, attempts at political organization, instances of violence. But escape, flight to the cities, emigration to other states—in the 1920s and 1930s, these comprised the dominant reaction, perhaps the form of resistance, to oppression. The meaning of this response was expressed eloquently in one piece of memorabilia of Mexican life during this period—a popular Texas Mexican ballad, "El Corrido de Texas," recorded in San Antonio in 1929.[53] In this *corrido*, the hero—a Texas Mexican laborer recruited to work for an Indiana company—feels dejected because he has to leave the woman he loves. Why must he leave? In the refrain he tells us repeatedly—the lyrics are straightforward and powerful at this point:

> Goodbye State of Texas
> with all your fields,
> I leave your land
> so I won't have to pick cotton.

An Underground Railroad

In large part, the harsh experience of the twentieth-century farm period can be understood in terms of a labor-repressive agriculture. Essentially, this repression consisted of the various measures and strategies commercial farmers and authorities used to attempt to maintain a low-wage Mexican labor force. Vagrancy laws, local pass systems, manipulation of labor contracts, and labor agency laws suggest the character of controls used to regulate the movement of Mexican farm workers. In one sense, the different restrictions illustrate the experimentation and various political steps that farmers took as they attempted to create an apparatus that could guarantee them a supply of cheap seasonal labor. These controls, however, were never crystallized in a coherent and effective system because of external political challenges undertaken by Michigan agribusiness.

Consequently, labor repression in Texas never progressed beyond an immature condition: it remained based, for the most part, on individual predilection, local custom, and administrative fiat. A good example of the latter can be seen in the common practice of Texas highway patrolmen to use any pretext—motor vehicle violations, even the diluted Labor Agency Laws—to interrupt the journey of Mexicans traveling out of state. In 1941, years after the federal court challenges to the Texas labor laws, McWilliams described the movement of Mexicans north as one "shrouded in conspiracy and intrigue." On the road Mexicans constantly had to be on watch for agents of the Texas Farm Placement Service or of the Texas Bureau of Motor Carriers as well as for patrolmen in other states. Thus, Mexican truck drivers, loaded with their cargo of Mexican laborers, usually drove at night, through back roads, following a zig-zag course to the beet fields of Michigan. Even when the Mexican workers "are not trying to evade the law, they are under the constraint of concealing, if possible, the nature of the enterprise in which they are engaged." The traffic of sugar beet workers from Texas to Michigan, in McWilliams' incisive characterization, was a virtual "underground railroad."[54]

10. The Culture of Segregation

FEW SETTLERS described their divided society solely in the pragmatic language of economic interest or political control. Most mixed their views and explanations with ethical statements, superstitions, biblical sayings, historical lessons, or just plain "gut feelings" about the proper place of colored people. In the minds of most Anglos, there was no question that Mexicans were an inferior people. Herschel Manuel pointed out the assumption in a 1930 report on Mexican school segregation: "The evidence that in general the Mexicans are considered inferior by non-Mexicans is not hard to find. It is so pronounced and so much a part of general knowledge in the state that it seems superfluous to cite evidence that it exists. To Texas readers one could almost say, 'Ask yourself,' or 'Consult your own experience.'"[1] Having described the material context of the farm society, I can now consider the images and ideas of race that were offered as common sense, as conventional wisdom, to explain the particular ordering of people and privilege.

My interpretation of race-thinking involves three tasks. The first is to identify the major themes expressed in the mass of racial opinions and beliefs of the Anglo settlers. What specifically did "Mexican" mean as a sign of inferiority? What ideas or images were associated with being Mexican? The second task is to outline how the farm order made the "races" of the region. Although in the 1920s and 1930s it seemed as if these commonsense ideas about Mexican inferiority had always been present—and in some sense, they had been—their emergence as public themes corresponded to the development of commercial agriculture. These ideas, in other words, were closely related to changes in the class order, a point I will discuss in some detail. The final task is to discuss how race ideas outlined the basis for an appropriate relationship between the two communities. Race ideas, in providing explanations for the position of Anglo and Mexican, also provided a basis for control of the Mexican, a critical element for the stability of the new farm order. To the extent that such ideas were accepted by both Anglo and Mexican, they served to legitimize the segregated order.

Ideas of Race or Class?

Playing the part of a devil's advocate, agricultural economist Paul Taylor tested the limits of the segregated order by asking Anglos about "equality with the educated Mexicans." Was segregation more a matter of class or of race? No straightforward answer was possible. Anglos were intransigent in their opposition to equality with Mexicans, and their comments generally made references to both race and class.

On the one hand, the question of skin color made equality with the Mexican, whether educated or not, impossible. A Nueces County professional man, although hedging a bit on the question, gave a typical response: ". . . you crowded me there [with the question]. Not as a rule, you can't give them social equality. Any other dark-skinned, off-color race is not equal to us. I may be wrong . . . but I feel, and the general public here, feels that way. They are not as good as Americans."[2] An "old salt" in Dimmit County handled Taylor's hypothetical question about equality by lecturing the testy young professor on Texas history: "They are a mixture, a mule race or cross-breed. The Spaniard is a cross between a Moor or a Castilian, and the Indian is a cross with them. I know a case in which the father is a mixture of Indian, white and Negro. The mother is Mexican. By intermarriage you can go down to their level but you can't bring them up to yours. You can put that down and smoke it. When you cross five races you get meanness."[3] A ranch manager's wife in the same county was willing to allow for "educating Mexicans" with one condition: "Let him have as good an education but still let him know he is not as good as a white man. God did not intend him to be; He would have made them white if He had."[4] And a West Texas dairy farmer familiar with anthropological theory was in favor of educating Mexicans but noted that they would "never amount to anything . . . [because] they are brunettes. The blondes organize and are at the head in giving directions."[5] The specific racial explanations were diverse and incorporated historical, religious, and scientific arguments.

The Taylor interviews make clear, on the other hand, that these wide-ranging race arguments derived a basic shared meaning from the class structure of the farm societies. The fact that Anglos were the owners and bosses and Mexicans the field workers provided the necessary ground for the elaboration of these various notions of Mexican inferiority. Thus, the dairy farmer never strayed far from the practical importance of his blonde-brunette theory: "Mexican labor is as essential at this degree of latitude as plows. We are blondes. They have pigment to absorb the actinic rays of the sun. . . . I paid $50 for the course of Homer Milton Baker, anthropologist. Now I can pick the man that I want for my work."[6] More direct in pointing out the combination of race and class was a newcomer school official in Dimmit County: "We have a high type of American and low class Mexican people. The inferiority of the Mexican is both biological and class. White trash is not superior in intellect to the Mexicans we have here, but we don't have any white trash here."[7] Even religious principles that supported a charitable view were constrained by the sharp class differences that separated Anglo from Mexican. In the words of a Winter Garden housewife: "I try to be a Christian, but whenever it comes to social equality I won't stand for it. Say 'Mr.' or 'Mrs.' to the Mexicans? No sir-ee!! Not to the class we have around here."[8]

In short, the elements of race and class were inextricably interwoven in the minds of Anglo residents. When the pragmatic language of interest or control was not used to explain the segregated order, the language of race entered in a critical way to fill out the details, to paint the color, of the regional society.

Themes in Race-Thinking

While Mexican inferiority was taken for granted by most Anglos, their specific views were complex and belied any appearance of a simple pattern. Mexican inferiority meant different things to different Anglos. Native Texans recalled Texas history or remembered the experiences of long-dead relatives who had fought against Mexicans. Newcomers, who had no easy recourse to Texas history, relied on their own experience with colored peoples in explaining their treatment of Mexicans. Transplanted southerners merely transferred their views of black labor to Mexican labor, and some ex-midwesterners saw Mexicans as "domesticated Indians."[9] For those new settlers with no strong racial bias on which to build, assimilation of Texan frontier lore quickly filled the void, and many who initially were taken aback at the conditions they found in South Texas often became, with a few years of residence, more Texan than the old-timers.[10]

In the Winter Garden town of Catarina, for example, the initial reaction of its northern homesteaders was one of shock; they were unaccustomed to the low wages and brutal treatment of Mexican laborers.[11] Nonetheless, as a local Texan put it, although it was not customary to "knock the hell out of Mexicans," there were limits to equality from the very beginning: "The Mexican is accepted at Catarina as a laborer but not as a servile laborer. . . . Here you find the northerners working out in the field with a straw hat beside the Mexicans, but not for a minute do they think the Mexicans equal to them."[12] The Texan predicted that such attitudes about equality as existed would erode with the passing of time, for Mexicans "don't assimilate as do the Germans and the Italians and take part in civic life. In this respect the attitude of the people of Catarina will probably become less free than it is now." The comments of a Winter Garden school official, a newcomer, suggested the social adjustments one learned to make: "The newcomer here seldom comes into conversation with the local people. After a few years he takes the views of the older people. At first I felt like doing a lot more for the Mexicans. At the beginning I would not have been opposed at heart to their coming over to the white school, but after I heard the old-timers I felt differently. There is a line between the two towns."[13] The assimilation process worked its magic in the American farm towns. The distinction between old-timer and newcomer, so sharp in the first twenty years of the farm developments, gradually broke down.[14] Despite the reputed arrogance of Texan natives, newcomers showed themselves capable of learning old-timer lessons about "cotton and Mexicans."

From this diverse mass of ideas and images, however, one prominent thread emerges: it makes sense to speak of old and new sets of ideas. If one identifies and distinguishes the racial beliefs and sentiments held by old-timers and newcomers, the following pattern surfaces. Old-timer ideas were rooted in frontier memories, in war and battle with Mexicans and Indians. Newcomer ideas, on the other hand, consisted of concern with hygiene and notions of germ theories. These two sets of ideas were not rigidly compartmentalized between the two groups; what separated old-timers and newcomers was the ease with which they referred to one or the other set of images. With the "amalgamation" of newcomer and old-timer, the distinction between historical and hygienic themes gradually became unimportant.

The Old-timer Theme: Remember the Alamo!

One common justification for anti-Mexican prejudice lay in the Anglo-Texan legends and folklore about Texas history. In these popular accounts, the Mexican was portrayed as the enemy that Texans had fought and defeated in several official and unofficial wars throughout the nineteenth century. By the early twentieth century the story of the Alamo and Texas frontier history had become purged of its ambiguities—of the fact that Mexicans and Anglos had often fought on the same side. The exploits of Texas dime novels had become woven into an Anglo-Texan saga, into a history of the triumph of Anglo over Mexican.[15] Texans, according to historian T. R. Fehrenbach, "came to look upon themselves as a sort of chosen race." This legacy, symbolized by the battle cry "Remember the Alamo!" was part of the folk culture, an integral part of school curricula, and the essence of Texan celebrations.

Thus, for native Texans the lessons of history (and the fruits of victory) explained the Mexicans' inferior place. Texas history made the issue of equality with Mexicans a rather absurd proposition, as a native Texan, a schoolteacher, explained: "Maybe some day these greasers can be (elevated) but Mexico is too near, and past Texas history. . . . They look at Texas with covetous eyes. We have border troubles here, and revolutionary cliques. . . . In one Mexican uprising their aim was the King Ranch. We were in fear at night even in Caldwell County. We heard the 'Mexican troops were pressing towards Texas.'"[16] Regardless of which aspect of the Mexican problem was mentioned, Texans frequently injected a historical element in outlining their position. An Anglo cotton picker, for example, explained his opposition to Mexican immigration in the following way: "The study of the Alamo helps to make more hatred toward the Mexicans. It is human nature if a man does you wrong, slaughters your kinsmen. In fact I just ain't got no use for a Mexican and I am in favor of not letting Mexicans come over and take the white man's labor."[17] Such historical memories made up the popular Texan culture of the time; they encapsulated the world view with which Texans approached their encounters with Mexicans.

Although in many ways unnecessary for the task, Texan war memories facilitated the denigration of the Mexican. They constituted a ready-made and well-developed body of myths, symbols, legends, and explanations that were readily invoked to explain the peculiar society of Mexican Texas. The ease and confidence with which the farm settlers directed the making of their segregated order and the repression of Mexican laborers were based in part on their view of Mexicans as subjugated enemies.

The point may be stated another way. Texan historical memories played a part similar to that of Reconstruction memories in the Jim Crow South of the same period. As a southerner described the latter (in the 1940s): "Stories of Reconstruction days in the South are kept vividly alive not because of historical interest, but because they provide the emotional set which any good Southerner is supposed to have."[18] In the first forty years of the twentieth century, the story of the Alamo furnished both old-timer and newcomer with the emotional set for being "good Texans." Américo Paredes has summarized the matter well: "The truth seems to be that the old war propaganda concerning the Alamo, Goliad, and Mier later provided a convenient justification for outrages committed on the Border by Texans of certain types, so convenient an excuse that it was artificially prolonged for almost a century. And had the Alamo, Goliad, and Mier not existed, they would have been invented, as indeed they seem to have been in part."[19]

The Newcomer Theme: Mexicans Are Dirty

Even as the newcomer farmers were assimilated as Anglo-Texans, they transformed the pioneer ranch country into a modern farm world—into a society with new classes, new social relations, new definitions, new symbols. The world of Mexican *vaqueros* and *bandidos* had passed for most of the region; the memory of frontier conflict with Mexicans appeared largely as history, as events and tales spun by old-timers and described in books. A more prominent, more relevant appeal among the farm settlers was a reference to hygiene: Mexicans were dirty. This characterization constituted the primary language in which segregation was discussed and assessed among the farmers. Germ theories, in particular, were an excellent vehicle for explaining the separation or quarantine of Mexicans in Texas.[20]

These ideas about dirtiness were imported by the new settlers. "Twenty-five per cent of the newcomers," estimated Cameron County sheriff Emilio Forto (in 1919), "usually look upon the Mexican as filthy, unsanitary and sickly makeshift."[21] As a result "everything relative to the Mexican and his habits becomes repulsive to the American who has been fed on anti-germ theories for a lifetime." The repulsion was evident in the responses to Taylor's questions about "mixing with Mexicans." As one Nueces County farmer put it: "I don't believe in mixing. They are filthy and lousy, not all, but most of them. I have raised two children with the idea that they are above the doggone Mexican nationality and I believe a man should."[22] A. H. Devinney, superintendent of Agua Dulce schools in the same county, explained that Anglos "would drop dead if you mentioned mixing Mexicans with whites. They would rather not have an education themselves than associate with these dirty Mexicans."[23] Several counties away in Dimmit, a school official noted that such intense opinions were commonplace: "There would be a revolution in the community if the Mexicans wanted to come to the white schools.

"American School," Nueces County, 1929 (Taylor, *American-Mexican Frontier*).

Sentiment is bitterly against it. It is based on racial inferiority. We have an exaggerated idea of their inferiority. The Mexicans have head and body lice and don't want to bathe."[24]

Concern with hygiene did not exhaust the meaning of "dirty Mexicans." Anglos commonly used the adjective "dirty" as a synonym for dark skin color and inferiority. Another common but more complex use of dirtiness was as an expression of the class order in the farm societies. For some Anglos, dirtiness stood as an appropriate description of the Mexican's position as a field laborer. Thus, farmers, when they talked about dirty Mexicans, generally didn't mean dirty in any hygienic sense; they meant dirty in the sense of being an agricultural laborer, in the sense of one who "grubs" the earth. For others who believed, as one bus driver did, that Mexicans were a "nasty" people who lived in "bunches and shacks," dirtiness referred to the living conditions of Little Mexicos.[25] Mexican dirtiness, in this sense, was a metaphor of the local class structure.

As a class metaphor, the caricature was supported, on the one hand, by the fact that farm labor was exclusively the work of Mexicans. On the other hand, the notion of Mexican dirtiness was suggested and reinforced daily by the physical condition of the Mexican towns in Texas. Mexicans did live in "bunches and shacks." In the Winter Garden, according to a federal survey conducted in the 1930s, the "typical houses of Mexicans" were unpainted one- or two-room frame shacks with single walls, dirt floors, one or two glass windows, and outdoor toilets.[26] The poorer houses were "patched together from scraps of lumber, old signboards, tar paper, and flattened oil cans." Some of the families had no stoves, and the women cooked outside over open fires or, when the weather made it necesssary, inside in open washtubs. Cleanliness was impossible: "Children slept on dirt floors, rolled up in quilts; clothing was kept in boxes under beds or cupboards; and although most of the Mexican housewives strove for neatness and cleanliness, these were qualities impossible to achieve in the face of such obstacles."[27]

Given these living conditions, added the federal report, it was not surprising that sickness and disease were common in the Mexican quarter. Serious epidemics of preventable diseases like diphtheria "broke out" occasionally. Tuberculosis, according to a federal official in the area, was extremely high among Mexicans because they "had been undernourished over a long period of years." Such poverty-related diseases, needless to say, validated the fear Anglos had of dirty Mexicans; they enabled, in the psychiatric language of Joel Kovel, "the entire complex of prejudiced fantasies to attain the certification of belief."[28]

In short, the theme of dirtiness resonated with meaning. In the minds of Anglos it referred to the race, work position, and living conditions, as well as hygiene, of Mexicans in Texas. Although these various meanings of dirtiness could generally be found together in segregationist statements, the most respectable way of making the point was through an emphasis on the problem of Mexican hygiene. Thus, the *Report of Illiteracy* in Texas, a University of Texas bulletin issued in 1923, called for separate schools on the basis of cleanliness: for "those who have not seen can scarcely conceive of the filth, squalor, and poverty in which many of the Mexicans of the lower classes live." The report elaborated: "Many of the children are too ill-clad to attend school with other children. The American children and those of the Mexican children who are clean and high-minded do not like to go to school with the dirty 'greaser' type of Mexican child. It is not right that they should have to do so. There is but one choice in the matter of educating these unfortunate children and that is to put the 'dirty' ones into separate schools til they learn how to 'clean up' and become eligible to better society."[29] As evident from the previous discussion, eligibility to better society was somewhat impossible for most Mexicans. Since dirtiness was not just a matter of hygiene but of race and class as well, the task of cleaning up the dirty "greaser" type of Mexican proved elusive.[30]

In one word, then, the idea of dirtiness portrayed the manner in which the farm settlers thought of the matters of race and class in their new society. The notion was not to be taken too literally, as Taylor discovered. Thus, a group of Nueces County farmers challenged Taylor to a sarcastic bet—they would pay him a dollar for every dirty Mexican he found in town on Saturday mornings. Some school officials acknowledged that Mexican dirtiness meant inferior or lower class. And a Dimmit County pharmacist who refused to serve Mexicans at the fountain explained that "it isn't a question of cleanliness or education, but race."[31] The idea of dirtiness was sufficiently ambiguous to accommodate the various interpretations of why the Mexican had to be kept separate; yet it was sufficiently meaningful to represent the collective sentiment—the Mexican was inferior, untouchable, detestable.

The Need for a New Understanding

In one sense, the emergence of old and new ideas of Mexican inferiority mirrored the Mexican problem—the need to find a place for the Mexican—that accompanied the development of commercial agriculture. Like the buildings and other improvements that were established, new definitions and rules concerning place and protocol for Anglo and Mexican had to be constructed. Anglos had to discuss and decide the particulars. Should Mexicans be served at the counter? Can they ride the public trolley? Can they shop in town on Saturday afternoons? Their ideas of race, in this context, underscored the need for vigilance. The settlers were explicit on this point. A Winter Garden school official, a newcomer familiar with the imagery of filth, commented in regard to education that "we take any reasonable steps to keep the Mexicans from putting their heads in our door. They outnumber us. We keep a strict tight rein on the Mexicans."[32] Likewise, the evidence suggests that the memories of Texan frontier history resurfaced as public symbols in the early twentieth century—acting, of course, to keep the Mexicans "in line." A Central Texas teacher, an old-timer with a sharp historical sense, was candid about the need to control the Mexicans: "The Mexicans have to be kept in subjection in some way. They have to understand they're not the masters, or they'll attempt to master the American. Don't misunderstand me. We want to give them a chance to reach as high a social standard as possible, but as for mixing with them and associating with them personally!!"[33]

The war memories and germ theories of the Anglos, in other words, betrayed an element of anxiety, an uneasiness, about the new order. As a class metaphor, the caricature of "dirty Mexican" belonged to the lexicon of inferiority—"white trash," "filthy niggers"—that farmers and landowners used to describe the laboring classes. As a reference to hygiene, however, the caricature also suggested a situation where the symbolic basis for separation and control rested on the specter of contamination: the laboring class was seen not only as inferior but also as untouchable. The notion of dirtiness, in particular, seemed to be a fitting expression of this anxiety. As anthropologist Mary Douglas has observed, such notions, whether directed against fingernails, feces, or people of color, guard against "threatened disturbances of the social order."[34]

The specter of contamination and the fear of the enemy, then, suggest the estrangement of Anglo and Mexican in the developing farm order. The anonymity between the two, between farmer and worker, lay at the base for the segregation of the two communities. Physical separation was necessary to control the strange Mexican; the elaborate social rules that defined the proper time and place and modes of deferences were designed to make sure Mexicans understood their inferior status in the social order. Germ theories and war memories provided a rationale, an explanation, for these segregationist rules.

One further point remains to be explored. These race ideas not only were justifications for policies and behavior; they also contained the elements of a new understanding. The segregated order was, of course, ultimately supported through physical force, but much more effective in regulating everyday life were the ideas and values that were taught and reinforced through the reality of segregation. More effective was the word of the superior that passed for truth, for beauty, for honor, for morality. Douglas Foley and his co-authors suggest this type of legitimation in their history of Frio County when they note that "paternalistic kindness and the Mexicano's acceptance of Anglo superiority were far more powerful forms of control than physical violence."[35] To the extent that the notion of dirtiness and other ideas were accepted by Anglo and Mexican as criteria of inferiority, these ideas offered the prospect of an organic reconstitution of the new class society. Having already described the opinions of Anglo adults. I can now turn to the opinions of children, particularly Anglo children, and to the opinions of Mexicans with respect to the segregated world in which they lived.

Learning about Supremacy

The truth about Anglo superiority and Mexican inferiority was taught to the youngest generation of the farm towns. Newcomers into this world, those who migrated as well as those born into it, were taught the morals and rules of living in a segregated society. In a world already divided into compartments, these lessons about the important differences between Anglo and Mexican came in numerous, diverse, and easy ways. Anglo and Mexican children, for example, understood that separate schooling meant separation of superior from inferior. This meaning was taught to them in countless lessons—the Mexican school was physically inferior, Mexican children were issued textbooks discarded by Anglo children, Mexican teams were not admitted to county athletic leagues, Mexican girls could not enter beauty contests, and so on.[36]

The Anglo children readily understood the catechism of segregation: Mexicans were impure and to be kept in their place. Anglo children understood this well, of course, because their parents and teachers made it clear to them. One notable demonstration of their comprehension of these tenets occurred in Dimmit County when anxious school authorities found themselves short of books at the Anglo school. They had the Mexican children send over their books but "the American children refused to use any of the books . . . because they said the Mexicans had used them."[37]

It was the lot of Anglo boys, naturally, to maintain and defend social standards. In the Winter Garden, observed an approving official, the Mexicans were considered "almost as trashy as the Negroes," and "the white boys are quick to knock their block off if they [the Mexicans] get obstreperous." In Nueces County, where a similar situation existed, a school official put it this way, "The white child looks on the Mexicans as on the Negro before the war, to be cuffed about and used as an inferior people." In Corpus Christi, where the American high school accommodated a few Mexicans, Mexican students spoke bitterly about hazing and wanted a separate high school. In Dimmit County, many parents, both Anglo and Mexican, believed that separation was necessary to keep the peace, that separation avoided fighting. And some school officials in both Dimmit and Nueces frankly attributed the low attendance of Mexican children to the antagonism they encountered from Anglo students and teachers. Such antagonism, not surprisingly, often relied on the lessons learned from Texas history. One Texas Mexican recalled that "when we were told of the Alamo in school, some of the Mexicans stayed away from school and some never returned."[38]

On and off the school grounds, schoolchildren and their parents often seemed to be re-enacting the battles of Texas history. The calls to war were not for the prizes of land or markets but for the prizes of honor, privilege, and purity. Thus, Anglo girls were protected aggressively from Mexican boys. Suspicion of any touch invited immediate and serious retribution.[39] The Mexican consul stationed in El Paso described a case in this connection: "A seven-year-old American girl stumbled and cut her face. The mother asked, 'Did the Mexican boy hit you?' The child replied yes, although this was not true. The result was that the Mexican mother was injured by [omission in manuscript], who also shot her two sons in alleged self-defense. These sons were American-born Mexicans."[40] The actions of Anglo children and their parents were, of course, understandable in the context of local norms and practices; they were normal. Mexicans were untouchable inferiors, and disciplining those who stepped out of place was no offense.

Learning about Inferiority

The inferior place of Mexicans, as mentioned previously, could not be maintained by physical force alone. The stability of the segregated order rested on Mexican recognition of their own inferiority. Mexicans had to be taught and shown that they were dirty and that this was a permanent condition—that they could not become clean. How well did the Mexicans learn?

There were diverse responses in the Mexican community to these notions of Anglo supremacy and Mexican inferiority. Mexicans in the Winter Garden, according to Foley's historical account, had "contradictory feelings" of gratitude, anger, frustration, and resignation concerning their experience with Anglos. Some Mexicans accepted Anglo beliefs about Anglo superiority, yet others could never admit such things because they "hated them [Anglos] too much." Mexican youth in the same region displayed their defiance of the racial order with some regularity: heckling, gang rumbles, and other confrontations with Anglo youth were commonplace. And among the small but growing class of professionals and propertied townspeople, the "educated Mexicans" of which Taylor spoke, there were vigorous campaigns against discrimination and prejudice.[41]

Much of the Mexican response to the racial order, however, occurred on the cultural field created by the Anglo settlers. Judging from the campaigns organized by the League of United Latin American Citizens (LULAC), the rhetoric of protest conformed to the dominant ideas of the time. The argument the educated Mexicans wished to make, and they made it forcefully, was that not all Mexicans were dirty. A no less important argument was that American-born Mexicans were loyal, patriotic Americans. Thus, the expressed purpose of the league, which in the 1920s saw itself "as a small nucleus of enlightenment" for the rest of the Mexican community, was "to develop . . . the best, purest and most perfect type of a true and loyal citizen of the United States of America." The standards that the league expected of its exclusive membership were the highest standards of respectability—speak English, dress well, encourage education, and be polite in race relations. Andres de Luna, a prominent leader of the Corpus Christi chapter, explained the approach as follows: "We try to teach our children to be clean and to tell the teachers to send them back home to be cleaned. Some of the other nationalities are dirty too."[42]

In other words, the race ideas of Anglos—ideas of cleanliness, of beauty, of respectability—constituted much of the cultural ground on which segregationist policies were discussed and debated. These ideas were diffused throughout the social order, among young and old, Anglo and Mexican. The notion of Mexican dirtiness, in particular, permeated the opinion of the time, influencing even opposition arguments to segregation. The campaigns of LULAC were one example, but there were others. For instance, sympathy for the Texas Mexican led Professor Herschel Manuel of the University of Texas to take issue with the popular and official opinion about dirty Mexicans. Interpreting the epithet literally, Manuel conducted a comprehensive survey in the region to measure hygienic conditions among Mexican children.[43] He discovered, contrary to the widespread belief, that many schools had no difficulty at all with Mexican dirtiness. In one South Texas school with nearly nine hundred children in the first three primary grades, the "ratio of dirty children to total enrollment" was 3, 2, and 2 percent for the first, second, and third grades, respectively. Head lice was a more serious problem: 62 percent of the first graders, 50 percent of the second graders, and 46 percent of the third had been infected with lice at some point in the school year. In another school, however, the first-grade infection rate had been reduced "from 80 percent in the first month of school to 8 percent in the second month." There was room for optimism, concluded Manuel: "The treatment for lice is a very simple one and very effective unless the child is reinfected." The results of Manuel's study, however, do not matter so much; what is important and ironic in this defense of Mexicans was that Manuel had operationalized the idea of "dirty Mexican."

The limits to such hegemonic ideas were always present. The very contrast in living conditions that validated race ideas for the Anglo also ensured permanent questioning by the Mexican. Thus, the idea of cleanliness was constantly in danger of exposure as self-serving rhetoric that justified segregation. Even the ambitious middle-class Mexicans could not reconcile the contradictions between their assimilationist posture and the intransigence of the Anglo community. The editor of the *LULAC News*, F. Valencia, posed the dilemma concisely in describing the problem of securing adequate education for Mexican children in 1931: "But how can we make rapid strides toward this goal, when at every turn we are confronted by the segregation question in various towns? In some towns they say it is for pedagogical reasons. At others they give no reasons, and perhaps don't care to give any, they taking it for granted that the reason is well understood (inferiority as they see it). Such are the obstacles placed before us by the same people whose standards we are trying to adopt."[44] Cleanliness, as the educated Mexicans continually discovered, was simply not enough.

A Concluding Note

I have described how ideas of Mexican inferiority acquired significance in the context of the developing farm order. The Anglo settlers, in explaining the racial divisions of the farm society, either reached back into Texas history to ground their views on Mexicans or pieced these sentiments and beliefs together on the basis of notions about cleanliness. Separation of Mexican and American appeared logical given these ideas: Mexicans were dirty and untouchable or they were the enemy and therefore detestable. In either case, they had to be controlled and their contact with Americans carefully regulated.

These race ideas, moreover, point to the historically specific character of the class order; in this case, to a society composed of farmers and migratory laborers. The rich, clean, and loyal were of one color, and the poor, dirty, and disloyal of another. But the effectiveness of much racial imagery was based on the politics and culture of a particular class context. Thus, already in the late 1920s, the civil rights campaigns of the small Texas Mexican middle class suggest what the emergence of this class signified for the culture of racism. Although these campaigns were presented in the name of the Mexican community, they were essentially class-specific protests: they pressed for the rights of the respectable educated Mexicans. The aim of these protests was not the abolition of all discrimination or the eradication of the cleanliness standard; the aim rather was to secure an acknowledgment from Anglos that some Mexicans could become clean.

11. The Geography of Race and Class

THE PRECEDING chapters in this section have explored various aspects of the segregated world of the farm counties. In this chapter I would like to temper the discussion by considering two "favorable" aspects of Mexican-Anglo relations during the 1920s and 1930s. This will enable us to unravel the puzzling evidence of extreme variations in race relations in the greater Texas border region.

The complex character of Mexican-Anglo relations was plainly evident in the 1930s. In some counties, Mexicans and Anglos were completely separate. In others, there was an easy mingling among the two "races" and few social distinctions were drawn between them. The abrasive nature of the racial order, according to Paul Taylor, varied according to the "political condition" of the Mexican. O. Douglas Weeks, who surveyed the area about the same time as Taylor's farm research, commented on the "variety of aspect and condition" he encountered: "Strong contrasts exist even in a single county, and the Mexican element may be observed in all stages of development."[1] Two general points help clarify the complex patterns.

In the first place, relations between Mexicans and Anglos in the farm counties were not simply based on coercion or repression. The tendency for complete separation and exclusion was sometimes relaxed, in terms of both everyday social relations and general policy. Like the repression described earlier, protection on the part of Anglos did not appear randomly: it, too, had a distinct class character and surfaced under certain economic and political conditions. Anglo merchants catering to the Mexican trade, in particular, represented vulnerable points in the segregated farm order.

In the second place, the development of an Anglo farm society in the midst of a Mexican ranch order introduced sharp contrasts in the region. In 1930 there were two distinct societies: a world of cattle ranchers and more-or-less permanent laborers and a world of commercial farmers and migratory wage laborers, each with quite distinct Mexican-Anglo relations. Again, the character of these social relations was understandable in the context of the local class order.

The following discussion will first consider the vulnerable points in the farm society and then will describe the dual character of the rural region.

The Logic of Protection   – *protecting labor from La Migra when labor in short supply*

As powerful as the growers were in shaping the segregated farm order, the political cohesion within the Anglo community was limited and tentative. This touches on a common misconception in class analysis that common interests necessarily lead to solidarity or unified action. On the contrary, shared interests have often produced intense competition among those in a similar situation.[2] Whether solidarity or competition prevailed depended on the extent of agreement between various factions, the strategy pursued by organized groups, and the results of political debate, that is, on the details that make for "political cohesion." The important point is that the same set of interests could be pursued in different ways, with distinct results for social relations. In other words, the same class actors that in one instance repressed Mexicans could in other instances protect them. This logic of protection can be sketched as follows.

As discussed previously, the inability of Texas commercial farmers to establish effective, statewide labor controls meant that they continued to compete with each other for labor. Farmers were thus forced to use other strategies to recruit their labor—offers of slightly higher wages, better working conditions, and paternalistic, benevolent treatment. One Dimmit County grower described the situation well: "The Mexicans' only protection is that they are the only labor available, and you can't treat them badly and hold them. The relations between Mexican laborers and American employers are fine, and are regulated under economic, not personal pressure."[3] Motivated by fears of labor shortages during the critical harvest seasons, some growers ironically sought to protect the Mexican in places where he was completely despised. Commercial farmers and county officials in the Winter Garden area, for example, were quick to protest the harassment of Mexicans by the newly formed Border Patrol. In the words of Dimmit County Judge Elmo O'Meara: "The immigration officers are violating the bill of rights against unlawful search and seizure, and are perjuring and throwing Mexicans in jail until they say they were born in Mexico. . . . They stop Mexicans who were born here and search them and throw them into jail and cuss them."[4] Immigration officials, in countering such accusations, pointed out the façade of righteousness, noting that farmers and local politicians never expressed such zeal in defending the rights of Mexicans in education or health.[5]

In short, the Texas farmer had to be concerned about events and incidents that could provoke the migration or flight of Mexican laborers to other counties or to another state. The urgent demands for seasonal labor, according to a Dimmit County deputy sheriff, had moderated the harsh treatment of Mexicans: "They have had their shot-gun settlements, but not in this county. They need the Mexicans too badly here." In Nueces County, the same situation prevailed, that is, when labor was "short." As one prominent Nueces County resident put it, "farmers will take Mexicans to town, and pet them when they are in a tight place, but not when labor is plentiful."[6]

The element of competition also figured critically in the situation of workers and merchants in Texas. Anglo and Mexican workers in the state were even more disorganized than farmers, a condition that resulted in a relentless competition for jobs. Such disunity meant, expectedly, that intense antagonism toward Mexicans would be found in union halls and workplaces. In the 1920s the uniform reflex of organized labor was to establish some "color bar" to protect "American workers." But for the greater unorganized part of the Anglo working population, there was no such protective "color bar." The agricultural fields, especially, "belonged" to Mexicans, and the situation of any Anglo working alongside them was seen as a "sorry one."[7]

The posture of merchants, who were generally more flexible in these race matters, depended on whether or not they found themselves competing with each other for the domestic trade. Like the situation in the fields, where a "free labor force" meant kindness on the part of growers, a "free clientele" promoted kindness among merchants, that is, if they could not capture this domestic market in some way.

Such politics affected the whole tenor of the racial order, from labor relations to educational policy to smiles at the local store. It was here, in the pursuit of their particular interests, that some Anglos often befriended and protected the Mexican. Texas Mexicans, of course, were quite conscious that class interests within the Anglo community furnished a contingent source of protection. Whenever they could, they used these interests to improve their situation in rural Texas.

Merchants and the Flexibility of Salesmanship

The manner in which economic interest shaped Mexican-Anglo relations is clearest in the case of Anglo merchants, who were anything but consistent in their relations with Mexicans. Every town, according to one report, had merchants who were scrupulously honest and highly respected and merchants who charged usurious prices and were disliked.[8] The inconsistency is superficial, however, for what underlay the various personalities of the merchants were differences in the way money could be made from the Mexican trade. Where merchants had no control over the domestic trade, friendliness was quick to flow from the store. Where a captive clientele was assured, usually through some arrangement between retailer and local landlord, merchants sensed no need to act kindly toward their customers. What mattered, in other words, was whether the merchant was an independent retailer or an ally of local growers.

As might be expected of people who make a living by selling merchandise and supplies, retail merchants were quite knowledgeable about the various circumstances affecting their consumer market. Their success as merchants depended on their sensitivity to the commodity market as well as on an impressive knowledge about the cultivation of local cash crops, be they cotton, onions, or grapefruit. Merchants were likewise quite perceptive in assessing the earning power of their regular clientele. One Nueces County merchant who catered to Mexican sharecroppers and pickers, for example, was able to provide Paul Taylor with estimates concerning the typical earnings and living expenses, including doctor bills, for a Mexican family of five with only one field worker.[9]

Since the wages or crop portion paid a worker by a landlord critically affected the store trade, retail merchants were understandably responsive to changes in the basic terms of tenant and migrant labor contracts. In protecting their economic interests, in fact, merchants sometimes found themselves opposed to the labor practices of local landlords. In Nueces County, for example, Mexican sharecroppers who needed assistance in making their written contracts with landlords would approach a local merchant by the name of Stokes Holmes for advice. Farmers naturally objected to Holmes' advising the Mexicans, but his reply was that "the Mexicans then make me bad customers" if they sign bad contracts. Holmes had no desire to lose money on advances made to Mexicans.[10]

Transposed on the social fabric of the region, the importance of these dynamics should be evident. The retail merchant who wanted the Mexican trade represented a point of tension within the Anglo community and a potential source of protection for the Mexican. Retail merchants who catered to the Mexican population were concerned about a poorly developed domestic market, a concern that ran counter to the interests of agribusinessmen. If a consumer market

Mexican School, Nueces County, 1929 (Taylor, *American-Mexican Frontier*).

were to develop, Mexican labor would have to be paid more, and farm diversification would have to be promoted, a position advanced forcefully by the Laredo Chamber of Commerce.[11] Despite the considerable backlash from grower-dominated chambers of commerce, the Laredo statement was no isolated critique, at least among merchants. One storeowner in Big Wells, Texas, in the Winter Garden area, assailed the growers' notion of development: "As an economic proposition there is nothing to cheap labor. It is just like the slaves before the war. There are no inventions where there is cheap labor. With fewer Mexicans there would be more dairies, etc. You could not convince the slave holders that freedom was better than slavery. The poor whites here can't ask for a better house, etc., because the landlords can get Mexicans who won't ask for more than $20 a month advances."[12]

The merchant-customer relation moved Anglo merchants to behave in a friendly manner in their everyday contact with Mexicans. Many of these acts were of a symbolic nature, to be sure, but within an inhospitable context such gestures (the friendly conversation at the store, attendance at Mexican community functions) were seen as important. In the Winter Garden region, for example, where separation was carried out to a considerable extent, it was the merchant catering to the Mexican trade who attended their fiestas and performed other acts of friendliness. As the Big Wells merchant put it, "The Mexican dances on the Fifth of May and Sixteenth of September are attended by some Americans who go over to eat tamales, listen to the speeches, and buy from the booths. The merchant desires to reciprocate so he attends their fiestas. They don't try to edge in any way or to force themselves into our community. A line between the two groups? Absolutely distinct."[13] The story was the same throughout the border: merchants did nice things because they "desired to reciprocate." Mexicans, in short, were a clientele to be protected and sheltered. Thus, in one Dimmit County town an effort was made to pass building codes on the Anglo side that would have restricted Mexican ownership, but the move was defeated by "persons genuinely friendly to the Mexicans as well as potentially interested in selling portions of the area to them."[14]

There was no inherent reason, however, for the retail merchant to be allied with his working-class clientele. Certainly there is much evidence to the contrary: of merchants who immobilized workers.[15] The most common method merchants had for securing a portion of the customer market was through some mutually profitable agreement with local landlords. The landlord would give his sharecroppers and pickers credit allowances at a particular store, and he would stand good on any unpaid bills they might leave. In turn, the merchants would give a rebate or kickback to the landlord on the bill his workers accumulated at the store. According to one Mexican consular official familiar with conditions throughout Texas, the landlord's share of the store bill his Mexican workers ran up was usually 10 percent.[16]

In this type of setting, increased competition among retailers sometimes moved them to initiate pacts with local landlords in order to guarantee a portion of the domestic market. The introduction of "cash and carry" chain stores throughout rural Texas in the early twentieth century, for example, placed credit stores on the defensive, for goods purchased in cash-and-carry stores like Piggly Wiggly and J. C. Penney were cheaper than those in credit stores.[17] At this point the agreement between landlord and credit merchant assumed added significance. The refund given by credit merchants became an incentive for landlords to continue giving their workers credit allowances rather than wages or cash advances. The agricultural agent of Caldwell County explained the system as follows: "There are about four credit stores here which cater to the Mexicans and Negroes. . . . The prices are 10 to 25 percent above cash prices. The landlord rents to Mexicans who receive cash or credit allowances. If the Mexican receives credit, the stores give a 10 to 15 percent refund to the landlord on the Mexican's account."[18] In short, where the merchant was able to secure agreements with landlords concerning supplies for Mexican sharecroppers and pickers, the merchant had no need to put on a show of salesmanship.

Another common arrangement that "attached" Mexican workers to a particular store was through the establishment of a farm commissary by a landlord or an agribusiness company. The merchant in this case was merely an employee of the grower or company, and the store debt just another means by which a work force could be controlled. On the Coleman-Fulton Pasture farms around Gregory, Texas, for example, the head storekeeper, a former Kansas merchant, had placed control of his "coupon system" in the hands of the Anglo foremen, who kept a running tab of each Mexican family's debt, applied it directly against their wages, and spared the storekeeper the headaches of bookkeeping. Commissaries, in short, were rarely run as mercantile enterprises and were considered satisfactory if they broke even.[19]

In sum, benevolence was no intrinsic characteristic of storekeepers. This type of salesmanship became important only when merchants had no ties with landlords and the consumer market was unattached. In other words, the benevolent side of the merchant—

protective, friendly, always careful to reciprocate—surfaced under a particular political circumstance: the condition that consumers remained free to buy where they pleased. Basically, the same market competition that made for bargain sales at one store made for friendliness, fairness, and so on. Considering the sensitivity of Mexicans to the way Anglos related with them, such "noneconomic goods" were particularly effective in the greater Texas border region. Local reputations were built on such matters.

Protests and Accommodation

The diversity in local conditions, then, owes much to class-related divisions within the Anglo community. But this portrays only one side of the picture. Accommodation and resistance on the part of Texas Mexicans figured as a basic element in the political calculus shaping Mexican-Anglo relations. The variation in racial practice and policy resulted in part because Mexicans used the divisions within the Anglo community to obtain concessions and protection. The response of Mexicans to the school policies of the farm counties illustrates the dynamic.

Texas Mexicans resented the schooling provided them and went to considerable lengths to challenge "Mexican school" policies. In Bishop (1926), Texas Mexicans asked for and received a favorable ruling from the state attorney general concerning admission into an "American school"; in Kingsville (1927), Mexican parents, by threatening a legal suit against the segregated system, pressured the school district into building a modern, well-equipped Mexican school; in Big Wells (1929), Mexican parents boycotted the Mexican school until the local board hired a teacher interested in teaching Mexicans; and in Del Rio (1930), Mexicans filed a suit against the separate school system, the first of many legal challenges to come.[20] The success of Texas Mexicans in modifying segregationist policies, however, came from the pressure they applied on the vulnerable points of the farm order. The 1929 boycott in Big Wells, a Winter Garden town, may serve as an example.

In the spring of that year, Mexican parents in Big Wells met and agreed, in the words of one parent, to keep their children "out of school until we get a teacher with a better disposition toward the Mexicans." The boycott, however, was not limited to the school system but threatened all business establishments that did not support the parents' demand for a new teacher. The reason why the Mexican parents were successful—that is, "catered to"—might be best related by one of the local merchants: "We want their trade and we want them to work for us, so they are catered to here, so there is a teacher. The Mexicans might boycott us too. If we refuse to admit them my competitors will tell them that I am doing it and that will injure me."[21]

In other protest activity carried out by Texas Mexicans during this time, the vulnerability of the Anglo retailer was quickly exposed and used. In Corpus Christi and Robstown, both Nueces County towns, the League of United Latin American Citizens (LULAC), the civic organization composed of rising middle-class Texas Mexicans, applied the boycott successfully to eliminate racial distinctions in business places. Pat Shutter, a real estate agent and prominent LULAC member, related to Taylor one case in 1923–1924 where a housing addition of "Stafford" ran newspaper advertisements in the *Robstown Record* stating "for whites only" and "no Mexicans allowed." As usually happened with such well-publicized incidents, an organized response proved unnecessary. The collective understanding of Mexicans, a bond of resentment, sufficed to make an informal boycott effective. Shutter described the outcome: "Another addition was put on sale by Clark, Huntley, and Griffin at the same time, which was open to Mexicans. I sold quite a few lots to Mexicans for them— about $18,000 worth. Finally, Stafford, whose addition had not sold well, came and asked me to sell to the Mexicans. But I would not sell, and they would not buy, because they knew of the former *distinción*. Now the addition has sold to some Negroes and a few Mexicans who don't know about the old signs."[22]

Many of the successes achieved by these middle-class efforts did not challenge the rule of discrimination, but only provided for "exceptions." Such was the result, to cite Andres de Luna, of direct action that LULAC had taken in Corpus Christi only a few years before: "About 1924 there was discrimination at the Palace Bathing house against Mexicans. They demonstrated against Cruz Gutiérrez's daughter. It is all right to discriminate against the individual but not against the race, so I took some ex-service men, the blackest I could find, some of whom were wounded in France and had the whitest record any man could have. One of them offered to beat up the proprietor and call it square, but I told him not to do it. They went to the bathing house and were refused."[23] LULAC then threatened legal action and the proprietor, after closing down and thinking about the situation for a day, modified his policy. "There is still some discrimination," de Luna noted, "but it isn't against all Mexicans."

Invariably only "qualified" Mexicans—that is, the middle-class

Mexicans themselves—were exempted from social discrimination. Although Anglo businessmen, from realtors to bathing house proprietors, followed a general practice of not doing business with Mexicans, they were often willing, especially if pressured, to accept the "Castilian" or "cleaner type" of Mexican as a customer. As one businessman put it, "if a Mexican dresses well and is clean and wealthy, he gets by; but the old greasers, no."[24]

Texas Mexicans used the interests and internal conflicts among Anglos to protect and improve their situation, but the manner in which these vulnerable points were used also reflected the various interests and divisions among Mexicans. As one middle-class Texas Mexican in the Winter Garden district explained to Taylor, there were different sentiments and tendencies in the Mexican community. On the one hand, the laboring Mexicans had only "ill feelings" for the Anglos: "It is almost like Mexico here; the laboring people have nothing to say about the government. The average Mexican knows these things and cusses them [Anglos] when they see them drive by, and ask how they [can] ride around in fine cars and smoke cigars." The "stable" Mexicans like himself, however, wanted to better relations with the Anglos and thus were more cautious. The situation, after all, was improving. As he put it: "We have the best relations with the Americans and we don't want to spoil it. We just talk between ourselves [the more stable Mexicans] . . . not in barber shops and around where it would stir up the others. They are ignorant and might do things when mad. I don't want them to think like they do in Russia. I just tell them that things are getting better here."[25] During the 1930s, these concerns led LULAC to take controversial positions against other segments of the Mexican community—to support, for example, the repatriation campaigns of the Border Patrol and the police suppression of the pecan shellers' strike in San Antonio. There would be no vigorous or unified opposition against segregation until after World War II, when Texas Mexican veterans would organize to challenge domestic conditions of race supremacy.

Two Worlds of Race and Class

Besides the variations due to political circumstances, another source of complexity in Mexican-Anglo relations stemmed from the checkered development of an Anglo farm society in the midst of a semi-Mexican ranch society. South Texas residents were well aware of the diversity in local conditions. One Winter Garden pharmacist informed Taylor that Mexicans from outside the district were not used to being treated like inferiors: "Some of the Mexicans get pretty hot about it when we don't serve them. Those who come here from elsewhere are not used to it, but the local Mexicans are pretty well used to it."[26] A poignant statement about these differences in protocol came from a school superintendent who had just moved from Central Texas to a Gulf Coast town where relations with Mexicans were more relaxed. The superintendent was repulsed by what he found: "In Caldwell County if a Mexican tried to sit by you someone would knock him for a row of stumps. At a barbeque here I saw some old Mexicans rubbing up along against white women. They mix here like one race. You don't know how disgusting it makes you feel."[27] Other settlers saw the personal bonds between Anglo and Mexican in a positive light. In the words of a Nueces County man, "The white man will cuss the Mexican, and then in the evening on the cattle ranches, he's down by the fire with him, with the frying pan, and eating tortillas with his coffee. There never was a grander companionship between men."[28]

In South Texas, then, there were a number of perplexing contrasts in human relations—"white primaries" in some places, political machines in others; segregation here, integration there; and so on. A succinct explanation of this diversity consists in outlining the class structure of the two worlds of ranch and farm. The diversity of Mexican-Anglo relations, in other words, reflected the various ways in which ethnicity was interwoven into the class fabric of these two societies. These combinations of ethnicity and class can be examined systematically by organizing the description and information from the thirteen counties of deep South Texas according to two important elements—the extent of Mexican landownership and the manner in which work was organized. Landownership patterns basically defined the status of the Mexicans in the local society, and work arrangements set the framework for the social conventions and norms expected in Mexican-Anglo interaction. What must be discussed first, however, is the methodology used to cluster the county-based information.

Arranging the region's counties into clusters was no straightforward task. Published census materials tell us nothing about Mexican landownership, do not distinguish ranches from farms (both were counted as "farms"), and say little about the character of work arrangements. On some critical questions, the census data are actually misleading. For example, according to the 1930 "racial" breakdown (when Mexicans were counted as "other race"), there were no significant differences in the ethnic composition of ranch and farm counties. The ranch counties of Zapata, Jim Hogg, and Duval (with a 47.3 percent, 46.8 percent, and 68.1 percent "native white" composition, respectively) were not distinguishable from the farm counties of Willacy (41.9 percent "native white"), Cameron (47.5 percent), Hidalgo (43.6 percent), and Nueces (48 percent). Yet Anglo settlers commonly placed the three ranch counties among the "Mexican counties" of the region and the four farm counties among the "Anglo counties."[29] As it turns out, these popular perceptions were correct, the census was wrong, and I was left with a curious discrepancy that called for an explanation, a matter that will be resolved shortly.

In order to assemble the basic information needed, then, indirect indicators had to be extracted from the census and primary and secondary descriptions of the region. Thus, although statistical information on landownership patterns was lacking, a rough but accurate division was drawn between counties with "many" Mexican landowners and those with "few" Mexican landowners. With ample data from the *Texas Almanac and State Industrial Guide*, the region's counties were categorized with some confidence according to their primary economy. Counties were classified as ranch or farm according to the monetary value of livestock and crops in the locality. In cases where the value of each was approximately equal, the counties were classified as mixed ranch-farm areas. The census data on the average "farm" acreage in South Texas counties—usually over a thousand acres in ranch areas and under three hundred in farm areas—also corroborated the classification.

This categorization of South Texas counties illustrates rather clearly the contours of the region's two societies (see Table 12). There is, on the one hand, a correspondence between ranching and counties dominated by Mexican landowners (what were called "Mexican counties") and between farming and counties dominated by Anglo landowners ("Anglo counties"). Zapata, Jim Hogg, Brooks, and Webb counties formed the core of the Mexican ranch society, and Willacy, Cameron, Hidalgo, and Nueces the core of the Anglo farm society. There were, on the other hand, some interesting exceptions. Duval and, especially, Starr represent cases where Mexican *rancheros* had made or were making a shift from cattle or sheep raising to cotton cultivation. Kenedy and, to a lesser extent, Kleberg and Jim Wells counties represent the stamp of Anglo pioneer ranchers in the region. This classification of South Texas counties, then, provided the framework for organizing various types of information regarding everyday life—educational statistics, county politics, evidence of segregation and integration, even ethnic "labels" and images.

Table 12. Selected Characteristics of South Texas, 1930

Economic Category	Approximate Value (in millions) Stock	Crop	% "Native White"	No. Farm Laborers & % "Unpaid Family"[a]	% Illiteracy "White"	% Illiteracy Mexican
"Mexican counties"[b]						
Zapata — Ranch	$ .6	$ .1	47.3	345 (16.8)	8.2	12.0
Jim Hogg — Ranch	1.5	.7	46.8	402 (48.2)	12.7	22.5
Brooks — Ranch	1.7	1.0	32.9	533 (37.5)	12.4	28.0
Webb — Ranch	2.3	1.3	27.9	3,286 (3.7)	6.5	18.6
Duval — Ranch-Farm	1.7	1.5	68.1	1,577 (29.5)	20.1	35.0
Starr — Ranch-Farm	.7	1.0	22.1	1,196 (61.8)	16.8	25.0
"Anglo counties"[c]						
Kenedy — Ranch	3.3	0	13.7	143 (0)	4.0	66.6
Kleberg — Ranch-Farm	2.0	1.3	51.4	865 (21.3)	3.0	30.0
Jim Wells — Ranch-Farm	1.8	2.3	43.3	1,366 (33.1)	4.6	30.6
Willacy — Farm	.9	2.0	41.9	1,159 (10.0)	2.9	44.0
Cameron — Farm	.8	7.4	47.5	6,687 (5.6)	7.0	38.3
Hidalgo — Farm	2.4	9.3	43.6	8,270 (8.4)	4.2	35.0
Nueces — Farm	1.2	15.0	48.0	3,761 (6.7)	.3	25.0

Source: Based on Texas Almanac & State Industrial Guide, 1930: U.S. Department of Commerce, Bureau of the Census, Fifteenth Census of the United States: 1930, Population, vol. III, part 2, and Agriculture, vol. III, part 2.
[a] Males only.
[b] Counties with Mexican landowners.
[c] Counties with Anglo landowners.

Landownership—the Social Basis of Privilege

The presence or absence of Mexican ranchers or farmers critically shaped all spheres of local social life—politics, access to public services, the determination of rights and privileges, and so on.[30] In the prosaic language of a "distinguished Southerner" in Nueces County: ". . . in Laredo there are many influential Mexican citizens and they can't be treated like a *pelado*. The treatment given to Mexicans depends partly on the individual Mexican, who may be of high class, and partly on numbers; in Laredo there are so many you have to give them social recognition. In Corpus Christi there are no prominent families. . . . There is absolutely no social recognition of Mexicans in San Antonio."[31]

The significance of Mexican landownership in local politics was plainly evident. According to Edgar Shelton's detailed political survey of the region, where Mexicans owned the greater portion of farms or ranches they directed county politics. In fact, argued Shelton, "there is a definite connection between ownership of land and 'ownership' of public offices."[32] Thus, between 1911 and 1946, Mexican representation on county boards ranged from "equal"—that is, equal to Anglo representation—to complete control in five of the six Mexican counties. Only Jim Hogg County appeared as an exception to this pattern. In the Anglo counties, on the other hand, there were no Mexican officerholders in this thirty-five-year period except for an occasional "token." These tokens merely strengthen the contrast, for their tenures cluster around the early years, that is, when the victory of farmer over rancher was still incomplete. Thus, Willacy, Cameron, and Hidalgo counties all had token Mexican officials at some point between 1911 and 1926, but none after.

The presence of landed Mexicans also made for access to public education, in contrast to places where Mexicans were solely migratory workers. In the Mexican counties, schooling was a matter of patronage and compensation for loyalty to the political machine. Even teaching appointments, as González described the practice, were a resource that the local *caudillo* (boss) used to reward and control landed Mexican families.[33] Whatever may be thought of patronage in terms of providing qualified schooling, it stood in sharp contrast with the Anglo counties where Mexican schooling was inferior and segregated or nonexistent. In the Anglo farm areas, keeping Mexicans away from school was explicitly seen as a way of safeguarding a cheap labor supply.

The relationship between Mexican landownership and education is suggested by the "illiteracy" rates of "native whites" and Mexi-

Table 13. *Mexican Illiteracy in South Texas, 1930*

Type of County	% Mexican Illiteracy				Average
	0–19	20–29	30–39	40+	
"Anglo counties"	0	1	4	2	38.5
"Mexican counties"	2	3	1	0	23.5

Source: Based on Table 12.

cans, a 1930 Census statistic.[34] The distribution of Mexican illiteracy in Mexican and Anglo counties, as shown in Table 13, reveals a clear pattern: where Mexicans owned land, there was less Mexican illiteracy; where Mexicans were landless, their illiteracy rates were high.

"Peonage" and Wage Contracts—the Organization of Work

If landownership settled the question of who merited certain privileges and rights, the character of landowner-worker relations essentially defined how the class society was held together. Since work in South Texas was organized in two distinct ways—through "peonage" and wage contracts—ethnic relations expectedly varied accordingly.

In the ranch counties, the bonds between landowners and workers were essentially *patrón-peón* relations characteristic of *hacienda* society. Labor needs were satisfied through relatively stable, long-term arrangements. Well-known folklorist J. Frank Dobie, describing South Texas ranch life in 1931, offered a revealing portrait: "On the larger ranches the *vaqueros* are still a part of something like a feudal domain, getting their supplies largely from the ranch commissary . . . depending on other Mexicans of the ranch for human association, voting as the *mayordomo* advises, and very often regarding the ranch, in the manner that other people regard a town or a county, as a unit of citizenship. For instance, a King ranch Mexican calls himself a *Kineño.*"[35]

In the ranch counties, this *patronismo* allowed a certain type of friendship to develop between owner and worker. This tendency, in fact, has long been an important element of the reputed egalitarianism of "horse cultures" and open frontiers.[36] For example, J. Frank Dobie, aware of the complex character of South Texas, frequently made clear to his audience that it was possible to form friendships with *ranch* Mexicans. Dobie's favorite illustration was drawn from personal experience, for an "old, faithful Mexican" who had worked on the Dobie ranch for over twenty years was "almost the best friend" he had ever had: "Many a time 'out in the pasture' I have put my lips to the same water jug that he had drunk from; at the same time neither he nor I would think of his eating at the dining table with me."[37] Mexican *vaqueros* and other hands, of course, needed no instruction on the limits of their friendship with the *patrón* or *amo* (master). Whatever the social conventions of life "out in the pasture," familiarity or life-long association did not mean equality.

The contrast with Mexican-Anglo relations in the farm counties could not be sharper. Here no loyal permanent work force was necessary, and no real or fictitious kinship bound Anglo owner and Mexican worker together. Instead the two were tied through impersonal anonymous contracts, a relationship that became generalized in the very organization of social life. This meant, essentially, that the terms of separation, deference, and so on between Anglo and Mexican had to be defined explicitly and enforced by law and policy—simply because there was no other way of teaching the moral code of the new farm society. What is striking about the segregationist codes of the Anglo farm counties, then, was not just their "racist" character but the fact that these explicit rules were even necessary in the first place. In other words, underneath the mass of segregationist rules that defined the proper place and protocol of Anglo and Mexican lay an element of anonymity.

Although no direct measures of these two types of work arrangements exist, the census classification of male farm workers as either "wage laborers" or "unpaid family laborers" suggests the distinct social character of work arrangements in the region (see Table 14).[38] In the Mexican counties the number of unpaid family workers constituted a sizable fraction of the local farm labor force. Nearly 40 percent of farm laborers in Brooks County were unpaid family; in Hogg, nearly 50 percent; and in the interesting case of Starr County, 60 percent of the farm laborers were unpaid family workers. On the aver-

Table 14. *Unpaid Family Farm Labor in South Texas, 1930*

	% Male Farm Laborers			
Type of County	*0–24*	*25–49*	*50+*	*Average*
"Anglo counties"	6	1	0	12.2
"Mexican counties"	2	3	1	32.5

Source: Based on Table 12.

age, nearly one-third of the local farm labor in Mexican counties consisted of unpaid relatives of the "farmer." In the Anglo districts, on the other hand, the great majority of farm laborers were wage workers, and unpaid family constituted a relatively minor segment, about 12 percent, of the local farm labor.

In other words, kinship and work were closely related in the Mexican counties, an association that underscored the personal and paternalistic character of work in these areas. In the Anglo counties, on the other hand, with the slight exception of ranch areas, family and work were completely disassociated, suggesting the absence of any personal bond between farmers and workers.

The distinct character of work arrangements in ranch and farm counties also left an evident imprint on the way politics were organized. No trained eye was necessary to discern, during the 1920s and 1930s, the contrast between election returns from the machine counties and those from the nonmachine areas. In the Mexican counties and the Anglo ranch county of Kenedy, the preferred candidate regularly received 75 percent or more of the votes cast, whereas in the Anglo farm counties the preferred candidate rarely won more than 60 percent of the vote.[39]

In the ranch counties, the paternalistic bond between landowner and worker assured the rancher control over the votes of his loyal *vaqueros* and provided the base for a well-disciplined political machine. Shelton described the organization of "Latin American voters" in some Valley counties as "an army, with the county boss as commander-in-chief." Under the boss were "various lieutenant generals, colonels, majors," and so on down the line, each of whom was responsible for maintaining the "strict discipline" of ten or more subordinates.[40]

No such personal bond existed in the farm society, and thus the idea of Mexican voting had a very different meaning than that in the ranch areas. The contrast appeared clearly in an editorial statement of the *Carrizo Springs Javelin,* which explained why Dimmit County had created a White Man's Primary Association: "Not that any bribery was alleged but it was 'loaning' money to this Mexican, 'standing good' for that Mexican's grocery bill, employing white men to act as 'interpreters' to present their cause to the Mexicans, and contributions to this or that Mexican baile, making the life of the candidate just one blamed thing after another."[41] Political practices that in ranch areas were seen as expressions of "friendship and love" were seen in farm areas as "just one blamed thing after another." Not only had wage contracts between farmer and worker made paternalism a thing of the past but they also made any paternalistic control over workers next to impossible. The loyalty of Mexican workers thus suspect, and undesired in any case, disfranchisement seemed to be a logical measure for the newcomer farmers to take. The White Man's Primary Association was the most obvious method newcomers used to control the Texas Mexican politically, but other means of accomplishing the same end—literacy tests, poll taxes, intimidation, for example—were no less effective.

Castilians and Mexicans—the Ordering of Ethnic Images

Class variations not only affected the organization of politics and the distribution of privilege in the region but also influenced the cultural side of ethnic relations, the signs and definitions of social status. As noted previously, Mexicans were generally seen as a "race"—an inferior people—in the modern farm era. The "Castilian" landowners as well as the small Texas Mexican middle class in the cities resented the "race" stigma attached to them in this period. Not surprisingly, then, the identification of Mexicans as a distinct "race" became, like the question of political representation and civil rights, an important issue to be settled locally.

Ironically, the most systematic evidence in this regard comes from the "flawed" census statistics mentioned earlier. These inaccuracies consist of overestimations of "whites," overestimations that did not occur randomly but were concentrated in counties with a landed Mexican class. Thus, although most observers of the period calculated the "American" element in Zapata, Jim Hogg, and Duval to fall between 10 percent and 25 percent of the total population, the 1930 Census reported 47 percent "white" in Zapata and Jim Hogg and 68 percent in Duval. A comparison with the Texas school census for the period suggests that as much as 30 percent of the reported "white" population in these counties may have referred to Mexicans. Similar reports leads us to suspect the percentage "white" in Brooks (32.9 percent), Webb (27.9 percent), and Starr (22.1 percent) as somewhat exaggerated. Whether these high miscounts occurred because landowning Mexicans identified themselves as "white," because the census taker classified them as such or because the local county government made sure they were counted as "white" is a question that cannot be answered. The answer would make little difference in any case, for this pattern of miscounts lends support to the general argument I have been advancing—that being "Mexican" derived its meaning within the social and political context provided by local class structures.

A Concluding Note

Various features of South Texas—political representation and organization, access to schooling, types of labor controls used, ethnic images—have been examined in the context of Mexican landownership and relations between owners and workers. The variations in ethnic relations reflected, in particular, the presence of distinct Mexican ranch and Anglo farm societies.

In ranch counties, where there were landed Mexicans, one found Mexican officeholders, access to schooling, lack of officially sanctioned discrimination, and other evidence suggesting that being "Mexican" carried with it no significant pejorative meaning. The work arrangements between landowner and worker were paternalistic and permanent, providing the social basis for disciplined political machines, loyal workers, benevolent *patrones*, and an "organic" understanding of the social standing of each. In the farm counties, where there were no Mexican landowners, everything was to the contrary and segregationist rules separated Anglo and Mexican thoroughly. Owner-worker relations were formal and anonymous, making explicit controls by the farmer elite necessary. Thus, the farm counties were characterized by political disfranchisement, repressed wage workers, absentee "town farmers," and a "rational-legal" code that defined the separate standing of Anglo and Mexican.

The exceptions to this duality strengthen the analysis by demonstrating how the class factors of landownership and work arrangements combined in different ways. Thus, the Anglo ranch county of Kenedy conformed in every way with what one finds when no Mexican landowners were present—no political representation, high illiteracy, and so on; but it also reflected the effects of *patrón-peón* relations—machine politics, the importance of patronage and paternalistic control, and emphasis on loyalty. In short, since the class composition of both Anglo and Mexican communities varied from county to county, racial policy and protocol also varied.

The farm settlers, of course, understood the reasons for mixing and leniency in the cities and along the border. As one Winter Garden grower told Taylor: "We segregate the Mexicans here. They have their own town. On the border they mix. . . . On the border you do business with the Mexicans and they were a great social class there once. You can't be quite so rough on them."[42] A Dimmit County merchant said likewise: "Politics is the reason for mixing of Americans in San Antonio and Laredo. There they can't offend the Mexicans."[43] Although the merchant was hardly the staunch ally of the Mexicans, nonetheless where they were a prominent class—in

cities like Brownsville, Laredo, Corpus Christi, and San Antonio—
Mexican-Anglo relations were more relaxed than in areas where
growers were more or less in complete control. As a political force to
be reckoned with, merchants represented a potential division within
the Anglo community that Mexicans could use to secure protection
and concessions.

The urban centers in the Texas border region thus appeared much
like the occasional oasis in a great desert: in the cities, a few "qualified" Mexicans could attend school with the *americanos*, sit in the
movie houses and buses without distinction, and attend official social functions. The presence of a large number of Anglo merchants
and Mexican consumers, particularly those of the small but influential middle class, was critical in this respect.

What gave "race relations" their specific expression, then, was
local politics. The complexity of Mexican-Anglo relations does not
suggest an unintelligible, amorphous phenomenon; rather, this diversity reflects the varying class politics in counties across the Texas
border region. The fact that merchants were important in urban
areas, that farmers ruled unchallenged in counties like Dimmit,
Zavala, and Willacy, that in some counties like Webb and Duval the
Mexican rancher retained his influence—this pattern goes far in explaining the complexity of Mexican-Anglo relations in Texas.

PART FOUR

Integration
1940–1986

Left: Striking farm workers on a march to Austin, outside Kingsville, March 4, 1977 (photo by Abel Cavada; *Caracol* 3, no. 9 [May 1977]). *Above:* Chicano school set up during boycott of school system, Houston, 1970 (*450 Years of Chicano History*, p. 135; courtesy Chicano Communications Center).

US press "discovers"
Mex-Am population

"A Minority Nobody Knows"
    —*Atlantic Monthly*, June 1967
"Texas' Sleeping Giant—Really Awake This Time?"
    —*Texas Observer*, April 1969
"No More Sombreros: The Chicano Rebellion"
    —*Nation*, December 1969
"Silent Minority Starts to Speak Out"
    —*U.S. News & World Report*, July 1970

*"The Gringo took your grandfather's land, he took
your father's job, and now he's sucking out your
soul. There is no such thing as 'mala suerte' [bad
luck]; there are only 'malos gringos.' He's keeping
us in slavery now through our jobs, through the
lousy education you're getting at school, through
everything that affects us."*

    —Pamphlet of the Mexican American
    Youth Organization, April 1969

A Struggle for Full Citizenship

[margin annotation: why was segregation weakened after WWII?]

On the eve of World War II, segregation was a formidable solution to the "Negro problem" in the South and the "Mexican problem" in the Southwest. The United States, according to C. Vann Woodward, was traveling a route parallel to that of South Africa. Sometime around World War II, for reasons still not fully understood, the paths of the two countries diverged.[1]

[margin annotation: agric labor less imp-tt]

One promising lead, suggested by the work of Stanley Greenberg, points to a shift in the primary economic sector from commercial agriculture to urban industrialism as a significant contextual factor in the decline of race segregation. In brief, farm mechanization and the rise of corporate farming made labor repression irrelevant for agricultural production. Urban businessmen, moreover, found labor stability and consumer markets more important than maintaining the old racial framework. Faced with pressure from below, the business community generally took the lead in abandoning an outmoded racial order.[2]

In Texas the limited economic and political role of commercial farmers was evident when they proved unable to institute their labor controls as a formal, coherent system. "Imperial Texas," as D. W. Meinig has described the pretensions of the former republic, was not a sovereign state that could chart an independent course of economic development.[3] Despite many heated defenses of "States' Rights," Texas could not hold its labor resources from midwestern and northern agricultural and industrial interests. Continued economic development thus gradually undermined the social base for "Jim Crow."

This erosion of segregation, which sociologists loosely attribute to industrialization and urbanization, reflected a change in the framework of Anglo-Mexican relations, a shift from a class order of growers and farm laborers to one where merchants and middle-class consumers were prominent. Such structural changes, however, were by themselves insufficient to upset the segregationist order. The demise was not predestined; rather, the system persisted, enduring constant tensions and contradictions, until finally worn down by the trauma of two major crises—World War II and the civil rights movement of the 1960s.

The tenacity of the racial order can be seen in the protracted, almost futile course that legal challenges followed through the state and federal courts. The legality of White Man's Primary Associations in Texas, for instance, was debated in federal courts in five major cases spanning a twenty-six-year period, from 1927 to 1953, and federal enforcement of these court decisions would not come for at least another decade. In a similar vein, the question of Mexican school segregation was adjudicated in two major cases—in the 1930 Salvatierra case and in the 1948 Delgado case. In the former, the "separate but equal" provision was held inapplicable for Mexicans but nothing was done beyond the particulars of the case. In the latter, school districts were enjoined from segregating "Latin Americans," but state authorities did nothing other than stop designating schools as "Mexican" in their official correspondence and publications.[4] In this context, the 1954 *Brown* v. *Board of Education* case, while a significant precedent overturning the "separate but equal" doctrine, produced few immediate results. On the contrary, the Brown decision stirred an Anglo backlash, which stalled desegregation attempts except where Texas Mexicans and blacks were active political communities.

In my use of the term, then, the "integration" of the Texas Mexican refers primarily to the granting of effective citizenship. This signified a dissolution of the authority principle, whose origins dated to the Mexican War. A century later, in the late 1940s, this principle was challenged aggressively by Mexican American veterans, who used the legitimacy they earned in World War II to press their claims to full citizenship. While these efforts produced some improvements in the cities of the region, it would take another decade and a major civil rights mobilization before the dismantling of the institutions of segregation—separate schools, voting restrictions, job discrimination—would seriously begin.

The national "discovery" of the Mexican American in the late 1960s apparently heralded the integrative process. As is common in such discoveries, the focus of this attention centered on the characteristics of the "new" group. The changed institutional context of which the discovery was symptomatic, on the other hand, was largely ignored. The monumental work of Leo Grebler, Joan Moore, and Ralph Guzmán, *The Mexican American People*, was representative of this unbalanced approach.

As Grebler and his co-authors put it, contrary to the "stubborn notions" that Mexican Americans were unassimilable, they were merely immigrants who were in need of "assimilative opportunities." Even the indigenous Spanish Americans were "a relatively recent immigrant group when *social* rather than legal status" was considered.[5] Of course, such a "social rather than legal" criterion would also have made Anglos "relatively recent immigrants" to the Southwest, but these writers seem to have been unaware of this possibility.

Such details in the work of Grebler, Moore, and Guzmán may perhaps be overlooked in light of their positive assessment for the future of the Mexican American. What cannot be ignored, however, is the striking but common paradox where the historical legends of the Alamo, cowboys, and Longhorns co-exist innocently alongside sociological studies of Mexican Americans as immigrants. Immigrant approaches, such as that of Grebler, Moore, and Guzmán, serve to shift the emphasis away from war and annexation, denying the memory of these origins for contemporary Mexican-Anglo relations. Rather than a people living under the shadow of the Alamo and San Jacinto, Mexican Americans are now seen as another immigrant group marching through the stages of assimilation. For the possibility of gaining full citizenship, such historical revisionism may be a small price to pay.

12. The Demise of "Jim Crow"

GREAT STRIDES in dismantling the segregationist order have occurred since the 1940s, but we—the generations that have lived through these decades—may not have a clear comprehension of the events we have witnessed. The more activist and "younger" of us may emphasize the critical place of the civil rights movement, believing that struggle and organization alone brought the old racial patterns down. Those with a more detached and "older" view may point to basic changes in economic and political structures as a primary cause. Both views contain persuasive elements but remain inadequate as separate explanations. A full understanding of the changes in race patterns must weave together the elements of social protest and structural change into one cloth, into one argument. The following chapter attempts to do this. Put in its barest, the argument is that, yes, we "living generations" have indeed made history but not in a world of our choosing. The demise of segregation was not a simple reflex reaction to an opposition movement; it was also the result of fundamental shifts in economic and political conditions.

"Jim Crow" may appear to be an odd description of the situation of Mexicans in Texas. There was no constitutionally sanctioned "separate but equal" provision for Mexicans as there was for blacks. According to the prevailing jurisprudence, Mexicans were "Caucasian."[1] But in political and sociological terms, blacks and Mexicans were basically seen as different aspects of the same race problem. In the farm areas of South and West Texas, the Caucasian schools were nearly always divided into "Anglo schools" and "Mexican schools," the towns into "white towns" and "little Mexicos," and even the churches and cemeteries followed this seemingly natural division of people. This was not a natural phenomenon, however, but the cumulative effect of local administrative policies. In the farm districts, the result was a separation as complete—and as "de jure"—as any in the Jim Crow South. To emphasize these commonalities, I use "Jim Crow" to refer to a situation of nearly complete separation and control of blacks or Mexicans. This use of Jim Crow also serves as a reminder that this demise was regional in nature. Throughout the South, the movement of people from farms to cities and industries

was accompanied by the collapse of the South's rigid race segregation. The institutional supports of southern conservatism, as V. O.
Key identified them—the one-party structure, malapportionment of
state legislatures, and disfranchisement of blacks—all crumbled.[2]
A similar institutional collapse occurred along the greater Texas
border region.

What caused the demise of Jim Crow for Mexicans? The segregated order was based ultimately on the political influence of the ✦
farmers, and herein lay the weaknesses of segregation in Texas and,
by extension, the Southwest. Already by World War II, growers had
begun to give way to urban commercial interests as a social and political force in Texas. Agribusiness itself gradually became "urbanized"
as resident farm ownership passed into corporate hands. The bottom
layer of the segregated order also collapsed as farm workers emi-
grated to the cities or to the fields of other states.

For their part, the new urban elites, in spite of their conservatism,
constituted a weakened foundation for Jim Crow. Financiers, industrialists, and merchants had never been as dependent as growers on
labor repression. In the absence of repression, an element of competition characterized the posture of Anglo merchants in their relations with Mexicans. Such competition signified vulnerable points
in the racial order, points that Texas Mexicans leveraged (as workers,
consumers, and voters) to secure concessions and "rights." Mexicans
in the cities remained second-class citizens, but Anglos were more
cautious and respectful. Thus, the character of Mexican-Anglo relations in recent memory has manifested a clear rural-urban dichot-
omy: segregation and repression in the countryside; partial integration and patronage in the cities. These differences were evident in
the 1940s but would become increasingly sharper over the following
two decades.

Such contrasts lent hope to liberal Texas intellectuals of the 1940s
and 1950s that industrialization and urbanization would weaken the
inefficient and counterproductive system of race segregation. Pauline
Kibbe, executive director of the first Good Neighbor Commission,
for example, recognized that a primary cause of anti-Mexican discrimination stemmed from the state's agricultural character. The
solution to the Mexican problem, reasoned Kibbe, lay in the expec-
tation that capital would be "liberal and progressive" and labor "co-
operative" in industrial society.[3]

Change in Mexican-Anglo relations did occur during the period
of industrialization, but not because of progressive capital or co-
operative labor. Likewise, the flexibility of the racial order in the
cities could not be attributed to some special "assimilative" quality

in urbanization; the fact that Texas cities in the 1940s were major "leaks" through which the Mexican escaped from the rural "caste system" has to be explained in the context of the various competing interests of local class groups.[4]

Social conflict and national crises provided the necessary impulse for the decline of old race arrangements. World War II, in particular, initiated dramatic changes on the domestic front. The need for soldiers and workers, and for positive international relations with Latin America, meant that the counterproductive and embarrassing customs of Jim Crow had to be shelved, at least for the duration of the emergency. In more lasting terms, the war created a generation of Mexican American veterans prepared to press for their rights and privileges. The cracks in the segregated order proved to be irreparable.

The cracks did not rupture, however, until blacks in the South and Mexican Americans in the Southwest mobilized to present a sharp challenge from below in the 1960s. In Texas the protest activity among all segments of the Mexican American community—farm workers, factory workers, students, professionals, businessmen— was unprecedented. This complex movement accelerated the decline of race restrictions in the cities and initiated a similar process in the rural areas.

The following discussion highlights, in overlapping sketches, four important events of recent Texas history: the emergency of World War II, the mechanization of labor-intensive agriculture, the emergence of urban-based political power, and pressure from below and outside—the civil rights struggle of the 1960s.

War and Industrialization

The industrial and urban revolution came to Texas abruptly under the "forced march" of World War II. The number of manufacturing establishments increased from 5,085 in 1940 to 7,128 in 1950; the number employed in these plants increased from 163,978 to 328,980. As a result of the building of a great war industry, nearly half a million people migrated from rural counties to industrial centers. Two hundred Texas counties lost population to the remaining fifty-four counties. The census figures suggest the remarkable growth in the urban population: from 2,911,389 or 45.4 percent of the state population in 1940 to 4,834,000 or 62.7 percent in 1950.[5]

Along with this sweeping transformation came a momentary relaxation of race segregation. This was not due, however, to "industrialization" or "urbanization" but rather to the war emergency. What makes this evident is that, prior to the war, industrialization and urbanization had merely incorporated the previous patterns of race exclusion.

In the prewar period, the urban situation for the majority of Mexicans was not vastly different from that found in the rural areas, in spite of some concessions. The urban Mexicans of Corpus Christi, San Antonio, and the bigger towns of South Texas, for example, attended school in relatively high proportions compared to rural Mexicans. Nonetheless, the public schools in these cities were segregated, businesses refused to serve Mexicans in places patronized by Anglos, and the Catholic churches conducted special services to prevent contact between Mexicans and Anglos. "Urbanization" merely signified the geographic expansion of segregation. Thus, as the "Mexican town" of San Antonio grew in the 1930s, new subdivisions on the Anglo side (such as the Jefferson and Harlandale areas) began to adopt restrictive covenants prohibiting the sale or rental of properties to persons other than of the Caucasian race—"implicitly excluding the Mexicans."[6]

Generally speaking, during the 1930s Anglo businessmen and skilled labor in the cities and big towns reproduced the prevailing racial practices of the countryside. The exceptions to this pattern were the border cities (El Paso, Laredo, Brownsville), where ethnic relations were flexible and pragmatic, that is, more a matter of class than of race. Away from the border, however, Mexicans were as a rule confronted with general discrimination. According to Kibbe, Mexicans experienced four kinds of discrimination: refusal of service in public places, real estate restrictions, police brutality, and employment barriers.[7] Of these, the employment barriers pointed most clearly to the castelike position of the urban Mexican.

Racial segmentation characterized the urban and industrial labor market across the state. In the oil industry, both Mexican and black workers received a lower wage (of several cents per hour) than did Anglo Americans in the same classification. The "Latin American" and black workers were not permitted to use the drinking fountains or the toilets and bathing facilities provided for Anglos. Nor were they permitted to punch the same time clock or receive their pay through the same window used by Anglos. A similar situation was to be found in the railroad industry.[8]

In San Antonio, according to a 1927 survey by the Texas Agricultural and Mechanical College, Mexican workers were limited to the unskilled labor market, while skilled occupations were nearly completely dominated by Anglos. Of twenty-eight skilled categories, Mexican employees had a significant presence in only three—structural iron (132 of 217), blacksmith (45 of 119), and automotive

Above left: Legal exhibit in school segregation case; modern school in Mathis, 1954 (courtesy George I. Sanchez Collection, Benson Latin American Collection, University of Texas at Austin). *Below left:* Legal exhibit in school segregation case: Mexican school in Mathis, 1954 (courtesy George I. Sanchez Collection, Benson Latin American Collection, University of Texas at Austin). *Above:* Executive Committee meeting of the School Improvement League, 1948; young man seated at far right is future Congressman Henry B. Gonzalez (courtesy E. Escobar Collection, Benson Latin American Collection, University of Texas at Austin).

painting (128 of 336). Among the categories that Mexicans were excluded from were retail sales, commercial trades (bookkeeping, general clerks, stenographic), and airplane and engine repair; and Mexicans were barely present in the printing and building trades; for example, of 2,551 carpenters only 150 were Mexicans. The same condition prevailed in employment by the city and the public utilities, where Mexicans were found only in common labor positions until World War II.[9]

In many cases job discrimination was not the result of management policy but of union policy. During the 1930s the great majority of labor unions (especially the skilled crafts) refused to admit Mexicans and blacks to membership, thus making their employment by management virtually impossible. The only unions readily open to Mexicans in the early 1930s were "Mexican unions" like the Hod Carriers and Common Laborers Union.[10]

In short, neither urbanization nor industrialization brought about the relaxing of race restrictions in the 1940s. Such relaxation as occurred had to do with the war emergency—with the need for soldiers and workers. Labor shortages opened job opportunities, military service presented many with training and experience, the need for stable relations with Mexico stimulated a drive to minimize discrimination, and the war emergency sanctioned such experimental measures as the Fair Employment Practices Committee.

These war-related necessities, however, did not require any real consensus, much less commitment, about a policy of nondiscrimination. The war years, in fact, saw a worsening of relations between Anglos and Mexicans in the Southwest. Increased discrimination, growing friction (including pogroms and police raids of barrios), and Mexican government irritation all reached new heights by 1945.

In rural Texas, Jim Crow conditions remained virtually unaffected by the war against Hitler and race supremacy, a situation that prompted Mexico to exclude the state from its international agreement regarding guest workers (*braceros*). The ban was not a "blacklist," as Mexican Consul General Miguel Calderón politely put it, but "merely exceptional measures for protecting Mexican Nationals in view of exceptional circumstances prevailing [in] this State." In 1943, in response to Mexico's blacklisting, Gov. Coke Stevenson established the Good Neighbor Commission (GNC) and had the legislature approve a "Caucasian Race Resolution," which forbade discrimination against "Caucasians." Pauline Kibbe, the first executive director of the GNC, called on Texans to remember that the state constituted "a living laboratory experiment in American unity" on which the eyes of the Americas were focused; that Texas was "a test case to prove or disprove the validity of the Good Neighbor policy."[11]

Such exhortations and other neighborly rhetoric did little to alter the shape of things. The Mexican government wanted "positive action and not bureaucratic lip service," as one GNC official put it. The strongest antidiscrimination plans devised by Texas authorities were based on voluntary cooperation. Nonetheless, Consul General Calderón noted, such steps would be "constructive and helpful in eliminating discrimination." In reference to a proposed "Stilley Plan," Calderón suggested to Texas representatives that they "experiment the Stilley Plan with American citizens of Mexican origin in order to appreciate its good results."[12]

In the cities, it also seemed that the war crisis would accommodate itself to previous employment patterns. According to one estimate, less than 5 percent of the Mexican American community in Texas was employed in war industry in the early 1940s. Those industries that did provide employment to Mexicans restricted them to common or unskilled labor jobs regardless of their ability or training. At San Antonio's Kelly Field, where approximately 10,000 of 35,000 civilian employees were Mexican Americans, none had a position above that of a laborer or a mechanic's helper. This pattern was common throughout the Southwest. Federal investigations in the mining, oil, ship, and aircraft industries in 1943–1944 revealed that in a good many cases "Latin Americans" classified as common laborers and semiskilled workers were in fact performing skilled jobs at the lower rate of pay.[13]

The weakening of labor barriers was due to direct federal intervention in the form of the Fair Employment Practices Committee (FEPC). Created by executive order, the FEPC was charged with the task of seeing that no federal agency or company doing business with the government discriminated against any person because of race, color, creed, or national origin. Field operations did not begin in the Southwest until 1943, and only then did Mexican labor begin to be integrated into the industrial plants. Carlos Castañeda, FEPC regional director for Texas, New Mexico, and Louisiana, stated that "the shipyards, the airship factories, the oil industry, the mines, the munition factories, and the numerous military and naval installations slowly, reluctantly, and with much misgivings, began to give the Mexican American a trial in semiskilled positions, and eventually in some skilled jobs."

These trials and experiments met general opposition from Anglo employees during the war years. In one dramatic episode in 1945, the oil union at Shell's Deer Park Refinery responded to the FEPC-ordered upgrading of three "Latin Americans" by going out on a wildcat strike in protest. Even within the FEPC administration, resistance to FEPC policy surfaced. Many staff members told Castañeda that when the war "was over the Mexican American would be put in his place."[14]

Whatever appearance of "fair employment" and unity existed during wartime rapidly evaporated during peacetime. One Sam Smith of Sonora expressed the opinion of many in West Texas when he complained to Texas officials that he and his fellow veterans did not fight for "ill-smelling Mexicans" who were overrunning movie houses and would soon probably move into swimming pools, dancing places, schools, and cafés; they were even taking veterans' jobs. Thus, with the return of the normal labor supply and the withdrawal of such controversial wartime agencies as the federal FEPC, job discrimination against Mexican Americans returned in force. When the United States employment offices were turned back to the states in November of 1946, they (in Castañeda's words) "relapsed to the discriminatory practices in general use before the war." Mexican Americans who registered for skilled jobs were never referred to the employers calling for such skills. The only openings to which the former U.S. Employment Service referred Mexican Americans were common labor jobs.[15]

Some observers saw an overall attempt to destroy any economic or social gains made by Mexican Americans during the war years. The South Texas newspapers had begun a steady campaign against the Mexican and his "lawlessness." And every attempt by Sen. J. Franklin Spears of San Antonio to check anti-Mexican discrimination was defeated. With the entry of thousands of "wetbacks" in the mid-1940s, the ineffective Mexican ban and the accommodating Good Neighbor Policy no longer mattered. When the matter of funding the GNC came up, the legislature refused to give the commission any power other than that of research. After a few years of further emasculation, the GNC devolved into the international public relations arm of Texas government.[16]

 It was too late, however, to turn the tide back. World War II had accelerated industrialization and the flight to the cities and generally had shifted the principal arena of Mexican and Anglo relations to the urban areas. The war had also exposed Texas Mexican soldiers to a world of greater freedoms and equalities, an experience that became especially important on the return home. According to Kibbe, "Latin Americans" who for years had tolerated discrimination "have acquired a new courage, have become more vocal in protesting the restrictions and inequalities with which they are confronted." A "new consciousness," to use Kibbe's words, was evident.[17]

Factories in the Field

Despite the apparent intransigence of Jim Crow in the rural areas, its social base began a gradual erosion before the repercussions of the war crisis. The massive migrations to the cities were the clearest sign of change—for these represented a displacement of two major classes, migrant laborers and small farmers. In their stead emerged the highly mechanized corporate farm, the basis of modern agribusiness.

After the war industrial capital and techniques "spilled over" into agriculture, intensifying a trend toward corporate ownership. In the Winter Garden, for example, several of the largest farms were branches of urban-based corporations that had similar operations in Florida, California, and Mexico. The modern basis of the corporate farm was "scientific farming," a loose term referring to mechanization, frequent agricultural research, and the development of highly integrated production systems. Del Monte, a branch of the California Packing Corporation, set the pattern, "the model which many area farmers were quick to imitate." Purchasing 3,200 acres of choice land around Crystal City, Del Monte established a highly mechanized farm, a cannery, and shipping facilities in 1946. In this fashion, Del Monte quickly became not only the leading scientific farming operation but also the region's most important economic institution.[18]

The small vegetable farmer, on the other hand, continued to operate on a marginal basis. In addition to increased operating costs, the small farmer had to contend with an unfavorable marketing situation. Because of limited acreages and a lack of facilities, small growers were forced to sell their produce through local sheds owned and operated by the area's larger growers. Marketing the produce of the small farmer was thus of secondary importance to that of the shed owner. As important, the packing sheds began to determine planting policies. Because sheds financed most Winter Garden growers, the vegetable acreage planted was largely determined by what individual shippers felt would be needed to satisfy their particular markets. The farmers of the Winter Garden's Northern District planted over 50 percent of the area's cabbage, carrot, lettuce, and onion acreage, a fact attributed almost exclusively to the planting policies of the local packing sheds. In the Southern District, the demand of Del Monte's cannery was the most significant factor influencing vegetable plantings. Del Monte itself produced virtually all of the Winter Garden's beet crop and grew or contracted over 50 percent of the spinach acreage in the southern area.[19]

In short, the postwar period saw the decline of the small owner-occupied farm. The drought of the 1950s, combined with marketing problems and rising costs, eliminated most of the smaller vegetable-farming operations in the Winter Garden. By the 1960s, the same was true of the Lower Rio Grande Valley. A report on the "swift changes" in Valley agribusiness described the matter in a straight-forward manner: "The small grower is virtually out of the game. The medium-sized operator is beginning to have king-sized troubles. And the era of the giant, vertically-integrated farm operations, usually corporate, seems to be at hand." As in the Winter Garden, the reasons for these changes reflected sharpening competition with Florida and California vegetables as well as with a booming Mexican vegetable industry. Another factor concerned the marketing practices developed with the age of supermarket chains. By linking consumer demand with planting policies and crop price, the new market practices had greatly weakened the bargaining position of independent growers.[20]

A few local families in the Valley and the Winter Garden weathered the shift to corporate farming through the development of integrated production systems that controlled the growing, packing, shipping, and marketing of produce. But whether organized by "native sons" or outside investors, the trend favored corporate farming. Agricultural statistics suggest the pattern. Between 1954 and 1959, the number of farms in Texas decreased at a record pace, from 292,947 to 227,054, a 22.5 percent decrease. At the same time, the size of the average farm increased by more than 25 percent, from 497.7 acres to 629.5 acres.[21]

Accompanying the decline in the number of small farmers was a decline in the size of the agricultural work force. During the 1940s and 1950s, competition for labor and labor flight to the cities continued to plague the farmer. For the farm worker, better wages and working conditions were sufficient motivation for migration to the cities or to fields in other states. On occasion, the excesses of Jim Crow moved Texas Mexican laborers to avoid entire counties, forcing federal and state farm officials to intercede in order to get the harvest picked. A farm labor official, for example, spent the entire month of October 1944 in Big Spring straightening out "difficulties." On the highway leading into the town, a constable had flagged down all migrant-filled trucks, instructing them not to stop in town under threat of arrest. The result was that the majority of the trucks did not stop in Big Spring; they didn't even stop in Howard County, and the farmers in that region experienced great difficulty in harvesting their crops.[22] Such were the contradictions between economic needs and the social divisions of the farm order.

The farmers responded to these contradictions in ways that further accelerated the exodus of Texas Mexican laborers. On the one hand, farmers shifted to Mexican nationals who, unlike Texas Mexicans, could be recruited and removed at will. Thus, thousands were imported in the early fifties; thousands were deported during "Operation Wetback" in the mid-fifties; and thousands were imported again as *braceros* in the early sixties. This shift in the labor source also made for more complicated migratory patterns. As Mexican nationals migrated into rural Texas, Texas Mexicans migrated to the West and the Midwest. In a sense, there was a "domino effect," as one migration reinforced the other.

On the other hand, farmers turned increasingly to mechanization as the solution to the labor situation. This trend had started in the 1930s and was accelerated by the unsettled labor market of the war and postwar periods. Thus, in spite of near-chronic labor shortages, extensive mechanization and improved techniques enabled farmers to increase productivity. Agricultural reports indicate that farm output increased nearly 40 percent between the mid-thirties and the late forties, while the number of farm laborers declined 40 percent for the same period. Only 550,000 laborers worked on Texas farms in 1949 compared to approximately 981,000 laborers in 1934. The number of tractors, on the other hand, increased from 98,923 units in 1940 to more than 250,000 in 1951.[23]

These trends—increasing mechanization and out-migration of Texas Mexicans—characterized the rural setting through the 1960s. The termination of the Mexican guest worker agreement (commonly known as the Bracero Program) in 1964, ironically, intensified these patterns. The repeal removed the supply of contract workers for midwestern and western agriculture. As a result, out-of-state growers and processors, faced with the prospect of labor shortages, concentrated their recruiting efforts in Texas. The number of interstate migrants swelled from 95,000 in 1963 to 129,500 in 1966, while the number of intrastate migrants declined in the same period from 36,800 to 32,500.[24]

By the 1960s, migration to the cities and large-scale mechanization had transformed the old Jim Crow order into a thin shell. In statistical terms, between 1950 and 1970 the number of Texas farms decreased from 332,000 to 214,000, a loss of one in every three farms. The number of those gainfully employed in agriculture declined even more sharply, from 446,000 to 195,000, or less than half of the work force in 1950. The "qualitative" changes were also apparent. In the Winter Garden, as Foley and his co-authors note in their study of Frio County, local farm workers had been replaced by *braceros* and machines, whereas local grower *patrones* had been replaced by absentee owners and manager-lease operators. Few permanent workers were left on the farms and ranches, and those with permanent work in the canneries and packing sheds were under a very different wage-labor system, with much of the earlier paternalism and labor controls absent. Most of the new owners had few personal relationships with their workers and did not expect to develop them. Moreover, the new absentee landlords had altered "the structure and solidarity of the Anglo community." The outsiders had little interest in running the local community or in solving ethnic conflicts.[25]

In short, with the widespread acceptance of scientific techniques and substantial corporate investment, the social base for agricultural production was no longer characterized by a society of "resident growers" and "cheap tractable labor." The most dramatic symptoms of these structural changes surfaced in the 1960s with wildcat strikes in the Lower Valley and aggressive political challenges in the Winter Garden. Other signs were a number of basic setbacks to rural interests—the shift in legislative power to the urban areas, the termination of the *bracero* program, the passage of a dollar-per-hour minimum wage in agriculture, and, finally, the enfranchisement of Mexican Americans. These acts fundamentally altered, to the dismay of growers, the region's "traditionally low-cost labor." Corporate farmers, as the manager of La Casita farms in Starr County commented, could live with a one-dollar-per-hour wage and restrictions on the supply of Mexican nationals, but he was less sure about the small grower. The minimum wage merely forced growers to eliminate many of their preharvest labor requirements through more extensive use of chemical pesticides and mechanical devices. As a consequence, migrants returning to the Winter Garden and the Valley have found fewer job opportunities awaiting them.[26] In the age of corporate farming, every advance for rural laborers merely hastened their eventual displacement.

Political Pluralism and the Urban Vote

In the 1940s, the increasing economic power of urban-based interests was not readily translated into political power. The emerging corporate elite were content to maintain a mutually beneficial relationship with growers. The growers controlled both houses of the

Texas Legislature, while the executive branch was virtually indistinguishable from the oil-insurance-banking-construction elite. In terms of political philosophy, the corporate leaders were not very different from their rural counterparts. In the pointed summation of Texas historian George Green, the corporate elite of the 1940s and 1950s were committed to upholding a regressive tax structure, anti-labor laws, oppression of blacks and Mexican Americans, and alleged states' rights.[27] The state Democratic Party, under the firm control of growers and their corporate friends, embodied these positions.

Thus, for awhile the rapid urbanization of the state did not matter, since conservatism, like so much else, left the countryside for a place in the cities. Jim Crow, in fact, seemed to be strengthened through "urbanization." Why not? Even as the businessmen began to take charge over economic and social matters, the conservative coalition remained intact. In the thirties and forties the new urban elite were busy, as one representative noted, making their first "ten or twenty million dollars." Then, in the fifties, "this Communist business burst" on them. Hugh Roy Cullen, H. L. Hunt, Sid Richardson, Clint Murchison, to name a few, became the financiers of militantly conservative causes. They became, along with other prominent businessmen, ardent supporters of Texas' "third Senator"—Joe McCarthy—whom they saw as ridding government and universities of radical New Dealers.[28] McCarthyism, in fact, swept Texas with the fervor of a religious revival. The major cities proved to be fertile ground for a score of archconservative organizations—minutemen, patriotic committees, citizen councils—all of which were dedicated to guarding against communists, atheists, and desegregationists.

In such climate, the reaction to the Supreme Court's overturning of the "separate but equal" principle (*Brown* v. *Board of Education*) in 1954 was predictably furious. The preservation of Jim Crow against federal intrusion was clothed in patriotic and religious dress. Preachers, retired generals, and politicians all railed against the evils of desegregation. A petition of 165,000 signatures of people objecting to desegregation was presented to Gov. Allen Shivers. In response, Shivers placed three segregationist referenda (preserving school segregation, strengthening laws against intermarriage, and supporting local rule over federal "intrusion") on the ballot for the state Democratic primary (July 1956). These passed by an overwhelming four-to-one margin in the state.[29] Sentiment in counties with large Mexican American populations, however, was sharply divided. Bexar, Kleberg, and Uvalde counties refused to put the referenda on their ballots; Webb County voted against the measures by an eight-to-one margin; and twelve of the sixteen counties where the referenda passed less convincingly (less than 60 percent approval) had significant Mexican American populations.[30]

Encouraged by the overwhelming support of segregation, East Texas legislators introduced a dozen bills in 1956–57 that, among other things, would withhold state funds from integrated schools, would require integrationists to register with the secretary of state (known as the "thought permit" bill), and would prohibit interracial sporting events. South and West Texas members of the House, whose school districts were partly integrated, fought a delaying action in the 150-member House. But the first nine bills rolled through by votes in the neighborhood of 85 ayes to 50 nays, with some members abstaining. When the bills reached the Senate, the senators from the major Mexican American districts (San Antonio, Laredo, Brownsville, El Paso) with support from the senators from Austin and Seguin began a filibuster to block the bills. Led by Henry B. Gonzalez of San Antonio and Abraham Kazen of Laredo, the *"filibusteros"* managed to mobilize sufficient support to block all but two of the bills. Newly elected Gov. Price Daniel, who had campaigned on the promise that he would use all lawful means to avert integration, signed the segregationist legislation. Despite his signing, Daniel attempted to assure his South Texas "Spanish-speaking supporters" that the new laws could not be used to segregate children of Mexican ancestry.[31]

After 1956 the race problem ceased to be a statewide factor in political campaigns and elections. In part this was due to the change in political guard that took place that year. Although supported by the same corporate interests, the new leaders—Lyndon Johnson, Sam Rayburn, and Price Daniel—were not as interested as the "Shivercrats" had been in maintaining a "red scare" mentality.

The renewed consolidation of a liberal wing within the Democratic Party (after its breakup during the McCarthy years) also helped to moderate the racist rhetoric in politics. A coalition of urban liberals, church groups, labor unionists, and minorities constituted the core of this faction. By the mid-1950s the "labor liberals," as they were commonly called, had developed a full-time leadership cadre, a fairly effective propaganda machine, an internal communications network, and a membership that thought it could win elections on occasion. Liberals began to challenge conservatives aggressively, if not always successfully. The election of Ralph Yarborough to the U.S. Senate in 1957 (after Yarborough had repeatedly lost the gubernatorial race) was a sign of liberal tenacity and influence. Another serious challenge was mounted in 1960 when the Kennedy campaign, antagonized by the hostile Texas party establishment, turned to groups excluded from the party machinery—Mexican Americans, blacks, labor, and liberals. Kennedy's narrow victory in Texas (50.5 percent of the vote) demonstrated the strength of this urban coalition.[32]

In spite of the rapid urbanization of Texas and the emergence of an important liberal Democratic faction, the rural conservatives were able to maintain tight control of the legislature. The key to such control was based on state constitutional limits on the number of representatives allowable per county and on pro forma redistricting, which had not significantly changed legislative boundaries since 1921. By the early 1960s, the counties containing the major metropolitan areas—Harris (Houston), Dallas, Bexar (San Antonio), and Tarrant (Fort Worth)—were grossly underrepresented. They were limited to 35 House representatives and 4 senators, when equal representation on the basis of population would have yielded them 54 House members and 10 senators.[33] In this manner, the rural conservative bloc was able to contain repeated liberal challenges in the fifties and sixties.

The entrenched position of the conservative bloc was abruptly upset in 1965 when the U.S. Supreme Court (*Kilgarlin* v. *Martin*) invalidated the districting schemas for both legislative houses as well as the limiting provisions of the Texas Constitution. The stakes were clear. As the *Texas Observer* put it, "the country boys stand to lose out, but they still had the most power in the 1965 legislature and juggled everything that would juggle with purposes as transparent as a country boy's leer."[34]

In the Senate, a split among rural representatives facilitated the transfer of 6 seats to the urban districts at the expense of the rural-based "old guard." Rural areas were reduced to 14 seats, urban-rural areas maintained their 7 seats, and urban areas increased their number to 10. In the House, the conservative leadership was able to delay the impact of reapportionment for a few years. The 1965 plan, which gave the cities 16 members at the expense of rural independents, was thrown out in federal court in 1967. In turn, the 1967 legislature, more urban oriented than the previous House, accelerated the breakup of rural control by distributing 9 more rural seats among urban and mixed urban-rural areas.[35]

A review of changes in the House composition illustrates the shift in power to the urban and urban-rural areas.[36] In 1961 the rural areas had 85 seats, compared to 35 for the four major urban areas. By 1967 the rural seats had been reduced to 63, a loss of 22 seats, while the

Table 15. *Texas House Redistricting, 1951–1967 (150 Seats)*

	Urban[a]	Urban/Rural[b]	Rural
1951	29	26	95
1961	35	30	85
1965	51	27	72
1967	52	35	63

Source: Based on *Texas Almanac,* 1958–1959, 1964–1965, 1966–1967, 1968–1969.

[a]Urban: counties with 300,000+ population in 1950: Dallas, Harris (Houston), Bexar (San Antonio), and Tarrant (Fort Worth).

[b]Urban/rural: counties with 100,000–300,000 population in 1950: El Paso, Jefferson (Beaumont), Galveston, Travis (Austin), Nueces (Corpus Christi), Hidalgo (McAllen), Cameron (Brownsville), and Lubbock.

major urban centers had gained 17 seats for a total of 52. In addition, the eight urban-rural areas increased their representation from 30 seats to 35 (see Table 15).

In terms of legislation, the impact of reapportionment has been clear. After 1967, there were fewer legislators to support what urbanites consider rural prejudices. Legislation favorable to the urban areas has passed: the optional municipal sales tax, the creation of a state Department of Community Affairs, the location of new colleges and state courts in metropolitan areas, to mention a few examples. Farm-to-market roads have become less popular subjects of legislation while state highway programs have become more urban oriented. With the increase of political power of organized labor in urban areas, the Texas Legislature enacted a minimum-wage law. Another way of summarizing the impact: in 1956 the House passed nine segregationist bills by comfortable margins. In 1969 the House rescinded the legislation with no vocal opposition.[37]

In sum, reapportionment was a major blow to the political strength of rural conservatives. Conservatism was by no means defeated—rather, the battle between conservatives and liberals had simply shifted to the urban front.

Pressure from Below, from the Cities

Commentators have suggested that the political "awakening" of the Texas Mexican in the late 1960s stemmed from the rise and development of a Mexican American business and professional class.[38] While this was certainly a significant factor, the urban class structure deserves the primary attention. Two particular events created an open-ing for the Mexican American middle class: the defeat of the old city machines by Anglo business leaders in the fifties and a momentary militance resulting from the joint efforts of middle- and working-class activists in the early sixties.

The first event brought about the initial incorporation of middle-class Mexican Americans into city government and resulted in the defeat of Jim Crow in the cities. Prior to the war, the Mexican American vote in Texas cities was largely controlled and manipu-lated by political bosses. Various Mexican American organizations (like LULAC) had attempted to develop a voice independent of the *patrones* but, on failing this, eventually found themselves vying for machine patronage. Laborers were controlled by job patronage and the middle class by symbolic appointments and honors. The break in the cities, despite some short periods of reform, did not come un-til the machines were deposed in the immediate postwar period by prodevelopment business groups. In San Antonio, for instance, the Kilday machine was undermined by a council-manager movement fi-nanced by prominent Anglo business leaders in 1949.[39]

The formation of numerous veteran organizations was also an im-portant factor in the death of city machines. World War II and the Korean Conflict created a group of politically conscious Mexican American veterans who launched vigorous protests against segrega-tion. In San Antonio the Mexican American veteran organizations included the Loyal American Democrats, the West Side Voters League, the Alamo Democrats, and the School Improvement League. From Corpus Christi came the most prominent new organization, the G.I. Forum, which rapidly formed chapters throughout the Southwest. The G.I. Forum had gained national recognition with its protest against a Three Rivers (Texas) funeral home that had refused to handle the body of a decorated Mexican American soldier.[40]

In general, these groups were oriented to mobilizing Mexican American poll tax registration and voting. In the early fifties, Spanish-speaking leaders were talking of organizing a "mass movement of over a million voters to the Texas ballot boxes." Such efforts did take place in the Rio Grande Valley in campaigns organized by the G.I. Forum and the CIO. Anglo-Texans reacted in fashion typical of the times by calling these efforts "Communist-inspired." The veterans' organizations, however, were able to withstand the "fifth columnist" slander commonly used against activists. As veteran activist J. Luz Saenz noted in speaking of racial discrimination, their "synopsis of The Number One Problem in Texas . . . might look Red-Hot due to the spirit that moves us to express it, but there is nothing of Red-

Communism in it as our enemies might presuppose or imply." Unlike previous community organizations, the postwar organizations were not defensive but aggressively sought the due owed to American veterans.[41]

In structural terms, the returning veterans, via the GI Bill of Rights and college degrees, formed the base for the expanding middle and skilled working classes among Texas Mexicans. The GI Bill of Rights, the compensation for WWII and Korean service, proved to be a most significant avenue for upward mobility for Mexicans and blacks. Its contribution, direct and indirect, has yet to be fully assessed. Although no figures are readily available, enrollment in state and private colleges increased substantially. Home ownership by Mexican Americans was facilitated by VA loans in the late forties and early fifties. The "military industrial complex," to use President Dwight Eisenhower's well-known phrase, provided permanent well-paying employment, thus laying a foundation for stable middle and working classes.[42]

These structural changes, evident in the growth of a profitable Mexican American consumer market, began to attract the attention of merchants, with moderating consequences for race relations. In 1955 the *Texas Business Review*, in a special issue on the Mexican American consumer market, noted that retailers who deal most successfully with Latin Americans tolerate no discrimination. "Latin American Texans" respond to fair and exceptional treatment in business and appreciate the efforts of only those who manifest a genuine interest in their welfare and comfort. A "haughty, lordly, or unfriendly attitude," on the other hand, "may be effectively dealt with by a group boycott of the guilty. Both favorable and unfavorable information travels amazingly fast by word of mouth." This, of course, was old advice for the political and economic elite of the border cities (Brownsville, Laredo, El Paso). Economically dependent on trade with Mexico and politically dependent on Mexican American voters, border city elites did not permit prejudicial expressions or practices that could antagonize their customers, clients, and voters.[43]

In San Antonio, the implications of a politically active Mexican American community were recognized by the reform-oriented Anglo businessmen and professionals who formed the Good Government League (GGL). The GGL leaders were primarily interested in economic growth and desired "an environment free of political and social conflict." To this end, the conservative business element was convinced by the liberals within the reform coalition that all groups in the city—specifically, blacks and Mexicans—must progress together if San Antonio was to progress in general. Accordingly, black and Mexican American representatives were regularly recruited to run on GGL-sponsored tickets. It was a means of allowing the minorities to have "visibility and ego input," as one GGLer put it. In San Antonio of the early 1950s, this was a notable departure from political tradition. For El Paso and other border cities, the symbolic inclusion of "successful" Mexican Americans on school board and city council slates had been the practice for some time. Pressure from the Mexican American community of El Paso, nonetheless, resulted in additional progress: El Paso elected its first Mexican American mayor, Raymond Telles, in 1957.[44]

In the urban areas, these changed political conditions steadily eroded the Jim Crow structure within a decade after the war. All types of discrimination were fought—restrictions in real estate, in voting, in access to public facilities and schools, and so on. San Antonio passed a desegregation ordinance of city facilities in the mid-1950s, and the same result was accomplished in Corpus Christi. These victories reflected the presence of a politically active Mexican American community. As prosperity and upward mobility occurred, the militancy of the veteran challenge gradually diminished.[45]

Urban ethnic relations stood in sharp contrast with the situation in the farm areas, which, as late as 1959, remained "blacklisted" by the Mexican government from any participation in the "guest worker" (*bracero*) program because of discrimination and abuse. South Texas farm towns, as William Madsen observed in 1961, were "separated residential districts divided by highway or railroad tracks." "Virtually the only relationship" between Anglos and Mexican Americans, noted Madsen, was that of "an employer to an unskilled employee."[46]

Through the 1950s and 1960s, despite some gains in the cities, the reign of Jim Crow in the rural areas stigmatized all Mexican Americans as second-class citizens. As long as Texas Mexicans in the countryside and the city, of working-class and middle-class backgrounds, followed unrelated and independent strategies, no major challenge to the entire segregationist edifice developed. In the cities, middle-class organizations were not sufficiently powerful to gain more than symbolic rewards. Their isolation, moreover, was reinforced by condescending attitudes toward working-class Mexicans. On the other hand, labor activism without outside support tended to be easily suppressed. The record is filled with episodes of repression by employers and authorities and of lack of support (and sometimes open antagonism) from Anglo unionists, middle-class Mexican Americans, and Catholic clergy. So long as these divisions remained, and middle-class and working-class organizations worked separately, nothing substantial was gained. What changed, on the urban side, was the emergence of an impatient middle-class organization willing to work with labor union activists. This "event" accelerated the demise of Jim Crow and introduced the process to the rural areas.

In 1960 the Viva Kennedy campaign, responsible for the John Kennedy victory in Texas, demonstrated the pivotal significance of the Mexican American vote. Just as important, the campaign demonstrated to Mexican American activists that the hold of conservative Democrats on local South Texas politics could be broken. As an organizational attempt to continue the momentum of the Kennedy victory, the Viva Kennedy campaign was transformed into a political coalition composed of Mexican American leaders from the established organizations (G.I. Forum, LULAC, and so on). The coalition was called the Political Association of Spanish-speaking Organizations (PASSO).[47]

From its founding, PASSO was split along moderate-militant lines, a tension that frequently erupted into open conflict at meetings. The moderates and conservatives favored gradual progress using established avenues, whereas the liberals urged more direct action and involvement in local issues. After a brief and inauspicious year of moderation, PASSO regrouped in 1963 under the aggressive liberal leadership of Albert Peña, Jr.

PASSO, along with the Teamsters, became involved in Crystal City in 1962–1963 in what eventually became known as the "first uprising." In 1963 the Mexican Americans of Crystal City organized and elected an all–Mexican American slate to the city council, a feat that attracted statewide and national attention. Teamster and PASSO strategy, which called for utilizing the large base of cannery and farm laborers through the small Teamsters union at the Del Monte cannery, was successful in turning the political structure of Crystal City upside down. To a large degree this success lay in the fact that the local elite no longer controlled the main economic strings of the local economy; rather, these now lay in the hands of corporate agribusiness, such as Del Monte. Local management did attempt to intimidate Del Monte workers active in the campaign but these were blocked by the local union with the help of high Teamster officials. One of the more dramatic incidents came on election day when Del Monte suddenly announced that it was going into overtime and that its workers would not have time to vote. Unable to change the company's decision, Teamster organizers placed an urgent call to their national president, Jimmy Hoffa, who in turn notified Del Monte headquarters in San Francisco that there would be action against the company. Management assented, and the Del Monte workers were

Community meeting of the Liga Pro Defensa Escolar (School Improvement League), San Antonio, 1948 (courtesy E. Escobar Collection, Benson Latin American Collection, University of Texas at Austin).

allowed time to vote. The mobilized Mexican American majority defeated— "overthrew" is not an excessive term—the long-established
rule of the Anglo minority. As a symbol of what was possible in
South Texas, the event far outweighed the takeover of a community
of 9,000. It symbolized the overthrow of Jim Crow.[48]

The repercussions of Crystal City widened the division between
moderates and militants within PASSO. In general the moderates
were against the Crystal City involvement and against working with
labor unions. By 1965 PASSO's middle-class membership, dissatis-
fied with its militancy, had largely dissipated. This defection by the
moderates permitted the remaining PASSO members to take a further step and become directly involved in labor organizing.

PASSO members in Starr County had been talking about a farm
worker strike for years when Cesar Chavez and the National Farm
Workers Association struck the Delano (California) grape vineyards
in 1965. The result was a wildcat melon strike in June 1966 against
eight major Starr County growers. Virtually all of the picketing and
boycott activity was aimed at La Casita farms, a huge integrated corporate operation that strikers called the "General Motors" of Valley
agribusiness. The wildcat strike appeared doomed from the start.
The general lack of preparation and coordination was a serious problem, but what made this a moot point was the breaking of the strike
by Texas Rangers, Starr County deputies, and imported Mexican
labor. In an insightful comment, a Valley banker suggested that the
labor organizing efforts would have been more effective and strategic
if they had been directed at shed workers, for the shed operators, not
the growers, controlled the marketing of produce.[49] Shed workers
could also be an efficient point for mobilizing farm workers, as the
Crystal City "uprising" had demonstrated.

Although the Valley strike failed, it succeeded in catalyzing the
Chicano civil rights movement in Texas. The farm worker cause,
while the lead element in this movement, was for most of the urban
Mexican American population important in a symbolic sense; it
ignited a broad resentment among all classes of the Mexican American community. Different agendas and energies were set off, some
moderate, some militant. The high school youth boycotted their
schools in Del Rio, Uvalde, Kingsville, Alice, Abilene, Pharr–San
Juan–Alamo, Laredo, and Robstown, to mention only a few places.
College students organized countless protest marches and meetings
and provided new ideas and directions as well as energy and impatience. Even the usually proper middle class became radicalized,
as they protested employment practices, boycotted companies (at

one meeting they burned their Humble Oil credit cards), and filed lawsuits against social inequities.

By the late 1960s, this movement was seriously challenging the dual structure of rural society. While the protest of the 1950s had focused on the cities, that of the 1960s was centered in the countryside. The major political events of a decade revolved around the farm worker strikes in the Lower Rio Grande Valley and the formation of a populist-nationalist party known as El Partido Raza Unida (The United People Party) in the Winter Garden region. The electoral take-over by Raza Unida of Crystal City and Zavala County in 1970—the "second uprising"—stunned the state, frightened the Anglo residents of South Texas, and prompted Gov. Dolph Briscoe to denounce Zavala County as a "little Cuba."[50]

In short, the social movement of the 1960s and 1970s accelerated the dismantling of the repressive social order known as Jim Crow. In its place were planted the seeds of a new ethnic order, one that is still being defined and molded. Much remains to be studied, for the Chicano movement was a complex collection of groups with various agendas and strategies, some of which were carried out with partial success. One of its more successful goals—one that the League of United Latin American Citizens (LULAC) had articulated in the 1920s—was the "opening up" of universities for Mexican American youth. LULAC had long called for this action, arguing that the Latin American people would be "uplifted" once they had more doctors, teachers, lawyers, and professionals of all types. The strategy essentially called for an expanded middle class. Such expansion may prove to be one of the more significant results of the great unrest of the sixties and seventies. Even the student activists were, in a sense, the cutting edge of a middle class frustrated by the narrow ethnic limits of the old Southwest. The militants among them succeeded and thus disappeared; in their wake, they left a modest booty of business and professional opportunities, the very stuff of LULAC dreams.

A Concluding Note

In the 1970s the legacy of segregation was still evident, especially in rural areas. The town of Ozona in West Texas illustrates the stubborn and uneven career of Jim Crow for Mexicans. In this town, drugstores were closed to Mexicans until the late 1940s; restaurants and movie houses did not open to Mexicans until the early 1950s; hotels were exclusively reserved for Anglo patrons until about 1958; barber and beauty shops were segregated until 1969; and in the early

1970s, the bowling alley, cemeteries, and swimming pools still remained segregated. Ozona, unfortunately, was somewhat typical of the Texas pattern. According to a mid-sixties study, nine of the eleven southwestern cities in which Mexican Americans were most rigidly segregated were in Texas. In descending order of magnitude, these were Odessa, Corpus Christi, Dallas, Lubbock, San Angelo, Houston, Wichita Falls, San Antonio, and Austin.[51]

The civil rights movement, nevertheless, was making some headway. In 1968 San Antonio and Corpus Christi joined Austin in adopting an open housing ordinance. And in the following year, the legislature set about the task of erasing the segregationist laws passed in 1957. In May 1969, the House and Senate passed five bills and sent them to Gov. Preston Smith with little dissent. The bills, introduced by San Antonio Representative David Evans and carried in the Senate by Joe Bernal, also of San Antonio, removed statutes that had provided for segregated schools, had empowered cities to enact segregation ordinances, had required railroads to provide separate coaches and facilities, and had banned sports events between persons of different races.[52] De jure segregation had ended in Texas.

In the meantime, a great social movement worked to eradicate de facto segregation and inequalities. The most dramatic successes occurred in the rural areas, a fact that, at first glance, may appear to weaken my argument about the ascendancy of urban commercial interests and the Mexican American middle class. On the contrary, these victories underscore one argument I have advanced—that local growers were no longer the dominant political force they had once been and that insurgent movements could be organized and sustained with urban support. The focus of the movement was on the countryside, but it emanated from the cities. It was a movement largely directed from the cities, decided in the cities. The strategy of key organizations—PASSO and later the Raza Unida Party (RUP), the Mexican American Legal Defense and Educational Fund (MALDEF), the Southwest Voter Registration Education Project (SVREP), to mention a few—consisted in large part of organizing "forays" into the countryside to accomplish some destructive mission among the remnants of Jim Crow. In the military jargon of the Vietnam era, these missions were basically "mopping up" operations.

Important questions remain to be addressed. What does the demise of Jim Crow signify for ethnic politics in the South and the Southwest? More to the point, what new forms of accommodation and control exist today? The answers rest, as this sketch has suggested, in a new order where Anglo business interests and those of the Mexican American middle class constitute the major political axis shaping contemporary ethnic relations. As political intermediary and broker for the Mexican American community as a whole, the Mexican American middle class has secured the role it has always aspired to. Anglo-Americans have by no means retired from political activity but, as Clark Knowlton suggests for El Paso, the pattern of race and ethnic relationships is beginning to resemble that of some eastern cities where the old Yankees, although retreating from local politics, still retain economic control.[53]

13. A Time of Inclusion

WHILE THE contours of the new order have not fully gelled in the 1980s, a few preliminary observations can be offered. Several signs—increasing use of English, intermarriage, upward mobility, for example—suggest a measure of integration for the Mexican American. Although the Texas Mexican community lags far behind on all mainstream indicators in the areas of education, health, income, and political influence, compared to the situation in the 1950s the current period has brought what Grebler, Moore, and Guzmán have described as "assimilative opportunities."[1] From the contradictory and conflictual events of the 1970s have come civil rights and opportunities for Mexican Americans. The most important sign in this regard consists of the contemporary public role of Mexican Americans as political actors in Texas.

In this concluding chapter, I wish to describe the current political influence of the Texas Mexican from both a near and a long view. From a near view, I wish to focus on the events of the past decade that have strengthened the political voice of the Texas Mexican. From a long view, I will emphasize the uneven connections of the present with the past, pointing out patterns of both continuity and discontinuity.

The Near View

To continue the argument presented in the previous chapter, two general factors underlying the relative progress of the Texas Mexican concern the political mobilization from below as well as structural changes introduced from outside. On the one hand, the political movement of the 1960s and 1970s broke the influence of Jim Crow Democrats in South Texas and, subsequently, in the state. The new Democratic Party in the greater border region is led by Mexican American politicians whose experience was gained, in large measure, during the days of Chicano militance. On the other hand, the breakup of political structures that had favored conservative rural interests continued. Reapportionment and the establishment of single-member urban districts were important constitutional changes in this regard. The most significant measure, however, was the extension of the Voting Rights Act in 1975 to include Mexican Americans in the Southwest.

The End of the Chicano Movement

By 1975 the civil rights movement in Texas and the Southwest had largely been exhausted. Many of its aims had become institutionalized and its more activistic elements accommodated. Exhaustion, however, came from internal friction about leadership and tactics, and from external pressure applied by state authorities.

Pressure by state authorities and politicians, especially those from South Texas, had a serious debilitating effect on movement activism. The Texas Rangers played a familiar role in the farm worker strike, arresting and beating strikers and supporters, including clergy and one state senator. The Rangers and their parent organization, the Department of Public Safety, were constant observers of the Raza Unida Party, as they harassed and occasionally arrested organizers and members of the party. Texas Attorney General John Hill took a special interest in a protracted investigation in Zavala County, the stronghold of the Raza Unida Party, for misuse of public funds and related corruption charges. The ten-month investigation resulted, with much media fanfare, in the indictment of three officials. Although the charges were later dropped or found baseless, the considerable publicity given to these charges placed Raza Unida on the defensive. Such media-based assaults underscored the strategy of state authorities.[2]

The enmity of state authorities toward the ethnic populism of Raza Unida was understandable on ideological grounds. There also were, however, pragmatic reasons for the antagonism. These centered on the real electoral threat that Raza Unida presented for Jim Crow Democrats in the greater border region. In 1972 the Raza Unida candidate for governor, Ramsey Muñiz, had surprised most political observers by capturing 6 percent of the state vote. More significant were the returns from forty South and West Texas counties: here Raza Unida captured 18 percent of the vote, a sizable defection from Democratic Party ranks. The result was an unexpectedly close race between conservative Democrat Dolph Briscoe, who won with a plurality of 48 percent, and a Republican "dark horse," Henry Grover, who had 45 percent.[3]

Governor Briscoe countered with legislative attempts to tighten the requirements for political party recognition. Briscoe, moreover, denounced the Raza Unida as a communist threat and blocked federal funding for Zavala County programs. Again, the publicity accompanying these denunciations had a disquieting effect on conservative Mexican American supporters of Raza Unida. More damaging, however, was the arrest on marijuana smuggling charges of key party leaders by the Department of Public Safety. The Raza Unida never recovered from these events.[4]

However, the most debilitating problem for the movement did not come from external causes, but from internal sources. The farm worker organizing campaign failed to gather strength and split into two contentious factions. Likewise, the Raza Unida Party became polarized into opposing factions over the question of leadership and direction.[5] The "gringo" no longer occupied the attention of the activists, who now exchanged accusations of "selling out" and "opportunism." Throughout the movement network there re-appeared the old tension between middle-class and working-class activists. Cultural nationalism, an attractive philosophy during the mobilization against the Anglos, provided no strategy or instructions once "los they" had been overcome.

But the impact of these movement organizations cannot be minimized. Both the farm workers and the Raza Unida campaigns provided invaluable training for a new generation of leaders, individuals who applied their experience and vision in other efforts. The movement energized old organizations like the League of United Latin American Citizens (LULAC) and gave birth to new ones. From relatively small networks emerged the leadership of the Mexican American Legal Defense and Educational Fund (MALDEF), organized in 1968; of community development agencies, such as the Mexican American Unity Council, organized in 1968; of neighborhood citizen groups, such as Communities Organized for Public Service (COPS), organized in 1973; and of various cultural centers, such as Centro Cultural Guadalupe and Centro Aztlán in San Antonio.

One of the more enduring victories of the Raza Unida Party was the breakup of Anglo control of the Democratic Party in the greater border region. As the Raza Unida Party dissolved, ex-members crossed over and took control of local Democratic Party chapters. As one former Raza Unida member in the Winter Garden put it, "We wouldn't have to change our philosophy or our politics or how we educate our kids just because we call ourselves Democrats. A name is a name."[6] Everywhere "new" political organizations were resurrected from the pyre of Chicano movement organizations. Thus, a critical core of the nonpartisan Southwest Voter Registration Education Project (SVREP), organized in 1974, the Mexican American Democrats (MAD), organized in 1976, and the influential Mexican American Legislative Caucus received its baptism in Raza Unida activities.

The influence on state politics of a mobilized Mexican American electorate can be suggested by the fact that Dolph Briscoe, a banker-ranchman from Uvalde, was the last of a succession of rural-based governors. In an interesting twist, the Raza Unida in its waning years could technically claim the credit for the end of this conservative dynasty. Although in 1978 Raza Unida gubernatorial candidate Mario Compean received less than 1 percent of the vote, this margin was sufficient to defeat Raza Unida's old nemesis, Democrat Attorney General John Hill. Bill Clements thus became Texas' first Republican governor in more than one hundred years.[7]

Four years later, in 1982, the liberal Democratic faction, with the critical support of the Mexican American electorate, assumed control of the state Democratic Party with the election of populists Jim Hightower, Ann Richards, and Jim Mattox to state office. The importance of the Mexican American electorate is indicated by one survey, which found that Democratic gubernatorial candidate Mark White had received a minority (or 49.6 percent) of the non–Mexican American vote while receiving an overwhelming majority (86.1 percent) of the Mexican American vote.[8]

The re-alignment of political party affiliation, which had begun in the mid-seventies, has been accelerated by these political dynamics. In the eighties, the flight of conservative Democrats to the Republican Party has in effect made Texas a two-party state. These shifts have further heightened the significance of the Mexican American electorate of West and South Texas. Recent legislative reform in school finance, farm worker compensation, and indigent health care, to name the most important, points to the new strength of the Mexican American.

These recent political currents can be interpreted in various ways. Historian Rudy Acuña has described this period in terms of the "return of the Democratic power-brokers," even though these power brokers are now frequently Spanish-surnamed Democrats. On the other hand, Gov. Mario Cuomo of New York referred to this process, at a 1986 banquet honoring Henry B. Gonzalez' twenty-five years in Congress, as the "politics of inclusion." By this, Cuomo meant that the one critical American thread is "the struggle to include" people of all the "colors and shapes" of the world, to work to extend the American dream to every American.[9] The political reality, unfortunately, is sufficiently complex to support both the cynicism of Acuña and the hope of Cuomo.

In Texas, the "inclusion" of Texas Mexicans did not occur through the good graces of the Democratic Party; rather, it unfolded through bitter "trench warfare" between the conservative and the labor-liberal factions. Much of the impetus for inclusion, curiously, spilled over from attempts to build the Raza Unida Party as well as from other ethnic-based efforts. In other words, an ironic consequence of the ethnic nationalism of the 1970s was the securing of a measure of political integration for the Mexican American community. The movement triggered a process that loosened the racial structure, providing opportunities for the moderate representatives of both communities to negotiate a new political understanding.

Reforming Electoral Structures

As in the South, there were in Texas and the Southwest numerous ways by which the minority vote was disenfranchised or minimized. These practices included the gerrymandering of districts, the use of at-large elections, the selective annexation of Anglo suburbs, voter intimidation, selective enforcement of electoral laws, and fraudulent ballot distribution and collection, to name a few. More systematic measures were the poll tax and, later, the annual registration requirements and the statutes that prohibited assistance to voters at the polls.[10]

As intended, these various obstacles resulted in the dilution of minority voting strength. According to a 1980 survey conducted by SVREP, of 361 school districts with 20 percent or more Mexican American enrollment, there existed an underrepresentation of elected Mexican American trustees in 92 percent of them.[11] Likewise, in 1981 MALDEF identified sixty-three counties with significant Mexican American population (ranging from 20 to 67 percent of the total) that had either token or no representation on the county commissioners court. Altogether these counties, located mainly in the Panhandle and in West Texas, had twelve Mexican American county commissioners when representative reapportionment would have produced approximately eighty-seven county officials.[12]

The major legal weapons against these practices have proven to be reapportionment lawsuits and the Voting Rights Act of 1965, which was extended to the Southwest in 1975. The reapportionment battles commenced with *Reynolds v. Sims* (1964), which established the "one man, one vote" principle, and were fought in federal and Texas courts from 1966 through 1977. Other legal barriers were ruled unconstitutional by federal courts: the poll tax in 1966, annual voter registration in 1971, and at-large state legislative districts in 1974.

The Voting Rights Act covered a wider range of electoral practices and in certain ways offered greater protection than reapportionment. The Voting Rights Act was explicitly intended to remove structural barriers that limited access of minorities to the political process.

Although the results of reapportionment and the Voting Rights Act have yet to be studied carefully, one apparent tendency has been an increase in the number of Mexican Americans elected to various levels of government. In the sixteen-year period from 1964 to 1980, the number of Mexican American state legislators has increased from 6 to 25. The number of county commissioners and judges has increased from 72 in 1973 to 105 in 1984.[13]

San Antonio remains the "showcase" for the success of the Voting Rights Act. Although the number of Mexican Americans elected to city council had increased since World War II, such representation consisted of token appointments made by the Good Government League, a business-civic group that governed San Antonio over a twenty-five-year period (1952–1977). This did not change fundamentally until 1976 when a letter of objection from the Justice Department (concerning suburb annexation) pressured San Antonio to adopt single-member districts. In the following election, five Mexican Americans and one black were elected, capturing a majority of seats on the city council, a first for modern San Antonio. This increased the voter registration of Mexican Americans and blacks. Then in April 1981, the first Mexican American mayor of San Antonio since Juan Seguin's tenure of 1840 was elected. Largely forgotten in the drama of the moment was another first: the Mexican American turnout (43 percent) had been higher than that of Anglos (39 percent).[14] Table 16 illustrates the relationship between increments in Mexican American representation on the city council and changes in the city's political system.[15]

In like fashion, voting rights–related objections have forced El Paso, Houston, Victoria, and the counties of Jefferson, Tarrant, and Nueces to adopt single-member districts or to redraw district lines. The results have in all cases been favorable to ethnic minorities: registration, voter turnout, and minority representation have increased considerably.[16]

The scope of Texas Mexican influence throughout the state can be illustrated by examining the composition of the central county government body, the five-member county commissioners court. Using a 1984 roster of county officials, a degree of political influence was assigned to each county according to the number of Mexican Americans elected to the commissioners court. Mexican Americans were deemed to have "some influence" if one member of the commis-

Table 16. *San Antonio City Council Members by Ethnicity,*
1933–1985

Political System	Period	Non-Spanish-Surnamed	Spanish-Surnamed
Mayor-commissioners (5-member boards)	1933–1943	15	0
	1943–1952	20	0
Mayor-council (9 at-large members)	1952–1961	51	10
	1961–1969	30	10
	1969–1977	28	13
Mayor-council (10 district members, 1 at-large)	1977–1985	31[a]	15

Source: Based on City of San Antonio, "Listing of San Antonio City Commissioners and Council Members."
[a] Includes 6 counts of blacks or Asian-Americans.

sioners court was a Mexican American, "swing influence" if two or three members were Mexican American, and "controlling influence" if four or five members were Mexican American.[17] The results of assigning such weights can be seen on the map "Mexican American Political Influence." Of forty-five counties with Mexican American county officials, Mexican Americans had "some influence" in nineteen, "swing influence" in seventeen, and "controlling influence" in nine.

A comparison of the 1984 roster of county officials with a 1973 roster provides us with some historical sense of the political momentum of the Texas Mexican. Between 1973 and 1984, twelve of the forty-five counties had progressed from no representation to "some influence," and another twelve had progressed from none or some influence to "swing" or "controlling influence." In short, twenty-four of the forty-five counties had experienced a noticeable increase in political influence during the past decade.[18]

The tier of lower border counties, where Mexican Americans comprise three-quarters or more of the population, is completely in the hands of Mexican American politicians. The counties of Maverick, Duval, Webb, Zapata, Starr, Brooks, and Jim Hogg have a long legacy of such representation. The Lower Valley counties of Hidalgo, Cameron, and Willacy, on the other hand, suggest the more recent mobilization of the 1970s. "It's a much friendlier place now," according to

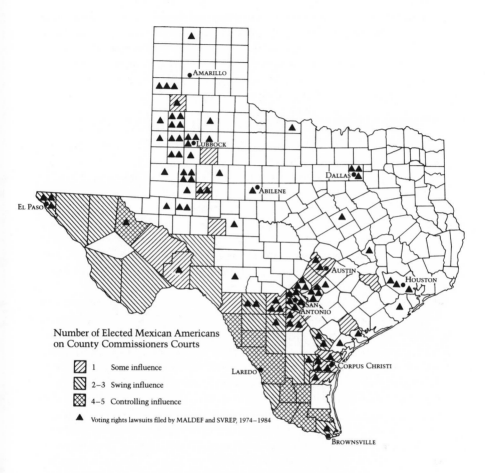

Number of Elected Mexican Americans
on County Commissioners Courts

▨ 1   Some influence

▧ 2–3   Swing influence

▨ 4–5   Controlling influence

▲ Voting rights lawsuits filed by MALDEF and SVREP, 1974–1984

Mexican American Political Influence, 1985 (based on data from
Mexican American Legal Defense and Educational Fund and
Southwest Voter Registration Education Project).

former farm worker organizer Gil Padilla. "The mayors of the small towns are Mexican and sympathetic to the farm worker."[19]

The Winter Garden counties of Zavala, Dimmit, and La Salle also point to the success of Mexican American political mobilization of the 1960s and 1970s, whereas the situation in Uvalde and Frio counties reflects more the handiwork of civil rights litigation. Whether because of movement organizers or lawyers, for many counties the "swing influence" of the Mexican American represents a novel departure from local history.

Similar results have been obtained in the intransigent rural areas of West Texas. The potential muscle of the Texas Mexican in this region has long been recognized, but only within the past twenty years has it surfaced (or resurfaced) effectively in Reeves, El Paso, and Presidio counties. In Crockett County, numerous suits and objections from the Department of Justice culminated in the election of two Mexican American county commissioners, signifying a virtual electoral revolution for the area. In the process, the registration rate of Mexican Americans increased to over 90 percent, probably the highest rate in Texas. Similar electoral revolutions occurred in Culberson and Hudspeth counties.[20]

Even where the Mexican American remains underrepresented, the voting rights lawsuits filed by SVREP and MALDEF demonstrate a persistent strategy to introduce the "Civil Rights era" to unresponsive rural areas. The geographic distribution of these lawsuits between 1974 and 1984 reveals two major clusters. Of eighty-eight voting rights lawsuits, thirty-eight had been filed against Panhandle or rural West Texas districts and another twenty-four had been filed in and around the Bexar County (San Antonio) area. A minor grouping of nine suits appears in and around Nueces County (Corpus Christi), with another nine scattered among the urban counties of El Paso, Dallas, and Harris (Houston).[21]

The progress resulting from these lawsuits and concerted voter registration drives has been slow but steady. Forty-six counties with sizeable Mexican American populations still have no Mexican American representatives on their county commissioners courts. But important margins have been reduced. William Velasquez, executive director of SVREP, explained the impact in this way: "West Texas used to go ten-to-one for Attila the Hun; now [because of Mexican American registration] it's three-to-one."[22]

The increase in voter registration among Mexican Americans has attracted the attention of state and national politicians. The number of registered Mexican Americans increased by 41 percent, from 591,950 in 1978 to 832,398 in 1982, whereas non–Mexican American registration increased by 25 percent during the same period. These new registrations accounted in large part for a doubling of the Mexican American turnout in the gubernatorial election, from 171,196 in 1978 to 318,742 in 1982. It also accounted for the winning margin of Democrat Mark White over Republican incumbent Bill Clements.[23]

The mathematical lesson of the 1982 elections has not been lost on the Democratic and Republican parties in Texas. The Republicans promise, in subsequent elections, to court the conservative Mexican American vote seriously, while the Democrats will attempt to maintain the enthusiasm of its Mexican American base.

The Long View

From the long view of a century and a half, Mexican-Anglo relations have traversed a difficult path, from the hatred and suspicion engendered by war to a form of reconciliation. The previous chapters have examined these changes in Mexican-Anglo relations in terms of the shifting class contexts of ranch, farm, and urban-industrial societies. The argument may be restated as follows.

In the nineteenth century, when a segment of the Mexican elite still held onto the land, an accommodative "peace structure" with the Anglo political and commercial elite mediated Mexican-Anglo relations. The loss of land and of control over markets, however, resulted inevitably in the erosion of the Mexican class structure. Several rebellions and bandit troubles represented the Mexican response, but no general uprising took place until the ranch order was confronted with a "newcomer" farm society at the turn of the century.

By the early twentieth century, except for a few border enclaves, the former ranch lands had been made "safe for farming," and the Mexican in Texas had become a farm laborer. This coincidence of race and class in the farm order made for a pervasive and brutal segregation. Such general control and separation emerged as the "natural" social policy of Anglo farmers in their dealings with Mexican farm workers.

The segregated farm order was undermined by the military mobilization and industrialization of World War II and the Korean Conflict. These war emergencies loosened the Jim Crow controls of the rural areas and laid the foundation for an elaboration of an urban-based class structure. The social transformation involved the mechanization of farm work, the migration from the countryside to the city, the politicization of Mexican American veterans, and the employment of Mexican Americans in war-related industry during the 1950s and 1960s. Such employment at the military bases provided the first stable income for many Texas Mexicans. The result was the creation of a sizeable middle class and skilled working class in cities like San Antonio.[24] In contrast to the farmer-laborer context of the farm world, the primary arena for Mexican-Anglo relations in the cities was that of merchant-consumer.

The Elaboration of Urban Classes

A suggestive outline of these structural changes may be seen if we review the census data on the occupations of Texas Mexicans in 1930, 1950, 1970, and 1980. By grouping the various occupations into "white collar," "skilled," and "unskilled" categories, a sharp outline of occupational trends emerges. Table 17 presents a summary of these broad changes.

In 1930, unskilled rural and urban workers comprised two-thirds of the Texas Mexican labor force: fully one-third (33.6 percent) of the gainfully employed Texas Mexicans were farm workers, while another third (32 percent) were service workers or laborers. The remaining one-third was composed of skilled and white-collar workers.[25]

By 1950, the effects of war-related industrialization in increasing

Table 17. *Occupational Distribution of Spanish-Origin Population in Texas, 1930, 1950, 1970, and 1980*

Occupation	1930[a] (%)	1950 (%)	1970 (%)	1980 (%)
White collar				
Professional/technical	1.4	2.2	7.6	8.0
Proprietor/manager	16.4	8.7	5.8	5.4
Clerical/sales	4.2	10.2	19.3	22.4
Skilled				
Craftsman/foreman	6.7	10.2	15.0	17.1
Operative	5.8	17.7	21.5	18.2
Unskilled				
Service worker/laborer	32.0	27.8	25.0	25.2
Farm worker	33.6	23.2	5.8	3.8

Source: Based on U.S. Department of Commerce, Bureau of the Census, Fifteenth, Seventeenth, Nineteenth, Twentieth Census of the United States: 1930, 1950, 1970, 1980.

[a]Includes a small number of Native Americans and Asian Americans.

the ranks of skilled and semiskilled laborers as well as of clerical workers were evident. The skilled and professional workers accounted for nearly half (49 percent) of the Texas Mexican work force, while the unskilled made up the other half.

By 1970 the occupational distribution of 1930 had been reversed. The unskilled category of farm workers and service workers-laborers comprised slightly less than a third (30.8 percent) of the work force, while the skilled and professional workers made up slightly more than two-thirds (69.2 percent). This occupational division of thirds is evident in the 1980 data, but with a further weakening of the unskilled categories and a strengthening of the white-collar categories. In 1980, 35.8 percent of Texas Mexicans had white-collar occupations; 35.3 percent had skilled occupations; and the number with unskilled jobs dropped to 29 percent.

The importance of these occupational changes for Mexican-Anglo relations cannot be overstated. The general effect of an expanding white-collar and skilled strata within the Mexican American community was the attainment of a measure of economic stability—sufficient stability to enable greater attention to the questions of education, housing conditions, sanitation, and matters of public service. This stability also made possible the support of community-based organizations. The conversion of the Texas Mexican from farm worker into war veteran, urban consumer, and civic actor expressed itself ultimately in the civil rights movements of the 1950s and late 1960s. Despite the conflict of those years, the rise of stable urban classes was ultimately a factor pushing for the moderation and inclusion of the present day.

In the 1980s, with the weakening of racial divisions as an issue, broadly defined class interests determine the arena of political discussion and debate. In contrast to the activities of the 1970s, the most active Mexican American organizations express and pursue class issues rather than explicit ethnic interests. For example, Communities Organized for Public Services (COPS), an Alinksy-style group based on San Antonio's Catholic parish network, is concerned with promoting the interests of its inner city members while keeping the monied suburban developers in check. In ten years, it has become the major nonbusiness political organization in San Antonio, and it has stimulated the creation of similar organizations throughout Texas and the country. For COPS and its sister organizations in El Paso and the lower Rio Grande Valley, Mexican American culture is an important cohesive factor. But explicit ethnic appeals are not relevant because the issues it raises and lobbies for are "nonethnic" issues concerning street drainage, improved streets, better housing conditions, and economic development. In a sense, these community groups represent an organizing strategy that used and then transcended the natural ties of family, parish, and ethnicity.[26] To put it another way, once the segregationist framework had been toppled, Mexican Americans could press for "previously ethnic" issues in a "nonethnic" manner.

The question of whether class divisions now overshadow race, a prominent issue in recent sociological literature, is irrelevant for Mexican Americans. Class divisions and tensions have always existed within the Mexican settlements of the ranch, farm, and city. However, since the rise of the urban middle class and skilled working class is a mid-twentieth-century phenomenon, the distance between poor and "well-off" may not yet be considerable. For the first-generation middle class, urban and rural poverty is still very much a part of their collective memory.

Patterns of Uneven Change

The movement from one period to another has been framed in terms of a succession from ranch to farm to urban-industrial orders. To speak only of a *succession* of class societies, however, would result in an incomplete view of historical change. Even today, three worlds—the ranch, the farm, and the urban, each with a distinct pattern of Mexican-Anglo relations—still co-exist, a testimony to 150 years of social change. Since the urban pattern of "inclusion" has already been described, I will direct my attention to the ranch and farm worlds of recent times.

The ranch world survives to the present day as the land of the *patrón*. The Klebergs still control Kleberg and Kenedy counties; the Guerras control Starr County and influence Jim Hogg; and, until recently, the Parrs ran Duval County. One commentator has described these deep South Texas counties as being run by landowners and authorities, "distrustful of democracy, who dominate their areas politically, economically, and socially."[27]

The key feature in the ranch counties remains the permanent, paternalistic bonds between rancher and *vaquero*. Cy Yeary, King Ranch liaison man, noted in a commemorative account in 1953, that "we hire about 10 percent of the employees and raise the rest." A large majority of the ranch employees have been grandsons and great-grandsons, grand-nephews, and cousins of all degrees of the original crew hired by Captain King. "Three generation teams" work the ranch, a combination that, according to the commemorative account, has produced "a well balanced mixture of experience and enthusiasm, age and youth, seasoned with loyalty to the boss of the outfit, loyalty to the foremen, and loyalty to the ranch."[28]

The key to such labor stability does not rest on debt or coercion but consists of the isolation from outside distractions and the family loyalty among the *vaqueros*. Thus, of the four King Ranch divisions, the employees at the more isolated Norias Division have been more stable. According to Yeary, these employees "have little contact with the world outside the ranch division, preferring to spend their weekends at home rather than in town. While none own automobiles, all have an opportunity to 'go into town' in ranch trucks occasionally." At the Santa Gertrudis, on the other hand, there has been "more changing about" because it is near Kingsville. The employees naturally have "greater opportunities of developing more 'off the ranch interests.'" Nonetheless, former Kineño José Luis Rivera remembers his village on the Santa Gertrudis as being quite isolated; in the late 1950s there were no televisions, one telephone, and few cars in his village.[29]

Another factor making for permanency on the King Ranch is the dense family network of the ranch employees. Yeary observed that when an employee leaves the ranch he is "not only breaking away from all that he has learned from childhood but is cutting loose his family ties also." Former Kineños like Rivera are reminded by ranch security on their visits home that they no longer have free rein at the Santa Gertrudis.[30]

The ranches have functioned as "total institutions," as organizations that have more or less complete control over the workers. Paternalism and the features of authority, deference, obedience, and permanency in a work arrangement are maintained by a cultural understanding generated on the ranches. The lines between owners and workers are sharply drawn. On the Kenedy Ranch, according to Roberto Villarreal's 1972 study, "a unique and significant degree of trust" defined the relations between the ranch owners and the *vaqueros*, especially the Mexican straw bosses (*caporales*) and foremen (*mayordomos*). Most workers, in fact, knew the weaknesses and the unethical practices of the owners. Their opinion on this was that the owners were "part of a different society that functioned under different rules. Their only contact was through their work and their relationship here was both formal and correct."[31]

In the ranch and ranch-farm counties where Mexican landowners have been a significant element, these paternalistic bonds also remain much in evidence, providing the basis for relatively stable political machines. In Starr County, where an estimated 50 percent of the land remains in the hands of the original grantees, the old land-

More than three thousand from throughout the state march to Del Rio, April 6, 1969 (photo by Shel Hershorn; *Texas Observer*, April 11, 1969).

"No Mexicans served."

"Anyone, even Texans."

Cabral's Cantinflas on Jim Crow Restaurants (Garcia Cabral, *Novedades,* 1944).

owning elite retain much of their traditional prominence in local affairs. Such local machines came under assault from the attorney general's office in the mid-1970s. The "Old Party" of Webb County (Laredo) was buried under a wave of court indictments in 1977. The affairs of Duval County, which periodically attracted statewide attention, also crumbled in the mid-1970s. One state investigator from the Texas attorney general's office put it this way: "We are going to drag Duval County kicking and screaming into the 20th century."[32]

Duval County had run on a system based on political patronage, misuse of public funds, and absolute political control. County Auditor Walter Meeks, age 72, described the political system as "frankly corrupt but fully benevolent." George Parr, who had inherited the political machine from his father, Archie, helped poor people "who were grateful and it did not matter that George got the money from the county." A young high school teacher said of the Parr machine: "It was good and it was bad. It maintained the unity of Mexican-Americans and it helped. Nearly 99 per cent of our high school kids graduate and about 70 per cent go to college. It was bad because most of those same kids never returned." In 1975, George Parr, having been convicted of charges of mail fraud and income tax evasion, committed suicide.[33]

The farm world of recent years reflects both "pre–civil rights" and "post–civil rights" settings. Political explosions occurred in the farm areas, with important ripples in small college towns like Edinburg, Kingsville, and San Marcos, where Jim Crow separation had been most acute. While Mexican Americans have increasingly taken over the governance of farm towns and counties, this fact itself has done nothing to stem the decline of agriculture and the out-migration of farm youth. Mexican Americans have taken political control of "declining farm counties," much like black politicians have done with "declining central cities."

Not all farm counties have been "liberated," however. The racial situation in some areas still provides stark reminders of how it used to be generally throughout the state. Thus, in 1975 in Castroville, a farm community only seventeen miles from San Antonio, the Anglo police chief applied the old *ley fuga*—the right to shoot an "escaping" prisoner—to a handcuffed Mexican American. The police chief, tried by a jury of eleven Anglos and one black in San Angelo, a West Texas farm community, was convicted of "aggravated assault." An intense protest from activistic organizations and the Mexican American community of San Antonio resulted in the intervention of the Justice Department on the basis that the victim's civil rights had been violated.[34]

Currently, rural West Texas, which seemed to have been by-passed by politics of the 1960s and 1970s, is experiencing some winds of change. Civil rights lawsuits and farm organizing campaigns and strikes have shaken the staid social order of the semiarid region. In 1980 onion pickers struck in Deaf Smith County (Hereford), and recently, in 1985, farm workers in Pecos County (Fort Stockton) began an organizing campaign in the new vineyards of the area.[35]

From the long view, the patterns and origins of complex development are rather obvious. Although the character of Mexican-Anglo relations in the cities sets the dominant tone for the state, the variations in rural areas serve as important reminders about the uneven road that links the past with the present.

A Concluding Note in 1986

In 1986 the origins of "American Texas" have again come into sharp focus. The Alamo, cradle of Texas independence, is at the center of this sesquicentennial celebration. Despite the uniform eulogies given this old mission, the Alamo has occupied an ambiguous place in the minds of many Texas Mexicans. This uncertainty does not stem from the actual historical events that took place there, for Texas independence was brought about through an alliance of the newcomer Anglo colonists and the established Texas Mexican elite. This history would be incomplete, for example, without the troops of Juan Seguin, who played a key role in the rout of Santa Anna at San Jacinto. The ambivalence stems rather from the long use of the Alamo as an everyday symbol of conquest over Mexicans, as a vindication for the repressive treatment of Mexicans. Historian-politician J. T. Canales of Brownsville explained the matter well in 1950: "Our Texas War of Independence in 1836 was one of those events, where human passions and prejudices were so stirred that for a time it blurred and clouded the acts of real heroes and heroines. . . . Then the War with Mexico, which occurred ten years later, again stirred up additional hatreds and prejudices and cast more dust and smoke which again choked the truth. To this followed the teaching in our Public Schools of Mrs. Pennybacker's History of Texas, the effect of this was to arouse more hatred and race prejudice between the Anglo-Saxon and Mexican peoples in Texas."[36] Conflict and war transformed the Alamo into a racial and nationalistic symbol, a shrine where a long line of American presidents, from Teddy Roosevelt to Gerald Ford, have come to pay their respects and praise American resistance against "foreign" aggression and tyranny.

This was the setting for a notable exchange between civil rights lawyers Gus Garcia and Maury Maverick, Jr., at the Gunter Hotel in 1947 when "both had too much to drink." According to Maverick, Garcia told him, "You damn gringos can have the Alamo. We Mexicans want Kelly Field."[37] Garcia's spirited comment was in a sense prophetic. In the following decades, Mexicans became increasingly entrenched at Kelly Air Force Base while the Anglos continued their annual parades before the Alamo.

Such background makes the sesquicentennial celebration all the more ironic and significant; for the host is Henry Cisneros, mayor of San Antonio, the first mayor of Mexican descent since Juan Seguin. In his public addresses before the Alamo, it is not surprising to hear Cisneros emphasize the American identity of Texas Mexicans, for Cisneros himself represents the reconciliation that has taken place between Anglo and Mexican in Texas. This does not mean that ethnic solidarity has become a matter of the past; it means rather that it has become subordinated to the voices of moderation from both communities. The politics of negotiation and compromise have replaced the politics of conflict and control.

Such an integrative climate is not an unchanging condition. The tenor of ethnic relations rests on a series of outcomes and social forces that can move a society in several different directions. There is no way to predict whether the "gentrification" of the Mexican American community will continue or whether some plateau has been reached. Regardless of the answer, poverty and associated ills will pose serious problems for some time to come. The manner in which the various levels of government respond to these needs will depend on local and state politics. These in turn may hinge on cross-cutting demographic movements, that is, on whether the out-migration of upwardly mobile Mexican Americans and the in-migration of retired military personnel and "snow birds" continue at their respective rates. Some of these movements, of course, are tied to larger questions concerning "sunbelt development," the border economy, and the world oil glut.

Another reason for caution stems from the considerable opposition among Anglos toward Mexican American assertiveness. Sentiment against bilingual education and affirmative action remains strong. Not to be overlooked or slighted are those who worry about the undermining of "American society," that is, Anglo-European culture. The "English-only" movement, the adverse reaction to the Voting Rights Act in some quarters, and the antiimmigrant sentiment all share a basic exclusivist strain. Indeed, one major controversy of the 1980s revolves around the rights of long-resident Mexican "illegals," a discussion that is reminiscent of the public debates of the 1840s, 1920s, and 1950s concerning the place of Mexicans in Texas.

In the 1980s, the struggle between exclusion and inclusion continues. What is different from previous battles, however, is that Mexican Americans have become an important factor in the political chemistry of the Southwest. It seems unlikely that such momentum can be stopped.

APPENDIX
On Interpreting Southwestern History

A fundamental characteristic of sociological or interpretive history is that, unlike most social history, it makes explicit the methods and theoretical points involved in the organization and writing of the narrative. Hence, this appendix. The theoretical points will be discussed first, the methods second.

Some Theoretical Points

This history has explored the political, economic, and cultural dimensions of race situations. The general argument in this regard has been that a succession of class societies explains change in race relations and that the uneven nature of this transformation explains variations in race relations. The key themes comprising this argument concerned the significance of annexation, the role of land and labor in historical change, Mexicans and the race question, and the notion of unevenness in development. Here I wish to examine these various themes and illustrate them with material from California and New Mexico. Presenting the theoretical points in this manner will make clear their significance to the Southwest as a region.

The Meaning of Annexation

Annexation set the context for the formation of "races" in the Southwest. These divisions were not necessarily an immediate result but were a predictable outcome of the political subordination and economic displacement set off by annexation.

Political subordination was an understandable point of departure for examining the significance of annexation. In situations of military occupation—examples include the "carpetbag rule" of the defeated Confederacy, the American occupation of Puerto Rico and the Philippines, Israel's "West Bank"—the power of "higher authority" has rested firmly in the hands of the victors. The military government does not allow the conquered to rule over the conquering soldiers, however lowly in rank. This applies by extension to the citizens (merchants and quartermaster employees) accompanying the army of occupation. Beyond this premise, however, the victor must formulate a policy of governance toward the defeated. The general options available to the victor may be suggested through a discussion drawn from "living memory"—a wartime article that asked, "What Shall We Do with Japan?"[1]

In a 1943 policy paper, written when Allied victory over the Axis powers appeared to be only a matter of time, Fred Gealy argued that the most difficult of the postwar problems would concern U.S. policy toward the defeated Japanese. In approaching this problem, Gealy turned to the lessons learned from experience with "minority races." "Annihilation" of the Japanese was ruled out—because the experience with the Jews and the blacks had shown that race problems could not be solved through extermination. Another possibility, which Gealy also discounted, was that of keeping the Japanese in "permanent subjugation." This was the "typical way" in which minority races and "backward" nations were treated, and it was also "the normal American pattern in our treatment of the Negro." Rejecting both annihilation and permanent subjection as inappropriate, Gealy argued for an "enlightened" approach. War presented a chance to start anew, to reconstruct: "The most significant fact about war as a method of social change is not that it is a means of securing immediate justice for anyone; but that by breaking up the rigidities of traditional social patterns it provides the fluidity requisite to the construction of political forms more relevant to changing history, and that it consolidates the victor or victors in power and enables them to create a *peace structure* which will further—not alone their own interests—but the political and social philosophy by which they interpret the War."[2]

Although, of course, the wars with Japan and Mexico were very different events, Gealy's policy analysis suggests a context for understanding annexation and Mexican-Anglo relations in the mid–nineteenth century. There were radical variations in these relations across the Southwest, as elements of all three options available to victors—annihilation, subjugation, and peaceful accommodation—were carried out in the immediate postwar period. Where the Mexican population remained a sizable population, the new authorities generally sought to establish a "peace structure." Under this arrangement, the Mexican settlements were usually allowed limited representation in the new government, but authority relations were structured so that in no instances would Mexicans stand over Anglos. In California, according to Leonard Pitt, "Americans saw the advantage of letting Californios control Californios, but they would give the native-born no license to govern Yankees." Thus many towns, such as San Jose, had a system of "dual *alcaldes,*" one Anglo and one Mexican, each of whom governed his respective community. In sum, victor and defeated, former enemies, had a distinct political status in the courts and governing agencies of the new order.[3]

The inferior political status of the Mexican was sanctioned by the Treaty of Guadalupe Hidalgo. At the treaty negotiations, the Mexican representatives had pressed hard for two articles—one that granted full citizenship rights to the Mexicans residing in the ceded territory and one that recognized the Spanish and Mexican land grants as valid. Neither of the articles survived the objections of the Senate. Article X, regarding the recognition of land grants, was deleted altogether, and Article IX, concerning the citizenship rights of Mexicans, was substantially rewritten. The senators, reflecting the popular opinion of the time (except for some dissent in the Northeast), were united in their belief that Mexicans were not ready for an "equal union" with Americans, and some senators argued like John C. Calhoun that they would never be. The substitute version of Article IX provided that Mexicans in the ceded territory "shall be incorporated into the Union of the United States, and be admitted, at the proper time (to be judged of by the Congress of the United States), to the enjoyment of all rights of citizens of the United States." The instrument that reflected Congress' intention was the long territorial status of New Mexico: the territory was not granted statehood until 1912.[4]

Another direct consequence of annexation was the rapid formation of a new elite in the Mexican settlements. From the initial Anglo-American presence—discharged soldiers, civilians who had been employed with the quartermaster service, and merchants who followed the army camps—emerged the nucleus of a mercantile group that would figure prominently in the political and economic history of the region. Everywhere in the frontier West an export-oriented elite took charge of development, acquired authority through the Spanish-Mexican elite, and displaced villagers or *rancheros* and, eventually, many of the elite from their landholdings. In New Mexico, for example, there was the Santa Fe Ring, a powerful clique of land lawyers and merchants, which did much to reorganize the old Spanish-Mexican society of *hacendados,* merchants, villagers, and *peones.* The collapse of this class structure was highlighted by fraud and violence, but this was basically a collapse accomplished legally and systematically through the play of the market, that is, through increasing dependence of Mexican landowners on Anglo merchants and lawyers. Throughout the Southwest, Anglo-American merchants, through access to credit and wholesale markets and knowledge of business techniques, eliminated much of their Spanish American mercantile competition.[5]

The Question of Land and Labor

Insofar as social change models have been discussed in western histories, many memorable statements have suggested a comparison to the transition from feudalism to capitalism. Walter Prescott Webb, for example, likened the strategy of Spanish colonization in the "great plains" to the European feudal system: ". . . like the feudal system, it rested on a foundation of service—serfs in Europe and pueblo Indians in America. Without serfdom in Europe feudalism could not have flourished; without pueblo Indians in America the Spanish colonial system did not stand."[6] In similar fashion, Howard Lamar described mid-nineteenth-century New Mexico as a "feudal frontier." The landed don occupied a hereditary position at the head of a vast family clan and numerous servants who were bound by debt peonage for a lifetime. The don had the powers of the American antebellum planter with his slaves, but, unlike the planter, the don "moved in a much more primitive, self-sufficient economic system which was more subsistence than commercial." More recently, T. R. Fehrenbach has described the eighteenth-century settlements of the Nuevo Santander province, which then extended from Tampico to Corpus Christi and Laredo, as a frontier society with "strong overtones of feudalism."[7]

In view of the economic subsistence and servitude of the time, "feudalism" has been an understandable description of Mexican frontier society. It is, however, a misleading description. The isolation and self-sufficiency were closely related to the exhaustion of mines, the lack of a stable market for livestock products, and the devastation of warfare with unpacified Indians in the early nineteenth century. The wars of Mexican independence also ruined the country's economic infrastructure. The *haciendas* of northern Mexico (and indeed of Latin America), however, were no less "commercial" than the antebellum plantations of the American South. In fact, like slave plantations and other types of manorial institutions, the *hacienda* possessed an economic resiliency: during periods of market expansion, the *hacienda* would become a unit of production and in periods of contraction, a self-sufficient institution.[8] Rather than describing it as feudalistic, it makes more sense to see the Spanish-Mexican colonial society as representing a form of early capitalism, as a commercial society still laden with aristocratic notions about land and labor services. The modernization of the annexed Mexican settlements, in other words, entailed the transformation of an early commercial form to a more "mature" form, where the enjoyment of land tenure and labor services was tied directly to market success.

Although the particulars vary across the Southwest, the "freeing" of land and labor provides a useful framework for understanding the economic and social history of the region after annexation. The nineteenth century was highlighted by the erosion of a Mexican land base, the twentieth by the organization of Mexican wage labor.

The nineteenth-century experience featured the development of a market in ranch lands and ranch products, which resulted in the dispossession of small and large Mexican landowners. The first American settlers found a landownership system of undivided "*derechos,*" or rights, a colonial practice dating back to the late sixteenth century. Most estates were owned jointly or were entailed so that individual owners could not sell their property, which remained indissolubly linked to a family name. Basically, there was no free arable land in the annexed Southwest.[9]

The displacement of landed Mexicans, according to many sources, was an experience characterized by fraud, intimidation, and violence. While such coercion was undoubtedly an important aspect of the story, what is generally overlooked is the systematic displacement that occurred through market competition. A general explanation for such displacement has been outlined by Jeffrey Paige in his work on rural class conflict.[10]

Paige has noted that, in societies where an agricultural export sector develops in competition with a "traditional" agrarian sector, the export organization introduces new patterns of conflict by creating new social classes and destroying old ones. In a traditional subsistence sector with weak or irregular ties to the world market, the upper classes generally draw their incomes exclusively from landed property and lack any financial assets beyond the land itself. With industrialization and world market penetration, however, the base of the agrarian upper class shifts from income derived from landownership to income derived from control of the processing, transportation, storage, and sale of agricultural products. While some traditional landed elite will weather the transition, generally the shift to market production will mark the ascendancy of a new cohort, a new upper class whose wealth and power stem from the organization and control of the export activity. Although the principal economic activity in the nineteenth-century Southwest involved livestock rather than agriculture, Paige's argument holds quite well.

Even as merchants supplanted the elite, they assumed the trappings of *patrones* and *hacendados* and relied on "traditional" arrangements to organize work and production. In California during the Mexican period, there were a number of Mexicanized Yankees who adjusted comfortably to Mexican life. They became Catholics, married local women, and obtained legal land grants. After annexation, the harmony of the races, especially in the southern portion of the state, rested on the "peace structure" established by these American *patrones*. In New Mexico, a similar process was evident in the fascinating personage of Lucien Maxwell, a Hispanicized Yankee merchant who married into the Hispano upper class and acquired the famous Maxwell land grant. According to historian J. Evetts Haley, "Don Luciano" had approximately a thousand Mexicans living in virtual peonage on his estate as well as a police force of five hundred "faithful" Apache Indians who had reduced cattle and sheep stealing to a minimum.[11] But these interesting *haciendas*, reflecting the hybrid character of the Southwest during the late nineteenth century, barely lasted a generation.

The twentieth century brings us to the second point in our story—the formation of a Mexican wage laboring class. The development of a labor market in the Southwest, given impetus with the railway and *rancho* bonanza of the 1870s and 1880s and consolidated with the farm boom of the early 1900s, undermined many of the remaining vestiges of the annexed Mexican settlements. The Mexicanized Anglo landowners, who had continued many of the old ways, were lured to a wealthy retirement by attractive offers or became realtors and bankers themselves and sold out their *ranchos* in parcels. With each land transfer and sale, the patterns and institutions that defined relations among *patrones*, *peones*, and villagers lost more of their meaning; at each turn, "tradition" had to be renegotiated. Thus, when Don Luciano Maxwell sold his ranch to an English company in the 1880s, the Apache tribesmen, although they threatened to go on the warpath, were forced to leave. Mexicans were apparently not much affected until the turn of the century when the English company began selling land to timber companies and other interested parties. As one source describes the results, families were forced off the land and "came to expect wages rather than a portion of the crop for their labor." This was no isolated instance; what was unfolding on the old Maxwell grant reflected the dire predicament of the vil-

lagers of northern New Mexico and southern Colorado as they became "gradually compressed into a single class of subsistence farmers, herders, and laborers."[12]

Mexicans and the Race Question

Beyond the turmoil and uncertainty of the immediate postwar period, from the perspective of a century and a half, the inconsistent
treatment of Mexicans reflected variations in local class structure.
Even during the immediate postwar period, the way Mexicans were
treated—whether subjugated or peacefully subordinated—had much
to do with class status. In spite of what many Anglo pioneers may
have thought generally of Mexicans, most were careful to make the
proper distinctions between different "types" of Mexicans. Mexican
landowners were "Spanish" or "Castilian," whereas Mexican workers were "half-breeds" or "Mexican Indians." The well-known aphorism explains the situation—"money whitens."

When the railroads and farm projects swept away a large portion of
the Mexican ranch society at the turn of the century, the converse of
this aphorism was shown to be equally valid. With the Mexican
ranch society removed by commercial farming, lack of money "dark-
ened" the Mexican. The Castilian-Indian distinction of the nineteenth century lost its meaning, and Mexicans became simply and
unambiguously Mexican. A similar process unfolded in the major
cities of the region, as the descendants of the Californios and Tejanos
became indistinguishable from the growing immigrant Mexican
community. Symbolic of the "darkening" of the Mexican was the
1930 Census reclassification of Mexicans as belonging to the "other
races." A more fundamental sign of this new racial status was manifested by the rise of segregation in the agricultural zones of California, Arizona, and Texas. The "factories in the field" brought about a
heightening of race distinctions. Agribusiness development gave rise
to "Anglo market towns" and "Mexican labor towns," a division that
laid the basis for pervasive social segregation.[13]

After World War II, the social base of segregation evaporated gradually as agribusiness passed into corporate hands and production became mechanized. Essentially, the Jim Crow class order collapsed:
small resident farmers were eliminated through market competition
and farm workers migrated to the cities and the fields of other states.
A new order took its place, one where urban business interests and
those of a growing Mexican American middle class constituted the
major political axis shaping ethnic relations. Since businessmen
were not as dependent on repression as farmers were, the shift from

rural to urban dominance was highlighted by a relaxing of race privilege. This moderation was accelerated by the aggressive labor organizing and civil rights protests of the 1960s and 1970s known as the "Chicano Movement."

Of theoretical import here is Stanley Greenberg's argument that change in a "modernizing" racial society can be explained in terms of shifts in the primary sector of the economy.[14] Thus, in both South Africa and the southern United States, capitalist development at an early stage brought about, along with wage labor, factories, and cities, the "intensification of racial discrimination." This intensification represented in large part the prominence of farmers who responded to commercialization and the increased mobility of farm laborers by elaborating a labor and racial repressive framework. Once the "commercial-industrial-urban complex" surfaced and dominated the economic and political scene, however, the period of intensification gave way and resulted in a "crisis of hegemony." The business sector, which can live with other ways of organizing society, led the way beyond the old racial framework. Moreover, with mechanization and the diversification of investments, even farmer groups lost interest in old racial practices. In this context, political challenges from below and outside were able to expose the obsolescence of old arrangements as well as the "uncertainty and disunity" within the dominant section.

Unevenness of Development

In the Southwest, as noted, there did occur the fabled "dance of commodities"; land and labor were transformed into marketable products. But with the exception of a few areas, such transformation did not unfold in a cataclysmic sweep. The *ranchos* of northern California were completely decimated within a few years because of the gold rush of 1849, but the southern portion of the state remained, in Pitt's words, a "semi-gringo" frontier for another thirty years. In New Mexico, the northern counties remained a stronghold for Hispanos while the eastern and southern counties became rangeland for an expanding Texas cattle industry in the 1870s. In Texas, dispossession and minority status were the lot of Mexicans above the Nueces River by 1850, but the old settlements along the Rio Grande in West and South Texas were spared the full effects of annexation until the turn of the century. For much of the Southwest, life in the countryside continued virtually unchanged for several decades after the war. The Anglo pioneers confined themselves to the towns, where they occupied themselves with merchandising and freighting.

In the nineteenth century, only a notable few engaged in ranching or agriculture. Thus, the country life of the *rancherías* maintained Mexican traditions, "apart from the world of commerce, news and ideas."[15]

For the study of development and social change, this type of "unevenness" suggests, as a basic point, that local class actors had considerable latitude in responding to "market impulses" from the outside. Market forces simply did not run roughshod over every intermediate or intervening factor. An especially important circumstance was whether local work arrangements were characterized by paternalistic and permanent relations or formal and contractual ones. These owner-worker relations were important because their effects were diffused throughout the social order, shaping all spheres of social life in their image. The character of work arrangements indicated the manner in which a class society was held together, that is, the way politics, coercion, incentives, protocol, and so on, were organized.

If this line of investigation were applied across the Southwest as a region, the mosaic character of development would become magnified many times over. Sorting through the differential impact of various industries (especially in labor needs and relations), the distinct political arrangements between Mexican and Anglo, and the demographics of class and ethnicity, to mention a few variables, would take us a considerable distance in understanding the distinct experiences of Mexicans in California, New Mexico, and Texas. Pursued far enough, such localized examination would suggest, for example, why the "Chicano politics" of the 1960s and 1970s assumed different expressions throughout the region—why a powerful farm worker movement emerged in California, a volatile land grant movement in New Mexico, and an aggressive political nationalism in Texas.

At a time when much recent historical sociology approaches the question of uneven development from a global perspective, it is important to underscore the value of a "provincial" viewpoint, that is, a recognition of the power of local class actors to shape local societies. Immanuel Wallerstein, a prominent exponent of the global perspective, has compared the world-system method for examining the history of development to that of astronomers who must deal with one universe.[16] The guidelines for provincial research, on the other hand, are drawn on an entirely different plane, a point that the political scientist O. Douglas Weeks emphasized in introducing a study of South Texas politics fifty years ago. Aware of the localized nature of his research, Weeks noted that the shifting social bases of politics "may readily be seen if one turns the telescope on the national political firmament, but it cannot be understood in the minutiae of its cease-less activity unless the microscope be applied to relatively small localities."[17]

Applying the microscope to uneven development demonstrates the centrality of local politics in shaping patterns of social relations. The result of such local initiative establishes the comparative perspective for regional studies, for a sufficiently large region will manifest the contrasts between "modernizing" and "nonmodernizing" areas. The larger global context, of course, is not forgotten; the outside world is always there, suspended, always intervening and affecting local matters. Local elites, however, possess sufficient influence to secure a measure of continuity for their social worlds.

On Methods in Historical Sociology

While conducting research for this study, I found that, outside of romantic social histories, little was actually known of the "Mexican region" of Texas. Primary sources were scarce; "facts" had to be discovered and given names; and even basic census figures often proved suspect or deficient. The secondary literature was not actually scarce but it was made up of scattered localized descriptions of varying quality. What was necessary was to tease out a pattern from the pieces offered in these unconnected studies, documents, and biographical materials. The "pieces" of sociology and history had to be pulled together and organized so that they could tell the complex story of social change and ethnic relations.

The distinct obligations carried by commitments to history and sociology at times were difficult to manage. It meant working on two fronts, balancing energies and emphases and blending the two into a coherent synthesis. This was risky business: there was the danger, on the one hand, of burdening the manuscript with descriptive detail and, on the other, of constantly interrupting the narrative with abstract terms and generalizations. A commitment to history meant, among other things, portraying the possibilities that human actors have at any particular moment, understanding their society as they did, and preserving the integrity of situations and events as much as possible. A commitment to sociology, on the other hand, meant teasing out patterns and sequences from a number of unique cases and moments in order to arrive at some general conclusions about society and social life.[18]

The contradictory pull of these obligations has created, for historical sociology or sociological history, a terrain where the concerns of both disciplines can be assessed, revised, and meshed in some way.

Quite self-consciously, historical sociologists must select general concepts or categories that bridge the distance between human experience and social forces.[19] Because historical sociologists must establish some kind of contact with those about whom they are writing, the working conceptions—the concepts used to convey the argument of the narrative—must be able to mediate between human activity and theoretical generalization. Thus, the most effective mediating concepts in sociological history have been the basic existential categories of social life—notions of class, race, religion, status, gender, and so on.

One way of describing the nature of sociological history is through an analogy to drama. In comparison to most social history, sociological history is sparse on details concerning character development, background setting, and dramatic movement. The dramatis personae are subsumed by social categories, the background limited to a few symbolic props, the movement of the story condensed and truncated by case studies. Symbolic and didactic in character, the effect of the sociological-historical narrative is rather like the allegory. Its effectiveness depends to a large degree on whether the chosen symbols or concepts can convey the theme or argument without subverting the human character of the story.

Juan Cortina, Charles Stillman, and Richard King, for example, were all important characters in South Texas during the nineteenth century. A social history of that period that did not describe the physical, cultural, and personal features of these actors would be, arguably, incomplete. In this sociological history, however, the only biographical characteristics that entered the narrative were those that make a point about class or ethnicity. Thus, Cortina's red hair, Stillman's Yankee Puritan background, and King's barroom behavior were details that, while important for re-creating some vivid scenes of this regional history, I omitted. For the allegory of development I wanted to present, what was important to know was that Cortina was a land grant owner, Stillman a merchant, and King a cattleman. The character details that appeared were selected and organized to illuminate these collective categories. I pointed, for example, to King's "eccentrically baronial" personality in order to stress the "Mexicanization" of the American pioneer ranchers during this time.

In short, the importance of general concepts in sociological history lies in the correspondence they establish and illuminate between facts and theory. An important consideration thus consists of the manner in which concepts are ordered or strung together. The constant search for correspondence guides the ordering of the general concepts. Each advance in conceptual understanding, each partial solution to a question, sets off a number of related questions to be asked of the theoretical and historical materials at hand. For example, the first sizable aspect of the twentieth-century history pieced together made sense of the difficult experience of Texas Mexican migratory laborers in the 1920s and 1930s. The Paul Taylor interviews of 1927–1930 contained rather frank references and discussion of the controls and restraints imposed on Mexican laborers. There seemed to be no order to these instances and episodes, however. Closer examination of these controls revealed that distinguishing between sharecroppers and migratory laborers helped bring some order to the experience of farm laborers. This, in turn, led to further investigation—to checking the fluctuations of the market, to surveying political conditions, and so on—until the diverse controls were woven together to form a comprehensible logic. The name I applied to this complex experience was "labor repression," a term borrowed from Barrington Moore, Jr.[20]

The clarity provided by this logic of repression set off a number of analytical probes. On one front, this experience led me to examine the culture of race-thinking that supported and reflected such repression; and this led, because of a need to achieve some closure, to an examination of protection and benevolence in such a society. On another front, the difference between ranching and farming, a distinction that had become apparent at an early stage of sorting through the historical materials, was given new significance by the notion of labor repression. The meaning of work arrangements for understanding the character of ranch and farm areas now became an important question. This line of questioning soon made it apparent that there were ranch counties and farm counties. The division was "too neat," however—a suspicion that led me to study the significance of county governments in the making of the local order, and this led me ultimately to see that in effect there were two distinct societies in the region.

In this way, sociological theory and historical facts interplayed to guide the journey. Sociological questions about ethnic relations and social change provided the broad outlines for approaching the history; the particulars suggested certain insights and clarified concepts and ideas about these questions; and these clarified concepts and ideas in turn helped organize a "grounded" historical interpretation.

NOTES

1. Introduction

1. This border zone includes all of South Texas and considerable portions of Central and West Texas. In these areas, the Texas Mexican population ranges from 40 percent to 90 percent of the local population.

2. Peter J. Parish states that the "triumphalist" tendency has characterized mainstream American historical writing since George Bancroft ("American History Arrives in Europe," *New York Times Book Review*, February 3, 1985, p. 29). See also Eric R. Wolf, *Europe and the People without History*, pp. 3–7.

3. For example, see Rodolfo Acuña, *Occupied America;* Albert Camarillo, *Chicanos in a Changing Society;* Mario Barrera, *Race and Class in the Southwest;* Mario T. García, *Desert Immigrants;* Arnoldo De León, *The Tejano Community, 1836–1900.*

4. T. R. Fehrenbach, *Lone Star*, pp. 256–257, 447–448, 678, 689.

5. For critical reviews of the manner in which the development literature has addressed the race question, see Stanley B. Greenberg, *Race and State in Capitalist Development*, pp. 29–50; Herbert Blumer, "Industrialisation and Race Relations, in *Industrialisation and Race Relations*, ed. Guy Hunter, pp. 220–270.

6. Robert Redfield, "Race as a Social Phenomenon," in *Race*, ed. Edgar T. Thompson and Everett C. Hughes, pp. 66–71; also see Pierre L. van den Berghe, *Race and Racism*, pp. 1–41; John Rex, "The Concept of Race in Sociological Theory," in *Race, Ethnicity, and Social Change*, ed. John Stone, pp. 59–74.

7. George M. Fredrickson, *White Supremacy*, pp. xi–xix; C. Vann Woodward, *The Strange Career of Jim Crow;* S. B. Greenberg, *Race and State*, pp. 29–50.

8. See Philip Anthony Hernández, "The Other North Americans: The American Image of Mexico and Mexicans, 1550–1850" (Ph.D. diss.); Raymund Paredes, "The Origins of Anti-Mexican Sentiment in the United States," *New Scholar* 6 (1977): 139–166; Arnoldo De León, *They Called Them Greasers;* Ronald T. Takaki, *Iron Cages.*

9. See Barrington Moore, Jr., *Social Origins of Democracy and Dictatorship.*

10. O. Douglas Weeks, "The Texas-Mexican and the Politics of South Texas," *American Political Science Review* 24, no. 3 (August 1930): 610.

11. For a theoretical discussion, see Moore, *Social Origins*, pp. 437–452.

12. For a concise description of the Paul Taylor Collection, see Abraham Hoffman, "A Note on the Field Research Interviews of Paul S. Taylor for the Mexican Labor in the United States Monographs," *Pacific Historian* 20 (Summer 1976): 123–131.

13. J. Frank Dobie, *A Vaquero of the Brush Country*, pp. 71, 81.

14. Frederick Law Olmsted, *A Journey through Texas; or, a Saddle-Trip on the Southwestern Frontier.*

PART ONE. **Incorporation, 1836–1900**

Ashbel Smith, "An Address Delivered in the City of Galveston on the 22nd of February, 1848, The Anniversary of the Birth Day of Washington and of the Battle of Buena Vista," in Smith, *Addresses, etc.*, pp. 11–17. The advice of the dons dates from the 1870s, according to Elena Zamora O'Shea (*El Mesquite*, pp. 68–69).

1. Mari Sandoz, *The Cattlemen*, pp. 39–40; also Dobie, *Vaquero of the Brush Country*, pp. 44–71; Walter Prescott Webb, *The Texas Rangers*, pp. 125–194.

2. Howard Roberts Lamar, *The Far Southwest, 1846–1912*; Ramón Eduardo Ruiz, ed., *The Mexican War*; Otis Singletary, *The Mexican War*; Glenn W. Price, *Origins of the War with Mexico.*

3. LeRoy P. Graf, "The Economic History of the Lower Rio Grande Valley, 1820–1875" (Ph.D. diss.), p. 62; Olmsted, *Journey through Texas*, pp. 452–453; Mrs. William L. Cazneau (Cora Montgomery), *Eagle Pass*, pp. 177–179.

4. Honorable E. Dougherty, *The Rio Grande Valley*, pp. 29–30.

5. Quoted by Graf, "Economic History," p. 55; also see pp. 89–93.

6. Quoted by Florence J. Scott, "Spanish Land Grants in the Lower Rio Grande Valley" (M.A. thesis), p. 116.

7. Graf, "Economic History," pp. 145–146; also see Tom Lea, *The King Ranch*, 1:52.

8. Lamar, *Far Southwest*, pp. 72–81; Frank H. Dugan, "The 1850 Affairs of the Brownsville Separatists," *Southwestern Historical Quarterly* 61, no. 2 (October 1957): 270–287.

9. See the report of John Haynes in U.S. Congress, House, *Difficulties on the Southwestern Frontier*, pp. 26–27. See also Francisco López Cámara, *La estructura económica y social de México en la época de la reforma*, esp. pp. 134–141; D. W. Meinig, *Imperial Texas*, pp. 38–42; Scott, "Spanish Land Grants," pp. 113–117.

10. Olmsted, *Journey through Texas*, p. 452.

11. Dougherty, *Rio Grande Valley*, pp. 28–29.

12. Ibid., pp. 26, 34, 35.

2. The Rivalship of Peace

1. For example, see Albert K. Weinberg, *Manifest Destiny*, and Frederick Merk, *Manifest Destiny and Mission in American History.*

2. Smith, "Address Delivered in the City of Galveston," pp. 11–17.

3. See Haynes' description in *Difficulties on the Southwestern Frontier*, p. 26.

4. James Ernest Crisp, "Anglo Texan Attitudes toward the Mexican, 1821–1845" (Ph.D. diss.), pp. 324–327.

5. Zamora O'Shea, *El Mesquite*, p. 59; also see Crisp, "Anglo Texan Attitudes," p. 329.

6. Olmsted, *Journey through Texas*, p. 262; Crisp, "Anglo Texan Attitudes," pp. 343–344.

7. A. B. J. Hammett, *The Empresario*, pp. v, 25, 28, 58–59, 189–190.

8. Juan Nepomuceno Seguin, *Personal Memoirs of John N. Seguin*, p. 18; also Frederic Chabot, *With the Makers of San Antonio*, p. 127.

9. José María Rodríguez, *Memoirs of Early Texas*, p. 60.

10. Cited by Crisp, "Anglo Texan Attitudes," p. 348.

11. John Bost Pitts III, "Speculation in Headright Land Grants in San Antonio from 1837 to 1842" (M.A. thesis), pp. 29–34.

12. Olmsted, *Journey through Texas*, pp. 502–503.

13. Ibid., p. 164; also J. Fred Rippy, "Border Troubles along the Rio Grande, 1848–1860," *Southwestern Historical Quarterly* 23, no. 2 (October 1919): 103.

14. Olmsted, *Journey through Texas*, pp. 156–160, 169; De León, *Tejano Community*, p. 88.

15. Olmsted, *Journey through Texas*, p. 164.

16. Ibid., p. 245.

17. Carland Elaine Crook, "San Antonio, Texas, 1846–1861" (M.A. thesis), pp. 34–35; Rippy, "Border Troubles," pp. 103–104; George Pierce Garrison, *Texas*, pp. 273–275; also see *Texas, a Guide to the Lone Star State*, p. 649.

18. For an account of the activities of Anglo filibusters, see Zamora O'Shea, *El Mesquite*, pp. 62–63; Rippy, "Border Troubles"; Marvin J. Hunter, comp. and ed., *The Trail Drivers of Texas*, 2:733.

19. Graf, "Economic History," p. 370; Rodríguez, *Memoirs of Early Texas*; Dugan, "The 1850 Affairs," pp. 270–287; Paul S. Taylor, *An American-Mexican Frontier*, pp. 179–190.

20. Oscar J. Martínez, "On the Size of the Chicano Population: New Estimates, 1850–1900," *Aztlan* 6, no. 1 (Spring 1975): 50–51.

21. James Thompson, "A 19th Century History of Cameron County" (M.A. thesis), pp. 70–71, 112–114; M. T. García, *Desert Immigrants*, pp. 13–15.

22. Terry G. Jordan, "Population Origins in Texas, 1850," *Geographical Review* 59 (January 1962): 83–103; and "The 1887 Census of Texas' Hispanic Population," *Aztlan* 12, no. 2 (Autumn 1981): 271–278; Abbé Emanuel Domenech, *Missionary Adventures in Texas and Mexico*, p. 9; Martínez, "On the Size," pp. 47–48.

23. Olmsted, *Journey through Texas*, p. 165; Graf, "Economic History," p. 413; Rippy, "Border Troubles," p. 92.

24. Rodríguez, *Memoirs of Early Texas*, p. 75; also Dugan, "The 1850 Affairs."

25. Domenech, *Missionary Adventures*, pp. 176, 228.

26. Ibid., pp. 238–239.

27. For accounts about Juan "Cheno" Cortina, see U.S. Congress, House, *Difficulties on the Southwestern Frontier*; Lea, *King Ranch*, 1:158; Webb,

Texas Rangers, pp. 175–193; Rippy, "Border Troubles," pp. 104–111; Charles W. Goldfinch, *Juan N. Cortina, 1824–1892*; José T. Canales, *Juan N. Cortina Presents His Motion for a New Trial*.

28. In U.S. Congress, House, *Difficulties on the Southwestern Frontier*, pp. 80–81.

29. Ibid., pp. 53, 70–72; Goldfinch, *Juan N. Cortina*, p. 47; see Webb, *Texas Rangers*, pp. 175–193.

30. Maj. S. P. Heintzelman to Lt. Col. Robert E. Lee, March 1, 1860, in U.S. Congress, House, *Troubles on the Texas Frontier*, p. 13.

31. James B. Gillette, *Six Years with the Texas Rangers, 1875 to 1881*, pp. 136–150; Webb, *Texas Rangers*, pp. 345–368; M. T. García, *Desert Immigrants*, p. 156.

32. See J. Thompson, "A 19th Century History," p. 48; Gillett, *Six Years*, pp. 136–150; also Webb, *Texas Rangers*, pp. 345–368, and *The Great Plains*, pp. 179–180; John L. Davis, *The Texas Rangers*, p. 89.

33. J. Thompson, "A 19th Century History," pp. 79–81.

34. Caroline Remy, "Hispanic-Mexican San Antonio: 1836–1861," *Southwestern Historical Quarterly* 71, no. 4 (April 1968): 567.

35. Rodríguez, *Memoirs of Early Texas*, p. 37.

36. Chabot, *With the Makers*; Remy, "Hispanic-Mexican San Antonio," pp. 566–567; William Bollaert, *William Bollaert's Texas*, ed. W. Eugene Hollon and Ruth Lapham Butler.

37. William J. Knox, *The Economic Status of the Mexican Immigrant in San Antonio, Texas*, pp. 3–5.

38. Goldfinch, *Juan N. Cortina*, p. 27.

39. See Rogelia O. García, *Dolores, Revilla, and Laredo*, pp. 36–39; Gilberto M. Hinojosa, *Borderlands Town in Transition*, pp. 68–71; also J. B. Wilkinson, *Laredo and the Rio Grande Frontier*; Kathleen Da Camara, *Laredo on the Rio Grande*.

40. Goldfinch, *Juan N. Cortina*, p. 6.

41. J. Thompson, "A 19th Century History," p. 12.

42. Jovita González, "Social Life in Cameron, Starr, and Zapata Counties" (M.A. thesis), pp. 27, 58; for intermarriages in Laredo, see R. O. García, *Dolores*, p. 39.

43. González, "Social Life," p. 27.

44. Evan M. Anders, "James B. Wells and the Brownsville Patronage Fight, 1912–1917" (M.A. thesis), p. 8.

45. De León, *Tejano Community*, pp. 51, 88; also Goldfinch, *Juan N. Cortina*, p. 31.

46. Virginia H. Taylor, *Spanish Archives of the General Land Office of Texas*, pp. 127–136; J. J. Bowden, *Spanish and Mexican Land Grants in the Chihuahuan Acquisition*; also see John H. McNeely, "Mexican American Land Issues in the United States," in *The Role of the Mexican American in the History of the Southwest*, pp. 36–37.

47. Quoted in P. S. Taylor, *American-Mexican Frontier*, p. 232.

48. Olmsted, *Journey through Texas*, p. 163; P. S. Taylor, *American-Mexican Frontier*, pp. 230–234.

49. Quoted in J. Thompson, "A 19th Century History," pp. 58–59. Another example is provided by Arnoldo De León, *In Re Ricardo Rodríguez.*

50. González, "Social Life," p. 84; M. T. García, *Desert Immigrants,* pp. 157–158; De León, *Tejano Community,* pp. 23–49; J. Thompson, "A 19th Century History," pp. 5, 28–31.

51. Remy, "Hispanic-Mexican San Antonio," p. 570; De León, *Tejano Community,* pp. 25, 28, 30–34.

52. This table was organized from information compiled by August Santleban, who attached an appendix of San Antonio's city officials to his memoirs. The ethnicity of an alderman was based on surname, a fairly reliable method. See August Santleban, *A Texas Pioneer,* pp. 314–321.

53. De León, *Tejano Community,* pp. 101–104.

54. Graf, "Economic History," pp. 129, 150, 207.

55. Scott, "Spanish Land Grants," pp. 125–126; J. Thompson, "A 19th Century History," pp. 80–82.

56. Olmsted, *Journey through Texas,* p. 152.

57. J. Thompson, "A 19th Century History," pp. 39–40; Graf, "Economic History," p. 361; see Lea, *King Ranch,* 1:1–92, for the full story.

58. J. Thompson, "A 19th Century History," p. 75; Graf, "Economic History," pp. 680–681.

59. Lea, *King Ranch,* 1:52–53.

60. See ibid., 1:95–99.

61. Graf, "Economic History," pp. 629, 661–662; also see Lea, *King Ranch,* 1:404–407; J. Thompson, "A 19th Century History," pp. 90–93.

62. *The King Ranch, 100 Years of Ranching,* p. 52; L. E. Daniell, *Types of Successful Men in Texas,* pp. 331–334; V. H. Taylor, *Spanish Archives,* p. 95.

63. For Maverick's story, see C. L. Douglas, *Cattle Kings of Texas,* p. 69; Green Peyton, *San Antonio,* pp. 25–28; Ralph A. Wooster, "Wealthy Texans, 1870," *Southwestern Historical Quarterly* 74, no. 1 (July 1970): 24–35; Maury Maverick, *A Maverick American,* p. 77.

64. See Wynema M. Lusk, "A Calendar of the Stephen Powers and James B. Wells Papers: 1875–1882" (M.A. thesis), pp. 2, 5, 9, 28–30, 145, 149, 159, 235, 248.

65. Quoted in ibid., p. iv.

66. Anders, "James B. Wells," p. 7; Jerry Don Thompson, *Vaqueros in Blue and Gray,* p. 100; also Weeks, "Texas-Mexican," p. 612.

67. Lea, *King Ranch,* I:52.

68. For a discussion of the role of Texas Mexican merchants in the Civil War trade, see Graf, "Economic History," pp. 558–559; J. D. Thompson, *Vaqueros,* p. 100; Jean Fish, "History of San Ygnacio, Texas" (typescript).

69. J. D. Thompson, *Vaqueros,* pp. 5, 7, 16.

70. Daniell, *Types of Successful Men,* pp. 324–330, 335–337.

71. See biographies of Don Blas María Uribe and Don Proceso Martínez in Fish, "History of San Ygnacio."

72. Goldfinch, *Juan N. Cortina,* p. 40; see Graf, "Economic History," pp. 273–332.

3. Cattle, Land, and Markets

1. Graf, "Economic History," p. 255.
2. David Dary, *Cowboy Culture*; Lea, *King Ranch*, 1:114–115; Richard J. Morrisey, "The Establishment and Northward Expansion of Cattle Ranching in New Spain" (Ph.D. diss.), pp. 226–232.
3. Lea, *King Ranch*, 1:114–115.
4. McNeely, "Mexican American Land Issues," pp. 36–37; also P. S. Taylor, *American-Mexican Frontier*, pp. 184–188; Fehrenbach, *Lone Star*, p. 510.
5. Arthur Rubel, *Across the Tracks*, p. 36.
6. *The World* (Corpus Christi), May 23, 1878, cited in Goldfinch, *Juan N. Cortina*, pp. 33–34; Paul Taylor interview with Catarino Lerma of Harlingen, Taylor Collection, no. 137–726; Américo Paredes, *With His Pistol in His Hand*, p. 31; Roberto M. Villarreal, "The Mexican-American Vaqueros of the Kenedy Ranch: A Social History" (M.A. thesis), pp. 18–19; P. S. Taylor, *American-Mexican Frontier*, pp. 179–190.
7. *Brownsville Sentinel*, April 20, 1869, cited in Graf, "Economic History," p. 481; Susan G. Miller, *Sixty Years in the Nueces Valley, 1870–1930*, pp. 86–87; Mexico, *Report of the Committee of Investigation Sent in 1873 by the Mexican Government to the Frontier of Texas*; U.S. Congress, House, *Texas Frontier Troubles*; Dale Floyd Beecher, "Incentive to Violence: Political Exploitations of Lawlessness on the United States–Mexican Border, 1866–1886" (Ph.D. diss.), esp. pp. 51–62.
8. Villarreal, "Mexican-American Vaqueros," pp. 17–18; see also Graf, "Economic History," pp. 642–644.
9. For example, see Webb, *Great Plains*, pp. 205–269; U.S. Congress, House, *Range and Ranch Cattle Traffic in the Western States and Territories*; Dobie, *Vaquero of the Brush Country*, pp. 20–29, 90–106; T. J. Cauley, "Early Business Methods in the Texas Cattle Industry," *Journal of Economic and Business History* 4, no. 3 (May 1932): 461–486; Frederic L. Paxson, "The Evolution of the Live Stock Industry," in *Readings in the Economic History of American Agriculture*, ed. Louis B. Schmidt and Earle D. Ross, pp. 381–389.
10. See Mexico, *Report*, pp. 92–101; Graf, "Economic History," p. 484; C. L. Douglas, *Cattle Kings*, p. 89; Lea, *King Ranch*, 1:122, 233; also Stirling W. Bass, "The History of Kleberg County" (M.A. thesis), pp. 75–76.
11. Webb, *Great Plains*, p. 217; also Cauley, "Early Business Methods," p. 472.
12. Webb, *Great Plains*, p. 223; Florence Fenley, *Oldtimers*, p. 137.
13. Philip Durham and Everett L. Jones, *The Negro Cowboys*, p. 45; Hunter, *Trail Drivers*, 1:404–411, 453, 470–474, 2:549–551, 574, 595; Villarreal, "Mexican-American Vaqueros," pp. 20–21.
14. Cauley, "Early Business Methods," pp. 474–475; also Dellos U. Buckner, "Study of the Lower Rio Grande Valley as a Culture Area" (M.A. thesis), p. 23.
15. Villarreal, "Mexican-American Vaqueros," pp. 20–21; Miller, *Sixty Years in the Nueces Valley*, pp. 86–87; Hunter, *Trail Drivers*, 1:367, 513.

16. U.S. Congress, House, *Depredations on the Frontiers of Texas*, p. 5.

17. Ibid., p. 4.

18. Cited in *Corpus Christi: A History and Guide*, pp. 146–147.

19. D. W. Hinkle of San Antonio in U.S. Congress, House, *Range and Ranch Cattle Traffic*, p. 111; William Curry Holden, *Alkali Trails, or Social and Economic Movements of the Texas Frontier, 1846–1900*, pp. 48–50.

20. *Corpus Christi*, p. 153; also see pp. 133, 146–147.

21. Taylor Collection, no. 28-621.

22. Fenley, *Oldtimers*, pp. 31, 140, 163, 246; "San Diego Has Romantic Past, Bright Future," *San Antonio Express*, October 18, 1954; *The Spanish Texans*, p. 31; Taylor Collection, no. 29-622.

23. Don H. Biggers, *From Cattle Range to Cotton Patch*, pp. 79–80.

24. Hunter, *Trail Drivers*, 2:888–889; J. Frank Dobie, *The Longhorns*, pp. 333–339; also De León, *They Call Them Greasers*, p. 31.

25. January 2, 1879, letter in Thomas Hughes, ed., *G.T.T. Gone to Texas*, pp. 35–38.

26. Rubel, *Across the Tracks*, p. 38; Zamora O'Shea, *El Mesquite*, introduction.

27. Biggers, *From Cattle Range*, pp. 94–101; also U.S. Congress, House, *Range and Ranch Cattle Traffic*; Webb, *Great Plains*, pp. 227–244.

28. Lusk, "A Calender," p. 159.

29. See King Ranch land purchase record in S. W. Bass, "Kleberg County," p. 239.

30. Dobie, *Longhorns*, p. 338.

31. Ibid., pp. 333–339.

32. Hunter, *Trail Drivers*, 2:888.

33. Ibid.

34. Ibid., 2:886–889; also Evan M. Anders, *Boss Rule in South Texas*, p. 45; Gene M. Gressley, *Bankers and Cattlemen*, pp. 201–202; also see Laurence M. Lasater, *The Lasater Philosophy of Cattle Ranching*.

35. Gressley, *Bankers and Cattlemen*, p. 194; Villarreal, "Mexican-American Vaqueros," pp. 3, 10; see Lea, *King Ranch*, 1:354–357, 2:533; William G. Kerr, *Scottish Capital on the American Credit Frontier*, pp. 128–129, 136–137, 183.

36. Lea, *King Ranch*, 1:145, 332, 366, 2:629; C. L. Douglas, *Cattle Kings*, pp. 92–93.

37. For King's secondary projects, see Graf, "Economic History," pp. 464–465; Lea, *King Ranch*, 1:335–336, 2:496–498; Bass, "Kleberg County," p. 248.

38. C. L. Douglas, *Cattle Kings*, pp. 92–93; Lea, *King Ranch*, 2:497–498, 629.

39. See Bass, "Kleberg County," p. 239.

40. Lea, *King Ranch*, 1:329–333.

41. Bass, "Kleberg County," p. 245.

42. Taylor Collection, no. 139-728.

43. *Corpus Christi*, p. 133; "San Diego Has Romantic Past, Bright Fu-

ture"; Elmer H. Johnson, *The Basis of the Commercial and Industrial Development of Texas*, pp. 85–87, 100–102.

44. Arnoldo De León, *A Social History of Mexican Americans in Nineteenth Century Duval County*; also Anders, *Boss Rule*, pp. 171, 192–193.

45. W. H. Chatfield, *The Twin Cities of the Border and the Country of the Lower Rio Valley*.

46. Rubel, *Across the Tracks*, p. 36.

47. De León, *The Tejano Community*, p. 63.

4. Race, Labor, and the Frontier

1. Terry G. Jordan, *Trails to Texas*, pp. 145–146; also J. Evetts Haley, *Charles Goodnight*, pp. 187–191.

2. Enrique Semo, *Historia del capitalismo en México: Los orígenes, 1521–1763*.

3. Domenech, *Missionary Adventures*, pp. 254–256; Robert Edgar Riegel, *The Story of the Western Railroads*, pp. 7–8; Graf, "Economic History," pp. 439–445.

4. Friedrich Katz, "Labor Conditions on Haciendas in Porfirian Mexico: Some Trends and Tendencies," *Hispanic American Historical Review* 54, no. 1 (February 1974): 32–33; Wilkinson, *Laredo*, p. 238; Mexico, *Report*; Cazneau, *Eagle Pass*, pp. 59, 80–81, 94–96; J. D. Thompson, *Vaqueros*.

5. Graf, "Economic History," pp. 449–450.

6. Knox, *Economic Status*, p. 3; also see M. García, *Desert Immigrants*, p. 72.

7. Wallace Thompson, *The Mexican Mind*, pp. 200–201; Lea, *King Ranch*, 2:501.

8. Wilkinson, *Laredo*, p. 237.

9. Richard Harding Davis, *The West from a Car-Window*, p. 132; J. L. Allhands, *Gringo Builders*, p. 21; Villarreal, "Mexican-American Vaqueros," p. 10; Lea, *King Ranch*, 1:148.

10. González, "Social Life," pp. 49–50.

11. Taylor Collection, no. 139-728.

12. P. S. Taylor, *American-Mexican Frontier*, pp. 116–117; González, "Social Life," pp. 49–50; James H. Cook and Howard R. Driggs, *Longhorn Cowboy*, p. 74.

13. Domenech, *Missionary Adventures*, pp. 308–309.

14. Lea, *King Ranch*, 1:347–351.

15. *The World* (Corpus Christi), May 23, 1878, cited in Goldfinch, *Juan N. Cortina*, pp. 33–34; also Lea, *King Ranch*, 1:350–351, 355.

16. Bass, "Kleberg County," p. 101; also Lea, *King Ranch*, 1:123–124, 146; Allhands, *Gringo Builders*, p. 21.

17. Villarreal, "Mexican-American Vaqueros," p. 11.

18. Sister Margaret Rose Warburton, "A History of the Thomas O'Connor Ranch, 1834–1939" (M.A. thesis), pp. 25, 34, 95, 111–116.

19. Lea, *King Ranch*, 2:483.

20. J. Frank Dobie, "Ranch Mexicans," *Survey*, May 1, 1931, p. 170, and "The Mexican Vaquero of the Texas Border," *Political and Social Science Quarterly* 3, no. 1 (June 1927): 23.

21. William Hale, *Twenty-Four Years a Cowboy and Ranchman in Southern Texas and Old Mexico*, p. 137; John H. Culley, *Cattle, Horses, and Men*, p. 103; Dobie, *Vaquero of the Brush Country*, pp. 54–56; González, "Social Life," p. 11; Hunter, *Trail Drivers*, 2:938–939.

22. Mary J. Jaques, *Texan Ranch Life*, pp. 361–362.

23. Ibid., p. 61.

24. Hunter, *Trail Drivers*, 1:187.

25. Lea, *King Ranch*, 2:497, 638–639; also *100 Years*.

26. Dobie, "Ranch Mexicans," p. 168; see also John Hendrix, *If I Can Do It Horseback*, p. 32.

27. Dobie, *Vaquero of the Brush Country*, p. 69; Graf, "Economic History," p. 625.

28. Miller, *Sixty Years*, pp. 15, 175.

29. Daniell, *Types of Successful Men*, p. 340.

30. Zamora O'Shea, *El Mesquite*, p. 59.

31. F. J. Turner, *The Frontier in American History*; Webb, *Great Plains*, pp. 206–207.

32. See Haley, *Charles Goodnight*, p. 16; for critiques, see George Rogers Taylor, ed., *The Turner Thesis*, esp. the contribution by Stanley Elkins and Eric McKitrick; for a Brazilian critique of the theme of *"la democracia gaucha,"* see Fernando Henrique Cardoso, *Capitalismo e escravidão no Brasil meridional*, pp. 119–132.

33. See Jordan, *Trails to Texas*, pp. 145–146; Webb, *Great Plains*, p. 230; Joe B. Frantz and Julian Ernest Choate, Jr., *The American Cowboy*, pp. 101, 105–106.

34. Biggers, *From Cattle Range*, esp. pp. 94–101; also Kerr, *Scottish Capital*, p. 189.

35. Gressley, *Bankers and Cattlemen*, p. 77; C. L. Douglas, *Cattle Kings*, pp. 52, 132–141, 218–225, 243, 252–253; Haley, *Charles Goodnight*, pp. 344–350.

36. Hunter, *Trail Drivers*, 1:439; Frantz and Choate, *American Cowboy*, pp. 105–106.

37. John Upton Terrell, *Land Grab*, pp. 225–226; Ruth Allen, *Chapters in the History of Organized Labor in Texas*, pp. 35–38; William Bennett Bizzell, *Rural Texas*, pp. 126–127, 132–133; for incidents, see Dobie, *Longhorns*, pp. 51–60, or *Vaquero of the Brush Country*, pp. 9–10.

38. See Webb, *Texas Rangers*, pp. 429–437; Fenley, *Oldtimers*, p. 246; Chester Allwyn Barr, "Texas Politics, 1876–1906" (Ph.D. diss.), pp. 92–94, 130–131.

39. Cited by Allen, *History of Organized Labor*, p. 37.

40. Ibid., pp. 35–39; also Haley, *Charles Goodnight*, pp. 363–380; Gressley, *Bankers and Cattlemen*, pp. 123–125; William Curry Holden, *The Spur Ranch*, p. 102; Arthur Stinchecombe, "Agricultural Enterprise and Rural

Class Relations," *American Journal of Sociology* 67 (September 1961): 174–175.

41. For a sociological discussion, see H. Hoetink, *Slavery and Race Relations in the Americas,* pp. 76–83.

42. Jonathan Speed, "The Hunt for Garza," *Harper's Weekly,* January 30, 1892, p. 103; Davis, *West from a Car-Window,* pp. 41–45.

43. Jaques, *Texan Ranch Life,* p. 38; Seymour V. Connor, *Texas: A History,* p. 269; Don M. Coerver and Linda B. Hall, *Texas and the Mexican Revolution,* p. 14; García, *Desert Immigrants,* pp. 14–17; Jordan, "1887 Census," pp. 271–278; Riegel, *Story of the Western Railroads,* pp. 1–16.

44. Holden, *Spur Ranch,* p. 90; Webb, *Great Plains,* p. 240; in U.S. Congress, House, *Range and Ranch Cattle Traffic,* p. 101.

45. B. Youngblood and A. B. Cox, *An Economic Study of a Typical Ranching Area on the Edwards Plateau of Texas,* pp. 308–312; A. Ray Stephens, *The Taft Ranch,* p. 130; Hunter, *Trail Drivers,* 2:853–854; Dobie, "Mexican Vaquero," p. 20.

46. Andrew García, *Tough Trip through Paradise, 1878–1879,* p. 6; J. Thompson, "A 19th Century History," p. 112; Dobie, "Mexican Vaquero," p. 23.

47. Allhands, *Gringo Builders,* p. 257; also Zamora O'Shea, *El Mesquite,* p. 65.

48. E. Johnson, *Commercial and Industrial Development,* p. 131.

49. Taylor Collection, no. 137-726.

50. Quoted in *Corpus Christi,* p. 153.

51. Davis, *West from a Car-Window,* p. 27.

52. Knox, *Economic Status,* p. 4; Johnny M. McCain, "Mexican Labor in San Antonio, Texas, 1900–1940" (typescript), p. 7; Jaques, *Texan Ranch Life,* p. 38.

53. Knox, *Economic Status,* p. 7.

54. Hunter, *Trail Drivers,* 1:461.

55. Chester Allwyn Barr, "Occupational and Geographic Mobility in San Antonio, 1870–1900," *Social Science Quarterly* 51, no. 2 (September 1970): 401.

56. Holden, *Alkali Trails,* p. 64; M. T. García, *Desert Immigrants,* pp. 16, 156–157; Connor, *Texas,* p. 269; Coerver and Hall, *Texas and the Mexican Revolution,* p. 14.

57. E. R. Tarver, *Laredo.*

58. Hinojosa, *Borderlands Town,* pp. 118–119.

59. Walter B. Stevens, *Through Texas,* p. 72; R. O. García, *Dolores,* pp. 36–39; Hinojosa, *Borderlands Town,* pp. 68–71; also Wilkinson, *Laredo;* Da Camara, *Laredo.*

60. Gressley, *Bankers and Cattlemen,* pp. 30–35; J. Thompson, "A 19th Century History," p. 79.

61. Graf, "Economic History," pp. 407–408; also see J. Thompson, "A 19th Century History," pp. 37, 60–61; Lea, *King Ranch,* 1:54, 248–252.

62. J. Thompson, "A 19th Century History," pp. 106–110; Graf, "Eco-

nomic History," p. 7; Edwin J. Foscue, "Agricultural History of the Lower Rio Grande Valley Region," *Agricultural History* 8, no. 3 (July 1934): 135; Lea, *King Ranch*, 1:252.

63. Chatfield, *Twin Cities*, p. 3.

64. González, "Social Life," p. 82; J. Thompson, "A 19th Century History," p. 70.

PART TWO. **Reconstruction, 1900–1920**

The Ranger song is the recollection of Ben Kinchlow, guide for the Texas Rangers (in Fenley, *Oldtimers*, p. 134). Jacinto Treviño, who in 1910 avenged his brother's murder at the hands of an Anglo and survived an ambush by a posse, was the hero of several *corridos* sung in the Lower Valley during the 1910s (see Américo Paredes and Raymund Paredes, eds., *Mexican American Authors*, pp. 5–7).

1. Webb, *Great Plains*, pp. 206, 242–243.

2. Otey Scruggs, "A History of Mexican Agricultural Labor in the United States, 1942–1954" (Ph.D. diss.), pp. 5–21.

3. Charles M. Harger, "The New Era of the Ranch Lands," *American Review of Reviews* 44 (November 1911): 580; also Scruggs, "Mexican Agricultural Labor," pp. 5–21; Gressley, *Bankers and Cattlemen*, pp. 269–272.

4. Jordan, "1887 Census," pp. 271–278.

5. Eric R. Wolf, *Peasant Wars of the Twentieth Century*, pp. 276–302.

6. Jovita González, "America Invades the Border Towns," *Southwest Review* 15, no. 4 (Summer 1930): 473.

5. The Coming of the Commercial Farmers

1. Ben F. Wilson, Jr., "The Economic History of Kleberg County" (M.A. thesis), pp. 16, 35; James W. Tiller, Jr., *The Texas Winter Garden*, p. 26; Lea, *King Ranch*, 2:534–535, 538.

2. Lea, *King Ranch*, 2:541–543.

3. Buckner, "Lower Rio Grande Valley," pp. 74–75; C. L. Cline, "The Rio Grande Valley," *Southwest Review* 25, no. 3 (April 1940): 239–255.

4. Cited in Buckner, "Lower Rio Grande Valley," p. 75.

5. Tiller, *Texas Winter Garden*, pp. 26, 28.

6. Hunter, *Trail Drivers of Texas*, 2:517–518, 611–617, 620; Duval County File, Daughters of the Republic of Texas Library, San Antonio, Texas; Harger, "New Era," pp. 580–590.

7. Tiller, *Texas Winter Garden*, p. 28; also Bass, "Kleberg County," pp. 182–185.

8. Dan E. Kilgore, "Corpus Christi: A Quarter Century of Development, 1900–1925," *Southwestern Historical Quarterly* 75, no. 4 (April 1972): 436.

9. Frank Putnam, "Texas in Transition," *Collier's Magazine*, January 2, 1910, p. 15.

10. Harger, "New Era," p. 580.

11. Kilgore, "Corpus Christi," p. 437.

12. Unless otherwise specified, all figures are based on U.S. Census information.

13. In 1900, "deep South Texas" consisted of Webb, Duval, Nueces, Cameron, Hidalgo, Starr, and Zapata counties.

14. González, "Social Life," pp. 48–52.

15. Ibid., pp. 22–23.

16. Bass, "Kleberg County," pp. 169–171; Lea, *King Ranch*, 2:545–551.

17. Weeks, "Texas-Mexican," pp. 616, 619.

18. Lea, *King Ranch*, 2:559; Anders, *Boss Rule*, pp. 142–146.

19. Taylor Collection, no. 2-25; P. S. Taylor, *American-Mexican Frontier*, p. 302; see also Edwin J. Foscue, "Land Utilization in the Lower Rio Grande Valley of Texas," *Economic Geography* 8, no. 1 (January 1932): 1–5.

20. Cited by Emilio Zamora, "The Chicano Origin and Development of the San Diego Revolt" (paper), p. 4; my translation.

21. The essays of Jovita González, generally completed in 1929–1930, describe in detail the effects of farm colonization on the Texas Mexican ranch society in the Lower Valley; see esp. "America Invades the Border Towns"; "Latin Americans," in *Our Racial and National Minorities*, ed. Francis J. Brown and Joseph S. Roucek, pp. 500–501; and "Social Life."

22. González, "America Invades," pp. 469–470.

23. González, "Social Life," p. 104.

24. P. S. Taylor, *American-Mexican Frontier*, p. 93; Dobie, "Mexican Vaquero," p. 17.

25. P. S. Taylor, *American-Mexican Frontier*, p. 93.

26. González, "America Invades," p. 474.

27. Ibid., pp. 472–473.

28. González, "Latin Americans," p. 502; P. S. Taylor, *American-Mexican Frontier*, p. 251; Paul S. Taylor, "Mexican Labor in the United States: Dimmit County, Winter Garden District, South Texas," *University of California Publications in Economics* 6, no. 5 (1930): 432; Rubel, *Across the Tracks*, pp. 38, 45.

29. Weeks, "Texas-Mexican," p. 618; Emilio C. Forto, "Actual Situation on the River Rio Grande," *Pan American Labor Press*, September 11, 1918. Forto, former county sheriff and county judge of Cameron, was a respected old-timer, a Spaniard, and a resident of Brownsville for fifty years. For a brief biography, see *Spanish Texans*, p. 30.

30. Frank C. Pierce, *A Brief History of the Lower Rio Grande Valley*, p. 112.

31. Ibid., pp. 77–115, 155–182; Forto, "Actual Situation"; Paredes and Paredes, *Mexican American Authors*, pp. 5–7.

32. Anders, *Boss Rule*, pp. 227–228.

33. *Primer Congreso Mexicanista, Verificado en Laredo, Texas, Los Días 14 al 22 de Septiembre de 1911*; and José Limón, "El Primer Congreso Mexicanista de 1911: A Precursor to Contemporary Chicanismo," *Aztlan* 5, nos. 1–2 (1974): 85–106.

34. Charles C. Cumberland, "Border Raids in the Lower Rio Grande Val-

ley—1915," *Southwestern Historical Quarterly* 57, no. 3 (January 1954): 301–324; William M. Hager, "The Plan of San Diego: Unrest on the Texas Border in 1915," *Arizona and the West* 5 (Winter 1963): 327–336; Webb, *Texas Rangers*, esp. pp. 471–516; Juan Gómez-Quiñones, "Plan de San Diego Reviewed," *Aztlan* 1, no. 1 (Spring 1970): 124–132; James A. Sandos, "The Plan of San Diego: War and Diplomacy on the Texas Border, 1915–1916," *Arizona and the West* 14 (Spring 1972): 5–24; Zamora, "Chicano Origin"; Charles H. Harris and Louis R. Sadler, "The Plan of San Diego and the Mexican–United States Crisis of 1916: A Reexamination," *Hispanic American Historical Review* 58, no. 3 (August 1978): 381–408; Rodolfo Rocha, "The Influence of the Mexican Revolution on the Mexico-Texas Border, 1910–1916" (Ph.D. diss.); Anders, *Boss Rule*, pp. 215–239; Coerver and Hall, *Texas and the Mexican Revolution*.

35. The Plan de San Diego also called for the death of all Anglo males over sixteen years of age, the return of tribal lands to Apaches and other Indian peoples, and the creation of a black nation between the new republic and what would remain of the United States. A translated version of the Plan de San Diego may be found in U.S. Congress, Senate, *Investigation of Mexican Affairs*, 1:1205–1207. Also see Pierce, *Brief History*, p. 100; Cumberland, "Border Raids," pp. 285, 289–291; Sandos, "Plan of San Diego," pp. 9–10.

36. "Lone Star State and Four Others to Be 'Freed' in 1915 Plot," *San Antonio Express and News*, May 9, 1954; Cumberland, "Border Raids," p. 308.

37. Sandos, "Plan of San Diego," pp. 10, 24; Harris and Sadler, "Plan of San Diego."

38. According to Forto, vigilante acts in the summer of 1915, especially the killing of Manríquez brothers from Mercedes, the "lynching of a boy named Muñoz" at San Benito, and the "indiscriminate killing" of Desiderio Flores and two sons at Arroyo Colorado, were the actual causes of the "alleged bandit raids" ("Actual Situation"). Also see Pierce, *Brief History*, pp. 89–91; Rocha, "Influence of the Mexican Revolution," pp. 279–283; Zamora, "Chicano Origin," p. 10.

39. U.S. Congress, Senate, *Investigation of Mexican Affairs*, 1:1263.

40. Ibid., 1:1262–1263.

41. Webb, *Texas Rangers*, p. 483; also see Lea, *King Ranch*, 2:581–591.

42. Pierce, *Brief History*, p. 114.

43. *San Antonio Express*, September 11, 1915; also Cumberland, "Border Raids," p. 300.

44. *San Antonio Express*, September 15, 1915.

45. Cumberland, "Border Raids," p. 301; Webb, *Texas Rangers*, p. 478.

46. *San Antonio Express*, September 9, 1915; Pierce, *Brief History*, p. 100; Anders, *Boss Rule*, pp. 226–227; Rocha, "Influence of the Mexican Revolution," pp. 316–318; Coerver and Hall, *Texas and the Mexican Revolution*, pp. 106–107.

47. Coerver and Hall, *Texas and the Mexican Revolution*, pp. 95–97.

48. Pierce, *Brief History*, p. 100; Coerver and Hall, *Texas and the Mexican Revolution*, pp. 99–100.

49. Sandos, "Plan of San Diego," pp. 21–22; Coerver and Hall, *Texas and*

the Mexican Revolution, p. 101; Rocha, "Influence of the Mexican Revolution," pp. 323–324; Zamora, "Chicano Origin," p. 13; Stephens, *Taft Ranch,* pp. 198–199.

50. Pierce, *Brief History,* p. 102; Webb, *Texas Rangers,* p. 478.

51. Cumberland, "Border Raids," p. 308; Hager, "Plan of San Diego," p. 336; Sandos, "Plan of San Diego," pp. 22–24.

52. Cumberland, "Border Raids," p. 294; Gómez-Quiñones, "Plan de San Diego," pp. 124–132; Zamora, "Chicano Origin"; Sandos, "Plan of San Diego," p. 15.

53. González, "Social Life," p. 24.

54. Rocha, "Influence of the Mexican Revolution," p. 265, n. 7.

55. Harris and Sadler, "Plan of San Diego," p. 391.

56. Maude T. Gilliland, *Rincon,* p. 47.

57. Forto, "Actual Situation"; Lea, *King Ranch,* 2:583–587, 638; Cumberland, "Border Raids," p. 306; Anders, *Boss Rule,* pp. 227–228, 231.

58. Forto, "Actual Situation."

59. Pierce, *Brief History,* pp. 114–115.

60. Emma Tenayuca and Homer Brooks, "The Mexican Question in the Southwest," *Political Affairs* (March 1939): 259.

61. Webb, *Texas Rangers,* p. 478.

62. Ibid., pp. 513–516; for a different interpretation, see Anders, *Boss Rule,* pp. 252–254, 266–273.

6. The Politics of Reconstruction

1. In Starr County, the colors were reversed, and red stood for Democrat, blue for Republican (González, "Social Life," pp. 83–93); Weeks, "Texas-Mexican," pp. 608–615; Anders, *Boss Rule,* pp. 3–25, 43; Edgar Shelton, Jr., *Political Conditions among Texas Mexicans along the Rio Grande.*

2. Texas Legislature, Senate, *Glasscock v. Parr, Supplement to the Senate Journal,* p. 1039.

3. Ibid., p. 848.

4. González, "Social Life," pp. 93–94.

5. U.S. Congress, House, *Report of the Select Committee to Investigate Campaign Expenditures,* p. 48.

6. Kilgore, "Corpus Christi," p. 439.

7. P. S. Taylor, "Mexican Labor," p. 400; William Leonard, "Where Both Bullets and Ballots Are Dangerous," *Survey,* October 28, 1916, pp. 86–87 (for Leonard's background, see U.S. Congress, Senate, *Report of the Commission on Industrial Relations,* 9:9044).

8. Weeks, "Texas-Mexican," p. 618; emphasis in original.

9. S. B. McAlister, "The County and Its Functions," in *The Government of Texas,* ed. S. D. Myres, Jr., p. 133; Stuart A. MacCorkle and Dick Smith, *Texas Government,* p. 394.

10. Shelton, *Political Conditions,* p. 48.

11. See Lea, *King Ranch,* 2:557–559; Neva V. Pollard, "The History of Jim

Wells County" (M.A. thesis), p. 17; Bass, "Kleberg County," p. 17; Lloyd N. Dyer, "The History of Brooks County" (M.A. thesis), p. 14.

12. De León, *Social History*, p. 3; Anders, *Boss Rule*, pp. 171–193.

13. *Remarkable Conditions in Duval County; Protest by Citizens against Proposed Division*, pp. 22, 37–40; also see Anders, *Boss Rule*, pp. 171–193.

14. *Remarkable Conditions*, pp. 3–8.

15. Ibid., pp. 9–10.

16. Ibid., pp. 32–33.

17. Ibid., pp. 37–38; see also Anders, *Boss Rule*, p. 192.

18. *Brownsville Herald*, September 25, 1928, as cited by González, "Social Life," pp. 90–91; Anders, *Boss Rule*, pp. 58–63.

19. *Glasscock* v. *Parr*, p. 1037; Anders, *Boss Rule*, pp. 63, 181.

20. Shelton, *Political Conditions*, p. 84.

21. Hunter, *Trail Drivers*, 2:888–889; González, "Social Life," pp. 22–23; also Ozzie Simmons, *Anglo-Americans and Mexican-Americans in South Texas*, p. 273.

22. The information is drawn from the 1930 Population and Agricultural Census and from the *Texas Almanac & State Industrial Guide*, 1925.

23. Pollard, "Jim Wells County," p. 99.

24. B. F. Wilson, "Kleberg County," pp. 4, 245.

25. See Lea, *King Ranch*, 2:558–559, 784, n. 91.

26. B. F. Wilson, "Kleberg County," pp. 87–88; Bass, "Kleberg County," pp. 232–233.

27. Barr, "Texas Politics," pp. 244–248, 285; *Glasscock* v. *Parr*, p. 1040.

28. The White Man's Primary Association was formally organized in Dimmit on February 12, 1914. A straw vote by mail of the 428 Anglo voters of the county recorded 262 voters in favor and 12 against it. The 133 Mexican voters were naturally not polled (see Taylor Collection, no. 164-335); P. S. Taylor, "Mexican Labor," pp. 302–304, 403.

29. Cited in Taylor, "Mexican Labor," p. 400.

30. Ibid., p. 399.

31. Ibid.

32. Ibid., p. 402.

33. Ibid.

34. Ibid., p. 404.

35. *Glasscock* v. *Parr*, p. 1037; Anders, *Boss Rule*, pp. 257–265.

36. *Glasscock* v. *Parr*, pp. 859, 1034, 1050.

37. Ibid., p. 1047.

38. Ibid., pp. 1034–1035.

39. This special congressional committee traveled to South Texas to investigate charges of election fraud in two congressional races, both involving Mexican voters and representing the struggle between old-line politician and newcomer challenger. In its probe of the Democratic primary election for the 15th Congressional District, the Select Committee found that incumbent John Nance Garner's victory was "clean as a hound's tooth." For the Democratic primary in the 14th Congressional District (Bexar County),

however, the committee found that the charges of fraud had reasonable grounds and recommended that the attorney general take appropriate action (see U.S. Congress, House, *Report of the Select Committee to Investigate Campaign Expenditures*).

40. Ibid., pp. 13–14.

41. Ibid., p. 25.

42. Shelton, *Political Conditions*, p. 78.

43. Election returns from South Texas counties were supplied by the *Texas Almanac & State Industrial Guide*, 1914, pp. 45–49; *Texas Almanac*, 1925, pp. 83–89. Also see *Almanac*, 1936, pp. 477–480, for the 1934 elections.

44. P. S. Taylor, *American-Mexican Frontier*, p. 93.

45. Taylor Collection, no. 164-335.

46. Douglas Foley et al., *From Peones to Politicos*; Lea, *King Ranch*, 2:546–547, 559.

47. Foley et al., *Peones to Politicos*, pp. 13–14.

48. See Pollard, "Jim Wells County," p. 102; Hunter, *Trail Drivers*, 2:834–836; Lea, *King Ranch*, 2:554, 556.

49. See *100 Years*, p. 5.

50. Webb, *Great Plains*, pp. 243–244.

51. Nonetheless, González added, folklore still abounded in "secluded communities untouched as yet by civilization," where people lived in "pastoral simplicity," retained their attachment to the land, disliked innovation, distrusted Americans, and refused to speak English ("Tales and Songs of the Texas Mexicans," *Publications of the Texas Folklore Society* 8 [1930]: 86).

52. Reading an obituary list was always the first order of business at the Trail Drivers' conventions. The association continued after 1920 by admitting sons of trail drivers as members. See Hunter, *Trail Drivers*, 2:665; for other farewells, see 1:9, 371, and 2:583, 595.

53. Ibid., 1:402.

54. Harger, "New Era," pp. 586–587.

PART THREE. **Segregation, 1920–1940**

Max S. Handman, "Economic Reasons for the Coming of the Mexican Immigrant," *American Journal of Sociology* 35, no. 4 (January 1930): 609–610; Américo Paredes Manzano, "The Mexico-Texan," in *First Year Book of the Latin American Population of Texas*, ed. J. Montiel Olvera, p. 20.

1. E. H. Johnson, *Commercial and Industrial Development*, pp. 21–23.

2. For characterizations of South Texas as a "caste-like" society, see Leo Grebler, Joan Moore, and Ralph Guzmán, *The Mexican American People*, pp. 322–325; Howard G. Raymond, "Acculturation and Social Mobility among Latin-Americans in Resaca City" (M.A. thesis); Simmons, *Anglo-Americans*.

3. Jorge Rangel and Carlos Alcala, "De Jure Segregation of Chicanos in Texas Schools," *Harvard Civil Rights–Civil Liberties Law Review* 7

(March 1972): 313–314; Foley et al., *Peones to Politicos*, p. 34; Wilson Little, *Spanish-Speaking Children in Texas*, pp. 59–60.

4. Moore, *Social Origins*, pp. 433–435.

5. Robert N. McLean, "Rubbing Shoulders on the Border," *Survey*, May 1, 1924, p. 204.

7. The Structure of the New Order

1. P. S. Taylor, "Mexican Labor," p. 396.

2. Bass, "Kleberg County," pp. 179–180, 198–204; Taylor Collection, no. 164-335; Buckner, "Lower Rio Grande Valley," p. 72.

3. Taylor Collection, no. 2-25; see also Cline, "Rio Grande Valley," p. 241.

4. Texas State Employment Service, Farm Placement Service, *Origins and Problems of Texas Migratory Farm Labor*, p. 11.

5. Ibid., p. 2. For a brief discussion, see Victor Nelson-Cisneros, "La clase trabajadora en Tejas, 1920–1940," *Aztlan* 6, no. 2 (Summer 1975): 239; Knox, *Economic Status*, pp. 2–21; P. S. Taylor, "Mexican Labor," p. 307; Dan Eggleston, "Birthplaces of Chicanos with Children Born in Kingsville, Texas, 1917–1920, 1928–1930," typescript; Tom Vasey and Josiah C. Folsom, "Survey of Agricultural Labor Conditions in Karnes County, Texas," in U.S. Farm Security Administration, *Survey of Agricultural Labor Conditions*, p. 5.

6. Knox, *Economic Status*, pp. 11, 20–22.

7. Letter to Mrs. J. L. Runnels, October 30, 1929, quoted in Bass, "Kleberg County," pp. 187–188.

8. Doris B. Brown, "Story of Freer, Texas: The Historical Background for the Educational System" (M.A. thesis), p. 5.

9. Buckner, "Lower Rio Grande Valley," p. 82; Peyton, *San Antonio*, p. 1.

10. Eggleston, "Birthplaces"; Taylor Collection, no. 20-530.

11. P. S. Taylor, "Mexican Labor," p. 397; Alonso Perales, *En defensa de mi raza*, pp. 34, 38–39; Taylor Collection, nos. 164-335, 166-337; Bass, "Kleberg County," p. 179; Rubel, *Across the Tracks*, p. 3; Stephens, *Taft Ranch*, pp. 117, 178, 183, 185.

12. Taylor, "Mexican Labor," p. 407; Foley et al., *Peones to Politicos*, pp. 42–44.

13. Taylor Collection, no. 101-69; see also Rangel and Alcala, "De Jure Segregation," pp. 313–314; Foley et al., *Peones to Politicos*, p. 34; Little, *Spanish-Speaking Children*, pp. 59–60.

14. Herschel T. Manuel, *The Education of Mexican and Spanish-Speaking Children in Texas*, pp. 70–75, 160–165.

15. Tiller, Jr., *Texas Winter Garden*, p. 26; E. H. Johnson, *Commercial and Industrial Development*, p. 44; also Cline, "Rio Grande Valley"; Lea, *King Ranch*, 2:549–550.

16. P. S. Taylor, *American-Mexican Frontier*, pp. 88–89; Taylor Collection, no. 188-777; Cline, "Rio Grande Valley," pp. 241–242.

17. W. A. Johnson, *Cotton and Its Production*, pp. 33–34; Fred A. Shan-

non, *The Farmer's Last Frontier*, pp. 88–95; Taylor Collection, no. 102-692.

18. Taylor Collection, no. 101-641; P. S. Taylor, *American-Mexican Frontier*, pp. 98–125.

19. Carey McWilliams, *Ill Fares the Land*, pp. 231–232.

20. For calculations, see David Montejano, "Race, Labor Repression, and Capitalist Agriculture: Notes from South Texas, 1920–1930" (Working Paper no. 102), p. 19; also P. S. Taylor, *American-Mexican Frontier*, pp. 98–115; W. A. Johnson, *Cotton*, pp. 33, 56–59.

21. P. S. Taylor, *American-Mexican Frontier*, pp. 188–190, and "Mexican Labor," p. 437.

22. Taylor Collection, nos. 31-36, 98-669, 101-641; P. S. Taylor, *American-Mexican Frontier*, pp. 188–190; Foley et al., *Peones to Politicos*, p. 16; Ruth Allen, *The Labor of Women in the Production of Cotton*, pp. 209–210.

23. U.S. Federal Works Agency, Work Projects Administration, *Mexican Migratory Workers of South Texas*, by Sheldon C. Menefee, pp. 3, 15; Vasey and Folsom, "Karnes County," pp. 2–3; Texas State Employment Service, *Migratory Farm Labor*, pp. 5, 70; P. S. Taylor, *American-Mexican Frontier*, pp. 92, 103, and "Mexican Labor," pp. 302–303, 325.

24. Unless otherwise specified, all statistical information is derived from the U.S. Agricultural Census of 1930.

25. P. S. Taylor, *American-Mexican Frontier*, pp. 88–89, and "Mexican Labor," p. 319.

26. P. S. Taylor, "Mexican Labor," p. 414.

27. P. S. Taylor, *American-Mexican Frontier*, p. 200, and "Mexican Labor," pp. 366, 434.

28. Vasey and Folsom, "Karnes County," p. 6; Allen, *Labor of Women*, p. 248.

29. P. S. Taylor, "Mexican Labor," p. 443.

30. Foley et al., *Peones to Politicos*, p. 13.

31. P. S. Taylor, *American-Mexican Frontier*, p. 299.

32. Foley et al., *Peones to Politicos*, p. 14.

33. Cited in ibid.

34. P. S. Taylor, *American-Mexican Frontier*, p. 299.

35. U.S. Federal Works Agency, WPA, *Mexican Migratory Workers*, pp. 13–14; also McWilliams, *Ill Fares the Land*, p. 241.

36. W. A. Johnson, *Cotton*, esp. pp. 33–47, 56–59, 73; P. S. Taylor, *American-Mexican Frontier*, pp. 98–115; U.S. Congress, Senate, *Report of the Commission on Industrial Relations*, 9:8960–8961, 9044–9056.

37. See *Report of the Commission on Industrial Relations*, 9:9001–9003; 10:9202, 9205; also P. S. Taylor, *American-Mexican Frontier*, pp. 325–329.

8. The Mexican Problem

1. For a concise view of the "Mexican problem" literature, see Emory S. Bogardus, *The Mexican Immigrant*; also see Carey McWilliams, *North from Mexico*, pp. 206–226.

2. U.S. Department of Labor, *Mexican Labor in the United States*, by Victor S. Clark, p. 507.

3. See Grebler et al., *Mexican American People*, pp. 64–65.

4. James L. Slayden, "Some Observations on Mexican Immigration," *Annals of the American Academy of Political and Social Science* 93, no. 182 (January 1921): 124–126.

5. C. M. Goethe, "Other Aspects of the Problem," *Current History* 28, no. 2 (August 1928): 767–768.

6. Duncan Aikman, "Statistical Terrorism," *Southwest Review* 13, no. 1 (October 1927): 116–118.

7. Robert N. McLean, *That Mexican As He Really Is, North and South of the Rio Grande*, p. 163.

8. Leonard, "Bullets and Ballots," pp. 86–87.

9. Handman, "Economic Reasons," pp. 609–610.

10. Allen, *History of Organized Labor*, p. 14, and *Labor of Women*, pp. 238–239.

11. Charles H. Hufford, *The Social and Economic Effects of Mexican Migration into Texas*; Robert H. Montgomery, "Keglar Hill," *Survey*, May 1, 1931, pp. 171–195.

12. P. S. Taylor, *American-Mexican Frontier*, pp. 282–283; Hufford, *Social and Economic Effects*, pp. 37–50.

13. P. S. Taylor, *American-Mexican Frontier*, pp. 282, 288–289, and "Mexican Labor," p. 338.

14. P. S. Taylor, "Mexican Labor," p. 339.

15. Taylor Collection, no. 153-742.

16. Hufford, *Social and Economic Effects*, p. 39; P. S. Taylor, *American-Mexican Frontier*, pp. 282–283.

17. P. S. Taylor, *American-Mexican Frontier*, p. 126.

18. Ibid., p. 300.

19. Taylor Collection, no. 160-160; also P. S. Taylor, "Mexican Labor," p. 343.

20. P. S. Taylor, *American-Mexican Frontier*, p. 291.

21. Taylor Collection, no. 124-127.

22. Abraham Hoffman, *Unwanted Mexican Americans in the Great Depression*, p. 26.

23. U.S. Congress, House, debate to suspend immigration, December 10, 11, 1920, *Congressional Record*, 60:173, 227.

24. Taylor Collection, no. 85-90.

25. Ibid., nos. 188-177, 57-647.

26. P. S. Taylor, "Mexican Labor," p. 457.

27. Ibid., pp. 343–344, 443–444.

28. U.S. Congress, House, Representative Hayden of Arizona speaking against the Box Bill, December 9, 1920, *Congressional Record*, 60:145.

29. P. S. Taylor, *American-Mexican Frontier*, p. 283.

30. Ibid., pp. 302–303.

31. Ibid., p. 299.

32. Montgomery, "Keglar Hill," p. 171.

33. Hufford, *Social and Economic Effects*, p. 40.

34. Nelson-Cisneros, "La clase trabajadora," p. 258; also see Joseph Raybeck, *A History of American Labor*, pp. 290–312; Allen, *History of Organized Labor*, pp. 129–131; U.S. Department of Labor, *Mexican Labor*, pp. 416, 494–495.

35. Allen, *History of Organized Labor*, p. 228; see *The Nation*, July 12, 1922, p. 53, and *La Prensa* (San Antonio), febrero 27, 1921.

36. Emilio Zamora has documented these various practices for selected factories in Austin, San Antonio, Waco, and Fort Worth ("Mexican Labor Activity in South Texas, 1900–1920" [Ph.D. diss.]); also see Ray F. Marshall, "Some Reflections on Labor History," *Southwestern Historical Quarterly* 75, no. 2 (October 1971): 137–157; also W. Wilson, *Forced Labor in the United States*, p. 117.

37. Allen, *History of Organized Labor*, pp. 100, 228, 233.

38. P. S. Taylor, "Mexican Labor," p. 341.

39. Ibid., p. 445; P. S. Taylor, *American-Mexican Frontier*, p. 301; Hufford, *Social and Economic Reasons*, p. 40.

40. Rangel and Alcala, "De Jure Segregation," pp. 313–314; Taylor Collection, no. 16-526.

41. P. S. Taylor, *American-Mexican Frontier*, pp. 191–214, and "Mexican Labor," pp. 437, 439.

42. Rangel and Alcala, "De Jure Segregation."

43. P. S. Taylor, "Mexican Labor," p. 437.

44. P. S. Taylor, *American-Mexican Frontier*, p. 194.

45. Manuel, *Education*, p. 77.

46. P. S. Taylor, "Mexican Labor," p. 441.

47. Ibid., p. 378.

48. Ibid., p. 333.

49. Ibid., p. 451.

50. Ibid., pp. 441–442.

51. Taylor Collection, no. 34-627.

52. P. S. Taylor, "Mexican Labor," p. 343.

53. William J. Knox, "Teaching Foreigners," address.

54. See P. S. Taylor, *American-Mexican Frontier*, pp. 213–214, and "Mexican Labor," pp. 431, 439, 441.

9. The Web of Labor Controls

1. For example, see Mexico, Secretaría de Relaciones Exteriores, *La Protección de Mexicanos en los Estados Unidos*, by Ernesto Hidalgo.

2. Carl N. Degler, *The Age of the Economic Revolution, 1876–1900*, p. 78.

3. Scruggs, "Mexican Agricultural Labor," p. 123; P. S. Taylor, *American-Mexican Frontier*, p. 119, and "Mexican Labor," p. 352.

4. P. S. Taylor, "Mexican Labor," p. 335.

5. P. S. Taylor, *American-Mexican Frontier*, pp. 105–113, and "Mexican Labor," pp. 325–335.

6. Manuel Gamio, *Mexican Immigration to the United States*, p. 39.

7. P. S. Taylor, "Mexican Labor," p. 340.

8. P. S. Taylor, *American-Mexican Frontier*, pp. 300, 308.

9. Taylor Collection, no. 188-177.

10. P. S. Taylor, *American-Mexican Frontier*, p. 200, and "Mexican Labor," p. 366; also McWilliams, *Ill Fares the Land*, p. 253.

11. Taylor Collection, nos. 78-699, 101-691; P. S. Taylor, *American-Mexican Frontier*, pp. 309–311.

12. Taylor Collection, no. 196-785.

13. Ibid., no. 123-294.

14. Ibid., nos. 59-64, 32-37; P. S. Taylor, "Mexican Labor," p. 350.

15. Taylor Collection, no. 83-673.

16. Mexico, *Protección*, p. 45.

17. Taylor Collection, no. 96-686.

18. Texas State Employment Service, *Migratory Farm Labor*.

19. U.S. Congress, Senate, *Report of the Commission on Industrial Relations*, 10:9200–9205.

20. Manuel Gamio, *The Mexican Immigrant, His Life Story*, pp. 150–151.

21. U.S. Congress, Senate, *Report of the Commission on Industrial Relations*, 9:9001–9003; P. S. Taylor, *American-Mexican Frontier*, pp. 168–169; also Taylor Collection, no. 102-692.

22. P. S. Taylor, *American-Mexican Frontier*, pp. 149–156, 325–329.

23. Taylor Collection, no. 169-758.

24. U.S. Congress, Senate, *Report of the Commission on Industrial Relations*, 10:9201–9202.

25. P. S. Taylor, "Mexican Labor," p. 331; McWilliams, *Ill Fares the Land*, pp. 231–232.

26. Mancur Olson, *The Logic of Collective Action*, pp. 148–149; Jeffrey M. Paige, *Agrarian Revolution*, pp. 36–37.

27. P. S. Taylor, *American-Mexican Frontier*, pp. 142, 281, and "Mexican Labor," pp. 331–333.

28. Taylor Collection, no. 206-377.

29. Paul S. Taylor, "Research Note," *Journal of the American Statistical Association* 25, no. 170 (June 1930): 206–207.

30. Taylor Collection, no. 203-376.

31. P. S. Taylor, "Mexican Labor," p. 333.

32. Taylor Collection, no. 51-641; P. S. Taylor, *American-Mexican Frontier*, pp. 281, 301, and "Mexican Labor," p. 331.

33. Texas State Employment Service, *Migratory Farm Labor*, p. 30; U.S. Federal Works Agency, WPA, *Mexican Migratory Workers*, p. 31.

34. Taylor Collection, no. 51-641.

35. P. S. Taylor, "Mexican Labor," p. 332.

36. Taylor Collection, no. 51-641; W. Wilson, *Forced Labor*, pp. 114–117.

37. McWilliams, *Ill Fares the Land*, p. 257.

38. P. S. Taylor, *American-Mexican Frontier*, pp. 281, 301.

39. P. S. Taylor, "Mexican Labor," p. 311; Taylor Collection, no. 51-641.

40. Texas State Employment Service, *Law Supplement to Texas State Employment Reports on Migratory Labor*, suppl. B, pp. 9–10.

41. McWilliams, *Ill Fares the Land*, pp. 232–233.

42. Texas State Employment Service, *Migratory Farm Labor*, pp. 30–32.

43. Texas State Employment Service, Annual Report, 1939, pp. 14, 67; Texas State Employment Service, *Migratory Farm Labor*, p. 50.

44. Texas State Employment Service, *Migratory Farm Labor*, pp. 23, 46, 56–57, 84–86; U.S. Federal Works Agency, *Mexican Migratory Workers*, p. 30.

45. P. S. Taylor, "Mexican Labor," pp. 332–333, 435–436.

46. Ibid., pp. 314–315, 332; McWilliams, *Ill Fares the Land*, p. 241.

47. U.S. Department of Agriculture, Bureau of Agricultural Economics, *United States Cotton Statistics, 1910–49 by States*, p. 28.

48. P. S. Taylor, "Mexican Labor," pp. 315, 330, 440; Taylor Collection, no. 19-529.

49. P. S. Taylor, "Mexican Labor," pp. 330, 335; Taylor Collection, no. 19-529.

50. McWilliams, *Ill Fares the Land*, p. 257.

51. P. S. Taylor, "Mexican Labor," p. 351.

52. P. S. Taylor, *American-Mexican Frontier*, p. 128.

53. "El Corrido de Texas" in *Chulas Fronteras* album, Arhoolie Records, El Cerrito, California.

54. McWilliams, *Ill Fares the Land*, p. 264.

10. The Culture of Segregation

1. Manuel, *Education*, p. 20.

2. P. S. Taylor, *American-Mexican Frontier*, p. 304.

3. P. S. Taylor, "Mexican Labor," p. 433.

4. Ibid., p. 436.

5. Taylor Collection, no. 20-192.

6. Ibid., no. 19-191.

7. P. S. Taylor, "Mexican Labor," p. 438.

8. Ibid., p. 443.

9. Ibid., pp. 432, 446, 449.

10. Peyton, *San Antonio*, p. 1.

11. Taylor Collection, no. 20-530; Taylor interview with Richard King III, ibid., no. 102-692.

12. Ibid., no. 20-530.

13. P. S. Taylor, "Mexican Labor," pp. 438–439.

14. Buckner, "Lower Rio Grande Valley," p. 82; Peyton, *San Antonio*, p. 1.

15. Annual Texas Independence Day celebrations before the Alamo, according to one Texas Mexican protest in 1926, deliberately omitted mention of its Spanish-surnamed defenders (see Perales, *En defensa de mi raza*, pp. 8–9, 24–28).

16. P. S. Taylor, *American-Mexican Frontier*, pp. 307–308.

17. Ibid., p. 313.

18. Olive Westbrooke Quinn, "The Transmission of Racial Attitudes among White Southerners," in *Race: Individual and Collective Behavior*, ed. Edgar T. Thompson and Everett C. Hughes, p. 452.

19. Paredes, *With His Pistol in His Hand*, p. 19.

20. Germ theories tapped a long tradition in English-speaking cultures about pollution rules concerning "dirt" (see Mary Douglas, *Purity and Danger*; Joel Kovel, *White Racism*).

21. Forto, "Actual Situation."

22. P. S. Taylor, *American-Mexican Frontier*, p. 310.

23. Taylor Collection, no. 66-656.

24. P. S. Taylor, "Mexican Worker," p. 391.

25. Ibid., p. 441; Manuel, *Education*, p. 76.

26. For a description of similar conditions in Central Texas, see Allen, *Labor of Women*, pp. 217–218; U.S. Federal Works Agency, WPA, *Mexican Migratory Workers*, pp. 41–43.

27. U.S. Federal Works Agency, WPA, *Mexican Migratory Workers*, pp. 41–43.

28. Kovel, *White Racism*, p. 82.

29. E. E. Davis, *A Report on Illiteracy in Texas* (Austin: University of Texas Publications, 1923), cited by Manuel, *Education*, p. 77.

30. Thirty years later, in the 1950s, farm settlers of the Lower Rio Grande Valley were still talking of "dirty Mexicans" to justify social segregation (see Simmons, *Anglo-Americans*, pp. 423–425).

31. P. S. Taylor, *American-Mexican Frontier*, pp. 218–219, and "Mexican Labor," p. 436.

32. P. S. Taylor, "Mexican Labor," p. 43.

33. P. S. Taylor, *American-Mexican Frontier*, p. 307.

34. *International Encyclopedia of the Social Sciences*, 1968 ed., "Pollution," by Mary Douglas.

35. Foley et al., *Peones to Politicos*, p. 15.

36. Manuel, *Education*, p. 71; P. S. Taylor, "Mexican Labor," p. 440.

37. P. S. Taylor, "Mexican Labor," p. 440.

38. Ibid., pp. 393, 438; P. S. Taylor, *American-Mexican Frontier*, pp. 221–222, 307; Taylor Collection, no. 190-779.

39. Also see P. S. Taylor, "Mexican Labor," p. 447.

40. Taylor Collection, no. 58-63.

41. Foley et al., *Peones to Politicos*, pp. 49–51; P. S. Taylor, "Mexican Labor," p. 393.

42. O. Douglas Weeks, "The League of United Latin-American Citizens: A Texas-Mexican Civic Organization," *Southwestern Political and Social Science Quarterly* 10, no. 3 (December 1929): 264; Taylor Collection, no. 192-781.

43. Manuel, *Education*, pp. 78–79.

44. "The Segregation of Mexican School Children at Del Rio," *LULAC News* (San Antonio), August 1931.

11. The Geography of Race and Class

1. P. S. Taylor, "Mexican Labor," p. 398; Weeks, "Texas-Mexican," p. 616.

2. Olson, *Collective Action*.

3. P. S. Taylor, "Mexican Labor," p. 351.

4. Taylor Collection, no. 16-526.

5. P. S. Taylor, *American-Mexican Frontier*, pp. 106–109, and "Mexican Labor," pp. 325–335.

6. Taylor Collection, no. 18-611; also P. S. Taylor, "Mexican Labor," p. 350, and *American-Mexican Frontier*, p. 132.

7. Raybeck, *American Labor*, pp. 290–312; Marshall, "Some Reflections," pp. 137–157; Ricardo Romo, "Responses to Mexican Immigration, 1910–1930," *Aztlan* 6 (Summer 1975): 173–194; also Zamora, "Mexican Labor Activity"; P. S. Taylor, *American-Mexican Frontier*, p. 314.

8. Foley et al., *Peones to Politicos*, p. 16.

9. Taylor Collection, no. 96-686.

10. Ibid., no. 99-686. For a case involving merchants and Anglo tenant farmers, see the testimony of Gov. James Ferguson, in U.S. Congress, Senate, *Report of the Commission on Industrial Relations*, 9:8956–8962.

11. Taylor Collection, no. 160-160; also P. S. Taylor, "Mexican Labor," p. 343.

12. Taylor Collection, no. 22-615.

13. Ibid.

14. Taylor, "Mexican Labor," p. 397.

15. Foley et al., *Peones to Politicos*, p. 16. Also see the hearings of the U.S. Congress, Senate, *Commission on Industrial Relations*, 9:8964–8966, for a description of common exploitative practices of merchants.

16. The consul added that this was one of the several devious means used by merchants and landlords to further "cheat the Mexicans" (Taylor Collection, no. 18-23); also see Foley et al., *Peones to Politicos*, pp. 15–16.

17. González, "America Invades," p. 471.

18. Taylor Collection, no. 31-36.

19. P. S. Taylor, *American-Mexican Frontier*, pp. 135–136; Taylor Collection, no. 96-686; U.S. Congress, Senate, *Commission on Industrial Relations*, 10:9217, 9223–9225.

20. P. S. Taylor, "Mexican Labor," pp. 437–441; Taylor Collection, no. 190-779; Perales, *En defensa de mi raza*; Rangel and Alcala, "De Jure Segregation," pp. 307–391.

21. Taylor Collection, no. 21-64; P. S. Taylor, "Mexican Labor," p. 375.

22. Taylor Collection, no. 146-735; and P. S. Taylor, *American-Mexican Frontier*, p. 228.

23. Taylor Collection, nos. 191-780, 194-783.

24. P. S. Taylor, *American-Mexican Frontier*, p. 251; González, "Latin Americans," p. 503.

25. P. S. Taylor, "Mexican Labor," p. 409.

26. Ibid., p. 436.

27. Taylor Collection, no. 66-656.

28. P. S. Taylor, *American-Mexican Frontier*, pp. 298–299.

29. See the closing argument of Mr. Pollard, lawyer for Glasscock (and the newcomer farmers), in *Glasscock* v. *Parr*, pp. 1040–1052.

30. The surveys and studies of the time showed this relationship clearly enough. In addition to the research of Taylor and Weeks, the most important "secondary" sources were two master's theses: González, "Social Life," and Shelton, *Political Conditions*.

31. P. S. Taylor, *American-Mexican Frontier*, p. 302.

32. Shelton, *Political Conditions*, pp. 105–106.

33. González, "Social Life," p. 78.

34. The 1930 Census classified as illiterate anyone ten years or older who could neither read nor write in any language. Figures for Mexicans were obtained following census instructions—that is, by adding the figure for "white" and black and subtracting the sum from the total population figures. All census information concerning Mexicans was extracted in this manner.

35. Dobie, "Ranch Mexicans," p. 168.

36. For a thorough discussion of this issue, see Taylor, *Turner Thesis*, esp. the contribution of Stanley Elkins and Erik McKitrick.

37. Dobie, "Ranch Mexicans," p. 169.

38. Women were excluded because they were almost exclusively agricultural laborers, a pattern that would sharpen the contrast between Mexican counties and Anglo counties even more. By considering only males, the changes in the family structure brought about by the agricultural economy are controlled.

39. See, for example, the county returns for the 1912, 1924, and 1934 gubernatorial and senatorial Democratic primaries as reported by the *Texas Almanac & State Industrial Guide*, 1914, pp. 45–49; 1925, pp. 83–89; 1936, pp. 477–480.

40. Shelton, *Political Conditions*, pp. 21–22.

41. Cited in P. S. Taylor, "Mexican Labor," p. 402.

42. Ibid., p. 434.

43. Taylor Collection, no. 19-612.

PART FOUR. **Integration, 1940–1986**

1. See Woodward, *Jim Crow*.

2. S. B. Greenberg, *Race and State*.

3. Meinig, *Imperial Texas*.

4. Rangel and Alcala, "De Jure Segregation," pp. 338–340; see Pauline Kibbe, *Latin Americans in Texas*, pp. 227, 229; Jack Greenberg, *Race Relations and American Law*.

5. Grebler et al., *Mexican American People*, pp. 3–11.

12. The Demise of "Jim Crow"

1. For a legal discussion, see Rangel and Alcala, "De Jure Segregation," pp. 307–391.

2. See Jack Bass and Walter DeVries, *The Transformation of Southern Politics.*

3. Kibbe, *Latin Americans,* pp. 208–209, 240.

4. Grebler et al., *Mexican American People,* pp. 322–325.

5. See Edwin Caldwell, "Highlights of Development of Manufacturing in Texas, 1900–1960," *Southwestern Historical Quarterly* 68, no. 4 (April 1965): 418; also Seth S. McKay, *Texas and the Fair Deal, 1945–1952,* pp. 1–2.

6. McCain, "Mexican Labor"; P. S. Taylor, *American-Mexican Frontier.*

7. See Kibbe, *Latin Americans;* also Alonso Perales, *Are We Good Neighbors?;* M. T. García, *Desert Immigrants;* Clark Knowlton, "Changing Patterns of Segregation and Discrimination Affecting the Mexican Americans of El Paso" and "Patterns of Accommodation of Mexican Americans in El Paso, Texas," in *Politics and Society in the Southwest,* ed. Z. Anthony Krusewski et al., pp. 131–154, 215–236.

8. Kibbe, *Latin Americans,* pp. 160, 162.

9. Texas Agricultural and Mechanical College, Department of Industrial Education, *An Occupational Survey of San Antonio, Texas* (1929), p. 22, as cited by McCain, "Mexican Labor," pp. 18–19; for a discussion of the "segmentation" of Mexicans as common laborers in industry, see Kibbe, *Latin Americans,* pp. 157–166.

10. Kibbe, *Latin Americans,* p. 245; McCain, "Mexican Labor," pp. 16–17; Nelson-Cisneros, "La clase trabajadora," pp. 239–265.

11. Kibbe, *Latin Americans,* p. 35; correspondence of the Texas Cotton Ginners' Association; also see Will Alexander, "Aliens in War Industries," *Annals of the American Academy of Political and Social Science* 223 (September 1942): 138–143.

12. The "Stilley Plan" was named after its author and chief advocate, Jay C. Stilley, executive secretary of the Texas Cotton Ginners' Association. According to the plan, members of the ginners' association in every town would monitor and mediate cases of discrimination (see correspondence to the Texas Cotton Ginners' Association).

13. Carlos E. Castañeda, statements, in Perales, *Good Neighbors?,* pp. 59–61, 95, 117; Kibbe, *Latin Americans,* pp. 163–164.

14. Castañeda in Perales, *Good Neighbors?,* pp. 59–61.

15. Ibid., pp. 60–61; Kibbe, *Latin Americans,* p. 161; McKay, *Texas and the Fair Deal,* p. 44; also letter from Sam Smith to Lt. Gov. John Lee Smith, June 4, 1945, cited by George Green, *The Establishment in Texas Politics,* pp. 256–257 n. 37.

16. See Green, *The Establishment,* pp. 80–81, 139–140; also Everett Ross Cluichy, Jr., "Equality of Opportunity for Latin-Americans in Texas" (Ph.D. diss.), pp. 45, 74–89, 180–184.

17. Kibbe, *Latin Americans,* pp. 222–223.

18. Tiller, *Texas Winter Garden*, p. 36.

19. Ibid., pp. 41, 79, 89.

20. Kemper Diehl, "Swift Changes Taking Place in Agribusiness," *San Antonio Express and News*, May 13, 1967.

21. Foley et al., *Peones to Politicos*, pp. 78–79; Fredolin J. Kaderli, "Changing Face of Texas Agriculture," *Texas Business Review* 35, no. 6 (June 1961): 8–11.

22. See Kibbe, *Latin Americans*, p. 179.

23. *Texas Business Review* 26, no. 6 (July 1952): 15; McKay, *Texas and the Fair Deal*, p. 6; Green, *The Establishment*, pp. 8–9.

24. Tiller, *Texas Winter Garden*, pp. 76–79, 89.

25. Bass and DeVries, *Southern Politics*, pp. 498–504; Foley et al., *Peones to Politicos*, pp. 83, 132.

26. Diehl, "Swift Changes"; Tiller, *Texas Winter Garden*, pp. 76–79, 89.

27. Green, *The Establishment*, pp. 16–20; Bass and DeVries, *Southern Politics*, p. 307.

28. Charles Murphy, "Texas Business and McCarthy," *Fortune* 49 (May 1954): 100–101.

29. See *Texas Almanac*, 1958–1959, pp. 455–456.

30. For county returns, see ibid.

31. See Stuart Long, "White Supremacy and the 'Filibusteros,'" *Reporter*, June 27, 1957, p. 15.

32. Green, *The Establishment*, pp. 190, 192, 199; also Robert Cuéllar, *A Social and Political History of the Mexican American Population of Texas, 1929–1963*, pp. 36–37.

33. Clifton McCleskey et al., *The Government and Politics of Texas*, esp. pp. 125–133.

34. *Texas Observer*, June 11, 1965, p. 8.

35. Ibid., pp. 7–14; Wilbourn E. Benton, *Texas*, esp. pp. 96–97; McCleskey et al., *Government and Politics*, pp. 125–133.

36. For the raw data, see *Texas Almanac*, 1958–1959, pp. 359–363; 1964–1965, pp. 534–539; 1966–1967, pp. 625–629; 1968–1969, pp. 624–627.

37. Benton, *Texas*, p. 97; McCleskey et al., *Government and Politics*, p. 132; *Texas Observer*, May 9, 1969, p. 9.

38. Knowlton, "Changing Patterns," p. 145; Foley et al., *Peones to Politicos*, pp. 136–137.

39. See Luther L. Sanders, "Nonpartisanism: Its Use as a Campaign Appeal in San Antonio, Texas, 1961–1971" (M.A. thesis), p. 51; Albert Peña, Jr., "A Marshall Plan for Mexican-Americans," *Texas Observer*, April 15, 1966, pp. 1, 4.

40. O'Lene Stone et al., "Life and Death of Mexican American Organizations," *San Antonio Light*, December 14, 1980; Carl Allsup, *The American G.I. Forum*.

41. In Perales, *Good Neighbors?*, p. 29.

42. For college attendance, see Herschel T. Manuel, *Spanish-Speaking Children of the Southwest*, pp. 57–62; for home ownership, see "Texas' Big-

gest Untapped Market: 1,000,000 Latin Americans," *Texas Business Review* 29, no. 12 (December 1955): 15–17; for the military industry, see *Texas Observer*, May 4, 1984.

43. "Texas' Biggest Untapped Market," pp. 15–17; Knowlton, "Patterns of Accommodation," pp. 215–216.

44. Sanders, "Nonpartisanism," p. 51; Knowlton, "Patterns of Accommodation," pp. 216–217.

45. *Texas Observer*, October 28, 1966, August 23, 1968; Knowlton, "Patterns of Accommodation," pp. 216, 218–219; also Rodolfo Alvarez, "The Psycho-Historical and Socioeconomic Development of the Chicano Community," *Social Science Quarterly* 53, no. 4 (March 1973): 520–542.

46. William Madsen, *Society and Health in the Lower Rio Grande*, p. 6; Meinig, *Imperial Texas*, p. 99.

47. Charles R. Chandler, "The Mexican American Protest Movement in Texas" (Ph.D. diss.), pp. 153–208; Cuéllar, *Social and Political History*, pp. 43–51.

48. John S. Shockley, *Chicano Revolt in a Texas Town*, pp. 24–41.

49. See *Texas Observer*, December 9, 1966, pp. 19–20; Cuéllar, *Social and Political History*, pp. 55–66.

50. Chandler, "Mexican American Protest Movement," pp. 231–252; see the following issues of *Texas Observer*: April 11, 1969; January 2, 1970; October 15, 1976.

51. Rangel and Alcala, "De Jure Segregation," p. 308; Grebler et al., *Mexican American People*, pp. 274–280.

52. *Texas Observer*, May 9, 1969.

53. Knowlton, "Patterns of Accommodation," p. 223.

13. A Time of Inclusion

1. See, for instance, the thematic issue in Rodolfo Alvarez, Frank Bean, Charles M. Bonjean, Rodolfo de la Garza, and Ricardo Romo, eds., *The Mexican Origin Experience in the United States*, special issue of *Social Science Quarterly* 65, no. 2 (June 1984).

2. *Texas Observer*, October 29, 1976, pp. 10–11; June 3, 1977, p. 15.

3. For county electoral returns, see Andrew Hernández, "A Study of Raza Unida's Strength in South and West Texas" (typescript).

4. Tom Curtis, "Raza Desunida," in *The Texas Monthly Political Reader*, pp. 40–44.

5. Joe Holley, "The Texas Farmworkers' Split," *Texas Observer*, April 17, 1981, pp. 4–8; Curtis, "Raza Desunida," pp. 40–44.

6. Cited by Curtis, "Raza Desunida," pp. 40–44; *Texas Observer*, May 15, 1981.

7. James W. Lamare, *Texas Politics*, pp. 79, 104–105.

8. Southwest Voter Registration Education Project, *Mexican American Voting in the 1982 Texas General Election*, p. 2; Robert R. Brischetto, "The Hispanic Electorates," in *The Hispanic Almanac*, pp. 139–152.

9. Acuña, *Occupied America; Texas Observer,* February 7, 1986, pp. 5–6.

10. Southwest Voter Registration Education Project, *An Inquiry into Voting Irregularities in Texas,* pp. 64–65; "Testimony of the Mexican American Legal Defense and Educational Fund on the Voting Rights Act before the Subcommittee on Civil and Constitutional Rights of the Judiciary Committee, U.S. House of Representatives," June 5, 1981, pp. 938–939.

11. Southwest Voter Registration Education Project, *Survey of Chicano Representation in 361 Texas Public School Boards, 1979–80,* pp. 4–8.

12. "Testimony of MALDEF," pp. 950–953; also see Rolando Rios, "Voting Rights Act: Its Effect in Texas" (typescript), p. 7.

13. See Frank C. Lemus, "National Roster of Spanish-Surnamed Elected Officials, 1973," *Aztlan* 5, nos. 1–2 (Spring–Fall 1974): 313–410; Southwest Voter Registration Education Project, "Roster of Elected Officials in Texas, 1984" (typescript).

14. See Rios, "Voting Rights Act."

15. City of San Antonio, "Listing of San Antonio City Commissioners and Council Members" (typescript).

16. Oscar Martínez, *The Chicanos in El Paso,* p. 35; Rios, "Voting Rights Act."

17. Southwest Voter Registration Education Project, "Roster."

18. See Lemus, "National Roster," pp. 313–410; Southwest Voter Registration Education Project, "Roster."

19. Conversation with Gilbert Padilla, August 8, 1984.

20. Southwest Voter Registration Education, *Inquiry,* pp. 86–118.

21. Information concerning Voting Rights Act lawsuits was based on listings provided by the Southwest Voter Registration Education Project and Mexican American Legal Defense and Educational Fund.

22. Conversation with William Velasquez, January 25, 1986.

23. Southwest Voter Registration Education, "Mexican American Voting," pp. 2–5.

24. See "The Military Presence in San Antonio," *Texas Observer,* May 4, 1984, pp. 9–11.

25. The seemingly large number of proprietors-managers-officials was due, as H. Manuel noted, to the numerous small storekeepers in Mexican American communities (*Education,* pp. 13–14).

26. Peter Skerry, "Neighborhood COPS: The Resurrection of Saul Alinsky," *New Republic,* February 6, 1984, pp. 21–23.

27. George N. Green, *The Establishment,* p. 6.

28. *100 Years,* p. 64.

29. Ibid., pp. 98–99; conversation with Jose Rivera, October 8, 1984.

30. *100 Years,* p. 99.

31. Villarreal, "Mexican-American Vaqueros," pp. 74–75.

32. Simmons, *Anglo-Americans,* pp. 3–4; Green, *The Establishment,* p. 6; "Hillitos Sift," *Austin American-Statesman,* September 28, 1975.

33. "Patrón System Part of Political Corruption," *Austin American-Statesman,* September 28, 1975; Green, *The Establishment,* p. 5.

34. "Hayes Case Won't Die," *Texas Observer*, September 3, 1976.

35. "Onion Revolt," *Texas Observer*, August 8, 1980; and "Labor Nouveau: Old Wine in Texas Bottles," ibid., December 20, 1985.

36. J. T. Canales, ed., *Bits of Texas History in the Melting Pot of America*, pp. 3–4.

37. Maury Maverick, "Remembering the 'Real' Alamo," *San Antonio Express-News*, December 29, 1985, p. 3-h; see Steven Kellman, "Remembering the Alamo," *Texas Observer*, January 14, 1983, pp. 15–16.

Appendix. On Interpreting Southwestern History

1. Fred D. Gealy, "What Shall We Do with Japan?," *Southwest Review* 28, no. 2 (Winter 1943): 105–124.

2. Ibid., p. 118; emphasis added.

3. Goldfinch, *Juan N. Cortina*, p. 31; Leonard Pitt, *The Decline of the Californios*, pp. 41–42.

4. For an excellent discussion of the congressional deliberations concerning the Treaty of Guadalupe Hidalgo, see P. A. Hernández, "The Other North Americans," pp. 262–269.

5. Lamar, *Far Southwest*; Clark S. Knowlton, "The Neglected Chapters in Mexican-American History," in *Mexican-Americans Tomorrow*, ed. Gus Tyler, pp. 26–27.

6. Webb, *Great Plains*, p. 90.

7. Lamar, *Far Southwest*, p. 27; Fehrenbach, *Lone Star*, p. 75; see also François Chevalier, *Land and Society in Colonial Mexico*, p. 313; Raúl A. Fernández, *The United States-Mexico Border*, pp. 1–12.

8. See Morrisey, "Cattle Ranching in New Spain," pp. 173–195; also Chevalier, *Land and Society*, pp. 112, 276, 309–314; Jaime E. Rodríguez-O, *Down from Colonialism*; also Graf, "Economic History," p. 425. On the nature of the *hacienda*, see Semo, *Historia del capitalismo en México*, p. 258.

9. Graf, "Economic History," p. 94.

10. See Paige, *Agrarian Revolution*, esp. pp. 1–71.

11. Pitt, *Decline of the Californios*, pp. 19, 123–124; Haley, *Charles Goodnight*, pp. 212–213.

12. Haley, *Charles Goodnight*, pp. 212–213; William Taylor and Elliott West, "Patrón Leadership at the Crossroads: Southern Colorado in the Late Nineteenth Century," in *The Chicano*, ed. Norris Hundley, pp. 79–80, 95.

13. Pitt, *Decline of the Californios*, pp. 262–267; Camarillo, *Chicanos in a Changing Society*; De León, *Tejano Community*; Ruth Tuck, *Not with the Fist*; Foley et al., *Peones to Politicos*, pp. 4–6.

14. S. B. Greenberg, *Race and State*, pp. 23–28, 385–410.

15. Paul Horgan, *Great River*, 2:793; Pitt, *Decline of the Californios*, p. 131.

16. Immanuel Wallerstein, *The Modern World-system*, pp. 8–9.

17. Weeks, "Texas-Mexican," p. 610.

18. Kai T. Erikson, "Sociology and the Historical Perspective," *American*

Sociologist 5 (November 1970): 331–338; Patrick Gardiner, "The Nature of Historical Explanation," in *Theories of History,* ed. Gardiner, pp. 62–63; Edward Carr, *What Is History?*; R. G. Collingwood, *The Idea of History.*

19. David S. Landes and Charles Tilley, eds., *History as Social Science;* Arthur L. Stinchcombe, *Theoretical Methods in Social History.*

20. Moore, *Social Origins,* pp. 437–452.

BIBLIOGRAPHY

Acuña, Rodolfo. *Occupied America: The Chicano's Struggle toward Liberation.* 2d ed. New York: Harper & Row, 1981.

Aikman, Duncan. "Statistical Terrorism." *Southwest Review* 13, no. 1 (October 1927): 116–118.

Alexander, Will. "Aliens in War Industries." *Annals of the American Academy of Political and Social Science* 223 (September 1942): 138–143.

Allen, Ruth. *Chapters in the History of Organized Labor in Texas.* Austin: University of Texas Publications, 1941.

———. *The Labor of Women in the Production of Cotton.* Austin: University of Texas Publications, 1931.

———. "Mexican Peon Women in Texas." *Sociology and Social Research* (November–December 1931): 131–142.

Allhands, J. L. *Gringo Builders.* Iowa City: private printing, 1931.

Allsup, Carl. *The American G.I. Forum: Origins and Evolution.* Mexican American Monographs, no. 6. Austin: University of Texas Press, 1982.

Alvarez, Rodolfo. "The Psycho-Historical and Socioeconomic Development of the Chicano Community." *Social Science Quarterly* 53, no. 4 (March 1973): 520–542.

———, Frank Bean, Charles M. Bonjean, Rodolfo de la Garza, and Ricardo Romo, eds. *The Mexican Origin Experience in the United States.* Special issue of *Social Science Quarterly* 65, no. 2 (June 1984).

Anders, Evan M. *Boss Rule in South Texas: The Progressive Era.* Austin: University of Texas Press, 1982.

———. "James B. Wells and the Brownsville Patronage Fight, 1912–1917." M.A. thesis, University of Texas at Austin, 1970.

Barr, Chester Allwyn. "Occupational and Geographic Mobility in San Antonio, 1870–1900." *Social Science Quarterly* 51, no. 2 (September 1970): 396–403.

———. "Texas Politics, 1876–1906." Ph.D. dissertation, University of Texas, 1966.

Barrera, Mario. *Race and Class in the Southwest: A Theory of Racial Inequality.* Notre Dame: University of Notre Dame Press, 1979.

Bass, Jack, and Walter DeVries. *The Transformation of Southern Politics: Social Change and Political Consequence since 1945.* New York: Basic Books, 1976.

Bass, Stirling W. "The History of Kleberg County." M.A. thesis, University of Texas, 1931.

Bean, Frank, and Benjamin Bradshaw. "Intermarriage between Persons of Spanish and Non-Spanish Surname: Changes from the Mid-Nineteenth to the Mid-Twentieth Century." *Social Science Quarterly* 51, no. 2 (September 1970): 389–395.

Beecher, Dale Floyd. "Incentive to Violence: Political Exploitations of Law-lessness on the United States–Mexican Border, 1866–1886." Ph.D. dissertation, University of Utah, 1982.

Benton, Wilbourn E. *Texas: Its Government and Politics.* 4th ed. Englewood Cliffs, N.J.: Prentice-Hall, 1977.

Biggers, Don H. *From Cattle Range to Cotton Patch.* Abilene: Abilene Printing, [circa 1905].

Bizzell, William Bennett. *Rural Texas.* New York: Macmillan, 1924.

Blumer, Hubert. "Industrialisation and Race Relations." In *Industrialisation and Race Relations*, ed. Guy Hunter, pp. 220–253. London: Oxford University Press, 1965.

Bogardus, Emory S. *The Mexican Immigrant: An Annotated Bibliography.* Los Angeles: Council on International Relations, June 1929.

Bollaert, William. *William Bollaert's Texas.* Edited by W. Eugene Hollon and Ruth Lapham Butler. Norman: University of Oklahoma Press, 1956.

Bowden, J. J. *Spanish and Mexican Land Grants in the Chihuahuan Acquisition.* El Paso: Texas Western Press, 1971.

Briggs, Vernon M., Jr., Walter Fogel, and Fred H. Schmidt. *The Chicano Worker.* Austin: University of Texas Press, 1977.

Brischetto, Robert R. "The Hispanic Electorates." In *The Hispanic Almanac*, pp. 139–152. Washington, D.C.: Hispanic Policy Development Project, 1984.

Brown, Doris B. "Story of Freer, Texas: The Historical Background for the Educational System." M.A. thesis, Texas Agricultural and Industrial College, 1940.

Buckner, Dellos U. "Study of the Lower Rio Grande Valley as a Culture Area." M.A. thesis, University of Texas, 1929.

Calcott, F. "The Mexican Peon in Texas." *Survey*, June 26, 1920, pp. 437–438.

Caldwell, Edwin. "Highlights of Development of Manufacturing in Texas, 1900–1960." *Southwestern Historical Quarterly* 68, no. 4 (April 1965): 405–431.

Camarillo, Albert. *Chicanos in a Changing Society: From Mexican Pueblos to American Barrios in Santa Barbara and Southern California, 1848–1930.* Cambridge: Harvard University Press, 1979.

Campbell, Ernest Q., ed. *Racial Tensions and National Identity.* Nashville: Vanderbilt University Press, 1972.

Canales, José T., ed. *Bits of Texas History in the Melting Pot of America.* San Antonio: Artes Graficas, 1950.

———. *Juan N. Cortina Presents His Motion for a New Trial.* San Antonio: Artes Graficas, 1951; reprint, New York: Arno Press, 1974.

Cardoso, Fernando Henrique. *Capitalismo e escravidão no Brasil meridional.* São Paulo: Difusão Européia do Livro, 1962.

Carr, Edward. *What Is History?* New York: Alfred A. Knopf, 1965.

Castañeda, Carlos E. "Statement before the Senate Committee on Labor and Education in the Hearings Held September 8, 1944, on Senate Bill 2048 to Prohibit Discrimination Because of Race, Creed, Color, National Origin, or Ancestry." In *Are We Good Neighbors?*, by Alonso Perales, pp. 93–98. San Antonio: Artes Graficas, 1948.

———. "Statement on Discrimination against Mexican-Americans in Employment Submitted to the President's Committee on Civil Rights, May 9, 1947." In *Are We Good Neighbors?*, by Alonso Perales, pp. 59–63. San Antonio: Artes Graficas, 1948.

Cauley, T. J. "Agricultural Land Tenure in Texas." *Southwestern Political and Social Science Quarterly* 11, no. 2 (September 1930): 135–147.

———. "Early Business Methods in the Texas Cattle Industry." *Journal of Economic and Business History* 4, no. 3 (May 1932): 461–486.

Cazneau, Mrs. William L. (Cora Montgomery). *Eagle Pass, or Life on the Border*. New York: Putnam, 1852.

Chabot, Frederic. *With the Makers of San Antonio*. San Antonio: private printing, 1937.

Chandler, Charles R. "The Mexican American Protest Movement in Texas." Ph.D. dissertation, Tulane University, 1968.

Chatfield, W. H. *The Twin Cities of the Border and the Country of the Lower Rio Valley*. New Orleans: E. P. Brandao, 1893; reprint, Brownsville: Harbert Davenport Memorial Fund, 1959.

Chevalier, François. *Land and Society in Colonial Mexico*. Berkeley: University of California Press, 1963.

City of San Antonio. "Listing of San Antonio City Commissioners and Council Members." Typescript, 1985.

Cline, C. L. "The Rio Grande Valley." *Southwest Review* 25, no. 3 (April 1940): 239–255.

Cluichy, Everett Ross, Jr. "Equality of Opportunity for Latin-Americans in Texas." Ph.D. dissertation, Columbia University, 1954.

Coerver, Don M., and Linda B. Hall. *Texas and the Mexican Revolution: A Study in State and National Border Policy, 1910–1920*. San Antonio: Trinity University Press, 1984.

Collingwood, R. G. *The Idea of History*. New York: Oxford University Press, 1956.

Connor, Seymour V. *Texas: A History*. New York: Thomas Y. Crowell, 1971.

Cook, James H., and Howard R. Driggs. *Longhorn Cowboy*. New York: G. P. Putnam's Sons, 1942.

Corpus Christi: A History and Guide. Corpus Christi: Corpus Christi Chamber of Commerce, 1942.

Cox, James. *The Cattle Industry of Texas and Adjacent Territories*. 2 vols. St. Louis: Woodward & Tiernan, 1895.

Crisp, James Ernest. "Anglo Texan Attitudes toward the Mexican, 1821–1845." Ph.D. dissertation, Yale University, 1976.

Crook, Garland Elaine. "San Antonio, Texas, 1846–1861." M.A. thesis, Rice University, 1964.

Cuéllar, Robert. *A Social and Political History of the Mexican American Population of Texas, 1929–1963*. San Francisco: R & E Research Associates, 1974.

Culley, John H. *Cattle, Horses, and Men.* Los Angeles: Ward Ritchie Press, 1940.

Cumberland, Charles C. "Border Raids in the Lower Rio Grande Valley—1915." *Southwestern Historical Quarterly* 57, no. 3 (January 1954): 301–324.

Curtis, Tom. "Raza Desunida." In *The Texas Monthly Reader*, pp. 40–44. Austin: Texas Monthly Press & Sterling Swift Press, 1978.

Da Camara, Kathleen. *Laredo on the Rio Grande.* San Antonio: Naylor, 1949.

Daniell, L. E. *Types of Successful Men in Texas.* Austin: Eugene Von Boeckmann, 1888.

Dary, David. *Cowboy Culture: A Saga of Five Centuries.* New York: Avon Books, 1981.

Davis, John L. *The Texas Rangers: Their First 150 Years.* San Antonio: University of Texas Institute of Texan Cultures, 1975.

Davis, Richard Harding. *The West from a Car-Window.* New York: Harper Bros., 1903.

Degler, Carl N. *The Age of the Economic Revolution, 1876–1900.* Chicago: Scott, Foresman & Co., 1967.

De León, Arnoldo. *In Re Ricardo Rodríguez: An Attempt at Chicano Disfranchisement in San Antonio, 1896–1897.* San Antonio: Caravel Press, 1979.

———. *A Social History of Mexican Americans in Nineteenth Century Duval County.* San Diego, Tex.: Duval County Commissioners, 1978.

———. *The Tejano Community, 1836–1900.* Albuquerque: University of New Mexico Press, 1982.

———. *They Called Them Greasers: Anglo Attitudes toward Mexicans in Texas, 1821–1900.* Austin: University of Texas Press, 1983.

Dobie, J. Frank. *The Longhorns.* Boston: Little, Brown & Co., 1941; reprint, Austin: University of Texas Press, 1980.

———. "The Mexican Vaquero of the Texas Border." *Political and Social Science Quarterly* 3, no. 1 (June 1927): 15–26.

———. "Ranch Mexicans." *Survey*, May 1, 1931, pp. 167–170.

———. *A Vaquero of the Brush Country.* Dallas: Southwest Press, 1929; reprint, Austin: University of Texas Press, 1981.

Domenech, Abbé Emanuel. *Missionary Adventures in Texas and Mexico: A Personal Narrative of Six Years' Sojourn in Those Regions.* Translated from the French. London: Longman, Brown, Green, Longmans, and Roberts, 1858.

Dougherty, Honorable E. *The Rio Grande Valley: A Lecture Delivered before the Lone Star Literary Association of Brownsville, Texas, May 29, 1867.* Brownsville: Ranchero Book and Job Printing Office, 1867; reprint, Brownsville: Runyon Bros., 1955.

Douglas, C. L. *Cattle Kings of Texas.* Dallas: Cecil Baugh, 1939.

Douglas, Mary. *Purity and Danger: An Analysis of Concepts of Pollution and Taboo.* New York: Praeger Publishers, 1966.

Dugan, Frank H. "The 1850 Affairs of the Brownsville Separatists." *Southwestern Historical Quarterly* 61, no. 2 (October 1957): 270–287.

Durham, Philip, and Everett L. Jones. *The Negro Cowboys.* New York: Dodd, Mead & Co., 1965.

Duval County File. The Daughters of the Republic of Texas Library. San Antonio, Texas.

Dyer, Lloyd N. "The History of Brooks County." M.A. thesis, Texas Agricultural and Industrial College, 1938.

Eggleston, Dan. "Birthplaces of Chicanos with Children Born in Kingsville, Texas, 1917–1920, 1928–1930." Typescript, 1966. Benson Latin American Collection, University of Texas at Austin.

Erikson, Kai T. "Sociology and the Historical Perspective." *American Sociologist* 5 (November 1970): 331–338.

Fehrenbach, T. R. *Lone Star: A History of Texas and the Texans.* New York: Macmillan, 1968.

Fenley, Florence. *Oldtimers: Their Own Stories, or Frontier Days in the Uvalde Section of South West Texas.* Uvalde: Hornby Press, 1939.

Fergusson, Harvey. *Rio Grande.* New York: Alfred A. Knopf, 1933.

Fernández, Raúl A. *The United States–Mexico Border.* Notre Dame: University of Notre Dame Press, 1977.

Fish, Jean. "History of San Ygnacio, Texas." Typescript, 1979. Daughters of the Republic of Texas Library, San Antonio, Texas.

Foley, Douglas E., Clarice Mota, Donald E. Post, and Ignacio Lozano. *From Peones to Politicos: Ethnic Relations in a South Texas Town, 1900–1977.* Mexican American Monographs, no. 3. Austin: University of Texas Press, 1977.

Forto, Emilio C. "Actual Situation on the River Rio Grande: Information Rendered to Colonel H. J. Slocum of the American Forces at Brownsville." *Pan American Labor Press,* September 11, 1918.

Foscue, Edwin J. "Agricultural History of the Lower Rio Grande Valley Region." *Agricultural History* 8, no. 3 (July 1934): 124–138.

———. "Land Utilization in the Lower Rio Grande Valley of Texas." *Economic Geography* 8, no. 1 (January 1932): 1–11.

Frantz, Joe B., and Julian Ernest Choate, Jr. *The American Cowboy: The Myth and the Reality.* Norman: University of Oklahoma Press, 1955.

Fredrickson, George M. *White Supremacy: A Comparative Study of American and South African History.* New York: Oxford University Press, 1981.

Fulmore, Z. T. *The History and Geography of Texas: As Told in County Names.* Austin: S. R. Fulmore, 1926.

Gamio, Manuel. *The Mexican Immigrant, His Life Story.* Chicago: University of Chicago Press, 1931.

———. *Mexican Immigration to the United States.* Chicago: University of Chicago Press, 1930; reprint, New York: Dover Publications, 1971.

García, Andrew. *Tough Trip through Paradise, 1878–1879.* Edited by Bennett H. Stein. Boston: Houghton Mifflin, 1967.

García, Mario T. *Desert Immigrants: The Mexicans of El Paso, 1880–1920.* New Haven: Yale University Press, 1981.

García, Rogelia O. *Dolores, Revilla, and Laredo.* Waco: Texian Press, 1970.

Gardiner, Patrick, ed. *Theories of History.* Glencoe, Ill.: Free Press, 1959.

Garrison, George Pierce. *Texas: A Contest of Civilizations.* Boston and New York: Houghton Mifflin, 1903.

Gealy, Fred D. "What Shall We Do with Japan?." *Southwest Review* 28, no. 2 (Winter 1943): 105–124.

Genovese, Eugene D. *The World the Slave Holders Made.* New York: Vintage Books, 1971.

Gillette, James B. *Six Years with the Texas Rangers, 1875 to 1881.* New Haven: Yale University Press, 1925.

Gilliland, Maude T. *Rincon: A Story of Life on a South Texas Ranch at the Turn of the Century.* Brownsville, Tex.: Springman Lithograph Co., 1964.

Goethe, C. M. "Other Aspects of the Problem." *Current History* 28, no. 2 (August 1928): 767–768.

Goldfinch, Charles W. *Juan N. Cortina, 1824–1892: A Re-Appraisal.* New York: Arno Press, 1974.

Gómez-Quiñones, Juan. "Plan de San Diego Reviewed." *Aztlan: Chicano Journal of the Social Sciences* 1, no. 1 (Spring 1970): 124–132.

González, Jovita. "America Invades the Border Towns." *Southwest Review* 15, no. 4 (Summer 1930): 469–477.

———. "Social Life in Cameron, Starr, and Zapata Counties." M.A. thesis, University of Texas, 1930.

———. "Tales and Songs of the Texas Mexicans." *Publications of the Texas Folklore Society* 8 (1930): 86–116.

González de Mireles, Jovita. "Latin Americans." In *Our Racial and National Minorities,* ed. Francis J. Brown and Joseph S. Roucek, pp. 497–509. New York: Prentice-Hall, 1939.

Goodwyn, Frank. *Life on the King Ranch.* New York: Thomas Y. Crowell, 1951.

Graf, LeRoy P. "The Economic History of the Lower Rio Grande Valley, 1820–1875." 2 vols. Ph.D. dissertation, Harvard University, 1942.

Grebler, Leo, Joan Moore, and Ralph Guzmán. *The Mexican American People.* New York: Free Press, 1970.

Green, George. *The Establishment in Texas Politics: The Primitive Years, 1938–1957.* Westport, Conn.: Greenwood Press, 1979.

Greenberg, Jack. *Race Relations and American Law.* New York: Columbia University Press, 1959.

Greenberg, Stanley B. *Race and State in Capitalist Development: Comparative Perspectives.* New Haven: Yale University Press, 1980.

Gressley, Gene M. *Bankers and Cattlemen.* Lincoln: University of Nebraska Press, 1971.

Gutiérrez, José Angel. "La Raza and Revolution: The Empirical Conditions of Revolution in Four South Texas Counties." M.A. Thesis, St. Mary's University, 1968.

Hager, William M. "The Plan of San Diego: Unrest on the Texas Border in 1915." *Arizona and the West* 5 (Winter 1963): 327–336.

Hale, William. *Twenty-Four Years a Cowboy and Ranchman in Southern Texas and Old Mexico.* Norman: University of Oklahoma Press, 1959.

Haley, J. Evetts. *Charles Goodnight: Cowman and Plainsman.* Norman: University of Oklahoma Press, 1936.

Hammett, A. B. J. *The Empresario: Don Martín de León.* Waco: Texian Press, 1973.

Handman, Max S. "Economic Reasons for the Coming of the Mexican Immigrant." *American Journal of Sociology* 35, no. 4 (January 1930): 601–611.

Harby, Lee C. "Texan Types and Contrasts." *Harper's Magazine* 81, no. 482 (July 1890): 229–246.

Harger, Charles M. "The New Era of the Ranch Lands." *American Review of Reviews* 44 (November 1911): 580–590.

Harris, Charles H., and Louis R. Sadler. "The Plan of San Diego and the Mexican–United States Crisis of 1916: A Reexamination." *Hispanic American Historical Review* 58, no. 3 (August 1978): 381–408.

Hawley, C. A. *Life along the Border: A Personal Narrative of Events and Experiences along the Mexican Border between 1905 and 1913.* Spokane: Shaw & Borden, 1955.

Hendrix, John. *If I Can Do It Horseback.* Austin: University of Texas Press, 1964.

Hernández, Andrew. "Mexican-American Voting Patterns in Bexar County, 1928–1941." Typescript, 1975. Southwest Voter Registration Education Project, San Antonio.

———. "A Study of Raza Unida's Strength in South and West Texas." Typescript, 1974. Southwest Voter Registration Education Project, San Antonio.

Hernández, Philip Anthony. "The Other North Americans: The American Image of Mexico and Mexicans, 1550–1850." Ph.D. dissertation, University of California, Berkeley, 1974.

Hinojosa, Gilberto M. *Borderlands Town in Transition: Laredo, 1755–1870.* College Station: Texas A&M University Press, 1983.

Hoetink, H. *Slavery and Race Relations in the Americas: Comparative Notes on Their Nature and Nexus.* New York: Harper & Row, 1973.

Hoffman, Abraham. "A Note on the Field Research Interviews of Paul S. Taylor for the Mexican Labor in the United States Monographs." *Pacific Historian* 20 (Summer 1976): 123–131.

———. *Unwanted Mexican Americans in the Great Depression.* Tucson: University of Arizona Press, 1974.

Holden, William Curry. *Alkali Trails, or Social and Economic Movements of the Texas Frontier, 1846–1900.* Dallas: Southwest Press, 1930.

———. *The Spur Ranch: A Study of the Inclosed Ranch Phase of the Cattle Industry in Texas.* Boston: Christopher Publishing House, [circa 1910].

Horgan, Paul. *Great River: The Rio Grande in North American History.* 2 vols. New York: Rinehart & Co., 1954.

Hufford, Charles H. *The Social and Economic Effects of Mexican Migration into Texas.* San Francisco: R & E Research Associates, 1971.

Hughes, Thomas, ed. *G.T.T. Gone to Texas: Letters from Our Boys.* London: Macmillan, 1884.

Hunter, Guy, ed. *Industrialisation and Race Relations.* London: Oxford University Press, 1965.

Hunter, Marvin J., comp. & ed. *The Trail Drivers of Texas.* 2 vols. Nashville: Cokesbury Press, 1925; reprint, New York: Argosy-Antiquarian Ltd., 1963; reprint, Austin: University of Texas Press, 1985.

Jaques, Mary J. *Texan Ranch Life.* London: Horace Cox, Windsor House, 1894.

Johnson, Elmer H. *The Basis of the Commercial and Industrial Development of Texas.* Bureau of Business Research Monographs, no. 9. Austin: University of Texas Publications, 1933.

Johnson, W. A. *Cotton and Its Production.* London: Macmillan, 1926.

Jordan, Terry G. "The 1887 Census of Texas' Hispanic Population." *Aztlan: International Journal of Chicano Studies Research* 12, no. 2 (Autumn 1981): 271–278.

———. "Population Origins in Texas, 1850." *Geographical Review* 59 (January 1962): 83–103.

———. *Trails to Texas: Southern Roots of Western Cattle Ranching.* Lincoln: University of Nebraska Press, 1981.

Kaderli, Fredolin J. "Changing Face of Texas Agriculture." *Texas Business Review* 35, no. 6 (June 1961): 8–11.

Katz, Friedrich. "Labor Conditions on Haciendas in Porfirian Mexico: Some Trends and Tendencies." *Hispanic American Historical Review* 54, no. 1 (February 1974): 1–47.

Kelley, Edna E. "The Mexicans Go Home." *Southwest Review* 17, no. 3 (Spring 1932): 303–311.

Kerr, William G. *Scottish Capital on the American Credit Frontier.* Austin: Texas State Historical Association, 1976.

Key, V. O. *Southern Politics in State and Nation.* New York: Vintage Books, 1949.

Kibbe, Pauline. *Latin Americans in Texas.* Albuquerque: University of New Mexico Press, 1946.

Kilgore, Dan E. "Corpus Christi: A Quarter Century of Development, 1900–1925." *Southwestern Historical Quarterly* 75, no. 4 (April 1972): 434–443.

The King Ranch, 100 Years of Ranching. Corpus Christi: Corpus Christi Caller-Times, 1953.

Knowlton, Clark S. "Changing Patterns of Segregation and Discrimination Affecting the Mexican Americans of El Paso." In *Politics and Society in the Southwest: Ethnicity and Chicano Pluralism,* ed. Z. Anthony Krusewski, Richard L. Hough, and Jacob Ornstein-Garcia, pp. 131–154. Boulder: Westview Press, 1982.

———. "The Neglected Chapters in Mexican-American History." In *Mexican-Americans Tomorrow: Educational and Economic Perspectives,* ed. Gus Tyler, pp. 19–59. Albuquerque: University of New Mexico Press, 1975.

———. "Patterns of Accommodation of Mexican Americans in El Paso, Texas." In *Politics and Society in the Southwest: Ethnicity and Chi-*

cano Pluralism, ed. Z. Anthony Krusewski, Richard L. Hough, and Jacob Ornstein-Garcia, pp. 215–236. Boulder: Westview Press, 1982.

Knox, William J. *The Economic Status of the Mexican Immigrant in San Antonio, Texas*. San Francisco: R & E Research Associates, 1971.

———. "Teaching Foreigners." Address delivered at a Teacher's Conference, Corpus Christi, Texas, 1915. Barker Texas History Center, University of Texas at Austin.

Kovel, Joel. *White Racism: A Psychohistory*. New York: Pantheon Books, 1970.

Krusewski, Z. Anthony, Richard L. Hough, and Jacob Ornstein-Garcia, eds. *Politics and Society in the Southwest: Ethnicity and Chicano Pluralism*. Boulder: Westview Press, 1982.

Lamar, Howard Roberts. *The Far Southwest, 1846–1912: A Territorial History*. New Haven: Yale University Press, 1966.

Lamare, James W. *Texas Politics: Economics, Power, and Policy*. 2d ed. St. Paul: West Publishing, 1985.

Landes, David S., and Charles Tilly, eds. *History as Social Science*. Englewood Cliffs, N.J.: Prentice-Hall, 1971.

Lasater, Laurence M. *The Lasater Philosophy of Cattle Ranching*. El Paso: Texas Western Press, 1972.

Lea, Tom. *The King Ranch*. 2 vols. Boston: Little, Brown & Co., 1957.

Lemus, Frank C. "National Roster of Spanish-Surnamed Elected Officials, 1973." *Aztlan: Chicano Journal of the Social Sciences* 5, nos. 1–2 (Spring–Fall 1974): 313–410.

Leonard, William. "Where Both Bullets and Ballots Are Dangerous." *Survey*, October 28, 1916, pp. 86–87.

Limón, José. "El Primer Congreso Mexicanista de 1911: A Precursor to Contemporary Chicanismo." *Aztlan: Chicano Journal of the Social Sciences*, 5, nos. 1–2 (1974): 85–106.

Little, Wilson. *Spanish-Speaking Children in Texas*. Austin: University of Texas Press, 1944.

Long, Stuart. "White Supremacy and the 'Filibusteros.'" *Reporter*, June 27, 1957, p. 15.

López Cámara, Francisco. *La estructura económica y social de México en la época de la reforma*. 2d ed. Mexico City: Siglo Veintiuno Editores, S.A., 1973.

Lott, Virgil N., and Mercurio Martínez. *The Kingdom of Zapata County*. San Antonio: Naylor, 1953.

Lusk, Wynema M. "A Calender of the Stephen Powers and James B. Wells Papers: 1875–1882." M.A. thesis, University of Texas, 1938.

McAlister, S. B. "The County and Its Functions." In *The Government of Texas: A Survey*, ed. S. D. Myres, Jr., pp. 130–137. Dallas: Southern Methodist University Press, 1934.

McCain, Johnny M. "Mexican Labor in San Antonio, Texas, 1900–1940." Typescript, n.d. Southwest Voter Registration Education Project, San Antonio.

McCleskey, Clifton, Allan Butcher, Daniel Farlow, J. Pat Stephens. *The Government and Politics of Texas.* 7th ed. Boston: Little, Brown & Co., 1982.

MacCorkle, Stuart A., and Dick Smith. *Texas Government.* New York: McGraw-Hill, 1949.

McKay, Seth S. *Texas and the Fair Deal, 1945–1952.* San Antonio: Naylor, 1954.

McLean, Robert N. "Rubbing Shoulders on the Border." *Survey,* May 1, 1924, pp. 184–185.

———. *That Mexican As He Really Is, North and South of the Rio Grande.* New York: Fleming H. Revell, 1928.

McNeely, John H. "Mexican American Land Issues in the United States." In *The Role of the Mexican American in the History of the Southwest.* Conference Proceedings of the Inter-American Institute, Pan American College, Edinburg, Texas, November 17–18, 1969.

McWilliams, Carey. *Ill Fares the Land: Migrants and Migratory Labor in the United States.* New York: Barnes & Noble Books, 1941; reprint, 1967.

———. *North from Mexico: The Spanish-Speaking People of the United States.* Philadelphia: J. B. Lippincott, 1949; reprint, New York: Greenwood Press, 1968.

Madsen, William. *Society and Health in the Lower Rio Grande.* Austin: Hogg Foundation for Mental Health, University of Texas, 1961.

Manuel, Herschel T. *The Education of Mexican and Spanish-Speaking Children in Texas.* Austin: Fund for Research in the Social Sciences, University of Texas, 1930.

———. "The Mexican Population of Texas." *Southwestern Social Science Quarterly* 15, no. 1 (June 1934): 29–51.

———. *Spanish-Speaking Children of the Southwest.* Austin: University of Texas Press, 1965.

Marshall, F. Ray. "Some Reflections on Labor History." *Southwestern Historical Quarterly* 75, no. 2 (October 1971): 137–157.

Martínez, Oscar J. *The Chicanos of El Paso: An Assessment of Progress.* Southwestern Studies Monograph, no. 59. El Paso: Texas Western Press, 1980.

———. "On the Size of the Chicano Population: New Estimates, 1850–1900." *Aztlan: International Journal of Chicano Studies Research* 6, no. 1 (Spring 1975): 43–68.

Maverick, Maury. *A Maverick American.* New York: Covici Friede Publishers, 1937.

Meinig, D. W. *Imperial Texas: An Interpretive Essay in Cultural Geography.* Austin: University of Texas Press, 1969.

Merk, Frederick. *Manifest Destiny and Mission in American History.* New York: Vintage Books, 1966.

———. *Slavery and Annexation of Texas.* New York: Alfred A. Knopf, 1972.

Mexico. *Report of the Committee of Investigation Sent in 1873 by the Mexican Government to the Frontier of Texas.* Translated from the official edition. New York: Baker and Godwin Printers, 1875.

————. Secretaría de Relaciones Exteriores. *La Protección de Mexicanos en los Estados Unidos.* By Ernesto Hidalgo. Mexico City, 1940.

Miller, Susan G. *Sixty Years in the Nueces Valley, 1870–1930.* San Antonio: Naylor, 1930.

Miller, Thomas Lloyd. *Bounty and Donation Land Grants of Texas, 1835–1888.* Austin: University of Texas Press, 1967.

————. *The Public Lands of Texas, 1519–1970.* Norman: University of Oklahoma Press, 1971.

Montejano, David. "Frustrated Apartheid: Race, Repression, and Capitalist Agriculture in South Texas, 1920–1930." In *The World System of Capitalism: Past and Present,* ed. by Walter Goldfrank, pp. 131–168. Beverly Hills: Sage Publications, 1979.

————. "Is Texas Bigger Than the World-System? A Critique from a Provincial Point of View." *Review* 4, no. 3 (Winter 1981): 597–628.

————. "A Journey through Mexican Texas, 1900–1930." Ph.D. dissertation, Yale University, 1982.

————. "Race, Labor Repression, and Capitalist Agriculture: Notes from South Texas, 1920–1930." Working Paper no. 102. Institute for the Study of Social Change, Berkeley, 1977.

Montgomery, Robert H. "Keglar Hill." *Survey,* May 1, 1931, pp. 171–195.

Montiel Olvera, J., ed. *First Year Book of the Latin American Population of Texas.* San Antonio: private printing, 1939.

Moore, Barrington, Jr. *Social Origins of Democracy and Dictatorship: Lord and Peasant in the Making of the Modern World.* Boston: Beacon Press, 1966.

Morrisey, Richard J. "The Establishment and Northward Expansion of Cattle Ranching in New Spain." Ph.D. dissertation, University of California, Berkeley, 1949.

Murphy, Charles. "Texas Business and McCarthy." *Fortune* 49 (May 1954): 100–101.

Myrdal, Gunnar. *An American Dilemma: The Negro Problem and Modern Democracy.* 2 vols. New York: Harper & Bros., 1944.

Myres, S. D., Jr., ed. *The Government of Texas.* Dallas: Southern Methodist University Press, 1934.

Nackman, Mark E. *A Nation within a Nation: The Rise of Texas Nationalism.* Port Washington, N.Y.: Kennikat Press, 1975.

Nelson-Cisneros, Victor. "La clase trabajadora en Tejas, 1920–1940." *Aztlan: International Journal of Chicano Studies Research* 6, no. 2 (Summer 1975): 239–265.

————. "La Frontera: A Case Study of Brownsville-Matamoros." Typescript, 1974. Author's collection.

Olmsted, Frederick Law. *A Journey through Texas; or, a Saddle-Trip on the Southwestern Frontier.* New York: Dix, Edwards & Co., 1857; reprint, Austin: University of Texas Press, 1978.

Olson, Mancur. *The Logic of Collective Action.* Cambridge: Harvard University Press, 1965.

Osgood, Ernest S. *The Day of the Cattleman.* Minneapolis: University of Minnesota Press, 1929.

Paige, Jeffrey M. *Agrarian Revolution: Social Movements and Export Agriculture in the Underdeveloped World.* New York: Free Press, 1975.

Paredes, Américo. *With His Pistol in His Hand.* Austin: University of Texas Press, 1958.

———, and Raymund Paredes, eds. *Mexican American Authors.* Boston: Houghton Mifflin, 1972.

Paredes, Eleazer M. "The Role of the Mexican American in Kleberg County, Texas, 1915–1970." M.A. thesis, Texas Agricultural & Industrial University, 1973.

Paredes, Raymund. "The Origins of Anti-Mexican Sentiment in the United States." *New Scholar* 6 (1977): 139–166.

Paredes Manzano, Américo. "The Mexico-Texan." In *First Year Book of the Latin American Population of Texas,* ed. J. Montiel Olvera, p. 20. San Antonio: private printing, 1939.

Paxson, Frederic L. "The Evolution of the Live Stock Industry." In *Readings in the Economic History of American Agriculture,* ed. Louis B. Schmidt and Earle D. Ross, pp. 381–389. New York: Macmillan, 1925.

Peavey, John R. *Echoes from the Rio Grande.* Brownsville: Springman-King, 1963.

Perales, Alonso. *Are We Good Neighbors?.* San Antonio: Artes Graficas, 1948.

———. *El méxico-americano y la política del sur de Tejas.* San Antonio: private printing, 1931.

———. *En defensa de mi raza.* 2 vols. San Antonio: Artes Graficas, 1936.

Peyton, Green. *San Antonio: City in the Sun.* New York: McGraw-Hill, 1946.

Pierce, Frank C. *A Brief History of the Lower Rio Grande Valley.* Menasha, Wis.: Geo. Banta Publishing, 1917.

Pilcher, J. E. "Outlawry on the Mexican Border." *Scribner's Magazine* 10, no. 1 (July 1891): 78–86.

Pitt, Leonard. *The Decline of the Californios: A Social History of the Spanish-Speaking Californians, 1846–1890.* Berkeley: University of California Press, 1970.

Pitts, John Bost, III. "Speculation in Headright Land Grants in San Antonio from 1837 to 1842." M.A. thesis, Trinity University, 1966.

Pollard, Neva V. "The History of Jim Wells County." M.A. thesis, Texas Agricultural and Industrial College, 1945.

Price, Glenn W. *Origins of the War with Mexico: The Polk-Stockton Intrigue.* Austin: University of Texas Press, 1967.

Primer Congreso Mexicanista, Verificado en Laredo, Texas, Los Días 14 al 22 de Septiembre de 1911. Laredo: Tipografía de N. Idar, 1912.

Pryor, Ike T. *Prospectus.* San Antonio: Nueces Valley Colonization Co., 1907.

Putnam, Frank. "Texas in Transition." *Collier's Magazine,* January 2, 1910, p. 15.

Quinn, Olive Westbrooke. "The Transmission of Racial Attitudes among

White Southerners." In *Race: Individual and Collective Behavior,* ed. Edgar T. Thompson and Everett C. Hughes, pp. 449–457. New York: Free Press, 1958.

Rangel, Jorge, and Carlos Alcala. "De Jure Segregation of Chicanos in Texas Schools." *Harvard Civil Rights–Civil Liberties Law Review* 7 (March 1972): 307–391.

Raybeck, Joseph. *A History of American Labor.* New York: Free Press, 1966.

Raymond, Howard G. "Acculturation and Social Mobility among Latin-Americans in Resaca City." M.A. thesis, University of Texas, 1952.

Redfield, Robert. "Race as a Social Phenomenon." In *Race: Individual and Collective Behavior,* ed. Edward T. Thompson and Everett C. Hughes, pp. 66–71. New York: Free Press, 1958.

Remarkable Conditions in Duval County: Protest by Citizens against Proposed Division. Pamphlet, 1915. Daughters of the Republic of Texas Library, San Antonio, Texas.

Remy, Caroline. "Hispanic-Mexican San Antonio: 1836–1861." *Southwestern Historical Quarterly* 71, no. 4 (April 1968): 564–570.

Rex, John. "The Concept of Race in Sociological History." In *Race, Ethnicity, and Social Change,* ed. John Stone, pp. 59–74. Belmont, Calif.: Wadsworth Publishing, 1977.

Riegel, Robert Edgar. *The Story of the Western Railroads: From 1852 through the Reign of the Giants.* Lincoln: University of Nebraska Press, 1964.

Rios, Rolando. "Voting Rights Act: Its Effect in Texas." Typescript, 1981. Southwest Voter Registration Education Project, San Antonio, Texas.

Rippy, J. Fred. "Border Troubles along the Rio Grande, 1848–1860." *Southwestern Historical Quarterly* 23, no. 2 (October 1919): 91–111.

Rocha, Rodolfo. "The Influence of the Mexican Revolution on the Mexico-Texas Border, 1910–1916." Ph.D. dissertation, Texas Tech University, 1981.

Rodríguez, José María. *Memoirs of Early Texas.* San Antonio: Passing Show Printing, 1913.

Rodríguez-O, Jaime E. *Down from Colonialism: Mexico's Nineteenth Century Crisis.* Chicano Studies Research Publications, Popular Series, no. 3. Los Angeles: University of California, 1983.

Romo, Ricardo. "Responses to Mexican Immigration, 1910–1930." *Aztlan: International Journal of Chicano Studies Research* 6, no. 2 (Summer 1975): 173–194.

Rubel, Arthur. *Across the Tracks: Mexican-Americans in a Texas City.* Austin: University of Texas Press, 1966.

Ruiz, Ramón Eduardo, ed. *The Mexican War: Was It Manifest Destiny?.* New York: Holt, Rinehart & Winston, 1963.

Sanders, Luther L. "Nonpartisanism: Its Use as a Campaign Appeal in San Antonio, Texas, 1961–1971." M.A. thesis, St. Mary's University, 1974.

Sandos, James A. "The Plan of San Diego: War and Diplomacy on the Texas Border, 1915–1916." *Arizona and the West* 14 (Spring 1972): 5–24.

Sandoz, Mari. *The Cattlemen.* New York: Hastings House Publishers, 1958.

Santibáñez, Enrique. *Ensayo acerca la inmigración mexicana en los Es-*

tados Unidos. San Antonio: Clegg, 1930; reprint, San Francisco: R & E Research Associates, 1970.

Santleban, August. *A Texas Pioneer: Early Staging and Overland Freighting Days on the Frontiers of Texas and Mexico.* New York: Neale Publishing, 1910.

Schmidt, Louis B., and Earle D. Ross, eds. *Readings in the Economic History of American Agriculture.* New York: Macmillan, 1925.

Scott, Florence J. *Royal Land Grants North of the Rio Grande, 1777–1821.* Rio Grande City: La Retama Press, 1969.

———. "Spanish Land Grants in the Lower Rio Grande Valley." M.A. thesis, University of Texas, 1935.

Scruggs, Otey. "A History of Mexican Agricultural Labor in the United States, 1942–1954." Ph.D. dissertation, Harvard University, 1957.

Seguin, Juan Nepomuceno. *Personal Memoirs of John N. Seguin: From the Year 1834 to the Retreat of General Woll from the City of San Antonio, 1842.* San Antonio: Ledger Book & Job Office, 1858.

Semo, Enrique. *Historia del capitalismo en México: Los orígenes, 1521–1763.* Mexico City: Ediciones Era, S.A., 1973.

Shannon, Fred A. *The Farmer's Last Frontier: Agriculture, 1860–1897.* New York: Farrar & Rinehart, 1945.

Shelton, Edgar, Jr. *Political Conditions among Texas Mexicans along the Rio Grande.* San Francisco: R & E Research Associates, 1974.

Shockley, John S. *Chicano Revolt in a Texas Town.* Notre Dame: University of Notre Dame Press, 1974.

Simmons, Ozzie. *Anglo-Americans and Mexican-Americans in South Texas.* New York: Arno Press, 1974.

Singletary, Otis. *The Mexican War.* Chicago: University of Chicago Press, 1960.

Skerry, Peter. "Neighborhood COPS: The Resurrection of Saul Alinsky." *New Republic,* February 6, 1984, pp. 21–23.

Slayden, James L. "Some Observations on Mexicans Immigration." *Annals of the American Academy of Political and Social Science* 93, no. 182 (January 1921): 121–126.

Smith, Ashbel. *Addresses, etc.* Private printing. Sterling Library, Yale University.

Smithwick, Noah. *The Evolution of a State or Recollections of Old Texas Days.* Austin: Steck-Vaughn, 1968; reprint, Austin: University of Texas Press, 1983.

Southwest Voter Registration Education Project. *An Inquiry into Voting Irregularities in Texas.* San Antonio, 1980.

———. *Mexican American Voting in the 1982 Texas General Election.* San Antonio, 1982.

———. "Roster of Elected Officials in Texas, 1984." Typescript, 1985.

———. *Survey of Chicano Representation in 361 Texas Public School Boards, 1979–1980.* San Antonio, 1981.

The Spanish Texans. San Antonio: University of Texas Institute of Texan Cultures, 1972.

Speed, Jonathan. "The Hunt for Garza." *Harper's Weekly,* January 30, 1892.
Spratt, John. *The Road to Spindletop: Economic Change in Texas, 1875–1901.* Dallas: Southern Methodist University Press, 1955; reprint, Austin: University of Texas Press, 1970, 1983.
Stambaugh, J. Lee, and Lillian J. Stambaugh. *The Lower Rio Grande Valley of Texas.* San Antonio: Naylor, 1954.
Steen, Ralph W. *Twentieth Century Texas.* Austin: Steck, 1942.
Stephens, A. Ray. *The Taft Ranch: A Texas Principality.* Austin: University of Texas Press, 1964.
Stevens, Walter B. *Through Texas: A Series of Interesting Letters.* St. Louis: Cotton Belt Route, 1892.
Stinchecombe, Arthur L. "Agriculture Enterprise and Rural Class Relations." *American Journal of Sociology* 67 (September 1961): 165–176.
———. *Theoretical Methods in Social History.* New York: Academic Press, 1978.
Stone, John, ed. *Race, Ethnicity, and Social Change.* Belmont, Calif.: Wadsworth Publishing, 1977.
Stowell, J. S. "Danger of Unrestricted Mexican Immigration." *Current History* 28, no. 2 (August 1928): 763–766.
Sutherland, Mary A. *The Story of Corpus Christi.* Published for the Corpus Christi Chapter of the Daughters of the Confederacy. Houston: Rein & Sons, 1916.
Takaki, Ronald T. *Iron Cages: Race and Culture in Nineteenth-Century America.* New York: Alfred A. Knopf, 1979.
Tarver, E. R. *Laredo: The Gate Way between the United States and Mexico.* Laredo: Laredo Immigration Society, 1889.
Taylor, George Rogers, ed. *The Turner Thesis: Concerning the Role of the Frontier in American History.* Lexington, Mass.: D. C. Heath & Co., 1972.
Taylor, Paul S. *An American-Mexican Frontier: Nueces County, Texas.* Chapel Hill: University of North Carolina Press, 1934; reprint, New York: Russell & Russell, 1971.
———. "Mexican Labor in the United States: Dimmit County, Winter Garden District, South Texas." *University of California Publications in Economics* 6, no. 5 (1930): 293–464.
———. "Research Note." *Journal of the American Statistical Association* 25, no. 170 (June 1930): 206–207.
Taylor, Paul S., Collection. Bancroft Library. University of California, Berkeley.
Taylor, Virginia H. *Index to Spanish and Mexican Land Grants.* Austin: General Land Office, 1976.
———. *Spanish Archives of the General Land Office of Texas.* Austin: Lone Star Press, 1955.
Taylor, William, and Elliott West. "Patrón Leadership at the Crossroads: Southern Colorado in the Late Nineteenth Century." In *The Chicano,* ed. Norris Hundley, pp. 73–95. Santa Barbara: Clio Books, 1975.
Tenayuca, Emma, and Homer Brooks. "The Mexican Question in the Southwest." *Political Affairs* (March 1939): 257–268.

Terrell, John Upton. *Land Grab: The Truth about "The Winning of the West."* New York: Dial Press, 1972.

"Testimony of the Mexican American Legal Defense and Educational Fund on the Voting Rights Act before the Subcommittee on Civil and Constitutional Rights of the Judiciary Committee, U.S. House of Representatives, June 5, 1981," pp. 936–1008. On file in MALDEF Office, San Antonio, Texas.

Texas, a Guide to the Lone Star State. New York: Hastings House, 1940.

Texas Adjutant-General. *Special Report of the Adjutant-General, September, 1884.* Austin, 1884.

The Texas Almanac, 1958–1959, 1964–1965, 1966–1967, 1968–1969. Dallas: A. H. Belo, 1959, 1965, 1967, 1969.

Texas Almanac & State Industrial Guide, 1914, 1925, 1930, 1936. Dallas: A. H. Belo, 1914, 1925, 1930, 1936.

"Texas' Biggest Untapped Market: 1,000,000 Latin Americans." *Texas Business Review* 29, no. 12 (December 1955): 15–17.

Texas Cotton Ginners' Association. Correspondence, 1947–1948. Barker Library, University of Texas at Austin.

Texas Legislature. Senate. *Glasscock v. Parr, Supplement to the Senate Journal.* 36th Legislature, regular sess., 1919.

Texas Observer, 1966–1967, 1976–1977, 1980–1981, 1984–1986.

Texas State Employment Service, Farm Placement Service. *Annual Report of the Farm Placement Service, 1939.* Austin, 1939.

———. *Law Supplement to Texas State Employment Reports on Migratory Labor.* Austin, 1941.

———. *Origins and Problems of Texas Migratory Farm Labor.* Austin, 1940.

Thompson, Edgar T. *Plantation Societies, Race Relations, and the South: The Regimentation of Populations.* Durham: Duke University Press, 1975.

———, and Everett C. Hughes, eds. *Race: Individual and Collective Behavior.* New York: Free Press, 1958.

Thompson, James. "A 19th Century History of Cameron County." M.A. thesis, University of Texas, 1965.

Thompson, Jerry Don. *Vaqueros in Blue and Gray.* Austin: Presidial Press, 1976.

Thompson, Wallace. *The Mexican Mind: A Study of National Psychology.* Boston: Little, Brown & Co., 1922.

Tiller, James W., Jr. *The Texas Winter Garden: Commercial Cool-Season Vegetable Production.* Bureau of Business Research Monographs, no. 33. Austin: University of Texas, 1971.

Tuck, Ruth. *Not with the Fist: A Study of Mexican-Americans in a Southwest City.* New York: Harcourt, Brace & Co., 1946.

Turner, F. J. *The Frontier in American History.* New York: Henry Holt & Co., 1920.

Tyler, Gus, ed. *Mexican-Americans Tomorrow: Educational and Economic Perspectives.* Albuquerque: University of New Mexico Press, 1975.

U.S. Congress, House of Representatives. Debate to Suspend Immigration.

H. Res. 14461, 66th Cong., 3d sess., December 9–11, 1920. *Congressional Record* 60, no. 1.

———. *Depredations on the Frontiers of Texas.* H. Exec. Doc. 39, 42d Cong., 3d sess., December 16, 1872.

———. *Difficulties on the Southwestern Frontier.* H. Exec. Doc. 52, 36th Cong., 1st sess., March 29, 1860.

———. *Range and Ranch Cattle Traffic in the Western States and Territories.* By Joseph Nimmo, Jr. H. Exec. Doc. 267, 48th Cong., 2d sess., March 2, 1885.

———. *Report of the Select Committee to Investigate Campaign Expenditures.* H. Exec. Doc. 2821, 70th Cong., 2d sess., 1929.

———. *Texas Frontier Troubles.* H. Report no. 343, 44th Cong., 1st sess., 1876.

———. *Troubles on the Texas Frontier.* H. Exec. Doc. 81, 36th Cong., 1st sess., 1860.

U.S. Congress, Senate. *Investigation of Mexican Affairs.* 2 vols. S. Doc. 285, 66th Cong., 2d sess., 1920.

———. *Message on Hostilities on the Rio Grande.* S. Doc. 21, 36th Cong., 1st sess., 1860.

———. *Report of the Commission on Industrial Relations.* Vols. 9–10. S. Doc. 415, 64th Cong., 1st sess., 1916.

U.S. Department of Agriculture. Bureau of Agricultural Economics. *United States Cotton Statistics, 1910–1949 by States.* 1951.

U.S. Department of Commerce. Bureau of the Census. *Twelfth–Twentieth Census of the United States.* 1900, 1910, 1920, 1930, 1940, 1950, 1960, 1970, 1980.

U.S. Department of Labor. *Mexican Labor in the United States.* By Victor S. Clark. Bulletin of the Bureau of Labor 17, no. 78. 1908.

U.S. Farm Security Administration. *Survey of Agricultural Labor Conditions.* By Tom Vasey and Josiah Folsom. 1937.

U.S. Federal Works Agency. Work Projects Administration. *Mexican Migratory Workers of South Texas.* By Sheldon C. Menefee. 1941.

van den Berghe, Pierre L. *Race and Racism: A Comparative Perspective.* New York: John Wiley & Sons, 1967.

Villarreal, Roberto M. "The Mexican-American Vaqueros of the Kenedy Ranch: A Social History." M.A. thesis, Texas Agricultural and Industrial University, 1972.

Wallerstein, Immanuel. *The Modern World-System: Capitalist Agriculture and the Origins of the European World-Economy in the Sixteenth Century.* New York: Academic Press, 1974.

Warburton, Sister Margaret Rose. "A History of the Thomas O'Connor Ranch, 1834–1939." M.A. thesis, Catholic University of America, 1939.

Waters, Lawrence Leslie. "Transient Mexican Agricultural Labor." *Southwestern Social Science Quarterly* 22, no. 1 (June 1941): 49–66.

Webb, Walter Prescott. *The Great Plains.* Boston: Ginn & Co., 1931; reprint, New York: Grossett & Dunlap, 1972.

————. *The Texas Rangers: A Century of Frontier Defense.* Boston and New York: Houghton Mifflin, 1935; reprint, Austin: University of Texas Press, 1965.

Weeks, O. Douglas. "The League of United Latin-American Citizens: A Texas-Mexican Civic Organization." *Southwestern Political and Social Science Quarterly* 10, no. 3 (December 1929): 257–278.

————. "The Texas-Mexican and the Politics of South Texas." *American Political Science Review* 24, no. 3 (August 1930): 606–627.

Weinberg, Albert K. *Manifest Destiny: A Study of Nationalist Expansionism in American History.* Baltimore: Johns Hopkins University Press, 1935; reprint, Chicago: Quadrangle Books, 1963.

Western Texas, the Australia of America; or the Place to Live. Cincinnati: E. Mendenhall, 1860.

Wilcox, S. S. "The Laredo City Election and Riot of April, 1886." *Southwestern Historical Quarterly* 45, no. 1 (July 1941): 1–23.

Wilkinson, J. B. *Laredo and the Rio Grande Frontier.* Austin: Jenkins Publishing, 1975.

Wilson, Ben F., Jr. "The Economic History of Kleberg County." M.A. thesis, Texas Agricultural and Industrial College, 1939.

Wilson, W. *Forced Labor in the United States.* New York: International Publishers, 1933.

Wilson, William J. *The Declining Significance of Race: Blacks and Changing American Institutions.* Chicago: University of Chicago Press, 1978.

Wolf, Eric R. *Europe and the People without History.* Berkeley: University of California Press, 1982.

————. *Peasant Wars of the Twentieth Century.* New York: Harper & Row, 1969.

Woodward, C. Vann. *The Strange Career of Jim Crow.* 2d rev. ed. New York: Oxford University Press, 1966.

Wooster, Ralph A. "Wealthy Texans, 1870." *Southwestern Historical Quarterly* 74, no. 1 (July 1970): 24–35.

Wyman, Walker D., and Clifton B. Kroeber, eds. *The Frontier in Perspective.* Madison: University of Wisconsin Press, 1965.

Youngblood, B., and A. B. Cox. *An Economic Study of a Typical Ranching Area on the Edwards Plateau of Texas.* Texas Agricultural Experiment Station Bulletin, no. 297. College Station: Texas Agricultural & Mechanical College, 1922.

Zamora, Emilio. "The Chicano Origin and Development of the San Diego Revolt." Paper presented at the 2d annual conference of the Chicano Social Science Association, Austin, Texas, 1973.

————. "Mexican Labor Activity in South Texas, 1900–1920." Ph.D. dissertation, University of Texas at Austin, 1983.

Zamora O'Shea, Elena. *El Mesquite: A Story of the Early Spanish Settlements between the Nueces and the Rio Grande as Told by "La Posta del Palo Alto."* Dallas: Mathis Publishing, 1935.

Zeichner, Oscar. "The Transition from Slave to Free Agricultural Labor in the United States." *Agricultural History* 13, no. 1 (January 1939): 22–33.

INDEX